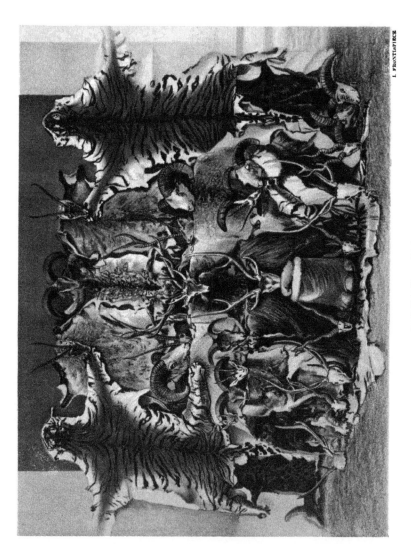

BAG MADE IN 1864-'65

LARGE
GAME SHOOTING

IN

Thibet, the Himalayas, and Northern India.

BY

COLONEL KINLOCH,
The King's Royal Rifle Corps.

ILLUSTRATED BY PHOTO-GRAVURES.

Calcutta:

THACKER, SPINK AND CO.
LONDON: W. THACKER AND CO.

1885.

CALCUTTA:
PRINTED BY THACKER, SPINK & CO.

PREFACE.

A good many years have now elapsed since I published the two volumes of "Large Game Shooting in Thibet and The North-West." Since then I have considerably extended my wanderings, and although I have not enjoyed such a large share of leave as formerly, I have had opportunities of enlarging my experience, and have added a good many animals to my collection.

I had hoped at one time to bag every sort of "Large Game" to be found on the continent of India, and to make my book a complete guide for the sportsmen of all three Presidencies.

As, however, I see no immediate prospect of my ambition being gratified, I have restricted the scope of my work, and confined myself to Northern India, within the limits of which, few " Large Game" animals exist, that are not described in the present volume.

The former volumes have been carefully revised ; mistakes eliminated as far as possible ; and much new matter added.

Modern improvements, and increased experience, have caused me to alter or modify my views regarding several subjects, and the chapter on equipment has been entirely re-written.

I am indebted to the courtesy of the proprietors of "The Civil and Military Gazette," of Lahore, for permission to partly reproduce a number of articles entitled " Reminiscences of Sport in India," which I wrote for that journal.

The photograph of my Camp is taken from a clever sketch by Lieut. Hobday, Royal Artillery, whose artistic talent is well known in India.

In addition to the Taxidermists whose names appear in the Introduction to my work I must mention Mr. E. Gerrard of College Place, Camden Town, who has most successfully mounted the heads of the Buffalo, Gaur, Musk Deer, and Bears.

ALEXANDER A. A. KINLOCH.

CONTENTS.

MAP.

ERRATA.

INTRODUCTION.

THE love of the chase is an instinct which centuries of civilisation have been unable to eradicate ; the pursuit which was a necessity to the savage, and in fact the business of his life, being now followed as a relaxation by those whose means place them in a position where physical toil and hardships are totally unnecessary.

That this instinct, like most of the promptings of healthy nature, is a pretty safe guide to follow, is generally admitted ; and there are few who question the advantages to be derived from field sports, among the votaries of which may be numbered some of the greatest names in history.

There is indeed a limited school who talk of the immorality and cruelty of all field sports, but it will be found that the professors of such doctrines have very peculiar views on other subjects, and seem to make it the business of their lives to prove that the world has been going on a wrong system, and that they have fortunately been born to set it right. If they had their own way, men would become effeminate, and women would lose much that now gives dignity and charm to their sex.

So general is the instinct which leads to the love of the chase in its many forms, that it may almost be said to be universal ; and when the taste is not developed, it will generally be found that the want of early initiation, or the absence of opportunity, are the causes to which its absence may be ascribed.

Some few there are indeed, who cannot appreciate the joys of the chase, like the famous Lord Chesterfield, who

> . . . . " though he rode beyond all price,
> Asked next day, if men ever hunted twice."

But probably even he would have become a constant attendant at the covert side if he had gone out that second time.

It is unnecessary to write a defence of field sports ; most of the charges against them have been often disproved ; but it must be admitted that of late years there has been some foundation for the assertion that men shoot for the love of slaughter and not for healthy excitement.

Without going into the question whether the battue system as usually conducted is, or is not, a high form of sport, nothing can possibly be said in favour of the practice of turning down pheasants, and even hares and rabbits, the day before a grand shooting party. It is hard to imagine what pleasure any one can find in butchering animals under such circumstances,

A

and the introduction of the system can only be attributed to a vulgar and childish desire to show a long list of slain at the end of the day, and obtain the cheap (in one sense only) notoriety of the heaviest bag of the season.

It will be observed that although "the chase" was the theme with which this article commenced, shooting is now particularly alluded to ; and it may, therefore, be well to explain that the word 'chase' is here used as comprising the pursuit of wild animals in any fair and legitimate way ; with horse, hound or hawk ; rifle, gun, spear or rod.

We have no word in English that properly embraces all these, but all are expressed by the Persian word '*shikár*.'

Although, as already alluded to, there has been a tendency of late years to debase sport in England by rendering it too artificial, and making everything subservient to the one object of obtaining the heaviest possible bag in the shortest time and with the least possible trouble, '*shikár*' hasnot yet degenerated in the East, and game cannot be killed in any quantities without considerable personal exertion.

Even Deer stalking in India is very different from the same sport at home, compared with which it has both advantages and disadvantages : the latter are obvious enough, but among the former may be reckoned the facts that it is within the reach of all at very moderate expense, and that you are shooting a really wild animal. Although I am perfectly aware that a Scotch stag takes very good care of himself, and is not to be approached without the exercise of perhaps as much skill as is required in the pursuit of most animals, still I cannot help fancying, that after all, the knowledge that the forester knows every stag on the ground, must somewhat detract from the pleasure which is experienced in circumventing an animal which owes nothing to human care ; whose wanderings are controlled by no fences or other arrangements for keeping him within certain bounds.'

In fact with all *preserved* game, one is apt to be reminded of *Punch's* admirable sketch some years ago, of a noble owner of coverts remarking to his keeper "*Dear me ! that is a very small pheasant* " and receiving the reply " *Yes m' Lord ; she allus wur a weekly bird : I never thought I should ha' reared her !* "

In India not only is the game varied, but the scenes among which it may be hunted are equally so. The sportsman may track the mighty Elephant and Gaur among the splendid Sub-Himalayan forests; rouse the Rhinoceros and Buffalo from their muddy lairs in the dense reeds on the banks of the Brahmapútra ; gallop his Arab at speed over the rocky soil of the Deccan in hot pursuit of the grey Boar; stalk the Ibex and Markhoor among the precipices of the pine-clad mountains surrounding the Happy Valley ; invade the solitudes of Thibet in hopes of adding to his trophies the massive head of the shaggy Yâk or the ever-watchful Ovis Hodgsonii ; or content himself by riding quietly over the cultivated plains of the North-West, express rifle in hand, and bringing to bag many a graceful Black Buck and Gazelle.

I have always been an enthusiastic lover of the rifle, and have devoted comparatively little time to small game shooting ; but should the sportsman prefer the shot gun to the grooved barrel, there are the gorgeous Moonal, the wary Argus (so called), the Cheer,

Koklass, and other Pheasants to be found in the cool and bracing atmosphere of the higher Himalayas; at the foot of the hills the Jungle Fowl, Peafowl, and Black Partridge abound; during the winter months, the lakes and marshes (*jheels*) teem with Wild Fowl of every sort; while the wet rice fields, and an unlimited extent of cultivation over which no permission is required to roam, at certain seasons shelter Snipe and Quail in such countless numbers that bags of from fifty to a hundred couple not unfrequently fall to a single gun.

Again, for followers of the "gentle craft," are there not deep pools and rippling streams in the Poonch, Jhelum, Ganges, Jumna,. Sunkose, and many another noble river, where it is nothing unusual for a 50℔ Mahseer to make the reel revolve at such a pace as would cause the canny Scotchman of story to be anxious, not only for the safety of his "*twa and saxpenny flee*," but for that of collar, two hundred yards of line, and perhaps even the rod itself !

Coursing is but little carried on in India now, but in former days there used to be a meeting of some importance at Ghazeeabad, near Delhi; and there are many localities where lovers of the leash can see the speed and working powers of their favourites well tested.

Except on the North-West Frontier, few Englishmen now keep hawks; but there the ancient sport of Falconry is well kept up; the Houbara, a species of bustard, being the usual quarry. Until lately, the Officers of the Guides used to hawk the Indian Gazelle—or Ravine Deer, as it is commonly but erroneously called. In Oudh many of the rich natives still keep up considerable hawking establishments, and in fact, in most parts of India where the country is suitable, professional Falconers could be obtained. .

The capabilities of India as a sporting country having thus been alluded to in general terms, it is proposed to give details of sport enjoyed in the pursuit of many different species, by one who has had unusual opportunities of following the chase; who looks back to each incident with the most lively pleasure; and who is still as great an enthusiast as when with fast beating heart he first brought the sights .of his rifle to bear upon the glossy shoulder of a "Master Buck." That was many years ago; but the scene is still vivid in his recollection, together with the memories of many a glorious day's sport. To those who have travelled much, and led a life a little out of the ordinary routine, there is a peculiar pleasure in looking back to bygone days, and in fancy fighting one's battles o'er again.

To interest other people in the same events is a very different matter; it is by no means easy to give life to the picture one is painting : it is very apt to be at best a stiff and formal delineation of a scene which, as it was witnessed, was full of light and color.

Numerous as are the books that have been written about Indian sport, I have still found that many good sportsmen are unacquainted with various animals coming under the comprehensive term of "Large Game," which inhabit the widely different countries constituting our Indian Empire. Most books have been written about one branch of sport, Tiger-shooting, Elephant-shooting, Pig-sticking, or shooting in the hills. Few books have been illustrated, and those in which the drawings give anything like a correct idea of the animals which they are intended to represent are still more rare.

In the present work, I have endeavoured to supply a want which I believe is felt by sportsmen, and to produce a book which, by means of photographs, shall give faithful portraits of most of the Large Game animals to be met with in the parts of India to which it refers. I have also given general descriptions of the beasts and of the districts they inhabit, and have added such notes on their habits and Natural History as I have gathered from personal observation. I have, for the most part, confined myself to the results of my own experience as I am aware how often common errors are perpetuated by people merely repeating what they have heard, without giving themselves the trouble of verifying its correctness. Of course, I do not pretend to say that I have not fallen into errors myself, but I have at least done my best to give as correct an idea as possible of the different animals described, and to afford some assistance to those who are fond of the chase.

During many years' residence in India, I have been fortunate enough to enjoy a large share of leave : most of it has been spent in travelling and shooting ; and I have thus been enabled to wander over a very large tract of country. There is hardly an animal, whose habitat I have visited, which I have not met with ; and there are very few which I have not shot. I have seldom made, nor indeed tried for, large bags. Travelling generally alone, after obtaining one or two good specimens of any animal, I have usually given up its pursuit, and set out in search of some other species, only to be found, perhaps, at the distance of many marches. My journal, therefore, if given entire, would often be very tedious, days of sport occurring only now and then during weeks of dreary marching ; so I have thought it better merely to make extracts from my diary, which was usually written every night.

One merit at least I may claim for my work—that of truthfulness : the descriptions are as accurate as I can make them, and I have in no instance drawn upon my imagination for the sake of adding to the interest of my anecdotes.

The photographs, to which I chiefly look for the success of my book, speak for themselves ; they are taken from heads of animals shot by myself, and for the most part admirably stuffed by Mr. Edwin Ward, Mr. Drake, &c.

When I have omitted to give a likeness of any animal, it has been either because it was unnecessary or impracticable (as in the case of the Elephant) ; or because I have not a sufficiently good specimen. All the portraits are those of at least average, and in many instances fine specimens.

When my first Volume appeared one of my critics was good enough to say that my rifle was my "better half" ! Since then I have made two more expeditions into Thibet, and it may interest my Lady readers (should I be fortunate enough to have any) to hear that I was accompanied everywhere by my wife. I mention this in order to show that the difficulties in travelling in remote districts are not so insurmountable as is generally supposed, and that any lady who enjoys a little adventure may accompany her husband if she can only make up her mind to undergo a certain amount of " roughing it." I need hardly say, however, that she must be a good walker and rider, and possessed of the ' pluck ' in which English ladies seldom fail.

My wife crossed some of the highest passes in the Himalayas, and traversed certainly the very worst paths, without any serious inconvenience. In Thibet she generally rode a Yâk, which, although slow, is more sure-footed than a pony, and is not so apt to go lame on stony ground. In the lower hills, when she did not walk, she travelled in a ' *dandy*,' which may best be described as a small hammock slung to a pole and carried by four men. A short walking dress of soft Kashmir woollen stuff, with loose pantaloons of the same material tucked into brown ' Elcho ' boots, is the best costume for a lady, who is then equally well equipped for riding, walking or climbing. A soft grey felt ' Terai ' hat, with a good thick ' *pugree* ' is the best head-dress, while a mask or thick veil is absolutely necessary to preserve the complexion from the cold dry wind and burning sun.

My wife saw nearly every species of game in the wild state, and actually saw me shoot Ovis Hodgsonii, Thibetan Antelope, Ibex, Bears, &c.

I have added some notes on tents, camp equipment, rifles, &c., together with simple directions for the preservation of Natural History specimens ; and I have appended a map showing all the routes I have travelled.

The " Kashmir Route Map " gives most of the marches in the more frequented parts of the Himalayas, but I should recommend the sportsman to procure the Government Survey map, on the scale of four miles to the inch, of each district that he intends to shoot over.

I trust that my work may be of use to real sportsmen ; and in conclusion I would express an earnest hope that those who may be induced, by these photographs and descriptions, to visit the distant lands where these noble animals are to be found, will enjoy good sport so long as they follow their pursuit as true sportsmen. This, I am sorry to say, has *not* always been the case. Too many instances have occurred of late years of " would-be sportsmen " becoming disgusted with the hard work, and (being ashamed to come back empty handed) employing their Shikaris to shoot game for them ; all thus obtained being counted in the bag.

This is not the only harm done ; rifles, guns and ammunition have been given to Shikaris—sometimes I fear in payment of wages—and they are consequently enabled and encouraged to kill game during the winter. A third evil is that of shooting females and young ones to swell the *numbers* of the bag.

All these practices I consider highly unsportsmanlike. Those who give guns and ammunition to natives may consider themselves very generous ; but it is selfish generosity at the expense of real sportsmen. No native—or not one in a hundred—shoots for sport, and it would be far better to give a man who had done good service a handsome present in rupees than to furnish him with the means of destroying a quantity of game whose value to him would be very little.

LARGE GAME SHOOTING.

CHAPTER I.

DESCRIPTION OF COUNTRY.

No country in the world affords such a variety of sport as our Indian Empire, and no part of it contains so many different animals as the region which lies between the great watershed of Asia and the plains of Hindostán.

There we have the extremes of a nearly arctic and a tropical climate; of precipitous and barren mountains, and plains clothed with the densest vegetation; and in each situation we find various descriptions of " Large Game," to understand whose habits we must be acquainted with the peculiarities of their natural haunts.

I shall attempt to give some idea of the different hunting grounds I have visited, although descriptions must always fall far short of conveying a proper conception of the magnificence of Himalayan scenery; and not even the word-painting of a Ruskin could do justice to the magical effects of light and vivid coloring to be witnessed among the wonderfully tinted hills of Thibet, through the medium of an atmosphere compared with which that of Italy is foggy.

Taking the northern and most elevated regions first, and gradually working southwards and downwards, I shall commence with that wild and little-known country—Thibet. Under this head several distinct provinces are included—Ládák, Báltistán, and some of the frontier districts of Chinese Tartary which are partially accessible to Englishmen.

Many people dislike Thibet, but in spite of its bleak, desert appearance, and severe climate, it has great charms for me. One there experiences a sensation of perfect freedom which I have never felt elsewhere : and a sort of mystery still hangs over the land, which modern geographical research has stripped from almost every other country in the world.

The greater part of Thibet is rugged and mountainous ; but the mountains, as a rule, are not very high above the plane of their actual bases, though the mean elevation of the country is somewhere about 14,000 feet above the level of the sea.

Few plains of any extent occur, but the country is much intersected by streams and rivers, which take their rise among the snows and glaciers of the Kara Koram, and other lofty ranges. The line of perpetual snow is very high, being about 22,000 feet. Although snow falls occasionally even in summer, it does not lie on the arid stony soil. Rain very seldom falls, and the sky is generally cloudless during the summer months.

Being thus exposed to the burning rays of the sun, the country appears almost a desert ; no trees, few bushes, and but little vegetation of any sort meet the eye: but here and there a tuft of some aromatic herb springs up among the stones and affords the only pasturage for the wild animals. That want of moisture and not the sterility of the soil is the cause, is clearly shown by the strip of bright green grass which always adorns the bank of any constant stream, and by the fine crops which grow around the villages where artificial irrigation is employed.

No part of Thibet perhaps excels in wildness and desolation the valley of Chung Chenmo. Here, on climbing to the top of one of the hills which immediately overlook the valley, one's eye rests on nothing but ridge after ridge of red stony hills (usually smooth and rounded, but here and there with craggy summits) stretching away in the distance till the view is at last bounded by a chain of snow-capped peaks. Beneath lies the arid valley, the stones and sand quivering in the blazing sunshine, causing a mirage which distorts all distant objects in an extraordinary manner. On either side of the stream are wide level flats richly clothed with a coarse grass, and a green plain also extends from the hot sulphurous spring of Keum nearly to the banks of the river. These grassy flats are the favorite feeding grounds of the Thibetan Antelope, and occasionally of the Yâk. On the gentle slopes of the hills on either side no traces of vegetation are at first apparent, but on a narrower inspection some scanty tufts will be observed.

A mile or two below the hot spring a tributary stream comes down from the valley of Kyobrung: ascending this for about thirty miles one reaches its sources among the glaciers which close the head of each of the little valleys, and there unite their streams to form the main river. A greater scene of desolation cannot be conceived : cold grey rocks, ice, and snow all piled up in the most fantastic manner in grand confusion ; not a trace of life, either animal or vegetable ; not a sound to be heard except the trickling of the water, the occasional crack of splitting ice, or rumble of falling stones. In the upper parts of the Kyobrung valley, below the glaciers, there is still more grass than in Chung Chenmo ; but it is later in the season before the snows are melted off it.

Four or five marches south of Chung Chenmo one reaches the shores of the Pangong Lake, or rather chain of lakes. This occupies a great valley of more than a hundred miles in length, bounded on the southern side by high, rocky, snow-capped mountains, while the hills which slope down to the water's edge on the northern shore are low and rounded. They are of almost every hue—brown, red, purple, pink, orange, yellow, and grey; and when seen from the southern shore, reflected in the deep blue waters of the lake, form a picture which, if produced on canvas, would probably be pronounced unreal by those who had never seen the original. Owing to the wonderful clearness of the air every outline is as sharp, every tint as vivid, at a distance of twenty miles, as if only a mile away.

These great lakes are a peculiar feature in Thibet : many exist in various parts of the country : some are salt, most are at least brackish, and there are evident signs that many of them were once of far greater extent than they now are. On the shores of these lakes are occasional marshy plains whitened by the efflorescence of various salts, and these are generally the pasture grounds of numerous herds of Kyang. On the rounded hills near the lakes are the favorite haunts of the king of Thibetan game, the Ovis Hodgsonii or Nyan.

The upper parts of the valleys of the great rivers are similar to those of the lakes, and the same fauna are met with, including the Thibetan Gazelle or Goa. Lower down, the valleys contract, and the hills become usually steeper and more rocky : vegetation, though still scarce, is more plentiful than in the upper regions ; and in many places wild flowers of great beauty may be found. On the steeper and more rocky hills, especially towards the sources of the smaller streams, the Burrell is everywhere to be met with, while on the more rounded and undulating hills its near relative the Shapoo is more common. On one occasion, in a small valley near Gya, I saw all three species of Wild Sheep, viz., the Nyan, the Burrell, and the Shapoo, in one day and on the same ground, but such an incident must, I fancy, be very rare.

Here and there, along the banks of the rivers, are situated villages which are really oases in the desert. Irrigation being largely employed, fine crops of barley, peas, and beans are grown ; while the eye rests with pleasure on groves of walnut, apricot, mulberry, poplar, and willow.

Although a few fields are cultivated in the neighbourhood of the villages, the Tartars are not an agricultural race. By far the greater number of them are pastoral, dwelling in tents of black hair cloth, and moving from place to place with their flocks and herds according to the season of the year, and the consequent necessity for changing the pasture grounds.

The Tartars are always cheerful, civil, and obliging, except where they have been corrupted by too much intercourse with the rascally Kashmiris. They are not, however, of much use as Shikaris, and it is not always that you can get them to take the trouble to show game : if you are lucky enough to find a willing man he is useful, as they generally know the haunts of the animals, and they have very good eyesight. There is no trouble when travelling with Tartars : the baggage animals having been provided, and sufficient store of provisions laid in, you can go where you like ; and you are not perpetually annoyed by their grumbling, as you often are with other natives.

Lower down the Indus—which is a good type of a Thibetan river—we come to Báltistán. Here the hills are quite as steep and rocky, but vegetation is rather more abundant, grass is pretty plentiful, and bushes grow naturally in the sheltered valleys. The Ibex and the Oorren take the place of the Nyan and the Burrell as the "Large Game" most frequently met with in the upper portions of the valley ; while still lower down, on the borders of Astor and Gilgit, the Markhoor, the Musk Deer, and the Snow Bear are found on the same hills.

The Báltis are a miserably poor, ill-clad, and apparently oppressed race, which probably accounts for the fact that they are great emigrants, wandering all over the Punjab, and even farther, in search of work.

B

After several months' residence in Thibet, it is very refreshing, on descending from any of the passes, to gaze once more on grass-covered hills and green trees. The difference of climate is perceptible as soon as one crosses the watershed. On the other side the air is clear and bright, while on the southern or Indian slope thick masses of cloud cling to the hills during the whole of the rainy season, causing a most luxuriant vegetation to spring up, even to the very limit of the snow line.

The hills on the southern slopes of the Himalayas are steeper and more precipitous than those in Thibet. The upper portions of the higher ones are, of course, covered with ice and snow, the limit of perpetual snow being about 15,000 feet. Below this the hills possess various characteristics, according to the elevation and the aspect of the slopes.

Vegetation is arranged in regular zones, commencing with the almost arctic plants just below the snow, and successively changing until a nearly tropical climate is reached at the foot of the Himalayas.

There is a considerable sameness in the character of the various hill provinces on this side of the snows, the chief difference consisting in the degree to which they are exposed to the influence of the summer rains.

As we proceed eastwards from Kashmir, we find that the rainfall during the summer months greatly increases; and, as a natural consequence, vegetation is much more luxuriant and of a different character.

Highest of all trees grow the juniper and a species of cypress; then the birch, the bush-rhododendron, the deodar cedar, half a dozen species of pine, the yew, oaks of several sorts, the tree-rhododendron, the horse-chesnut, and many other trees too numerous to mention, succeed one another nearly in the order named, until at last the bamboo and the 'máljan' creeper show that we have nearly reached the foot of the hills.

It must not, however, be supposed, that the trees and other flora are restricted by as well defined horizontal as vertical limits; but a visit to the several hill sanitaria, the elevations of which are all between 6,000 and 8,000 feet, will show a marked change in the character of the forest from one end of the Himalayas to the other.

At Murree the forest consists chiefly of pine and horse-chesnut : at Dalhousie and Dharmsala of oak (ilex). At Simla the deodar is most plentiful ; while at Mussourie and Naini Tal, we again find the evergreen oak, but much interspersed with the beautiful tree-rhododendron, which is, however, more or less generally distributed.

Going still farther east, we find, at Darjiling, a still more marked change ; the magnolia, the tree-fern, climbing arums, screw-pines, and creepers of many sorts forming a denser jungle than is ever met with in the western hills.

A general description of Kashmir, together with brief sketches of other parts of the hills and the country at their feet, may perhaps convey sufficient information to the sportsman regarding the various hunting grounds. For accurate and detailed accounts of the Himalayas, and especially of Kashmir, I must refer the reader to the many books that have been written about them.

Kashmir is a nearly level valley about one hundred miles long and thirty miles wide surrounded by a circle of mountains and watered by the river Jhelum, which, having taken its rise in the north-eastern corner of the valley, flows through the city of S'rinugger, and, after having had its waters augmented by many tributaries, leaves the valley at the south-western corner. The mountains do not rise abruptly from the edges of the plain, but irregular spurs from the chief snowy range run down to the valley, and these, having again their offshoots, form an extensive ramification of ridge and valley, the drainage from which goes to swell the waters of the Jhelum. The height at which game may be found here depends entirely upon the season. In the winter everything is driven down by the snow, and as this melts the animals usually ascend. The lower valleys are covered with dense jungle of various trees and shrubs, where the ground has not been cleared for cultivation, and amongst this forest the Black Bear abounds, living in the neighbourhood of the villages, so that it may plunder the crops and fruit trees. A little higher up one frequently meets with green and beautifully wooded slopes, where the forest is diversified by open glades, reminding one of an English park ; the likeness may be rendered still more striking by the appearance of a herd of deer on one of the open spots. A Snow Bear may occasionally be found as low down, but it is not till the verge of the snow is reached that there is much certainty of finding one. As one ascends through the pine forest, a Musk Deer or two may be met with, if there is also some undergrowth. Above the pines the forest becomes much thinner, and with more frequent open spaces ; one side of a ravine may be clothed with a thicket of birch trees, while the other is nearly bare ; patches of snow lie in the more sheltered hollows (I am supposing that it is the end of May or beginning of June), and where the snow has recently melted, bright colored flowers are in profusion. Tender sprouts of grass are coming up through the decayed stalks of last year's growth which strew the surface of the ground, and frequent uprootings of the soil show that Snow Bears have been at work. Here, too, in the soft soil, the marks of a deeply cleft hoof may be found ; it is the track of an Ibex, which has been feeding here in the morning, but has now doubtless betaken itself with the rest of the herd to the crags which surmount the hill. These slopes are not always mere gentle inclines ; they may be nearly perpendicular and diversified with rocky and precipitous ground, rendering a slip extremely dangerous. Some of the ravines on a steep slope will be filled with hard snow, and in order to cross them, it may be necessary to cut every footstep.

The walking is not, however, as a rule, nearly so dangerous as that on the southern slopes of the Pir Punjal, where the Markhoor is hunted ; there the ground is frequently most difficult, being far steeper and more slippery than most of the Ibex ground.

The hills become gradually lower and tamer looking as one approaches the plains, until the lowest ranges are hardly deserving of the name of mountains, being merely a succession of ridges covered with dense thorny jungle. Among these the Pig and the Barking Deer, with an occasional Tiger or Panther, are the only large game.

The Kashmiris are a lazy, lying race ; the men are generally large and powerful, but they are sadly deficient in pluck, and are often most troublesome as coolies. There are some very good Shikaris among them, but for one good one there are at least forty useless wretches who know nothing about the country, and care nothing about sport, but endeavour to obtain service by exhibiting a lot of worthless certificates, and then devote all their energies to plundering and cheating their employer.

The valleys of the various great rivers which cut their way through the hills are, as a rule, more contracted as we go further east. The Jumna and Ganges have their sources in eternal snow, and their upper waters flow between huge rocky mountains, the grassy slopes of which are the home of the Burrell and the Snow Bear.

Lower down, the sides of their valleys become more or less dotted with cedars and pines, which gradually become more frequent, until at length the vegetation completely changes, and the slopes on either side instead of being merely sprinkled with forest trees are clothed with the densest jungle, consisting principally of oaks and ringal cane. In addition to this, a thick undergrowth of balsams and other fast growing herbaceous plants springs up after the first rains, and frequently attains a height of six or seven feet. These rocky forests are the favorite resort of the Tahr and the Serow. Where more open slopes occur, covered with short grass and sparsely sprinkled with pine trees, Gooral are nearly sure to be found. On some of the hills where the ground is not quite so precipitous and the forest more park-like, the Jaráo or Sambur may be met with.

Descending to the foot of the hills from Mussourie, we find forests of sál, sénd, and bamboo ; then comes the wide flat valley of the Doon, watered by several rivers, and bounded on the southern side by the curious Sewalik hills, which seem as if they had slipped away from the Himalayas.   .

The valley of the Dehra Doon, where not under cultivation, is covered with heavy grass jungle and beautiful forests intersected by many streams, and is the resort of the Elephant, the Tiger, the Panther, and of herds of deer and antelope of various species, including Sambur, Spotted Deer, Hog Deer, Barking Deer, Nilgai, and Four-horned Antelope.

The Sewalik hills are a perfect paradise for the sportsman who is fond of stalking, and prefers a mixed bag on foot to the larger numerical bag that may be made off Elephants in a less broken country. The Sewaliks are composed of a series of abrupt rocky ridges intersected by deep, narrow, and tortuous ravines with stony watercourses. These ravines are called '*sotes*' ; the rocky watercourses are called '*ráos.*' The hills between the '*ráos*' are more or less densely covered with jungle, consisting chiefly of sál, sénd, bamboo, and máljan creeper, with, of course, an undergrowth of rank grass. Here and there are flats and hollows among the hills ; and on following up some narrow branch of a '*sote*' one may find it debouch into a shady amphitheatre with pools of water, probably the favorite standing place of some old solitary Tusker. In addition to the beasts met with in the Doon itself, the Black Bear (*Ursus labiatus*) and the Gooral are also to be found.

The 'Terai,' or belt of forest extending for some distance from the foot of the hills, from the Doon on the west to our very eastern frontiers, is the home of countless " Large Game," including all those species that have already been mentioned as occurring in the Doon, with the addition of the Swamp Deer, the Buffalo, the Gaur, and two kinds of Rhinoceros.

The vegetation of the Terai is very rank and luxuriant: in addition to noble forest trees, which are frequently grouped in masses affording ample shade, there are copses of leafy bushes whose tangled branches are almost impenetrable ; wide plains covered with high grass here and there occur ; while on the margin of some treacherous swamp or on the banks of some sluggish stream, are wide belts of ' *nul* ' and ' *burroo* ' reeds growing to the height of twenty feet or more, and so dense that none but the most powerful animals could possibly force their way between their stems. On the edges of such cover, or in the shade of some cool ' *boja* ' (as a thick grove of trees with bushy undergrowth is called) Tigers and Panthers delight to spend the hottest hours.

It is a grand sight to see a long line of Elephants beating through the Terai for Tigers —the solemn silent manner in which the line advances, each Elephant forcing his way straight ahead, only deviating from his course when some large stem or branch which it is beyond his power to break down, impedes his progress. The silence is occasionally broken by the crash of a tree levelled by the huge beaters, by the angry trumpet of an enraged animal as he is forced through an unusually thorny thicket, or by the abuse heaped upon a lazy or restive Elephant by the Mahout.

The howdah Elephants on which the sportsmen are mounted are distributed at intervals along the line, and, as the beat progresses, some commotion may be observed as various species of game are roused. Rifles may be raised as a rush through the high grass, and the moving stems, show the direction taken by some Chítal or Hog Deer ; but as yet it is not allowable to fire at such small deer, and the rifles are again lowered. A little later, and another rush accompanied by an angry grunt, and immediately followed by the shriek of one of the more timid pad Elephants, raises the hopes of those who are not near enough to see that it is only a sounder of Pig, headed by a surly old boar, whose ill temper at being roused from his noonday slumbers made him charge back through the beaters with a vicious cut at the legs of his nearest disturber.

The line advances half a mile further ; and an old Tusker, who probably saw Tigers shot before any of the sportsmen present were born, raises his trunk in an ominous manner, then strikes it angrily on the ground, and shows plainly that he is aware of the presence of something that displeases him. He is too staunch and experienced to be afraid of Pig, and he does not even *fear* a Tiger, but would, if permitted, rush in on one as soon as he saw it ; however, his uneasiness is pretty certain proof of a Tiger being near. The belt of cover is not here very wide, so the pad Elephants are ordered to close in, and they advance in compact order with a howdah on each flank, while one or two more guns have been sent half a mile further on to where there is a break in the cover.

The Tiger,—or there may be a family of them,—ought now to be considered as bagged ; and it entirely depends upon circumstances whether they are shot down at once as soon as seen, or only 'padded' after a prolonged and exciting fight. Most of my readers have probably read enough "Tiger stories" to prevent the necessity for my giving a long account of a Tiger fight now, more especially as I have related what I have actually seen in the chapter devoted to that animal.

This is the way in which Tigers are shot in the Rohilkund, Oudh, and Nepal Terai, in all of which hunting is frequently successfully carried on by beating every likely place, regardless whether Tigers are actually known to inhabit them or not.

In the Sikkim Terai, the Bhútán Dooárs, and still further east in Assam, however, the jungles are so extensive and dense, and the grass and reeds so high, that unless Tigers are marked down, it is in many places utterly useless to look for them. Even if found they could not be killed in the dense beds of reeds which frequently prove a safe asylum for the Rhinoceros and the Buffalo. The Gaur also occasionally takes refuge in such fastnesses, but as a rule he prefers to spend the day under the shade of the umbrageous trees, whose heavy masses adorn the lowest skirts of the hills.

The habits of each animal will, however, be more fully treated of in the proper place.

Having thus conducted the reader in fancy from the west of Thibet to the south-east end of the Himalayan range, I will ask him to accompany me to our north-west frontier.

Here he will find that between Peshawur and Jhelum, from the foot of the Himalayas to the junction of the Punjab rivers, the land is broken up in a most fantastic way. Low ranges of hills, of which the Salt Range is the highest and most conspicuous, run in various directions ; while, besides these upheavings of the soil, it is also hollowed out in an extra-ordinary manner, producing as it were a second series of hills and valleys, the summits of these lower hills only reaching the level of the bases of the ranges above.

Thousands of ravines of various depth and width intersect the country in every direction, and any one unacquainted with the locality would find the greatest difficulty in making his way from point to point, even on foot. To wheeled carriages, and even to beasts of burden, the country is impassable, except along two or three lines of communication, of which the grand trunk road is the only good one. An invading army would have hard work in fighting its way from Attock to Jhelum. Water has evidently been the power at work which has so furrowed the country, and it would be interesting to know how many centuries were required to produce such results.

Oorial and Chikara are scattered all over this country, inhabiting alike the hills and the ravines.

On the Indus leaving the rocky hills—between which it has hitherto been imprisoned—at Kalabagh, it opens out into a wider channel ; the soil being soft and sandy, the course of the river is constantly changing ; the bank on one side may be seen falling in at the rate of many acres a day, while the earth and sand thus swept away accumulate and form islands in other places. These islands and the banks of the river where not cultivated, are generally covered with long grass and '*jhdo.*' In former times the Swamp Deer (or '*Goind,*' as it is here called) used to be common, but it is now very rare.

A large expanse of sandy desert extends from the right bank of the Indus to the low rocky ridges which form the line of our western frontier ; and a more inhospitable looking country cannot be imagined than the 'Deraját.' From Dera Ismail Khan, one of our Frontier Stations, to the hills, is a distance of about forty miles. On one of the highest peaks the small Sanitarium of Sheikh Boodeen has been established, to which people from Bunnoo and Dera Ismail Khan principally resort during the hot months. The hill is very steep and rugged, and there is little vegetation on it ; a few wild olive trees, palm trees and thorny bushes being the only green things to relieve the eye. On the top of the hill is a tolerably level space around which the houses are built. Rain water for washing purposes is collected in tanks constructed at the top of the hill, but the supply is very precarious, and all drinking water is brought from the foot of the hills, a distance of eight miles, with an ascent of about 4,000 feet !

This hill, barren as it is, is the resort of great numbers of Markhoor and also of a few Oorial.

The Suleiman Range and other mountains just beyond our frontier are said to abound with Markhoor of the largest size, and with other sorts of game ; but as yet these hunting grounds are inaccessible to the English sportsman.

The plains of India require little description. One monotonous deadlevel, generally under cultivation, but with occasional tracts of low jungle, and expanses of waste land, possesses no charms in the way of scenery, and the sport to be obtained is hardly more varied Antelope and Gazelles, and here and there Nilgai, are the only large game to be shot. One sport indeed to be obtained here can never be called tame,—I allude to Pigsticking, which will be duly described in the chapter on the Boar.

CHAPTER II.

THE TIGER.

FELIS TIGRIS.

Generally throughout India—*Bágh—Shér—St.*

THE Tiger is found in suitable situations all over India, and even occasionally ascends the Himalayas nearly to the limit of the snows. The broad belt of forest at the foot of the Himalayas, termed the Terai, and the lower spurs of the hills, are the great strongholds of Tigers in Northern India ; from which stragglers occasionally stray to great distances, and are found where they would be little expected.

Tigers vary much in height, in girth, and in length of tail. The fairest mode of comparison, if it could be carried out, would be by weighing. The color varies a good deal, some being darker than others : and the number and arrangement of the stripes also varies much. As a rule the color becomes lighter, and the stripes fewer and less distinct, as the animal advances in age. Young Tigers have longer and more *fluffy* hair than the old ones, though I. have seen a very old male with a great deal of long hair about his throat, forming, indeed, a sort of mane.

Although I do not pretend to be an authority on Tiger-shooting—having only been in at the death of fifteen or twenty—I have the pleasure of the acquaintance of men who have shot hundreds, and I only state what is corroborated by the unanimous testimony of all the experienced men with whom I have conversed on the subject, when I express my belief that the size of the enormous Tigers of which one frequently reads, has been immensely exaggerated. The measurements of eleven, twelve, and even thirteen feet, which have been frequently given, could only be obtained from stretched skins, or by some error in the measuring tape, or defect in the memory of the writers. Even by measuring along the curves of the body instead of in a straight line from nose to tip of tail (the only fair way), not more than a few inches would be gained.

It is, of course, not beyond the bounds of possibility that there may be giants among Tigers as among the human race, but when one individual asserts that he shoots many of these Brobdignagians, while others with far greater experience never have the good fortune to meet with a single specimen, the conclusion forced upon the impartial mind is, that the man of exceptional experiences must have been travelling with Gulliver in the land of Romance.

Captain Forsyth, in his admirable book on the Highlands of Central India, fully bears out what I have just written, and adds that "the British Public demands twelve feet Tigers!" As I am writing for sportsmen, and endeavouring to give reliable information, I trust that I may be excused from truckling to the popular demand.

The Tiger, as is well known, delights in thick cover in the vicinity of water. In the cold weather, when water is plentiful, the Tigers are much scattered; a great many of them betaking themselves to the lower hills and wandering about a great deal. At this season there is no certainty of finding them. As the hot weather approaches water becomes scarcer; much of the grass jungle is burned; and the Tigers frequent the shady jungles on the banks of rivers, beds of reeds on the margins of swamps, and such cool and moist retreats. They are then disinclined to move during the heat of the day, and may be found for a certainty in the places which they are known to frequent, and when once found can be generally accounted for. At this time they frequently do great damage among the herds of cattle, which are of course obliged to be kept in the neighbourhood of water.

It is rarely that Tigers become man-eaters in Northern India, probably on account of there being such abundance of game and cattle for them. Unless provoked the Tiger will rarely attack a man, but does his best to get quietly away. Tigers vary much in their dispositions, some fighting desperately, and others dying like curs without attempting to be revenged on their assailants.

Tiger-shooting is such a well worn theme that I would dispense with all notice of it were it not that no series of anecdotes of Indian sport would be considered complete without it; and as I am not in the fortunate position of the man who was congratulated by his friend as being the only old Indian he had ever met who had *not* shot a Tiger, I suppose I must add a few reminiscences under this heading.

The different methods of shooting Tigers, *viz.*, from the backs of Elephants, from platforms on trees, and on foot—by beating, driving, or watching, have been written about a hundred times. I will not, therefore, weary the reader with "vain repetition," but will merely mention that all the different methods are adapted to different circumstances; and that as there are times when shooting off Elephants is not merely the *safest*, but the *only* way in which a Tiger could possibly be brought to bag, so, on the other hand, there are places where Elephants cannot go, yet Tigers may be shot on foot with but little risk. Even the usually despised plan of sitting in a tree over "a kill" may be the only feasible way of getting a shot; and tedious as this undoubtedly is, the man who is a naturalist as well as a sportsman will find much to interest him during his solitary watch. I say *solitary*, advisedly, for no one, who does not wish to have his labor for nothing, will ever permit a native to sit with him. I have never yet seen the native who could keep quite still and absolutely silent. All that I have met with either become excited, or fidget, or cough, or talk, or go to sleep and snore!

In the Terai the only way of shooting Tigers is off Elephants: shooting them on foot is simply impossible: the grass is so high that the Tiger could not be seen. Those who have shot Tigers on foot in the Bombay Presidency and other parts, where Tigers are driven out of nullahs, may disparage the Terai shooting, but the nature of the countries is so different

C

that it is impossible to apply the same rules to both. Some will decry all Tiger-shooting on foot as foolhardiness, and others will compare Tiger-shooting off an Elephant to "shooting a mad dog from the roof of an omnibus!" I can speak with no authority on the subject, never having had the opportunity of shooting a Tiger on foot, with the exception of one wounded one, as described hereafter. I think, however, that there is little doubt that Tiger-shooting on foot may be carried out with very little risk in favorable localities if properly conducted, as described by Mr. Rice in his most interesting book. For my own part, I should not have the slightest hesitation in firing at a Tiger if he were going away from me, or if I had the advantage of being above him or behind a tree ; but I think that no one who values his life should walk up to a Tiger which is expecting him, however confident he may be in his own shooting. Every one has heard how Tigers, which have been mortally wounded, have struck down men in their dying agonies ; and almost every year some fatal accident occurs to add to the warnings, but they are still too often unheeded. Young sportsmen are usually ready to laugh at the danger which more experienced ones acknowledge, and though men are to be found who have made a practice of shooting Tigers on foot, still more have paid the penalty of their rashness, and those who do survive will usually be *among the first to point out the danger*. The blow of a Tiger's paw is irresistible, and though he may generally be turned from his charge, if he *does* charge home, death is nearly inevitable. With other animals this is not the case : the Elephant or the Gaur may be dodged and avoided ; while, however unpleasant, a "rough and tumble" with Bear, Leopard, or Pig is by no means necessarily attended with fatal consequences.

My first introduction to Tigers was in May, 1863. I was invited by M. to join his party, which consisted of his brother C. M., and B. He had upwards of fifty Elephants out, but as I had not been expected there was no howdah for me ; so I was provided with a '*Chár-jámá,*' a sort of padded seat with a light iron rail round it, not very comfortable nor easy to shoot from, but superior to an ordinary pad.

On the 5th of May the camp being at Kheree, not far from Roorkee, we proceeded to beat the jungles behind the bungalow. Tracks of Tigers were abundant, but we beat for a long time in vain. Coming to the end of what we intended to be the last beat, and seeing nothing but deer, we fired at them. I had just missed a Chítal, and finished reloading, when I saw a large Tiger going slowly up the high bank about fifty yards off. I fired at him, and he fell back and lay for several seconds. I thought he was done for, but he got up again, and as the Elephant moved, I missed with my second barrel. Dismounting, I reloaded and ran up the bank with my Shikari. We found a row going on up above, the Tiger having charged and scattered the Elephants ; and on M.'s coming up, he insisted on my mounting the Elephant with him. Two Tigers were on foot, but the Mahouts funked and let them get away. M. and I went in search of my Tiger, while the other two went after the second one. We had a long hunt without success ; but they were more fortunate, found, and killed their Tiger.

We returned to camp to breakfast, and again went out in the evening. After going a very short distance we saw a Tiger returning from the water and went after him at once.

M. fired at him and sent him my way. He cantered out of the jungle and stood still, offering a splendid shot within twenty-five yards, but before I could fire, my Shikari had the impertinence to fire my small rifle at him. As he sprang forward I fired, and heard the shell burst, but could not see whether it struck the Tiger or not. We found blood, and followed up the track, but it soon became dark, and we had to give it up. I was much disappointed with my bad luck.

Next day we hunted all forenoon without seeing a Tiger. After breakfast a man came in with news of a cow having been killed a short distance off. On proceeding to the place in the afternoon we found a Tiger, C. M. had a shot, and I followed the beast up. I came on him once, but had to turn round to fire, and only had a snap shot at his tail as it disappeared in a bush. We then lost him.

May 7th. The Tigers carried off the dead cow last night, so this morning we went to look for them. As we approached the bushes in which the carcase was, there was a roar, and *three* Tigers came charging out, tail on end ! I was outside the jungle, and only got a long snap shot. C. M. dropped one of the smaller ones, and I followed the other into some very long grass. I came right on him, and he jumped up under my Elephant's trunk. I blazed at him, but as I did so the Elephant backed, and my Shikari took a 'header' right under the Tiger's nose, carrying my second rifle with him ! This alarmed the Elephant so much that she turned and bolted, followed by the Tiger, who was so close under my Elephant's tail that I could not get a shot at him. At last I fired off a barrel without any aim, and the Tiger went back into the grass, where C. M. and the Shikari finished him. The Shikari only got a very slight scratch, and his jacket torn ; but the stock of my rifle was broken. Meanwhile M. and B. had killed the old Tiger and Tigress, which had gone to the other side of the covert. The former had an old shell wound on his shoulder, from the edges of which the hair had been licked away, so he was without doubt the one I fired at on the first day : the shell must have burst too soon, or it must have killed him. The young Tigers were about three parts grown. All four were polished off in less than ten minutes.

On the 9th we had a long day, and were beating homewards across a level grassy plain, when some of the Mahouts who had lagged behind luckily saw a Tiger, which we had passed by. We went back after him, but he lay very close, and B. and I were nearly on the top of him before he would show. We both blazed at him as he went off, but both missed. We now chased him in view for about a mile across the open, he keeping just in front of us. B. fired several shots, and M. joining in, did the same without effect. I kept my Elephant going as hard as she could until I got a good chance, when I fired, and sent a shell into the Tiger, which completely paralysed him, and M. gave him a finishing bullet. He was very lean, and bore the scars of fights, though he never made the slightest attempt to attack us.

On the 12th we beat two Tigers out of a regular network of ravines. C. M. had all the fun, and shot them down in capital style.

While shooting on foot in the Sewaliks, after M. had left, I on one occasion came close upon a Tiger, but did not get a shot. I was walking across an angle of the Undera Kohl, between two bends of the stream, when I saw a branch move and heard a rush about fifteen yards in front of me. Thinking it was a deer, I walked slowly on, and found the fresh tracks of a large Tiger, with the water still oozing into them, but I could see nothing more of him. On one or two occasions at night I heard Tigers close to my tent, and once sat up in bed with my rifle cocked, so close had the brute approached; but he seemed to dread the fires which I kept burning all night, and I heard him walk away. Another evening I waited for a Tiger by a pool of water; he did not appear, but as I was walking home in the dark we distinctly heard him snuffing within thirty yards of us. I sat down on a stone and tried to make him out; but though I knew the very bush he was under—a large '*máljan*' creeper— I could not see him.

In 1865 I went out after Tigers in the Bijnour district. On the 18th of April I shot a Tigress at Burrapoora, and on the following day I shot a Tiger; neither of them gave particularly good sport, though the Tiger made one fine charge at me, which I stopped with a bullet in the shoulder. For several days afterwards I got nothing, but missed one Tigress.

On the 27th, having sent away all the Elephants except one, which I rode, I proceeded to beat some ground which I had hunted the previous day, in hopes of getting a few Hog' Deer. Going over a nearly bare and most unlikely-looking plain, I had sat down in the howdah, when, on reaching some thin but longish grass, a Tigress suddenly sprung up. Before I was ready she was out of shot, but soon brought up in a thick clump of grass. I went after her, and found her crouched ready for a spring. I fired, and her head dropped between her fore-paws. Seeing a wound in the nape of her neck, and the blood streaming over her face, I thought she was done for, so would not give her another bullet, but went in search of men to assist in padding her. Having taken off the howdah, I returned on the pad, and was surprised to find that the Tigress had moved into the grass. I felt sure that she was past doing mischief; so, as I was anxious not to spoil her skin, I slipped off the Elephant and walked into the grass. I found the Tigress sitting up, but evidently quite stupid, so I fired a bullet into her chest from a distance of two or three yards. She dropped to this, and we pulled her out by the tail. After some minutes, as she still continued to breathe, I fired a bullet with a small charge of powder into her chest, and thought for a moment that I had finished her; to my amazement, however, she got on her legs and began to crawl away, creating a panic among the bystanders. This would not do! so I had to shoot her through the heart. I then found that the wound on her neck was an old sore occasioned by fighting; my first bullet had struck below the eye, merely splintered the bone and gone out again without doing much harm; it had luckily stunned her. We now padded her, and took her home.

On the 29th of May I was encamped at Rikki Kase, on the Ganges, in the north-east corner of the Doon. I had shot an Elephant the day before, and this morning I sent out my first gun-carrier (a hill man, Moti by name), in company with two villagers, to cut out the teeth. About twelve o'clock one of the villagers came in with a story of having met with a Rogue Elephant, and feared that he had caught the other two men. I rather laughed at the story, and waited for the others to arrive. In about half an hour the other villager came in howling and declaring that Moti had been killed by the Elephant. On cross-examination, however, I found that he had merely heard a noise, and had at once bolted without waiting to see what had become of Moti; and from his account I was quite certain that it could not have been an Elephant which they met, but probably a Tiger, or perhaps only a Pig. I at once set off for the place, and, guided by. the villagers, came to a patch of '*nul*' (a species of high thick reed), close to where I had shot the Elephant. I entered this, and soon found the axes and other things which the men had thrown away in their flight; and a pace or two further on I found poor Moti lying on his face. I lifted him up, and found that he was quite dead, with the marks of a Tiger's teeth in his throat. He had evidently come upon the Tiger asleep, and the brute must have jumped up and killed him instantly. I had given him a gun before he went out, but he had foolishly fired off both barrels immediately after leaving camp; the gun and a jungle fowl which he had shot were still-in his hand. I was sorry for poor Moti, as he was a plucky, willing fellow. His brother was with me, and helped to carry him to camp; he was soon deposited in the Ganges.

None of the Hindoos at Rikki Kase would sell a cow or a buffalo to be tied up as a bait for the Tiger, so I took a buffalo calf by force, and fastened it under a tree, close to the '*nul*' where poor Moti was killed. I made a '*machán*' in the tree, and took my station in it about four o'clock. I waited till about nine o'clock, when it became too dark to see to shoot, and I had ordered men to come to meet me with torches. No Tiger came; in fact I hardly expected it; as it had evidently only killed Moti on being surprised, and not with any intention of eating him. I heard a Tiger roar at a great distance, and several Elephants came to drink at a pool near the tree, and when I descended to go home, I heard them all round me.

Talking of Tigers *roaring*, the word is rather out of place: the sound heard at night is more a sort of moan than a roar, and when a Tiger charges, it utters a series of loud angry grunts.

Tigers are met with so unexpectedly, that it is wise never to walk in jungles frequented by them without a loaded gun or rifle in one's hand; a shot in the nick of time will very probably either stop or turn a charge. I had on the previous day walked through the very patch of '*nul*' in which Moti was killed, without any gun in my hand, but I have taken good care to be armed ever since when walking through ' Tigerish' places.

When spending the hot months at Murree in 1874, I used frequently to make short shooting excursions, and used occasionally to hear of kills by Tigers and Panthers. I promised a reward to any one who would bring me immediate news of a fresh kill, and consequently many days seldom passed without my receiving '*khubr*' of some sort. On enquiry, however, it usually turned out either that a cow or goat had been killed about a week before, or else that the village Shikari had been trying to get a shot at the wild beast,—whatever it was,—and so spoiled my chance of success.

On one occasion, however, a villager came in with the news that a Tiger had recently killed three cows, and that he was known to be in a certain heavy jungle on a steep hill-side.

I at once started for the place, and after a walk of about seven miles, most of which was down hill, I reached two or three small houses situated in a low hot valley. A few hundred yards from these houses was the jungle in which the Tiger was said to live, and the people declared that they heard him nearly every night. I now made enquiries as to the situation of the kill, and found that it was on a rather open spot on the top of a low ridge where several nullahs joined. There were only a few bones left, but as Tigers sometimes visit the scene of a kill when hardly anything remains, I determined to watch the place. There were no large trees near, so I had a shelter constructed of green boughs on the ground, and tied up a cow in a conspicuous position within about twenty-five yards of the ambush. About four o'clock I commenced my watch, giving orders to the villagers to come at once if they heard a shot, but otherwise not to come for me until about nine o'clock, when they were to bring torches. There was no moon, so it was useless to sit up very late. The hours passed away slowly enough until the approach of dusk, when it became necessary to be particularly on the alert, and to strain every sense to prevent the possibility of the Tigers approaching without being discovered.

On such occasions the ear becomes wonderfully sensitive to the slightest sounds, but it is extremely difficult to educate the eye to see at all clearly at night, and the best eyesight is frequently entirely at fault. In the present instance there was nothing to see, for not even a Jackal paid me a visit, but my hopes were raised to the highest pitch by hearing the distant moan of the Tiger. This was early in the evening, but the sound was not repeated, and the Tiger must have taken his walk in some other direction, for although I left the cow tied up when I returned to the village, we found her untouched in the morning. I could not spare another night at this time, so I returned home, leaving my Shikari with orders to picket a cow every evening, and to send me immediate news if it was killed.

Two days afterwards a man came in hot haste, with the intelligence that the cow had been killed. It did not take me long to make my few preparations and again set out for the scene of the kill.

I reached the village early in the afternoon, and found that my Shikari had gone to view the carcase of the cow in the morning and had found that very little of it had been eaten. Without loss of time I made him guide me to the spot, which was indeed plainly indicated by the vultures which soared over it, and perched on the surrounding trees. It was close to where I had watched for the Tiger, and on this occasion he had dragged his prey a little way down one of the ravines. On reaching the bush under which the Shikari had left the dead cow, we found it was gone, but a few paces farther on we found the remains, a great part of the flesh having been devoured since morning. The grass was much trampled down, and it seemed as if two Tigers had been at work, while from the appearance of the carcase it was evident that they had only just left, probably on hearing our approach. There was only one tree of any size from which a view of the carcase could be obtained ; I at once ascended it, and having made a slight screen of green boughs hastily adjusted, I dismissed my attendants with orders to come for me about an hour after dark, as on the previous occasion. There was but little shade from the tree in which I was perched, so I had the full benefit of the hot afternoon sun ; this I did not much mind, but I *did* mind the swarms of mosquitoes which came out a little before dusk and attacked me savagely at the very time when I most expected the Tiger. I have not yet met the man with sufficient stoicism to bear the bites of mosquitoes unflinchingly; and on this occasion, although I tried to avoid moving, it was beyond human endurance to refrain from occasionally brushing away the tormentors from my face. Whether the Tiger came and caught sight of me, or whether he never returned, I could not ascertain; but just before dark I heard some animal rush through the jungle, and I caught a glimpse of something red. It struck me at the time that whatever it was moved too quickly for a Tiger, and that it was probably only a Jackal or a Barking Deer. Be this as it may, I neither saw nor heard anything more, and returned to the hut where I was staying considerably disappointed.

As the Tiger had had a good feed, I thought it best to leave him alone for a few days and tempt him again when he was hungry; I therefore returned home and waited till it was nearly full moon. I then revisited the Tiger's jungle, and this time tied up three cows on different parts of the hill-side, and had them watched from a distance during the day. The animals were provided with food and water, and were left out all night.

On the evening of the second day the cows were still unmolested, and as we had not seen a fresh track nor heard the Tiger's voice, we began to think that he had left his favorite haunt for a time. At daybreak on the third morning however, on going my rounds as usual, I found a cow missing. A broad trail through the adjoining bushes showed plainly what had become of her, and I proceeded to follow it up. The peg to which the cow had been tethered had been torn up, and the cow dragged down the hill into very thick cover. As the cow was a good sized one it must have been a large Tiger which could carry it through so many obstacles. After following the trail for about a quarter of a mile, I found the cow lying under a thick bush; she was still warm, and the tooth holes in her throat were the only marks of violence. For several yards in every direction was a dense cover of low bushes, and it would have been absolutely impossible to have obtained a shot at the Tiger had I left the cow where she lay. I therefore dragged her four or five yards into an open space which I found I could command very well from a tree which grew near its edge. I at once made my men cut a quantity of branches with as little noise as possible, and with them I constructed a capital nest in the tree and within a quarter of an hour I had comfortably established myself in it. I then dismissed my attendants with orders to bring me some sandwiches and a bottle of beer at midday, when they would be least likely to disturb the Tiger. The morning passed away without incident; some vultures collected on the neighbouring trees, but they seemed to know that they must wait for the master of the feast to take his share before they could regale themselves. About midday my dinner arrived, and was handed to me in silence, my men being again dismissed by a sign.

During the afternoon several birds of various species visited my tree, and as I remained perfectly motionless, they sometimes came within a few inches of me; and once a slender snake came gliding along the branches and passed close to my face with a most graceful undulating motion.

About four o'clock a skulking Jackal made his appearance, and it was most amusing to observe the cautious manner in which he approached the carcase: with his tail tucked in he sneaked along, casting uneasy glances in all directions, and frequently stopping and raising his head to sniff the tainted air, partly doubtless to enjoy the gamey flavor of the beef, and partly to try and detect the presence of the enemy whom he evidently suspected.

Gradually gaining confidence, he at last walked up to the carcase and began tugging at it. He could not make much impression on the nearly unbroken skin, but while busily engaged in his occupation he suddenly darted away. Now, I thought, the Tiger is coming; but it was only another Jackal whose tread the first comer had heard, and, with the cowardice of a guilty conscience, mistaken for that of the rightful owner of the beef.

Both Jackals now turned their attention to the cow, but they were evidently not at all at their ease, and before long slunk away. Not long after their departure, my hopes were again roused by hearing the low suppressed voice of the Tiger as he approached from a neighbouring ravine. Nearer and nearer he came, at a very leisurely pace, and at last I could plainly hear him within thirty yards. How I strained my eyes to penetrate the screen of leafy bushes, and gain a view of even a square inch of his hide; how motionless I sat with finger on the trigger, hardly even venturing to breathe, and momentarily expecting to see the Tiger emerge from the bushes and take possession of his property. But I was doomed to disappointment. Whether the Tiger got my wind, or suspected that all was not right, I do not know; but after lingering in the vicinity for some time without showing himself, merely uttering a few low whines, he moved away. I still hoped that he had only come to reconnoitre and would again return at night: I, therefore, remained at my post.

Towards evening the vultures, which had been collecting all day, became bolder; they approached nearer and nearer to the carcase, until at length one adventurous spirit hopped up to it and gave it a tug with his beak. This was the signal to the others: immediately there was a rush of wings, and from every point of the compass the foul birds poured in in rapid succession, until the dead cow was completely hidden by a surging mass of feathers, as about a hundred vultures, piled one on the top of the other, struggled and fought to get at the flesh which they had long gloated over. Not that those in the foremost, or lowest rank gained much by it; for the hide had not yet decomposed sufficiently for them to tear it; so they had to content themselves with pecking at the eyes and tongue, the holes made by the Tiger's teeth, and other vulnerable parts.

Soon they were disturbed by the return of the two Jackals, who rushed in amongst them, snapping right and left, and pulling out numerous feathers.

The vultures, however, did not treat the new comers with much respect; merely hopping away a few yards when a Jackal became demonstrative, and again returning to pick up what they could. Just before dark, both Jackals and vultures went away, the former apparently satiated, and the latter to roost in the trees around, in hopes of finding their breakfast ready for them in the morning.

"*The sun set, and up rose the yellow moon*" and as its full orb rose above the trees I could see the outline of the dead cow as plainly as by daylight. Anxiously I listened for the moan of the Tiger, and grasped my rifle at every rustle of the leaves, but the night passed away without another sign of him.

At daylight, my Shikari made his appearance, and, tired and disgusted, I descended from my tree after a weary watch of twenty-four hours.

The Tiger never returned to the cow, and although I subsequently tied up other baits for him he would never take them, and I left the neighbourhood without even getting a glimpse of the animal which I had taken such pains to secure.

Perhaps this unsatisfactory ending is disappointing to the reader : I cannot help it. Shooting adventures do not always end—as three-volume novels ought to—to the satisfaction of every one ; though even in novels there is generally a villain who has to be punished. In this instance, I suppose, I must have been the villain ; at any rate the Tiger had the best of it !

On one of my last expeditions against Tigers, in 1878, I was accompanied by two friends, S. and L. We had only a few days to spare, and we did not intend to confine ourselves to Tigers alone, but to take whatever came in the way. L., however, had never shot a Tiger, so I was anxious that he should bag one. I preceded my friends by a couple of days, to procure Elephants and make other arrangements. The Elephants which were lent to us were anything but staunch, as my narrative will show ; all the best Elephants at the station being *hors de combat* from one cause or another. Having reached the place where I intended to commence operations, I pitched the camp, and sent men in all directions for '*khubr*' of Tigers. I soon heard of two ; one had killed a calf within a mile of the tents only a day or two before, while another had killed a buffalo about three miles off. The former Tiger was said to inhabit a grass jungle, where there was much '*fussun*' (quicksand) and consequently impracticable for Elephants. The latter had killed the buffalo on the edge of a sál jungle, which was pretty extensive and rather open, so that there was no particular place in which we could reckon upon finding the Tiger at home. On the second morning after my arrival, my friends joined me, having lost their way and spent the whole night wandering about on a pad Elephant ! Breakfast, however, soon set them to rights, and about midday we started in search of the slayer of the buffalo.

On reaching the small collection of thatched huts, which represented a village in that part of the world, we were shown the place where the Tiger had seized the buffalo, and the track by which it had been dragged away was still visible, though nearly obliterated by recent rain. The villagers could give us no idea as to where we were likely to find the Tiger, but on enquiry I found that the sál forest was intersected by two or three narrow watercourses which eventually joined a large river which bounded one side of the forest. Although the jungle had been burned, there were dense patches left every here and there, where the grass had been too wet to burn, and there were many places where a Tiger might find the cool shade in which he delights.

I determined to beat along one of these watercourses to begin with : we had ten Elephants, so I asked L. to take the left of the line and follow the course of the stream. S. took the centre, and I was on the right, the pad Elephants being distributed between us, and our front

D

extending to about two hundred yards. Slowly and silently we beat for about a mile and a half, our progress being considerably impeded by the very rough ground in which L. soon found himself, the watercourse occasionally sub-dividing into several branches. As we approached the river, the stream which we had been following widened considerably: we had come along its right bank, and now crossing it at its junction with the river, we proceeded to beat back along the left bank, all of us still occupying our original positions in the line. The jungle now became much heavier, consisting of high forest trees, with an undergrowth of various creepers, and that tall rank grass in which Tigers are so fond of lying. We had proceeded about four hundred yards, when I heard an Elephant trumpet on the left of the line. We had already found out that several of the Elephants were very nervous, and evidently not to be depended upon, so I did not think much of the circumstance. Directly afterwards, however, I heard a shot, and a large Tiger came galloping down the rear of the line, till he came behind my Elephant, when he pulled up and stood gazing at me within thirty yards. I got a beautiful shot at his chest with my Express rifle, and he dropped on the spot, apparently dead. I had not much time to see, however, for my Elephant, apparently realising for the first time what was going on, took to flight, and I was fully occupied in endeavouring to avoid the branches of trees against which I was in danger of being dashed. The Mahout succeeded in stopping him before he had gone very far, but nothing would induce him to move a step in the direction of the fallen Tiger. I therefore shouted to the other Mahouts to bring up a female Elephant on each side of me, so as to give my Elephant confidence: not a man would move. There they sat motionless on their Elephants, pretending either not to hear or not to understand me. In vain I endeavoured to have my Elephant driven up to them—it was in the direction of the Tiger, and not a step would he stir, except away from the foe. In vain did I exhaust my stock of Hindustani invective, and make use of every threat that I either could or could not have carried into execution: the whole lot of Mahouts and Elephants were utterly demoralised, and it seemed hopeless trying to get them under command again.

At last S. and L. who were on the only two tolerably staunch Elephants, came along the line, and by dint of more strong language, and the advantage of being able to get within reach of the Mahouts, they managed to bring some pad Elephants to my assistance. I told them that I had knocked the Tiger over, and believed that he was dead. S. then said that he had hit him hard with his first shot, the beast having been roused in front of L.'s Elephant, and gone right down the line. We now contrived to get a few Elephants together, and force them up to the spot where the Tiger had fallen: here we found a great quantity of blood, and a bloody trail leading away from the place. Following this for a short distance we found that we were "hunting heel," the blood being that from the Tiger's first wound. Retracing our steps, we soon took up the proper track, and in two or three hundred yards came to a wet nullah filled with immense masses of a thick creeper, and long rank grass. I forced my Elephant through this without rousing the Tiger, but as there was no sign of his having gone out at the other side, S. went through it again. His Elephant soon showed signs of uneasiness, but he went ahead pluckily enough, and presently the Tiger bounded out from under his trunk and made off up the stream, L. and S. both getting shots at him. I saw him go into some dense reeds by the water's edge, and on hurrying up I saw the grass shaking, and fired into it. The Tiger was evidently there and nothing would induce my Elephant to go in. L. and S. soon came up, and their Elephants also objected to come to close quarters, and it was not for some time that the exact position of the Tiger could be ascertained, so as to give him a finishing shot.

The next thing was to beat down the grass so as to get at him, and this was also a work of some time and difficulty. When we were at last able to examine him, we found that he was a very heavy old male, measuring exactly nine feet nine inches in length. S.'s bullet, from a heavy 12-bore rifle, had caught him fair on the shoulder, and my Express bullet had hit him nearly in the centre of the chest; it would have been difficult to place two bullets better, and it was another instance of the uncertainty of ever dropping a Tiger on the spot, however straight the aim may be.

Our troubles were not yet at an end, for Elephant after Elephant absolutely refused to allow the Tiger to be placed on its back; and when we at last got one to submit, it was all that we could do to hoist the Tiger on to the pad; he was certainly a very unusually heavy one.

Altogether we had had a very exciting half hour, and had killed our Tiger under exceptionally difficult circumstances; for nothing is so hard to contend with as timid Elephants and unwilling Mahouts. I am afraid that some of the language used was not exactly what would have been approved of at an evangelical meeting, where I believe it is customary to express displeasure by praying for people. I dare say it comes to pretty much the same in the end!

We beat through a considerable extent of forest before we returned to camp, but saw nothing except a few deer and Pig. The only incident that took place was a savage onslaught by S.'s Elephant (a big tusker, with a very uncertain temper) on another and smaller tusker. Making a sudden rush at the unsuspecting pad Elephant, which had only time to turn its stern, he gave it a tremendous blow with his tusks, the tips of which had fortunately been sawn off. The pursued Elephant made the most of the forward impetus thus given to him, and bolted at full speed with his assailant close behind him. It was an amusing race for every one, except the riders of the two Elephants, to whom it was anything but a joke, as it led straight to the sál forest, in which there would be every chance of being dashed against a tree. Luckily, the extra weight told on the howdah Elephant, so that although he succeeded in reaching his victim once just after the start, he gradually dropped behind, and the Mahout contrived to stop him, just before reaching the forest, by throwing a cloth over his eyes. The next day we marched several miles, and on the day following we had a very long beat, but without seeing anything except a few deer.

On the third morning we were just about to leave the house of the hospitable Tea-planter, with whom we had been staying for a couple of days, when two natives came up and implored us to come and shoot two Tigers which had been fighting close to their village all night: they declared that the Tigers were still there, and that the people dared not stir out of their houses. This was an opportunity not to be lost, so we at once set out for the village.

It was about four miles off, and on reaching it we found that we had beaten close past it the day before.

The village consisted of about half a dozen thatched huts with the cowsheds belonging to them ; there were two or three small fields of maize ; and for several hundred yards on every side there was a level and tolerably open expanse of grass, with a few clumps of carda-mums, high reeds, and bushes scattered here and there. On approaching the village we saw the inhabitants clustering on the roofs, and at the doors of their houses, and we were assured that the Tigers were still somewhere quite close, though it was not known exactly in what part of the cover they then were. The guide, who had brought us, pointed exultingly to the marks in the grass, which showed unmistakably where the Tigers had been fighting or play-ing together in the morning, within a hundred and fifty yards of some of the houses.

I enjoined the strictest silence on all the Mahouts and other attendants, and proceeded to lay plans to cut off the retreat of the Tigers from the dense forest on either side of the small valley in which the village was situated, and from the impracticable grass jungle which was to be found both higher up and lower down the small stream, which flowed past the village.

Forming the Elephants in a semicircle between the nearest forest and the village, with S. on the right of the line, L. in the centre (which I thought the best place) and myself on the left, we proceeded to draw the first clump of cardamums, which was not above twenty-five yards square. The Elephants were hardly in motion, and had not yet reached the edge of the cover, when a Tiger walked out of it on my side and made off to the left. L. could not see him from where he was, and there was no use in standing on ceremony and letting the Tiger escape ; so I had to fire, and knocked him over. His roar, in response to the shot, was the signal for a general stampede among the pad Elephants, and mine followed suit. It was some minutes before I could get my brute round, but I at length succeeded, and managed to get another shot at the Tiger, which had only been able to drag itself a few yards. L., whose Elephant, though very slow, was tolerably staunch, now brought him up and gave the Tiger the *coup de grâce*.

I had only seen the one Tiger at which I fired, the precipitate retreat of my Elephant having prevented me from seeing much of what was going on, but I now learned that on my firing the first shot, another Tiger had been seen to bound away in the direction of the forest. We much feared that he had altogether escaped us, but being determined not to lose a chance we hurried off to the margin of the forest, and proceeded to beat each likely piece of cover in the direction of the village. It was too late, however, the second Tiger had evidently gained some stronghold ; and we saw no more of him. During our beat we had to explore one particularly thick piece of long grass, which actually extended to the margin of the village, and in this we found indications showing that the Tigers went up to the very doors of the houses ! Habit is second nature, and people accustomed to the vicinity of Tigers soon cease to be afraid of them. We now padded my Tiger and returned to the house, but on arrival there I found that the skin had been too long exposed to the rays of the sun, and was now utterly useless, the hair coming off in large patches at the slightest touch.

CHAPTER III.

THE PANTHER.

FELIS PARDUS.

Generally throughout India—*Shér—Gúldár Shér*. In Central India—*Téndwá*. In the
Himalayas—*Chítá—Chitrá—Lagá bagá*.

IT has long been a vexed question, both among naturalists and sportsmen, as to whether
the Panther and Leopard are distinct species ; and some writers have even gone so far as to
insist that there are at least three species of the large spotted cats which are as often called
by one English name as the other.

I use the word Panther so as to prevent the possibility of confusion with the Hunting
Leopard or Chíta (*Felis jubata*), which latter name is frequently wrongly applied to
the subject of the present chapter.

The Panther—in all its varieties—is a true cat, and is furnished with retractile claws.
It stalks its prey and kills it by suddenly springing on it from some hiding place. The
Chíta on the other hand, although it also stalks its game as far as possible, so as to place
itself in a favorable position, is enabled by its immense speed to run down the swiftest
animals. The paw of the cat would be ill adapted for this purpose, and accordingly we find
that the Chíta's foot is more like that of the dog, and that the claws are only semi-retractile.

Panthers undoubtedly vary much, in size, color, markings, and—to a certain extent—in
habits ; and if the most widely differing specimens were only considered, two or more species
might be established with much show of reason.

I have seen many specimens, both wild and in confinement ; I have inspected hundreds
of skins from various parts of India ; and I have heard or read most of the arguments in
favor of and against the theory that there is more than one species.   And I have come to the
conclusion that there are not sufficient grounds for separating the Panthers or Leopards into
anything but varieties.   Even the varieties are not, in my opinion, sufficiently defined to be
looked upon as permanent.

The largest are eight feet long or more, and are sometimes nearly as powerfully made as
a small Tiger, and they exhibit their power by preying upon full grown cattle, horses, and even
buffaloes. These large Panthers have frequently light-colored skins, with rose-shaped spots,
rather sparsely distributed ; the ground color of the skin forming a centre to each spot.

Again, the smallest Panthers—or, as many would call them, Leopards—may be found,

even when evidently adult, to measure not more than five feet six inches, or six feet, in length ;
and their skins are usually of a much darker hue than those of the largest variety, with the
spots much smaller, more irregular, and closely clustered together.   These Panthers, for the
most part, confine their attention to goats, sheep, dogs, and the smaller deer.

From the above descriptions, it might be inferred that the two species differ so widely,
that they might be separated with more propriety than in the case of many acknowledged
species of other genera.   But if a large number of skins were collected from different districts, the most strongly marked types of each variety placed at the extremities of a long
line, and the remainder carefully arranged between them, in the order of their resemblance to
the selected specimens, it would be found that there was a regularly graduated scale between
the two, a clearly established chain, without a missing or a faulty link.   In fact, it would be
impossible for any unprejudiced observer to say where the Panthers ended and the Leopards
began.   I *believe* that, if the same test were applied to the skulls, the same result would be
obtained.

The Panther is widely distributed throughout India, from the snow line of the Himalayas
to Ceylon, and from Kashmir to Bhútán ; it is found wherever there are hills, or jungles of
any extent.   Its habits vary to a certain extent in different localities ; and I believe that
climate and other causes, influencing its choice of prey and general mode of life, are the
origin of the wide variations in size and color.   Wherever it may be found, the Panther is a
fierce and destructive brute ; and although shy and cunning to the last degree, it is bold and
determined in its attack, when pressed by hunger, or roused to anger by interference.   It will
occasionally enter villages and houses, in broad daylight, and carry off its prey in spite of
man and dog ; and it will even attack human beings, who have never molested it : but, as a
rule, it is an animal rarely seen unless sought for. · Instances have been known of Panthers
becoming man-eaters, in which cases they are perhaps more to be dreaded than Tigers ; but
such instances are very few and far between.

In the Himalayas, Panthers always haunt the neighbourhood of sheep-folds, moving up
with the shepherds to the summer pasture grounds, and levying toll on the flocks and herds,
whenever they have an opportunity.   Dogs are also a very favorite prey of the Panther, and
the shepherds' dogs are all furnished with heavy spiked iron collars.   These dogs are sometimes splendid beasts and one has been known to kill a Panther single-handed in a fair fight.
The way in which these dogs frequently come to an untimely end is from the Panther suddenly springing on them from behind and taking them at a disadvantage.

In the less elevated parts of India Panthers delight in low rocky hills and ravines, and
regularly take up their abode in deep caves, where they spend the hottest hours.   They
appear to be more patient of thirst than Tigers, and are not so frequently found in close
proximity to water.   Although not possessed of the crushing power of the Tiger, the smallest
Panther is a formidable antagonist, and the wounds which it inflicts, though not fatal at the
time, often prove mortal owing to their poisonous nature.

Common as Panthers are, they are comparatively seldom shot by English sportsmen
except in certain favorable localities.   In large jungles, or where huge collections of rocks

and boulders afford secure retreats, it is frequently impossible to drive Panthers out ; and unless one is actually marked down, beating for them is often in vain.

Panthers of all varieties are extremely cunning and wary in their movements. They have an extraordinary faculty of concealing themselves in the most scanty cover ; their beautiful spotted skins harmonizing with almost any ground they may be lying on. They hide in thick cover during the day and prowl about in search of their game at night. Occasionally one may be seen sunning himself in the early morning on some exposed rock ; but a sportsman may wander for months, find tracks of Panthers every day, but never meet with the beast himself ; and it is only by the merest chance that a shot may be obtained.

The greater number that are killed by natives are shot over the carcases of animals that they have destroyed ; but few Englishmen have the patience to wait long enough for them, to ensure success. Unless much frightened, a Panther will almost invariably return to its ' kill ;' but sometimes not for two or three days, when the carcase of its victim has become perfectly putrid.

When beating for Tigers, Panthers are occasionally killed ; but very often they contrive to sneak away in cover where a Tiger would have no chance of escape.

I have often sat up for Panthers, but have not been very successful, on the whole ; and I should recommend the sportsman, who tries the plan, to be prepared for repeated disappointments. It frequently occurs that the Panther does not come till after dark, and under these circumstances it is impossible to shoot with any accuracy, even at a distance of ten or twelve yards. It is therefore a good plan, when there is no moonlight, to place a lantern so as to throw its light upon the carcase ; contrary to the popular notion that no wild animal will come near a light, the Panther does not take the least notice of it, and I have killed one within a couple of yards of a lantern. On two occasions, when I have neglected to take a lantern, I have had the mortification of hitting the goat which I had tied up as a bait, when actually in the Panther's jaws!

I have not killed very many Panthers, but I give an account of some that I have shot, and have also two or three instances of their ferocity which came under my immediate notice, to relate.

In 1863, when hunting for Tigers to the south of the Sewalik hills, we surrounded a small Panther. A shell from my rifle was the first that struck him, but as he did not at once die, he was fired at by every one and his skin quite spoiled. A few days afterwards as I was going up one of the 'ráos' in the Sewaliks, I came upon an enormous Panther crouching by some water. He was a long way off, and as I approached he sneaked off and I missed a difficult shot.

In 1865, while halting during a shower of rain under the shelter of a Brinjara's hut in Kansrao, I saw the head of some beast appearing above the long grass at the top of a cliff opposite to us. We could not make out what it was for a long time, but at length the animal got up and showed that it was a Panther. We went in pursuit, but the brute concealed itself, and we could not find it again.

On September 5th, 1869, on our return march from Ládák to Mussourie, my wife and I reached the dâk bungalow of Jahree, at the foot of the Deobund hill, and a few miles from the new station of Chakrátá which was then being built. We had with us a couple of Ládák goats, which were tied up in the verandah. About dusk I was sitting in the bunga-low when I heard a clattering noise outside, and on calling out to ask what was the matter, I was informed by my servants that the goats had run down the hill. I sent after them, and they were presently brought back, and I thought nothing more of the matter. A few minutes afterwards my wife happened to go into the verandah, where she found splashes of blood. She called me out to look at them, and we were puzzled to account for them. I then thought of examining the goats, and I found that the blood was pouring from a wound in the throat of one of the poor beasts. I now knew what had happened, and finding that the goat was badly injured, I gave orders for it to be killed. It was now dinner time, and our servants kept passing backwards and forwards between the bungalow and the cook-house, which was only a few yards off. After dinner I got the dead goat and tied it to a heavy log of wood which lay just outside the verandah. The road in front was only a few feet wide, and then came a sunk fence, beneath which was the grassy slope of the hill-side. I loaded my rifle, placed it in the corner of the room, and went to bed with very small expectations of hearing anything more of the Panther.

I had not been in bed more than five minutes before I heard the goat being dragged away. I jumped up, seized the rifle, and ran out, but it was too dark to see anything. I frightened away the Panther, however, and recovered the dead goat, which I replaced in the old spot, set a lantern by it, and sat down just inside the door of the room. I had not sat two minutes when the head and shoulders of the Panther appeared above the sunk fence. I allowed him to walk up to the goat, and as he was about to carry it off, I shot him through the heart. He was not four yards from the muzzle of my rifle, and he dropped dead. The explosion put out the light, but on procuring another, we had the satisfaction of finding a beautiful Panther lying by the body of the poor goat. He had a very handsome skin, which I was much afraid would be spoiled, as the weather was very wet; but thanks to the kindness of a friend at Chakrátá, it was taken the greatest care of, and I eventually had it splendidly cured.

Panthers wander about a great deal, and occasionally stray into places where they are little expected.

During the time that my Regiment was quartered at Meerut (in 1864 or 1865—I forget which) S. and F., two brother Officers of mine, were one day riding through cantonments when they saw an animal cross the road and go into a garden. They rode up to see what it was, but the beast had disappeared. They accordingly began hunting for it, and F. had reached the last bush when a Panther rushed out of it. F. had just time to wheel his horse round when the Panther sprang upon its hind quarters, seized F. by the arm, and pulled him off. The Panther then retreated into the garden, and F. having picked himself up, rode off to hospital, where his wounds were dressed. He had been badly bitten through the elbow, and had some claw marks on his sides. In the meantime S. had managed to procure a gun, and, accompanied by an Englishman who had formerly been a soldier, proceeded to beat for the Panther. It was now nearly dark, but they obtained torches, and after some rather exciting work they shot the Panther dead in the act of charging. He had a beautiful skin with the rose-shaped spots described as being characteristic of the largest Panthers.

On another occasion when my Regiment was marching down country near Kurnal, our Paymaster and a soldier servant who accompanied him, came upon a Panther in long grass and actually succeeded in killing it with small shot, but not without a tough fight, during which the soldier got severely clawed. It was a plucky but dangerous experiment to try.

I was staying at the hill station of Murree during the hot season of 1874, and knowing that there were a good many Panthers in the neighbourhood, I employed a man to go about and bring me news of cattle and goats having been recently killed. On the 10th of July he came in and informed me that a Panther had early that morning carried off a goat out of a sheep-fold about six miles from Murree: the carcase, of which very little had been eaten, was discovered in the jungle not far off, and the remains had been hung up in the fork of a tree. It was about four o'clock when I got the news, but I at once started and reached the place about an hour before dusk. I immediately procured a kid and tied it up on the spot where the dead goat had been found, which was a small open space on the edge of a densely wooded ravine. Sending away my Shikari I sat down behind a bush about fifteen yards from the kid, and made up my mind for a tedious watch. I had not waited more than a quarter of an hour when a small round head appeared above the edge of the ravine, and in another moment the whole animal came in sight, and I saw that it was a cub. It was quickly followed by *three* others! and all four stood looking at the kid, which was naturally in a great fright. In another moment the old Panther sprang out of the jungle, made a pat at the kid, and then crouched by its side. If there had been more space, I should have waited and watched the Panther's proceedings, but as I was afraid that she would drag the goat into the jungle, I fired at her at once, and immediately jumped up so as to see above the smoke. The Panther sprang into the air, fell backwards, and then disappeared among the bushes. I followed her tracks, and found her lying dead about one hundred yards down the hill. She only measured six feet four inches in length, but the skin was a good one. I had intended to have slept in the open, but a heavy thunderstorm came on which compelled me to take shelter in a cow-house where I was nearly devoured by fleas.

Two of the cubs, which had vanished when I fired, were caught and brought into Murree about a fortnight afterwards. The poor little beasts were nearly starved, but they soon recovered with good feeding, and although rather savage at first, they gradually became perfectly tame. One was for a long time in my possession, and was as quiet and playful as a kitten. It was chained up, and was great friends with a little terrier, though it would kill any other dog that ventured within its reach. It at last became so powerful, that I feared it might kill or seriously injure one of my children, so I reluctantly gave it away.

On the 11th of September I went out in the afternoon to look for Kakur in the forest

E

below the village of Dhanda. Not expecting to see anything else, I had only taken a minia-ture single barrelled Express rifle ('360 bore) by Henry, while my Shikari carried a shot gun. After a time we heard a Kakur barking about a mile below us, but I thought it was too late to go after him. A villager with me, however, declared that we had plenty of time, so we went down the hill at best pace. There were some old fields, now uncultivated, in the middle of the jungle at the foot of a steep hill : it was close to these fields that the Kakur was bark-ing, but it left off before we reach the place. The path led along the hill-side, and we followed it, keeping a good look-out below us. Suddenly Futteh Dín (my Shikari) called my attention to a Panther which was lying on its back, with all its legs extended, in one of the fields. It looked so large in this position that I at first thought it was a Tiger. I now regretted that I had only brought the miniature rifle, but I determined to try it, and at once commenced the stalk. I found that it was impossible to get very near the Panther, as after descending some way, I saw that if I went any lower, a belt of high trees at the foot of the hill would conceal the beast. I had, therefore, to climb along the face of some steep rocks till I could get a clear view, when I found that I was still about one hundred and forty yards from the Panther, which was now crouching with its tail towards me, but was looking back over its shoulder. As soon as I fired, it sprang forward with a roar and took a regular 'header' into the thick jungle below : there was a growl or two, the bushes shook for a short distance, and then all was quiet. On going down to the place where the Panther had been lying, I found some of its fur and the base of the bullet flattened out to about the size of a fourpenny bit. My Shikaris declared that the beast must be dead, but I did not feel at all sure of this, and insisted upon caution. I gave Futteh Dín the gun loaded with No. 5 shot, and made over my hunting-knife, together with a couple of rifle cartridges, to the village Shikari, telling him to hand the cartridges to me quickly if necessary. I then led the way into the ravine, telling Futteh Dín to be careful not to shoot me if the Panther seized me. The jungle was very dense and thorny, and I had to go in on my hands and knees, naturally keeping a very bright look-out ! After going about fifty yards I saw the Panther lying under a rock within five yards, with its broadside to me, but looking round at me. I whispered to the men that it was still alive, upon which they rapidly retreated a few paces. The beast seemed to be rather stupid, and I crept towards it till I could get a clear view ; but in order to do this, I had to pull aside the bushes and grass. I then aimed between the eyes and fired : the brute jumped and tumbled about for a minute or two, and again lay down under the rock, but was evidently past doing mischief. This was perhaps rather lucky, for on putting out my hand for a fresh cartridge, I found that the Shikari had carefully tied up those I had given him—to be ready in case of emergency—in his 'kummerbund.' Of course I had others in my belt, with one of which I quickly gave the Panther a finishing shot in the head. On dragging her out I found that she was a great beauty, but it was very lucky that I had followed her up so promptly. My first bullet had only hit her on the cheek, splintering the bone, but doing no further injury, and she would probably have completely recovered in a very short time.

On another occasion I received information of a Panther which haunted a certain village. Having provided myself with a pariah dog as a bait, I went to the village, and by the advice of the local Shikari, I tied up the dog at a point where several paths met, a few hundred yards from the village. The spot chosen was an open space in the jungle, where there were only a few bushes scattered about ; and I sat down behind one of these, within about twelve yards of the bait. It was full moon, and a beautiful still night, and as the wretched dog howled lustily there was a very fair chance of getting a shot at the Panther, if he was in the vicinity. I watched patiently for several hours, until at last the pariah appeared to resign himself to his disagreeable position, coiled himself up, and went to sleep. I fancy that I was not long in following his example, and I slept soundly until just before dawn, when I was awoke by the frightened yelping of the dog. Sitting up with my rifle in my hand, I saw a large Panther bound across the open space and seize the dog. It was nearly as light as day, but as the two animals struggled together, I waited till they should be still for a moment, so as to get a steady shot. Before the opportunity offered itself, the chain by which the dog was tied up suddenly snapped, and the dog escaping from the Panther's grasp made off at full speed, with his enemy in hot pursuit. All happened so instantaneously, that I had not a chance of a shot, and although I ran after the retreating animals I saw nothing more of them. Day was now commencing to break, so I shouted to my Shikari, who was sleeping in the village, and on his arrival told him what had happened. On examining the chain I found that it had been broken before, and mended by my servant with a bit of string, which naturally soon gave way. Of course, it was my own fault for not carefully inspecting the chain before making use of it, but that did not make the fiasco the less annoying. On searching for the dog, we found that he had made his way to the village, and scratched · violently at the door of a house. On the owner's opening it the dog rushed in, and the man saw the Panther turn away disappointed. The dog was very slightly injured, having only received a few rather deep scratches. On a subsequent night I again sat up for the same Panther, but I never saw him again.

In the Bhútán Dooárs in 1880 when out Tiger shooting with a friend, we received *khubr* of a Tiger having killed a cow about two miles off. The man who brought the news was very positive of its accuracy, and informed us that the jungle where the dead cow lay was a small one and easily beaten. We were soon on our way to the place, with about fifteen Elephants, and on arriving at our destination, we found a small and extremely tortuous stream, whose steep banks were fringed by belts of high and dense reeds. The cover only extended a short distance, so the guns were sent to the end, while the pad Elephants formed line and proceeded to beat. For some time none of the Elephants gave any indication of their having detected the presence of any wild beast ; but as they entered a very thick patch in a loop of the stream, two or three of them trumpeted, and we at once saw that game was on foot. The Elephants forced their way onwards in a dense mass, and presently something glided along the edge of the stream and crossed to my left. I could only see the grass move, but made my Elephant advance a pace or two, upon which the Panther (for such it was) raised its head to look for an opening to escape by. It was only twenty-five yards off, and a bullet from my heavy rifle immediately crashed through its neck, and it dropped without a struggle. This Panther was, of course, the slayer of the cow.

In 1882, I was at Falákátá in the Bhútán Dooárs, when I again received news of a kill. I had only two Elephants in camp, but at once set out. I had not gone above a mile before I heard shouting, and saw a Panther galloping across the open plain, pursued, at the distance of three or four hundred yards, by several men armed with big sticks, and their dogs. I shouted to the men to desist ; but it was some time before I could get them to obey. In the meantime, the Panther had disappeared among some tufts of grass, which formed the only cover that was to be seen for a considerable distance. Riding my Elephant up to these tufts, I commenced to examine them carefully : they were much scattered, and none of them seemed large enough to hide a peafowl. After closely inspecting a few of them, and satisfying myself that they were untenanted, I approached another, in which I felt confident that I could make out the spotted skin of the Panther. So certain was I, that I at length fired into the tuft from a distance of about twenty yards ; and as there was no response to the shot I made sure that I had either killed the Panther outright, or else that I had been firing at nothing. My Shikari evidently thought the latter ; but I rode my Elephant close up to the tuft, and bending over the front of the howdah peered down into the grass. The Elephant's trunk was actually touching the grass, but there was not a movement nor a sign of any animal. In another moment I again fancied that I could see spots, and a still more careful scrutiny showed me the heaving flanks of the Panther. He was evidently untouched, so I fired for his spine, and this time there was no mistake. He bounded out with a roar, and cantered slowly across a strip of meadow, making an angry demonstration against my pad Elephant. He was too much crippled to do harm however, and he soon lay down, and finally rolled over on his side, apparently nearly at his last gasp. I was unwilling to spoil his skin by giving him another shot, so I dismounted, and, standing close over him told my Shikari to finish him with a blow on the head with a thick stick. On being struck, the Panther gave an angry growl and struck at me with his claws, but his hind quarters being paralysed, he was unable to spring at me. He was so close, however, and his attack was so sudden, that I fired from my hip, smashing his shoulder to pieces, and singeing his fur. This effectually settled him.

One cannot be too careful, when approaching seemingly dying animals : many lives have been lost by neglecting the most ordinary precautions.

THIBETAN LYNX

FELIS ISBELLINA

Published by Thacker, Spink & Co., Calcutta.

CHAPTER IV

THE THIBETAN LYNX.

FELIS ISABELLINA.

In Thibet—*Ee.*

THE Lynx appears to be very rare in Thibet. During seven summers which I have spent there, I have only twice met with it, and know very little about its habits.

The Lynx stands about seventeen inches at the shoulder, but is enormously powerfully made, with teeth and claws large enough for an animal of twice its size. The color of its fur is a lightish red, merging into a very pale tint on the lower parts, which are faintly spotted. The tips of the ears are beautifully pencilled and jet black. The tail is very short, and black at the tip. The fur is soft and close.

The Tartars informed me that the Lynx frequently killed sheep and goats, and it is certainly armed quite formidably enough to do so. Hares, however, appear to be its favorite food ; and as they literally swarm in some places, it can have no difficulty in killing them whenever it likes.

In 1864, I saw a Lynx in the Kyobrung Valley, but as I was in hopes of finding Yâk, I would not fire at it.

On the 4th of July, 1866, I was hunting Oves Hodgsonii on the high ground between Hanlé and Nyima, when I suddenly came upon a female Lynx with two young cubs. I shot the mother, and as the cubs concealed themselves among some rocks, I barricaded them in, and went on with my hunting. On arriving in camp, I sent men back to try and catch the cubs : in this they succeeded, and brought them to me. They were about the size of half-grown cats, and more spiteful, vicious little devils cannot be imagined ; they were, however, very handsome, with immense heads and paws. For two or three days they refused all food, but at the end of that time they fed quite ravenously from the hand. They soon became very tame and playful, though always ready to set their backs up if at all teased, or if a dog came near them. They lived in perfect health for nearly a month, when one suddenly died without any apparent cause. I have since learned that its death was probably occasioned by its having its meat cut up for it. The cat tribe are accustomed to masticate their food thoroughly before swallowing it, and this they naturally do when cutting and tearing the flesh from their prey : when, however, the meat is cut into pieces they are apt to swallow it in lumps, which disagrees with them. The other Lynx lived to accompany me to the plains, and was in perfect health when, to my great annoyance, it was lost off my dâk gharry, near Delhi, owing to the carelessness of my servant. I had intended to have sent it to England.

In 1878, I saw a full grown Thibet Lynx in the possession of Dr. Anderson, the Curator of the Calcutta Museum. It had been brought down through Darjiling, and strange to say, it did not appear to be injuriously affected by the hot damp climate of Bengal : it was very tame and playful.

This Lynx is still living in the Zoological Gardens at Calcutta.

CHAPTER V.

THE INDIAN WOLF.

CANIS PALLIPES.

Throughout India—*Bhériá.* In Afghanistan—*Gúrg.*

THE Indian Wolf is generally distributed throughout the continent of India, and is also met with in Afghanistan. It appears to prefer the drier and more open provinces, and to avoid damp climates and extensive forests.

It is a smaller and lankier animal than the European Wolf, and its coat is considerably shorter. The general color is a brownish grey, with a sprinkling of black hairs.

The head is large in proportion to the size of the animal and the jaws are long and immensely powerful. The eyes have a peculiarly sinister expression.

Indian Wolves do not assemble in large packs, but are usually found alone or in pairs, though they occasionally hunt in small parties.

They are destructive brutes, and kill large numbers of sheep, goats and children, besides wild animals. They are generally cowardly beasts, but they not infrequently take to killing human beings, though in such cases they are very cunning in their selection of victims, and as a rule, only attack the weak and unarmed.

When impelled by hunger they sometimes become bolder, and when we were encamped at Jalálabád during the winter of 1878-79, sentries were on more than one occasion attacked by Wolves, which nightly visited our camp.

It is singular that it is matter of general belief in India that Wolves sometimes nurse and rear children that they have carried away—a story that appears to have gained credence in every country and every age, since the days of Romulus and Remus.

Although I have not infrequently met with Wolves, it has so happened that I have never shot, nor even fired at, one. I have, however, on two or three occasions reared cubs, and have found them most interesting pets. They have exactly the manners of dogs, and they become much attached to their master, though apt to be suspicious of strangers, and inclined to resent interference from any one who shows any fear of them.

In 1875, I became the possessor of a young cub which I christened ' Rom.' He was brought up with my dogs, and soon became perfectly tame. He was generally chained up, but when let loose, he would run about the house, or accompany me in my walks.

I could do what I liked with him, but he was the terror of a weak-minded cook, whose kitchen he used to invade with a view to plunder ; and on one occasion I found ' Rom ' standing on the lawn guarding a saddle of mutton, which he had abstracted, spit and all from the kitchen fire ; the cook being too much frightened to hinder him !

CHAPTER VI.

THE THIBETAN WOLF.

CANIS LANIGER.

THE THIBETAN BLACK WOLF.

CANIS NIGER.

In Thibet (The grey), *Chánko* ; (The black), *Chánko Nágpo*.

WOLVES of at least two sorts are found all over Thibet, and I am not sure that there are not three varieties. I know of two, the common grey 'Chanko' and the black one, called by the Tartars 'Chanko Nagpo' (Black Wolf) and which they say is fiercer and larger than the other, and will even kill Kyang. I have heard of a so-called 'Golden Wolf,' but whether it was a light colored specimen of the common Chanko, or a different variety, I am unable to say.

The Chanko is not gregarious in its habits, being usually found singly or in pairs ; but such is its strength and ferocity, that it commits considerable havoc among the flocks and herds belonging to the Tartars, apparently preferring the slaughter of tame animals to the harder task of circumventing wild ones. At any rate they are always to be found hanging on to the outskirts of the Tartar flocks. The common Chanko is about the same size as the common Wolf ; he is of a yellowish grey color, with very long and soft hair. The black Chanko is rather larger than the grey one ; he is of a beautiful glossy black, with a small white star on the chest, and a few grey hairs about the muzzle.

I have only a few times had the luck to meet with the common Chanko. The first I ever saw was at the head of the Kyobrung Valley, amidst the desolate solitude which I have already attempted to describe. I had penetrated to the very sources of the streams in search of Yâk, and had begun to retrace my steps without having seen a sign of life, when I suddenly caught sight of a Chanko, trotting quietly along the bottom of a ravine below me. I whistled to attract his attention, and on his stopping to listen fired a shot at him ; he dropped with a howl, but quickly recovered himself, and made off with a broken shoulder, and though I immediately followed him up, I soon lost the trail and failed to bag him. On other occasions I saw Chanko in the neighbourhood of Hanlé, and wounded another, but lost him.

On the 5th June, 1866, I was encamped at the foot of the Lanak Pass, between the Tsomoriri Lake and Hanlé, when one of my servants brought in a young Black Wolf apparently about three weeks old. He had procured it from some wandering Tartars, and informed me that they had another one. I at once recognized the value of my prize, and sent off a man to secure the other cub, which arrived next morning. I had only heard of one other Black Wolf having been met with by Englishmen, and that had been shot the previous year in the neighbourhood of the Mansarovara Lake. I was, therefore, particularly anxious to keep the young Wolves alive, and in this I was fortunately successful. Emptying a ' kilta ' I converted it into a kennel for the cubs, which I fastened to opposite ends of the only dog chain I possessed. I made the middle of this fast to an iron tent peg, which was driven into the ground, and thus the little beasts were secured. They fed ravenously on raw meat, and before long became pretty tame. When I marched they were bundled chain and all into the ' kilta,' the lid of which was then tied on, and thus they journeyed to the next halting place, the ' kilta ' being slung horizontally either to the pack saddle of a Yâk, or behind a coolie's shoulders. On camp being pitched they were taken out and pegged down. One night they managed to draw their peg, but they were fortunately discovered next morning, the chain having become entangled in a bush, about a mile from my tent. They accompanied me for more than two months, and before that time had become a good deal too large for their abode : they gnawed holes in it, and used to travel with their heads sticking out at opposite ends.

As I was quartered at Meerut, whither I had to return by the 15th of August, I was afraid that the heat of the plains would be too much for them ; so I left them in charge of a friend at the hill station of Kussowlie, near Simla, till the end of October, when I had them sent down to me. By this time they had immensely increased in size, but although they had not seen me for so long, they recognized me, and also my greyhound, of which they had previously been very fond. They soon became much attached to me, and would fawn on me like dogs, licking my face and hands ; they were always, however, ready to growl and snap at a stranger. I took them down to Agra at the time of the great Durbar there, and used to let them loose in camp with my dogs, so tame had they become.

I presented them to the Zoological Society, and they reached the Regent's Park gardens in safety : they lived there for eight or nine years, and produced several litters of cubs.

All the cubs were black, a fact which, I think goes far to prove that the Black Wolf is a separate species,* or at any rate a permanent variety, and not a mere instance of *melanism*, as some naturalists have supposed.

It has been stated, however, that a grey Wolf has been seen with a black cub: this might be accounted for by the not improbable explanation that black and grey Wolves, although distinct species, occasionally interbreed. It is well known that the Wolf will readily cross with the Dog, and that the progeny is fertile, showing how closely the two species are allied.

---

* The Black Wolf is now recognized as a distinct species, and has been named Canis niger by Dr. Sclater.

III

WILD DOG
CUON RUTILANS

Published by Thacker, Spink & Co., Calcutta.

CHAPTER VII.

THE WILD DOG.

CUON RUTILANS,

Throughout India—*Jangli Kútá.*   In Thibet—*Hási.*

THE Wild Dog is found in all parts of the hills, from the highest ranges of Thibet down to the foot of the Himalayas.

Wild Dogs frequently go in pairs, sometimes in packs, and wander about a great deal. They are fearfully destructive to game, and if their fresh footmarks are to be found upon a hill, farewell to any chance of sport in the neighbourhood ; for every wild animal will have been driven away. The Ibex seems to be a very favorite prey of the Wild Dogs, but nothing comes amiss to them ; ponies, cattle, sheep, deer, are indiscriminately slaughtered. Even the Tiger is said occasionally to fall a victim to the attacks of a pack, but this story requires confirmation. The Serow, it has been stated, is the only animal that is at all able to make a successful stand, occasionally transfixing his adversaries on his sharp and powerful horns.

Mr. Wilson and others have remarked that during the breeding season the Wild Dogs will, with extraordinary sagacity, drive a hunted animal to the vicinity of their earths before killing it, in the same way as an African hunter will drive an Eland up to the waggons before despatching him, thus saving the trouble of carrying the meat.

The Wild Dog stands considerably higher than the common Jackal ; he is also much longer in the body, and more wolfish looking.   The color is a reddish yellow ; the hair is soft and woolly, and about two inches in length.   The tail is long and bushy and carried like a Fox's, but it is not so full as the brush of the latter animal.

Although I have often, to my cost, been in the vicinity of Wild Dogs, I have very seldom seen them.   The first I met with were near the hot springs in the Furiabad Valley in 1862. A pair crossed the path as I was marching along ; I fired a snap shot and knocked one over, but although hit with a shell it managed to escape.

In 1864, I found two Dogs feeding on the offal of a Burrell which I had killed the previous day, but I did not get a shot at them.   A few days afterwards (July 16th) I was walking along the road between Meroo and Oobshi, on the way to Leh, when I saw a Wild Dog drinking at the other side of the river.   I quickly uncased my rifle and shot him dead, and sent a Tartar across the river to bag him ; he proved to be a fine specimen, and his head is well represented in the photograph.

I have no more personal experience of the Wild Dog.

F

CHAPTER VIII

THE SNOW BEAR.

Ursus Isabellinus.

Generally throughout the hills—*Lál Bhálú.* In Kashmir—*Hárpat.*

THE Snow Bear, Brown Bear, Red Bear, or White Bear, as it is variously called, inhabits most of the highest forest-clad ranges, but it is by far most numerous in Kashmir. In that country, in 1864, a friend of mine saw twenty-eight in one day, and shot seven. I have myself seen thirteen. Forty years ago, the country must have been literally swarming with them, and I have heard that the people were afraid to go from one village to another, after dark. Now-a-days every one who visits Kashmir shoots a few Bears, and the only wonder is that the race is not quite exterminated.

I think the name of Snow Bear is most appropriate, as the animal is usually to be found in the summer months along the margin of the snow, and it never descends, like the Himalayan Black Bear, to the lower ranges.

The Snow Bear varies a good deal in size and color, partly doubtless according to age and sex ; but the variations are also individual, and it would be impossible to tell the sex of a Bear from its size or color.

As a rule the old males are the darkest, and young Bears of both sexes the lightest color- ed, the very young ones having a white collar. I have not kept any accurate measurements, but a very large Bear would be about seven feet long, from snout to tail, the latter appendage being only two or three inches in length.

The hair is about eight inches long, and when killed early in the season, the skin is exceedingly handsome.

This Bear lives more upon roots than other species, not being such a fruit-eater as the Black Bear, probably for the reason that he would have to resort to the warmer valleys to procure it. His arms and claws are admirably adapted for digging, the former being enor- mously muscular, and the latter powerful, slightly curved, and three or four inches in length.

The Snow Bear invariably hibernates, retiring to some cave at the commencement of winter, and reappearing in April or May when the snows begin to melt. Bears have very seldom been found during their winter-sleep, and I am not aware whether they actually

IV

SNOW BEAR

URSUS ISABELLINUS

Published by Thacker, Spink & Co., Calcutta.

become torpid like the Hedgehog and Dormouse, or whether they still retain their faculties. The reason why they are not found is, of course, that their retreats are probably buried under many feet of snow, while there is no clue to their whereabouts. Their skins are in best order when they first show themselves in the early spring, as not only is the hair longest at this season, but the hide itself is comparatively free from grease, and therefore more easily cured.

When they first appear, the Bears may be found on all the open spots on the hill-side where the snow has melted, turning over rocks in search of insects, digging for roots, or feeding on the young sprouts of grass and various herbs. About this time the young ones are born, and may be seen accompanying their mother when little bigger than Skye terriers. As the season advances, the Bears scatter all over the hills, and may be frequently found at great elevations, far above the forest.

Although endowed with most acute powers of scent, the Bear is a very blind animal, and if care be taken to avoid giving him the wind, no animal is more easily stalked. He is uncouth and grotesque in all his movements, and I, for one, can never watch a Bear without laughing at his absurd appearance. The Kashmiris have so low an idea of Bruin's intelligence, that they apply the name of '*Hárpat*' to any peculiarly stupid and loutish individual.

One whiff of the human scent, and however busily a Bear may be employed, up goes his nose in the air; he may probably rise on his hind legs to try and obtain a view of his unseen enemy; and after looking very uncomfortable and highly ridiculous for a few moments, he will shuffle off to the nearest cover. Get well to leeward of him, however; keep your eye on him so as to remain motionless when he looks up; and by moving slowly you may approach within easy shot on the most open ground. On receiving a shot which is not immediately fatal, the Snow Bear usually utters a grunt or two, and then rushes off with a peculiar rolling action which is very laughable. He does not always seem to know where he is going to, and he may rush close past a sportsman's legs without having the least idea of his proximity. This rush is often called *charging*, the real fact being that the poor brute is merely trying to escape. If any one happens to be in the way he will probably suffer, a hastily aimed blow with the formidably armed forepaw causing a terrible wound if it does take effect. Though I have shot a good many Bears I have never seen one charge, and I think I am justified in saying that it is very seldom indeed that one of this species will deliberately attack a man.

In our childish days Bears were always associated with Wolves, Lions, and Tigers, as being most ferocious and terrible wild beasts. We were told of their deliberate way of hugging their victims to death; while their taste for wholesale slaughter was exemplified by the Biblical story of the fate which befel the hapless children who ventured to 'chaff' a prophet. Even in those days of infantine orthodoxy we probably thought the punishment rather out of proportion to the crime, though we may not have ventured to say so : in the present age of scepticism the reader may perhaps not be shocked at being told that those murderers of the innocents must at least have been very exceptional Bears!—probably provided for the occasion!

Certainly there are Bears and Bears, and some species are undoubtedly cross grained and occasionally dangerous, but the subject of the present chapter, which is either identical with, or closely allied to, the Syrian Bear, is, as a rule, a most inoffensive and harmless animal.

Until recently, and I believe even now, any one visiting Kashmir might make a very large bag of Snow Bears; but as they are found on hills which are also the habitat of much more worthy objects of the chase, the energetic sportsman will soon get tired of slaughtering beasts which require so little skill. I am sorry to say, however, that some Englishmen not only shoot every Bear they can come across in a legitimate way, but fire absurdly long shots at them, thereby often merely wounding the poor brutes; and others who are not satisfied with their bag, employ their Shikaris to shoot Bears for them. Such unsportsman-like conduct requires no comment.

A few old Bears, however, are worth shooting for the sake of their skins, provided that there is no danger of disturbing nobler game.

When I first visited Kashmir, I was of course anxious to kill a Bear, and well remember my delight, when, on the first day of my arrival in the valley, I was awoke from a sound sleep by a coolie who came running up to inform me that he had just seen two Bears. Being a Kashmiri, he could not deny himself the gratification of telling a lie, but it turned out that he had seen *one*. Seizing my rifle, I quickly ran out, and had not proceeded more than two hundred yards from the tree under which I had been sleeping, before I saw a Snow Bear leisurely sauntering along, occasionally stopping to dig up a root or turn over a stone. Ensconcing myself behind a tree towards which he was making, I waited until he passed within thirty yards, when a bullet from my rifle dropped him, and one or two more finished him. His skin, though not particularly large, was as soft and handsome as any I have ever seen. This took place on the 4th of May, 1861.

After paying a visit to S'rinugger and engaging a new Shikari (poor fellow! he was accidentally shot next year by an officer), I went into the district of Dagowan in search of Bears. For the first two or three days I did not see a single animal, although pretty recent traces were abundant.

On the 15th, as I was dressing at the door of my tent, a Snow Bear made his appearance a few hundred yards off. I was soon in pursuit of him, but as he was travelling and not feeding, I had a long stern chase and only wounded him by a long shot. We then determined to try another hill which was not very far off.

The ground was a series of high ridges of rock running from top to bottom of the mountain, with green ravines between them, and occasional patches of jungle. We went down along one of the ridges, and the Shikari soon discovered a Bear feeding far below us. Shortly afterwards he saw a Serow about four hundred yards lower down. As he was pointing it out to me, a fine Bara Sing stag crossed the same open space with a Snow Bear in hot pursuit of him, and immediately afterwards another Bear appeared coming up the ravine. Being on a high cliff I had to make a long circuit in order to get near this collection of beasts, and had an awkward climb for it. At last we got near the place, and I saw a

Bear a short distance below us. The Shikari, however, first wished to have a look at the exact place where we had seen the Serow, and which was only a few yards off. He had only gone a few steps, when he drew back and handed me my rifle, saying there was a Bear close by. I went to the rock from which he had seen it and looked down into the ravine, but could see nothing. The Shikari pulled my arm and pointed to the corner of the rock, and there, to my amazement, was a Bear standing on her hind legs, coolly looking at me not five yards off! I was so surprised that I fired in a hurry at her chest, and must have made a bad shot, for she tumbled off the rock and made off, and though I put two more bullets in her, she managed to get away, leaving a good deal of blood behind her. As I was re-loading I discovered her cub, and told my coolie to catch it : he did so, but as the little brute was savage the stupid fellow let it go again.

For several days I shot nothing, being a young hand at the work, and losing several chances, but on the 20th I shot another Bear.

On the 25th as I was stalking a Bear she suddenly galloped past about forty yards above me. I rolled her over, and as she came tumbling down the rocks I had only just time to step out of her way, and give her the *coup de grâce* as she passed.

In the Furiabad valley in 1862, I was detained for a day or two by a heavy fall of snow which rendered it impossible to move camp. At last the weather cleared up, and although it was still too wet to strike the tents, I determined to explore a little further up the valley.

One May morning, I started before daylight, and following the rugged and ill-defined path which wound along some way above the river, had proceeded about four miles, when we saw a couple of Snow Bears on the grassy slopes ahead of us. They were a long way apart, one being some distance up the hill, and the other below us near the river bank. We determined to try for the one on higher ground first, and accordingly went after him. Just as we were getting within long shot of him he moved off, for some reason best known to himself, as he could neither have seen nor smelt us. I was a young hunter then, and foolishly fired at him as he was moving fast, at about two hundred yards. My bullet hit, but apparently too high, and Bruin escaped. I now turned my attention to the other Bear, which was still feeding quietly, close to the stream, the noise of which had probably prevented him from hearing my shots. I had little difficulty in getting within easy range of him, and on looking over a rock, I saw him digging up roots about thirty yards below me. A shell behind the shoulder tumbled him over, and he rolled down the bank, howling and roaring considerably. As he regained his legs I had to give him another shot, on receiving which he rolled down to the water's edge, where he seized hold of a branch in his teeth and hung on. I now placed a third bullet in his chest, which unfortunately dropped him into the river : he was at once swept away by the torrent, and carried under a snow bridge, where he was, of course, irretrievably lost.

The sun was now high, and as this was evidently a favorite feeding ground, I determined to wait till the Bears came out again towards evening. It was a cloudy afternoon, and before three o'clock, two or three Bears showed themselves on the opposite side of the river. These it was impossible to approach, but before long a very light colored and unusually large Bear came out of the forest a little further up the valley on our side of the stream. I was in hopes that he would begin feeding, but either some eddy of the wind wafted our scent to him, or he changed his mind, for he presently hurried back into the forest, and we saw him no more.

Half an hour afterwards a large dark colored Bear made his appearance out of a deep ravine and fed to within a hundred yards of us. I took a most deliberate aim, but though my bullet struck about the right place, and the Bear rolled over, he managed to scramble down to the river, crossed it, and escaped.

It was now time to return to camp, and I reached it about dark, very much disgusted with my want of success. The failures were doubtless owing to my defective rifle, or rather ammunition. I then possessed a double barrelled rifle ·577 bore, which, although accurate enough at known distances, had a very high trajectory, the charge being only one and a half drams of powder. Shells had then been recently invented, and I supposed that nothing hit by them could possibly escape : as it was, I really diminished the power of my rifle rather than increased it by using them. The mixture with which the shells were loaded was very sensitive, and the charge of powder in the rifle was very small ; the result was that the shells burst on striking, and on a tough beast like a Bear inflicted only superficial wounds.

The next day's sport made amends for a day of bad luck. On my way back to camp I had seen some Ibex in the rocks above me, but too far off to go after at such a late hour of the day. In the morning I ordered camp to be moved up the valley to the farthest point which I had reached the day before, and, instead of following the path, I at once ascended the hill and went along the ridge on which I had seen the Ibex. We found them, and I shot a couple. Going down to where the second one had fallen, my Shikati and I began to skin it ; as we were thus engaged, two Bears suddenly cantered past within thirty yards. The man with my rifle had not yet joined us, so I picked up my gun, which was loaded with ball, and hit the foremost Bear, but not severely. I missed the second one, and both went up the hill, passing so close to my gun-carrier that he pelted them with stones and actually struck them ; he was in a great fright, but the Bears seemed to have no intention of harming him.

Having skinned the Ibex we went down to the place which we had selected for the camp, but had hardly reached it when a Bear appeared on the hill-side which we had just quitted. Up we went again, and after an easy stalk I found myself within about thirty yards. I placed a shell between his eyes, but he walked slowly on ! Two more shots, quickly fired, dropped him dead, and on going up I found the smoke of the shell still issuing from the hole between his eyes : owing to the peculiar position his head was in, the brain had not been touched. He was a very large Bear, and as he was in an awkward place for skinning we rolled him down the hill right into our camp.

In the evening I went to the strip of forest out of which the light colored Bear had appeared yesterday. On the verge of it I found another Bear, but though I rolled him over, he managed to make his escape, as we lost the trail in dense jungle.

Passing through the forest we came to another grassy hill-side, and on this, within a few hundred yards of each other, were no fewer than six Bears. Very little daylight remained ;

the hill-side was very open ; and a ravine full of snow lay between me and the Bears. This it would be difficult to cross without being seen ; the only chance being to crawl across it very slowly, for which there was no time. The alternative was, to risk the long shot at one of the two nearest Bears, which were, as nearly as I could estimate, two hundred yards from me. One of these Bears was nearly white, so I determined to have his skin if possible. Making a rest for my rifle with a grass shoe on the edge of the bank of snow, I fired very steadily. The Bear started, rushed up hill a few yards, and then rolled to the water's edge—stone dead. The skin was a very large one, and one of the handsomest I have ever seen.

During many subsequent shooting expeditions a fair number of Snow Bears have fallen to my rifles, but no incident of special interest has ever occurred to render a detailed account worth recording. With the powerful low trajectory weapons of the present day, no one with the most ordinary degree of coolness should fail to bag nearly every Bear at which he fires.

CHAPTER IX.

THE HIMALAYAN BLACK BEAR.

URSUS TIBETANUS.

Generally throughout the hills—*Kálá Bhálú—Rích.* In Kashmir—*Hárpat.*

THE Himalayan Black Bear is not, as its specific name would seem to imply, a dweller at very high altitudes. It is doubtful, indeed, whether it is found in Thibet at all ; certainly those parts of that country with which I am acquainted are totally unsuited to its habits, and if banished to them it would probably starve.

This Black Bear is to be met with all along the southern slopes of the Himalayan Range, from its very skirts up to an elevation of about 12,000 feet. Being an essentially forest-loving animal, it probably seldom ascends above the last mentioned elevation ; and it does not, like the Snow Bear, delight in digging for roots on the grassy slopes immediately below the snow line.

The Himalayan Black Bear is, as a rule, a considerably larger and heavier animal than the Indian Black Bear (*Ursus labiatus*), with which it has frequently been confounded ; but I know of no animal in which individuals vary so much in size. To judge by appearances, the Himalayan species must go on increasing in bulk for many years, a very old male being sometimes, I should say, double the weight of a middle-aged female. The color is a deep glossy black, with a white V-shaped mark on the chest, and a white lower lip. In the winter, the hair on the shoulders is considerably elongated, giving the appearance of a sort of hump. The head is shorter and rounder than in most Bears, and the eyes are small. The claws are short and stout, and are better adapted for climbing than for digging ; and consequently we find that this Bear is very arboreal in its habits, and does not dig so much as either the Snow Bear or the Indian Black Bear, whose claws are much more developed. The extreme length of a full grown male may perhaps be stated as about seven feet.

While the Snow Bear is comparatively a shy animal, living on the bare mountain tops and content with simple fare, the Black Bear is a thorough *gourmand*, and shifts his quarters so as to be within reach of the delicacies of the season, whatever they may be. In the forest he will put up with roots, berries, acorns, scorpions, ants, or such other trifles as he may meet with during his wanderings ; but as the various cereals and fruits ripen in the vicinity of the villages, he takes up his abode in some well-wooded ravine or tangled copse within easy reach of the fields and orchards, and plunders them regularly every night. Maize and buck-

BLACK BEAR

URSUS THIBETANUS

Published by Thacker, Spink & Co., Calcutta.

wheat among grains, and mulberries, apricots, and walnuts among fruits, are his favorite food. At times he likes to vary his usual vegetarian diet, and takes to killing sheep, cattle, and ponies ; and, like the rest of his race, he is extremely fond of honey.

The Black Bear does not thoroughly hibernate like the Snow Bear, but appears to pass a great deal of his time during the cold months in a state of semi-torpor ; occasionally wandering out in search of food, when an unusually mild day thaws his blood, and awakens him to the sense of hunger.

As already mentioned, this Bear is to be found all along the Himalayas, but it is most plentiful where fields and gardens alternate with thickly wooded hills and ravines. It perhaps exists in greatest numbers in some parts of Kashmir ; and owing to its preference for dense jungles, it is comparatively less subject to destruction by sportsmen than the Snow Bear. Few keen hunters, indeed, devote much time to its chase, as its skin is not much of a trophy, and its pursuit affords but little interest or excitement.

Occasionally, certainly, the Black Bear proves a formidable antagonist, and I have known more than one British officer killed by them, while one constantly meets with natives who have been terribly mutilated in encounters with one of the species ; but these accidents have usually occurred when the animal has been attacked, or suddenly met with, in thick cover, where the Bear had every advantage. For my own part, I have never seen a Bear charge, although I have shot a good many at different times.

I never thought it worth while to devote much time to Black Bear shooting, and I have never, since my earlier hunting days, gone out of my way to search for them. When I have come across them accidentally, however, and there was no chance of disturbing nobler game, I have frequently shot them.

When I first visited Kashmir I was of course anxious to get one, and well remember my disgust at losing the first I ever saw on the Pir Punjal in 1861. I was returning to my tent one evening in April, after a long unsuccessful day, when I suddenly saw a Black Bear feeding on a green flat below us. I stalked carefully down, and having got within fifty yards, bowled him over ; after howling and rolling about for a little, he regained his legs and rushed into the jungle. As he bled plentifully I was in hopes of bagging him, but after a long chase I found that he had crossed a river, and I had to give him up.

The same year I went out beyond the Shalimar Gardens, on the 2nd of June, to try a place where many Bears were said to resort to feed on the mulberries. Next morning I was out before daylight, and soon saw a Bear returning from his feast. As he leisurely strolled along, he found a bone, and lay down under a rock to gnaw it. This gave me time to stalk to within thirty yards of him. He was nearly straight below me, and I took great pains to shoot him dead, but somehow or other my bullet only grazed him ; I missed with the second barrel, and he went into some jungle, but as he passed an open space I killed him with my single barrel. On skinning him I found that he was literally stuffed with mulberries ! Early next morning I saw a large Bear go into some jungle, so, in the evening, I went to wait for him near the place. Bruin was punctual, and I soon saw him coming towards me. I went to meet him, and got a shot, within about fifteen yards, as he was feeding among some rose

G

bushes. A twig must have turned the bullet, for the Bear went off untouched, but my second bullet catching him in the loins, as he turned away, raked him completely, and after galloping about two hundred yards down hill he stopped in a patch of jungle, where I found him lying dead. He was a large Bear and had a very good skin.

In Pangi, in 1870, I was one day marching with my wife along a narrow valley, on my way to some favorite Ibex ground, when one of the coolies came to tell me that he had seen two Black Bears. Hurrying on along the mountain track, I soon discovered the animals lying fast asleep on a flat rock close to the opposite bank of the stream which ran through the valley. I easily got down to within eighty yards, and rudely awakened the larger of the pair by a bullet in the chest. He rolled off the rock, roaring and howling, and the other having joined him, the two scrambled over the stones by the river's edge. I soon saw that the wounded one was about done for, but I gave him another shot to make sure, and then turned my attention to his partner. She was ascending the opposite bank when I fired at her, and by the time that the smoke cleared away she had crept under a fallen pine tree. I could just make out something black, so I fired my second barrel, but nothing moved, and it was evident that she was also disposed of. My wife, who remained on the path, had a good view of the fun.

It was impossible to cross the river where we were, and as skinning the Bears would occupy some time, I pitched my camp about a mile farther on, where there was a bridge, and went back with a few men to strip off the skins. We found that the male was a remarkably large one, and the female so old that her teeth were worn down to mere stumps: being early in the season both skins were in first-rate order.

The people of the village close to which the Bears were killed were delighted, as the brutes had long haunted the place and done much damage both to crops and cattle.

On another occasion, having hunted in vain for Markhoor on a hill which used to be famous for them, I one morning, just as the sun began to make its rays unpleasantly felt, discovered a large Black Bear in the act of making himself comfortable for the day. He had chosen the base of a large tree, which afforded ample shade, for his noonday siesta, and as soon as I saw that his arrangements were complete, I stalked quietly down to him. I easily approached to within fifteen yards, and poor Bruin never awoke until a bullet behind the ear from my express rifle gave him his *quietus*.

The best way of getting Black Bears is to beat any wooded ravines that may be in the vicinity of the fields or fruit trees where they are known to feed. By sending men out at daylight to mark them down as they return to the ravines much time may be saved, but the sport is not a very exciting one. Early in winter the Bears may frequently be found on the oak trees, and may be quietly 'potted' as they sit!

CHAPTER X.

THE ASIATIC ELEPHANT.

ELEPHAS INDICUS.

Generally throughout India—*Háthí—Gaj—Fíl.*

THIS Elephant is an inhabitant of the forests at the base of the Himalayas, being found as far west as the Western Doon, and from thence eastwards all the way to Assam, as well as in parts of the Central Provinces.

The Asiatic Elephant is too well known to require description, being the only one which had been exhibited in England until within the last few years.* There are several varieties which differ slightly in size, shape, and color. The facial angle varies a good deal, the forehead being nearly perpendicular in the Doon Elephant, and receding in the Assam and Burmese varieties. In Ceylon 'Tuskers' are very rare, while at least two-thirds of the male Elephants in the Sub-Himalayan forests are furnished with tusks.

As with most large animals, the size of the Elephant has been greatly exaggerated, and some years ago I saw a paragraph in an English newspaper alluding to an Elephant *fourteen* feet high, which had been exhibited in some provincial town! I cannot say exactly what is the extreme height which the Elephant has been known to attain, but I should fancy that eleven feet was the very outside. A ten-foot Elephant is a *very* large one, measured at the shoulder. Baker mentions having shot an Elephant whose height he calculated at more than eleven feet, but he states the average height of the Ceylon Elephant to be only about seven feet, which is much smaller than the Doon and Terai Elephants.

The Elephant is principally nocturnal in its habits, remaining concealed in some shady retreat during the day, and often wandering long distances at night in search of its favorite food. During the cold and dry months the Elephants betake themselves to the forests at the very foot of the hills, usually retiring during the daytime to some secluded valley, and coming out to feed in the evening. During the rains the Elephants leave the hills and often resort to some jungle in the neighbourhood of villages, hiding among the high grass which there springs up in a few weeks, and committing great ravages among the crops.

---

* When this was written, the ridiculous Jumbo sensation had not developed, and the English public had not yet proclaimed that they had more sympathy with the imaginary woes of an Elephant than with the real distress of widowed and impoverished Irish ladies.

Elephants usually go in herds, varying in number from four or five, to sixty or seventy. When in herds they are generally quite harmless, and a child might put a hundred to flight ; but a solitary bull is often a savage and dangerous brute, attacking and killing everyone he can. Occasionally one of these 'rogues' will haunt a certain road and completely stop the traffic as long as he remains.

There was one which used to haunt the Dehra Doon, and which was said to have killed many people, and even destroyed houses. I fancy, however, that the depredations of several Elephants were laid to the charge of one. He was always described as the 'khúnní' or murderer Elephant, with one heavy tusk and one stump. I once thought I had shot him, but was disappointed, as hereafter related, and I do not know what was his ultimate fate.

I have often heard people talk of Elephant-shooting as cruel and unsportsmanlike ; for what reason I cannot imagine. I do not think that anyone who has stood the charge of a wild Elephant could describe the sport as tame ! I certainly think it is a great shame to slaughter numbers of female Elephants which might be caught and made useful, and which have no tusks to make them worth the shooting ; but if the sportsman confines himself to old males he will be doing more good than harm by their destruction, while he will enjoy one of the most exciting sports in the world.

I have been singularly unlucky in Elephant-shooting, and am still unable to account for not having bagged several fine tuskers ; but I am aware that there is a certain knowledge of angles which one must acquire before one can be successful, and that I am not the only man who, though otherwise a fair shot, has failed in his early attempts at Elephant-shooting. The brain is the deadly spot in which to hit the Elephant, but in order to do this the aim must be taken according to the position of the head, and this is what requires great experience. In order to succeed, it is necessary to get as close to the Elephant as possible, anything over fifteen yards being considered a long shot. In approaching an Elephant, the direction of the wind is of paramount importance ; no animal has a more delicate sense of smell, though its sight is by no means so acute.

I know few more exciting sensations than that of tracking an Elephant among high grass and jungle, when one expects every moment to come upon him. I know I have felt my heart beat pretty quickly while doing so, and have felt it " come into my mouth " when a Chítal has uttered its sharp bark, or rushed through the jungle within a few yards of me ! But as soon as the mighty game is viewed, excitement gives place to perfect coolness. A short account of my own adventures with Elephants, unsuccessful though they have been, may give some idea of the sport.

I first saw wild Elephants in 1863. On the 2nd of June I was encamped in the Undera Kohl (dark glen), near the Mohun pass through the Sewalik hills. I had come to the 'kohl' on purpose to look for a herd of Elephants which I had heard had lately arrived there. In the evening I went up to the head of the 'kohl,' directing my camp to follow me. I had not hunted very long before I discovered a herd of about fifteen Elephants standing on an open sort of table-land. I lay down and watched them, but could see no tusker. I had intended to fire at no tuskless Elephant, but I found the temptation too strong, and attempted the stalk. On reaching the place I found that the Elephants had moved off, and had entered some thick jungle. I ran round to head them, and soon saw the backs of several above the high grass. They were moving away, and I thought they were the last of the herd. I went after them, and as I was climbing up a bank I heard a noise behind me, and on turning round saw eight or ten Elephants going away at full speed, and not more than twenty yards off. I had walked nearly under their trunks without seeing them. I ran as hard as I could in pursuit of the herd, and as they stopped to have a look I could not resist firing at the side of the head of the largest, though nearly seventy yards off. The bullet (a steel-tipped one) cracked loudly on her head, and she staggered a little, but went off with the remainder of the herd right down the stony watercourse which formed the bed of the '*kohl*.' I followed, half expecting to find my camels, &c., smashed by the retreating Elephants, but they left the watercourse, and I met my camels about a mile back. I now chose a spot for my tent, and while I was assisting to pitch it, sent out my gun-carrier to look after the Elephants.

He came back again directly, having found some of the herd close by. I at once went out, and found seven Elephants, four large and three small, standing on the summit of a low hill which was nearly surrounded by a rather deep ravine. I went round to leeward, but could not get nearer than about ninety yards on account of the ravine. I lay watching them until they at length moved, and were passing along the opposite bank within sixty yards of me. I took steady aim at the head of one and fired. She merely shook her head, and I don't know where my second bullet struck. The Elephants then hurried across the ravine to my left and halted in a slight hollow about thirty yards below me, where they stood with their trunks up, uncertain which way to go. I was standing on the open hill-side with no tree to get behind, and only a little low jungle about fifty yards off to retreat to in case of a charge. I loaded as fast as I could, but could only find one rifle bullet, and had to put a small gun bullet in the left barrel. My gun-carrier stood by me well, and, just as I put the caps on, the Elephants wheeled round and came straight towards me. I picked out the nearest and largest, and gave her both barrels in the head : she staggered and seemed quite bewildered, and as she moved slowly off with the rest of the herd I fired a heavy single rifle and struck her again. The herd made for the bed of the stream and rushed down the bank within thirty yards of my tent, frightening my servants considerably. They reported that the wounded Elephant was a long way behind the others, and appeared very sick. There was lots of blood on her track, so I hoped to find her in the morning.

I had returned to camp about half an hour, when down came an Elephant into the watercourse within two hundred yards. I jumped up and loaded my rifles and had a large fire lit, but the beast would not go away, but occasionally startled us with a crash, and we could sometimes hear him chewing within one hundred yards. In the middle of the night I was awoke by a cry of '*Háthí díd hai :*' jumping out of bed and seizing my rifle, I saw ten Elephants come down the bank within forty yards. One or two of them stopped, and I could easily have hit them in the head, as it was bright moonlight, but I thought that if I merely wounded one it might bring the herd down on us, when, in the dim light, there might have been a catastrophe, so I did not fire. One of them seemed inclined to have a long look at us, until a hill dog of mine went at him and drove him away screaming.

Next day I tracked the herd for many miles, but could not come up with them. I hunted without success for several days, until I became so lame from a boil on the leg, that I had to return to Delhi.

Early in September of the same year, I disregarded all warnings about jungle fever, and set out to have another try for Elephants in the Sewaliks. I took the precaution of swallowing a glass of sherry with a good dose of quinine every morning when I got out of bed, and I never had a touch of fever. The grass was tremendously high and thick, and the heat in the narrow '*sotes*' very oppressive. It was generally impossible to move through the jungle except by following the Elephant tracks.

On the night of the 6th of September, soon after I had gone to bed (I was encamped at the village of Russoolpoor, about sixteen miles from Roorkee), a man came to say that an Elephant was feeding in a field not far off. At daylight next morning I started and went to look for the tracks ; the man who had brought the news soon joined me and pointed out the field in which the Elephant had been feeding. The crop was Indian corn, and it was half eaten and trampled down by the brute, whose footmarks showed him to be a very large one. Taking up the track where it left the field, we followed it towards the Sewaliks, and after going a couple of miles found ourselves in thick jungle, where the tracking, which had been sometimes rather difficult, now became easy enough. We reached the place where he had drunk, and from which he had returned to the jungle. Further on we came to a place where he had evidently stood for a long time ; and still further on, to where he had again drunk. I had several times heard deer bolt through the jungle, but soon after leaving the water I heard a rush which I felt sure must be the Elephant, and on following the track a little further we found that I was right. After a time I again heard him, but the jungle consisted of thick trees and creepers, and I could not see five yards. About a mile further on I once more heard the Elephant in front of us, and the jungle being more open I exchanged the double gun I was carrying for a heavy single rifle, and ran forward for a shot. Immediately there was a crash and a trumpet, and back charged an immense Elephant. My men at once concealed themselves ; I was a few paces in front and saw no available cover. Two stems, not thicker than my leg, were on my left, and I stepped behind these and placed my rifle to my shoulder. The Elephant charged up to within ten paces and then stood still with his trunk raised, his ears cocked, and his vicious little eyes searching in every direction. He was not, although so close, in a favorable position for a deadly shot, so I waited with the rifle to my shoulder for fully half a minute, hoping that he would turn his head a little. He would not do so however, and as I expected him to discover me every moment I thought it best to fire, and therefore aimed as I best could for the brain and pressed the trigger. Under cover of the smoke I ran back to the nearest tree. The Elephant stood apparently stupefied for a moment, and then turning, rushed into dense reed jungle, where, as I had only a single barrel, I thought it unadvisable to follow him.

Next day I moved camp a few miles and hunted several '*sotes*' without success. Towards evening I met some woodcutters, who informed me that they had seen a tusker in Golni Kohl. On going to the place we found the recent track of a large Elephant, and selecting a likely spot near some water sat down to listen. After about half an hour a loud crack, as of a breaking branch, disturbed the silence, but the sound was not repeated. After a time I went towards the place whence the sound had proceeded, and found the perfectly fresh footmarks of an Elephant which had passed since we came up. Following the track, I found that the Elephant had entered a long belt of high grass on the margin of the watercourse, so I went down to the end to wait for his appearance. Taking up a good position, I sent my gun-carrier up the high bank above me to look out ; he presently saw the Elephant cross the ' *rdo* ' and enter the jungle on the opposite bank. I soon got across to him and found him feeding on some bamboos. Getting in his path, I waited for him to feed up to me, and got a steady shot within fifteen yards between the eye and ear, which I felt certain must prove fatal. To my disappointment, however, after blundering about for some time in such a cloud of dust that I could not see to fire again, he made off, and as it was becoming dusk I had to leave him till next morning, when I took up the track.

I followed it for many miles, and at last lost it among those of a herd of Elephants which I found in another ' *kohl*.' I had a look at a number of them, but as they were all females and young ones, I would not fire at them.

For several days I hunted in vain for a tusker, but saw females and small ones nearly every day. I sometimes lay for hours watching their habits with great interest. Their extraordinary faculty of scent was one of their most observable characteristics. I noticed that whenever an Elephant went to leeward of me, though at many hundred yards' distance, up went her trunk, the signal of alarm was given, and the herd collected together, betraying the greatest uneasiness. On one occasion I had a peculiarly good opportunity of watching them, as I was lying on a high rock overlooking a level valley in which the herd had taken up their station.

Finding no tuskers, I left the Sewaliks and went down to the open country below Hurdwár. Here I was told some tuskers resorted, and I had only been three nights in the village of Bhoorper when three Elephants came at night to the fields close to the village.

Next morning I followed the tracks, which showed that they were all large ones, and one, judging from the height of the mud marks on the trees, must have been an enormous one. They had, however, gone straight down wind ; it was impossible to move through the dense jungle except in their path, and when I at length came up with them and heard them chewing under a tree forty yards ahead of me, they had already scented me, and at once made off. As they went down wind, pursuit was unsuccessful. That night they again visited the gardens, but my leave was up and I was obliged to return.

In May, 1865, I again visited the Doon and Sewaliks, determined to do my best against the Elephants. I had a most powerful battery, which I felt confident would enable me to give a good account of any Elephants I might come across. The result shows how useless the heaviest guns are unless used scientifically.

My battery consisted of a single-barrelled two-grooved five-bore rifle, weighing sixteen pounds, carrying a spherical belted ball (hardened with quicksilver), and a charge of *one ounce* of powder; and two double-barrelled ten-bore rifles, fourteen pounds in weight, carrying hardened spherical bullets with nine drams of powder. My friend F. accompanied me, and I lent him one of the double rifles; he had also a single-barrelled Whitworth.

We began hunting at Poordooni, about five miles above Hurdwár. The first two days we found fresh tracks, but no Elephants; on the third day we were more fortunate. After in vain attempting to follow up the fresh track of an Elephant which we soon lost on stony ground, we suddenly came upon him as we were descending a small valley. He was unconscious of our presence, so we stalked behind a bamboo bush and waited for him to pass us. As he was leisurely passing within fifteen yards I made a slight noise to attract his attention, and as he cocked his ears to listen I took a steady aim at his temple. To my disgust the cap snapped! The Elephant at once turned and made off. I ran after him, but could not get a fair shot, so I let him go, so as to give him time to get over his alarm. We now went to some water which he was in the habit of frequenting, and sent a man on his track with orders to watch him and bring us word if he stopped. After an hour or two the man rejoined us at the water with the news that the Elephant had halted under a shady tree. We at once set out after him, and on approaching the place soon heard him. Going carefully towards the sound we discovered that he was lying on his side. Creeping quietly round we got within fifteen yards of his head; the ground was quite open, with the exception of a few bare stems. I now wished to walk up and shoot him in the head, while F. covered my retreat from behind a tree in case I did not kill the beast. F., however, wished to accompany me, which I did not think safe, and during the momentary hesitation the opportunity was lost and the Elephant began to rise. As he straightened his forelegs I fired at his forehead with the heavy rifle; F. gave him right and left about the ear, and I gave him one from the double barrel as he went off. After going a few yards he fell on his knees, but recovered himself directly; I fired the remaining barrel in hopes of making him bleed and thus assist in tracking him. We followed him as hard as we could for several miles, but had at last to give up the chase as hopeless.

Next day we were unable to track him, so we shifted our ground, and crossing the Sewaliks by Kánsráo, went to Russoolpoor, and from thence hunted the various 'kohls' in the neighbourhood. For four or five days we could meet with no Elephants, but on the 13th we heard of some in Undera Kohl.

Taking the man who had seen the Elephants with us, we started early and went up the 'kohl.' We could find no tracks in it, so we ascended the hills between the Undera and Beenj 'ráos' to the place where the Elephants had been last seen. Taking up the tracks, we followed them through all sorts of extraordinary places, across Beenj and another 'ráo.' In the latter we saw an Elephant with one small tusk, and got down to within twenty-five yards of him, but he was very wary, and either heard or winded us and made off without giving us a chance. He went up the very path we had come down, passing close to some men whom we had left there.

We returned on his track for a short distance, but gave it up, and had just sat down to rest when we heard a crash on the other side of the valley, and on looking up saw a magnificent old tusker forcing his way through the trees. We at once set out after him, but on reaching the place, he had gone, and we could see nothing of him. After some time we discovered that he had crossed to Boolawalla, whither we followed him, but lost his tracks in the stony ' *rdo.*'

Returning to Beenj we met some woodcutters, who informed us .that they had seen an Elephant go into Amsote. We went to the place and found plenty of tracks, among others a large fresh one which led along a path which went up the ' *sote.*' I followed it for some time, but at last reached a spot where it appeared that the Elephant had been going the other way, so I turned round. I had hardly done so when I heard a noise, and on looking round, saw a tusker about thirty yards off. Had I gone a few paces forward I should have come right on him : as it was, he heard or saw us and made a rush. I ran as hard as I could to get a shot, but he would not give me a very good one, and I had to fire hurriedly behind his ear at about twenty-five yards. He reeled to the shot, and F. gave him one with one of my heavy double barrels. I took the other, and gave him a second shot behind the ear. He seemed quite stupefied ; but on F.'s hitting him again he trumpeted and went down the ' *sote.*' I gave him my last barrel behind the right ear, but away he went, slowly, and bleeding a good deal. We followed for some distance, and then gave up, as it was becoming dark, but left directions with the woodcutters to keep a sharp lookout, promising a reward if they found him.

Next day we sent several men out to look for tracks, but none having returned by two o'clock, we went up Beenj and explored various curious dark ' *sotes,*' but without success. On the 15th, we had no better luck, and F.'s leave being up on the 16th, we parted, and I marched for Rikki Kase, in the north-east corner of the Doon, where the Ganges leaves the hills. Arriving there on the 19th, I spent two days in searching for a Rogue Elephant, who was said to be in the neighbourhood, but I was unable to find him.

On the 22nd, I crossed the Ganges, and encamped at a village called Kánkar. Here I obtained news of Elephants. I was out early on the morning of the 23rd, and soon found fresh tracks, which I followed in an easterly direction for several miles ; they then turned and brought us back nearly to the place where we first found them, a large jungle of ' *nul* ' and ' *burroo* ' reeds extending in a belt along the foot of the hills. Ascending a low hill above this, I sent a man up a tree to look out, and he soon saw an Elephant not far off. I went round to the place, and found five Elephants standing in some thick jungle at the foot of the hill. I crept carefully down to within twenty yards, and watched them for some time. There were an old tusker with a good pair of tusks, another with one tusk, two ' *maknás* ' or females, and a young tusker. The single tusker was nearest me, and I carefully studied his head to make out where the brain lay, and waited for him to turn it in a good position. At length he turned straight towards me, and taking a most careful and steady aim, I fired. I made certain of bagging him, but, whether from being above him or some other cause, I must have miscalculated the angle, for he merely staggered, and went off with the rest of the herd without giving me the chance of another shot.

H

I returned much disgusted to Kánkar, and in the afternoon sent my camp to Kúnar, while I again went along the foot of the hills to the '*nul*' and '*burroo*' jungle. About half way along this I heard an Elephant in it, and went in after him. I got within twenty-five yards, but the reeds were so high and thick, that I could hardly see him, and I think he must have heard me, for he put up his trunk, and after looking uneasy for some time moved off into the thickest reeds without giving me a chance: he had one large tusk. As I was stalking him a Tiger roared in the reeds not far off.

Next morning I hunted along the foot of the hills without seeing anything. During some showers of rain I rested in a '*Banjárd's*' hut opposite the centre of the '*nul*.' As I was preparing to start again, an Elephant made his appearance at the edge of the reeds. I at once went after him, but he moved into the jungle where it was so thick that I could not get at him, and after following him a short distance I came out again and went round to the other side, sending men up trees to watch him.

Not seeing anything of him for some time, I went back to where I had first seen him, and found that he had taken up his old position at the edge of the reeds. Outside was a level plain covered with short grass, and no tree or shelter of any kind near; however, I resolved to go up to him, trusting to my heavy rifle. Under cover of a slight angle in the reeds I walked close up to him (I could have touched him with a fishing rod !) and stood for a minute waiting for him to turn his head, and as he did so, fired between the eye and ear. He staggered at the shot, and went blundering about, sinking down on his hind knees. As he turned round, I aimed behind his ear with the double barrel, which was quickly put into my hands, but the cap snapped, and he was too much turned away when I gave him the second barrel. He then disappeared in the reeds, and having reloaded I enquired from the men in the trees where he had gone to. They informed me that he was moving off very slowly, so I ran on, and turning down an open ride in the '*nul*,' headed him. I heard him coming up very slowly, and as he halted in the ride, I fired at the orifice of his ear from a distance of about fifteen paces. He seemed completely stupefied, and stood stockstill ; my double rifle was handed to me, but as I was raising it a brute of a gun-carrier fired from behind me and struck the Elephant somewhere about the ear. Round he came, and attempted to charge, but he was too much shaken, and rolled over with a heavy crash. Up went his legs in the air, and I shouted Whoo-Whoop ! and ran up . to him. But I was too soon : his great head rose above the reeds, and I had just time to give him a shot in the forehead as he regained his legs and charged. I dodged behind a tree, and the Elephant went on. I reloaded and followed him with difficulty through a tremendous thicket of reeds of various sorts, where it was impossible to move except in the path which he had made, and which few animals but an Elephant could have forced their way through. At length I again heard him in front of me, and on emerging from the cover and ascending a slight rising ground I saw him moving slowly about among the reeds not a hundred yards off. I could of course have easily hit him, but I would not fire, as I expected him every minute to come out and give me a fair shot. There was no way of getting at him in the impenetrable reeds, and at last, as it became dusk, I reluctantly left him, though feeling sure of being able to track him in the morning. He had one fine tusk, and was the same Elephant I saw on the previous evening.

It rained in torrents all night, so that tracking was out of the question. In the morning I went out without my guns, but though I hunted all that day and the suc- ceeding one, I never found a trace of the wounded tusker. He must have died, as he had two five-bore bullets propelled by sixteen drams of powder, and three ten-bore bullets with nine drams behind them, in his head ; all fired from the distance of a few paces only.

On the 28th, I had returned to Rikki Kase, and was sitting at breakfast, when a man came in a state of breathless excitement with the news that the ' *Khúnní Háthí*' was by the roadside not a coss off, having just stopped his bullock cart.

Having finished breakfast and looked to the caps of my rifles, I accompanied the man, and had not gone much more than a mile when I saw a huge pair of hind quarters and a swinging tail through a vista in the trees. The wind was in the wrong direction, so I sent my guide up a tree, and making a long detour, regained the road on the other side of the Elephant. Here I found two men with the bullock cart, in an abject state of terror. Telling them to keep quiet, I went after the Elephant, and soon came in sight of him again. He moved towards some thick jungle, so I ran on and placed myself in the direction which he seemed most likely to take. He came straight on to within twenty yards, but the branches and high reeds prevented me from getting a clear view of his head, so I would not fire. He passed me and went round to leeward, so, fearing that he would scent me, I determined to try the effect of laming him, and accordingly fired the heavy single barrel at his shoulder from a distance of about forty yards. He turned round and bolted.

Finding plenty of blood, I followed as fast as I could, and had tracked for perhaps half a mile, when I heard an Elephant a little to my left. Going in the direction of the sound, I saw him standing under a thick ' *máljan*' creeper. I fired at his off shoulder, thinking that as he had stopped so soon for one bullet, he would not go far with both shoulders lamed. He made off, and I had to wait a short time for bullets. On taking up the track I found blood on the right side, and plenty of it.

I had gone but a short distance when I again heard an Elephant in front of me, and soon saw him standing under a tree among very thick undergrowth, where I could not very well get at him. I therefore watched him for some time from a distance of about thirty yards. I could only see the top of his head and his ear, so I could just make out what position he was in. At length he turned straight towards me ; and kneeling down, I took a very steady shot at the centre of his forehead. I heard one crack, as the sound of the rifle died away, and then all was still. Walking up to the place, I found the huge beast lying stone dead, my bullet having struck him just above the bump on the forehead. To my great disgust he was a ' *maknd*' (tuskless male). I had been unable to see whether he had tusks or not, on account of the very thick jungle, but had taken it for granted that he had, and my gun-carrier, Moti, had declared that he saw one large tusk. Blood was oozing from under his left shoulder, on which side he had fallen, but to my astonishment there was no wound on the right shoulder. I could not at first make this out, but soon came to the conclusion—which was of course correct—that I must have fired at *two* Elephants.

Going back to where I had left the track of the second Elephant on (as I thought) seeing him, I found that it turned off in another direction. I followed it at best pace for several miles, but at last gave it up, as the Elephant seemed to have no idea of stopping.

Returning to the dead one, I cut off his tail and forefoot, and took his measurements very carefully. He stood ten feet one inch at the shoulder, and his forefoot was exactly five feet and half-an-inch in circumference. The rule, that twice round an Elephant's forefoot gives his height, is more accurate than might be supposed. It will generally be found correct within an inch or two.

I also set men to work to cut out his grinders, and it was after completing this work on the following day that poor Moti was killed by a Tiger, as elsewhere related.

After in vain endeavouring to avenge Moti's death, I gave up shooting in the Doon, and walked from Rikki Kase to Dehra on the 30th of May—a long and hot walk.

Since then I have only hunted Elephants once, for two days in the Patli Doon in 1866. I saw two tuskers, but the fallen leaves which then (in March) covered the ground rendered it impossible to walk without noise, and I did not get a shot.

I hope still to have an opportunity of bagging a few tuskers, though Elephant-shooting is quite properly prohibited in most districts in India.

Mr. Sanderson states that so far from there being any scarcity of Elephants they are actually on the increase ; and the extensive captures which he has made during the last few years show that there is at any rate an ample supply for immediate wants.

CHAPTER XI.

THE GREAT INDIAN RHINOCEROS.

RHINOCEROS UNICORNIS.

Generally throughout India—*Gaindá—Gairá.*

THE Great Indian Rhinoceros appears in former times to have inhabited the Terai throughout its whole length, but it has been gradually driven eastwards, until at the present day the Nepal Terai is its western limit. Even there its numbers have been much thinned, and it has lately been so highly prized that it has been reserved as Royal game, the late Sir Jung Bahádoor permitting no one to shoot it but himself.

Many Rhinoceros have been shot within the last few years in the vicinity of Julpaigori ; but there, partly owing to being constantly hunted, and partly owing to the clearance of large tracts for Tea cultivation, they are rapidly becoming scarcer, and the sportsman must travel still farther east before he finds them at all plentiful. In the eastern portion of the Bhútán Dooárs and in Assam, wherever there are heavy reed jungles on the banks of rivers or on the margin of swamps, Rhinoceros may be met with, and occasionally several congregate in one covert. I have myself known six to be roused in a belt of '*nul*' not more than half a mile long and three or four hundred yards wide.

The marvellous growth of the long grasses and reeds, which spring up during the rainy season in the long belt of country lying along the foot of the Eastern Himalayas, and on the '*churs*' in the valley of the Bráhmápútrá and other great rivers, has often been described ; and the accounts received with incredulity by those who have never seen how vegetation thrives under the combined influences of a tropical sun and abundance of rain. Let those doubt who may, however, the fact remains that, year after year, in the short space of two or three months, these giant grasses shoot up to a height of from twenty to thirty feet, forming, with the wild cardamum, various other broad-leaved plants, and numerous creepers, a tangled cover which shelters the Elephant, the Rhinoceros and the Buffalo, as effectually as a field of standing corn affords concealment to the partridge or the quail.

I have seen a line of about fifteen Elephants beating a strip of reeds not more than two hundred yards in width, and I could hardly see the grass shake. There was not as much commotion or indication of what was going on, as would be caused by a pack of beagles drawing a gorse covert.

Runs or tunnels among the high reeds, like magnified 'meuses' of hares and rabbits, show that the same paths through the thick jungle are generally made use of ; and the

Rhinoceros, like several of the deer and antelope tribe, has the habit of dropping its dung in one place. Vast heaps of these droppings, the accumulation of years, are constantly to be seen, and native Shikaris frequently watch these spots and obtain a shot at easy distance.

The Great Indian Rhinoceros is by no means 'a thing of beauty.' Huge and unwieldy in form, with an enormous head and general pig-like appearance, it is enveloped in what seems at first sight impenetrable armour, the thick and tuberculated skin hanging in massive folds, which attain their greatest thickness on the neck, shoulders, and quarters.

So thick and tough do these folds or shields appear, as to have given rise to the popular belief that the animal is nearly invulnerable, and that it is only by striking the joints in his harness that a bullet can penetrate.

I recollect an amusing story of a soldier in the Mutiny who was placed in the guard-room for shooting a tame Rhinoceros which had been captured by his regiment. His defence was that he had read in a book that the hide of the animal was bullet-proof; and being of an enquiring turn of mind, had determined to put the theory to the test! As the shot was well directed, the unfortunate subject of the experiment fell dead, and the prize fund was several thousand rupees the poorer.

As a matter of fact, the skin is quite soft when fresh; a bullet will penetrate anywhere with the greatest ease, and a hunting knife can be driven through it with the slightest amount of force. When dried, of course it becomes extremely hard, and used to be in great request for the manufacture of shields. The hide, when polished, is very handsome and semi-transparent, and when held up to the light looks exactly like tortoise shell, the tubercles giving it a beautiful mottled appearance.

The horn of this species seldom exceeds a foot in length; it is composed of agglutinated hairs, and is not firmly attached to the skull, but rests on a slight bony excrescence on the snout, from which it is easily removed, a day or two after death. Contrary to general belief, the Rhinoceros does not make use of its horn as a weapon of offence; the wounds which it occasionally inflicts on Elephants are caused by its long sharp incisors, with which it can give a very formidable bite.

The horn is highly valued by natives both of India and China, and fetches a high price in the market; being worth from Rs. 50 to Rs. 100 according to weight. Hindoos use it in some of their religious ceremonies, while the Chinese ascribe to it the virtues of the famous Venetian glass, and believe that drinking cups manufactured from it possess the property of indicating the presence of poison.

The foot of the Rhinoceros is peculiarly formed, having only three toes, and its trefoil-shaped track cannot be mistaken for that of any other animal.

Ungainly animal as the Rhinoceros is, it is possessed of considerable speed, and although its usual gait when disturbed is a long swinging trot, it occasionally breaks into a lumbering gallop, the pace of which is surprising.

Owing to their formation Rhinoceros do not readily roll over on their sides, and when shot they almost always die in a recumbent position, as if they had quietly sunk down to sleep.

The flesh is excellent, and cannot easily be distinguished from beef; indeed it is better than most beef that one sees in India. The tongue, which is very curiously formed, is particularly good.

The following are the measurements of an old male which I shot, but larger specimens are to be met with :—

Height at withers	5 feet 9 inches or 17 hands 1 inch.	
Length from nose to root of tail	10 „ 6 „	
Length of tail	2 „ 5 „	
Girth	9 „ 8 „	
Girth of forearm	3 „ 2 „	

.There are two ways in which Rhinoceros may be hunted ; one by quietly tracking up the animal on a single Elephant until he is at last found in his lair, or perhaps standing quite unconscious of danger—the other, by beating him out of jungle with a line of Elephants, the guns being stationed at the points where he is most likely to break cover. In the latter case it is necessary to have reliable men with the beaters, who can exercise authority and keep them in order, for both Mahouts and Elephants have the greatest dread of the huge brute, who appears to be much more formidable than he really is. When disturbed he makes a tremendous noise crashing through the reeds, and grunting and snorting with steam engine power, but unless driven to extremities by being hemmed into a corner, I believe that it is but seldom that he will really charge home. I have not yet witnessed an instance of his doing so.

In April, 1878, I received an invitation from a friend, who had the command of many Elephants in one of the best heavy-game shooting districts in Bengal, to join him in an expedition against Buffalo and Rhinoceros. Of course I gladly accepted, and on arriving at my friend's house I was pleased to find that our shooting party consisted of only three, the very best number for such sport. Large shooting parties are very good fun, and probably (though not always) more game may be bagged than with a smaller party ; but as far as the actual sport is concerned, I infinitely prefer to have not more than two companions.

When there are many guns out there is nearly always a lot of wild firing, and it is frequently impossible to tell who has actually shot an animal.

With three guns, and a manageable number of Elephants, the cream of sport may be enjoyed, and each sportsman is independent and has his fair share of the shooting, without being interfered with by, or interfering with, others.

Our first day was blank as regarded the bag, although one Rhinoceros was wounded ; much of our time being lost owing to an Elephant sticking in a quicksand, from which we had the greatest difficulty in extricating her, after laboring hard for several hours.

The second day we only shot Buffaloes, which inhabited the same jungles as the Rhinoceros, so that we could never tell which animal would be likely to break covert in any given beat, and it so happened that we several times found both together.

Our third day's sport afforded an instance of this, and I succeeded in killing my first

' Rhino,' as we always called them for the sake of brevity, and as I shall henceforth call them in this narrative.

We had tracked a wounded bull Buffalo into a large and very thick covert, into which it was useless to follow him with any idea of getting a shot. The three guns therefore went on ahead, and took up their positions at the other end of the covert, while the pad Elephants were ordered to form line and beat steadily through the jungle. After waiting a long time at my post, I heard some large animal crashing through the reeds, and as the line of beaters advanced, the waving of the grass betrayed its movements. It came on very slowly, occasionally stopping for some time to listen, and again making a cautious advance. I remained still as death, but I was in a great state of anxiety lest my Elephant should become uneasy, and give the alarm. Fortunately, he remained silent, and at length the ' Rhino,' anticipating no danger ahead, and pressed by the steadily advancing line of Elephants behind him, poked his ugly head out of the reeds within twenty yards of me. I could only see his snout and his horn, and aimed above the latter for his forehead. I either took a bad aim, or my Elephant moved slightly as I fired, for, as I afterwards found, my bullet merely grazed the snout, cutting a deep furrow along the base of the horn. As the ' Rhino' wheeled round, I gave him another bullet in the centre of his ribs, and he rushed back into the reeds and through the beaters with an angry grunt.

I was using a 12-bore rifle with hardened spherical bullets, and seven drams of powder, so I felt certain that the ' Rhino ' was mortally wounded, and accordingly two or three of the beaters were ordered to follow his track. They had not gone far before they shouted that they had found him, and on hastening to the spot, I had the satisfaction of contemplating my first ' Rhino.' My second bullet had struck him in the ribs, and passing forward into his lungs, had caused death by suffocation. The huge animal lay with his legs doubled under him, as if fast asleep, and it required some exertion on the part of one of our largest Elephants to roll him over. The horn was an average-sized one, thick at the base, but not very long.

Although it was a blazing hot day, we celebrated the event with a glass of whisky, and then superintended the cutting off his head and the removal .of the shields, while a number of long strips were cut from his hide, to be afterwards made into whips. We selected a few choice pieces of meat for ourselves, and in a very short time scores of villagers from the neighbourhood flocked to the spot, delighted at the chance of obtaining a good supply of flesh.

I took the measurements of this ' Rhino' very carefully : they are those given above.

Another ' Rhino ' was wounded during the afternoon, but we lost it among high reeds, and a savage bull Buffalo created a *divertissement*, which prevented us from continuing our search.

Next morning D. was unable to go out shooting, so S. and I went to look for the animals wounded yesterday, at least two Buffaloes having been severely hit in addition to the ' Rhino.' We were not long in finding a cow Buffalo, which had fallen in a sandy nullah;

and some vultures wheeling over the thickest part of the jungle drew our attention to the spot where we discovered the ' Rhino '—a small female—lying dead.

A little separated from the large covert was a belt of high reeds on the bank of a river, and as it was a most likely looking place, we proceeded to beat it. S. went to the end of the covert, while I skirted the edge, keeping just ahead of the line of beaters. It was not long before I heard a ' Rhino,' which moved slowly along some two hundred yards in front of the Elephants, occasionally approaching the edge of the covert and again plunging deeper into it. At length he made up his mind to at least see whether the coast was clear or not, but hardly had his head appeared, when he drew back, and grunting loudly, charged through the beaters. I immediately called them out of the jungle, and taking them back half a mile, re-formed the line, and recommenced the beat. On coming to the end, however, I found that we had not gone back far enough, and that the ' Rhino ' was still behind us.

S. therefore went to the other end, and we proceeded to beat in the reverse direction. The ' Rhino ' was again roused, and after dodging about for some time he at length trotted out close to me. My Elephant was unsteady and I missed the shot at the head, and as the ' Rhino ' turned away, my second bullet struck him close to the root of the tail, a pretty deadly place with the heavy charges that I was using. The ' Rhino ' now went straight to S., who dropped him with a couple of shots. On examining him, we found that he had a very perfect sharp horn, about a foot long. He was covered with scars from fighting, and had lost one eye !

On subsequent days we shot with varied luck, bagging several more ' Rhino,' and losing others which we ought to have got. The greatest difficulty was to get the beaters to keep their places when a ' Rhino ' was on foot. As soon as the great beast began grunting and rushing about, they would scream out that he was attacking their Elephants, and with few exceptions they would do their best to get out of the way, and afford the ' Rhino ' a clear line of retreat.

At length, after a very enjoyable week, we came to our last beat, a long narrow belt of reeds with a small marshy stream trickling through it. D. went to the extreme end ; I was about a hundred and fifty yards from him, and S. came along with the beaters. As they approached I heard a ' Rhino ' coming on ahead of them, and he passed me within a few yards, but without showing himself. Directly afterwards, two shots from D., both of which hit him hard, sent him back in my direction, and as he passed me at a swinging trot within thirty yards, I got a clear shot at him. My bullet struck him fair in the very centre of the shield, and the enormous brute rolled heels over head like a rabbit—stone dead. This was the only instance we witnessed of a ' Rhino ' dying otherwise than in a recumbent position, but none of the others were thus shot dead in full career. This was the largest ' Rhino ' that we killed during the trip, and had the most massive horn. I regret that I did not keep his measurements.

CHAPTER XII

THE KYANG.

EQUUS HEMIONUS.

In Thibet—*Kyang*.

THE Kyang can hardly be considered a game animal, but, as he is one of the most conspicuous beasts to be met with in Thibet, and is moreover interesting from being so closely allied to the horse, he is certainly worthy of mention. There has been great discussion as to whether he is a horse or an ass ; whatever scientific name he may receive, to the casual observer he is as unlike one as the other. He belongs to the same family as the Zebra and Quagga.

Kyang are found all over the elevated plateaux and valleys of Thibet with which we are acquainted. They are especially numerous in the neighbourhood of the Salt Lake, and in the valley of the Indus below Hanlé. When full grown, the Kyang attains the height of about fourteen hands. He is strongly and compactly built, stands on short legs, and has capital quarters and shoulders. His feet are tough and hard as iron, and appear to bear any amount of battering on the rocky ground which he frequents. The worst point about the Kyang is his disproportionately large and ugly head, which quite spoils his appearance, which is otherwise extremely graceful. The prevailing color is a reddish brown, verging into white on the lower parts of the body. The short hog-mane, dorsal stripe, and tail are dark brown. The hair of the winter coat is very warm and thick-set, and rather woolly in texture.

The Kyang prefers the most barren and desolate plains in the vicinity of the lakes and large rivers ; it seems to delight in the coarsest and most wiry pasturage, a description of rough yellow grass, hard and sharp as a pen-knife, appearing to be its favorite food. Kyang are usually found in small parties of four or five, but on being disturbed these parties will join others until a large number are collected in one common herd. Later in the season, as the foaling time approaches, the mares congregate in certain favorite localities, while the old stallions are scattered about the hills, either solitary, or in twos and threes.

No animal is a greater nuisance to the sportsman. Very inquisitive by nature, as soon as Kyang observe a strange object they seem anxious to find out all about it ; and often, when stalking, one is annoyed by a brute who snorts, cocks his ears, and then trots up to have a look at one. Any of his friends who may be near at once follow his example, more distant ones are attracted, and in a few minutes a herd of fifty or sixty may be galloping in circles, effectually alarming all the game in the country.

They will also sometimes spoil sport by actually chasing and driving away other game from their pastures. I witnessed a case of this in the Indus Valley in 1866, when some Goa which I was stalking were hunted right away by some Kyang. A friend of mine had his stalk at some Antelope in Chung Chenmo spoiled in a similar manner.

In places where they have not been disturbed Kyang will frequently gaze at the sportsman within fifty yards, without betraying any fear, but merely curiosity. On the more frequented routes which are annually traversed by tourists the Kyang are much more shy, and seem to know the range of a rifle well. Of course there is no sport in shooting such an animal, but the skin of one is occasionally useful to mend one's shoes with, and in some parts of Ládák the Tartars eat the flesh with avidity. I have tried it, and found it tough and coarse ; but as the Yankees would say, " Poor bull is better than no meat," and in case of need one might fare worse.

The Tartars never seem to attempt to domesticate the Kyang. I saw one which belonged to the Thannadar of Léh, and I was informed that the boy who attended to it could mount it ; it was, however, secured by a strong iron chain, and I was warned against going near it. I was present at the birth of a foal in the valley of the Sutlej, to the north of the Niti Pass in 1865. I walked up to the little thing, while the mother trotted off a short distance and stood anxiously watching me. If I could have procured a mare to act as foster mother I should have attempted to rear the foal, but having no milk even at my disposal I left it alone.

I saw in a newspaper some years ago that a cross had been obtained between the Kyang and the ass at the Jardin des Plantes. I should imagine that the cross between the Kyang and the horse, could it be effected, would be a most valuable animal, possessing all the good qualities of the ordinary mule, with greater size and strength, and better shape. As there are Kyang in the Regent's Park Gardens, surely the experiment might be tried.

CHAPTER XIII.

THE INDIAN WILD BOAR.

Sus Indicus.

Generally throughout India—*Súr—Bad—Bandla*.

THE Wild Boar appears to be distributed over nearly the whole of the old world, varying only slightly in different countries. In India it is found almost everywhere throughout the plains, and also in the hills to a great elevation. It is most numerous in the belt of forest commonly called the Terai, at the foot of the Himalayas.

The Wild Boar varies much in size, according principally to the nature of the country he inhabits ; those found in the lower ranges of the hills are generally the largest. The biggest I ever saw was in the Patli Doon, one of those valleys which lie among the spurs of the Himalayas. I was hunting for Elephants when this Boar suddenly got up under a bush, within twenty yards, and quietly stood watching me. I did not fire at him, and he walked leisurely off, looking very much as if he wanted but slight provocation to induce him to charge. He was an enormous brute, and I wished that I had him on an open plain, where, with a good horse and a spear, we might have had a fair fight. I believe thirty-nine or forty inches is about the greatest height to which the Boar grows, but they vary very much in bulk, some being lean and lanky, others fat and heavy. The color also varies a good deal from nearly jet black to a reddish hue..

The tusks of the Boar are most formidable instruments ; they are as sharp as razors, and protrude nearly three inches from the jaw of a large Boar, the total length of whose tusk may be as much as nine inches, two-thirds being imbedded in the jaw.

The Sow is considerably smaller than the Boar, and has merely the rudiments of tusks ; she is, however, more active, and is sufficiently formidably armed to be a very dangerous opponent.

In the hills, the Wild Boar lives in any thick jungle he can find, often in the vicinity of villages, on whose crops he nightly levies tribute. In the plains, the Pig delights in grass jungle, in beds of reeds in the vicinity of water, and above all in sugar-cane. If the latter is not in sufficient quantity to afford good cover, Pig will live in the nearest jungle and pay nocturnal visits to the sugar, of which they destroy an immense quantity ; they will often travel many miles in search of their favorite food. Frequently, however, an old Boar will take up his abode in the cane, and will not leave it, attacking every one who ventures to disturb him.

No animal exceeds the Pig in ferocity, nor equals him in courage and determination Once roused, nothing will stop him ; he will boldly charge the largest Elephant who may have disturbed him, without further provocation ; or, if desperately wounded, he will receive spear after spear without flinching, rushing fearlessly at every horse or man whom he can see, utterly reckless of the wounds he receives, and fighting gallantly, until at last he sinks from a mortal thrust. This gameness, added to considerable speed, has made him much sought after, as affording the most exciting and delightful sport in the world, when legitimately hunted with horse and spear.

Pig-sticking (for in these days it would be pedantic to call it Hog-hunting) is, I think, generally allowed by those who have thoroughly joined in it, to possess all the requisites of real sport in an unequalled degree ; and in no other species of hunting is the animal pursued treated with such fairness. With two or three horsemen after him, an old Boar can, and often does, make a good fight of it, and the wounds are not always all his. In Pig-sticking many sports are combined ; racing, steeple-chasing, hunting, and (is it not a sport ?) fighting. I think no one would ever forget the day when he first experienced the delightful sensation of taking *first spear*.

This glorious sport has often been written about by abler pens than mine, and by men with a hundred times more experience ; so I shall not presume to lay down rules, nor to give my own views on horses and riding ; but will merely quote Colonel Shakespear with regard to the latter, and record my opinion that it is not necessary to have very expensive horses in order to enjoy this sport. Of course, with equal riders the best horse will have the best chance of the spear, and among a large field of first-class horses a slow screw would probably see little of the run ; still among ordinary horses, a man very indifferently mounted will find that he can see a good deal of the fun, and that his turn for 'first spear' will frequently come round, if he will only ride his best. If you have lots of money, buy the best horses you can find ; but don't stay at home and give as your reason "that you can't afford to give 1,500 rupees for an Arab up to weight." Besides, unless you are *very* rich, you will probably not enjoy your sport so much, if you are riding on a "lot of money."

But with regard to riding, Colonel Shakespear says, " Ride to the front, there is hardly any ground that a Hog crosses where your horse cannot follow. Blot the words *impossible* and *impracticable* out of your dictionary."

I suppose there are many more falls, in proportion, out Pig-sticking, than there are across a stiff hunting country in England. This arises from the 'blind' nature of the ground ridden over, and the pace at which it is necessary to go, giving no time to pick one's away.

In the 'Khádir' or old valley of the Ganges, for instance, the ground consists of level plains covered with grass and intersected with deep nullahs or ravines, some dry, others full of water ; with deep but invisible ditches ; holes varying in size from pits large enough to swallow up horse and rider, to others just big enough to admit a horse's leg ; hidden stumps, and tangled bushes of '*jhdo* ;' and over this one has to gallop at racing pace. What wonder if 'croppers' are the rule, and not the exception? Still, I have rarely known any one hurt; the pace is too good.

The Meerut Tent Club hunt over this ground, and enjoy splendid sport. I think the day's sport, which I now record, was the first regular meeting of that Club. As most of us were then beginners, we did not, I fear, spare the Sows sufficiently, but the grass was so long that one sometimes had a longish gallop before the sex of the Pig could be discovered, and then it was hard to pull up! Afterwards we were more particular.

On the 23rd of March, 1865, a party of eleven of us met at Hastnápúr, on the Ganges, about eighteen miles from Meerut. Most of us went out shooting in the evening and killed a few partridges and snipe. Early next morning, three of us rode over to Shérpúr, a village a few miles off, where the coolies had been ordered to await us. In the grey of the morning we saw some Pig returning from their night's ramble, but not having our spears in our hands we could not ride them. Having reached Shérpúr, and made all preparations, we were just starting to beat, when we met the rest of the party: two of them had met with a Sow and killed her. C. had obtained first spear.

All being in readiness, we commenced beating, but for some time without success. At last I saw three Pig coming back towards the right of the line where I was posted, and at once gave chase, but getting into a thick clump of palm trees I was thrown out, and when I got clear I saw F. with the lead. I raced up to him and overtook him just after he had turned the Pig. We gave turn and turn for some time without spearing, the Sow being a very active one, and my horse (a powerful grey Arab), very violent and difficult to turn. At one turn he sprang clear over the Pig. F. at length got first spear, and some of the others coming up, the Sow was quickly despatched. Shortly after we had recommenced beating a good-sized Boar started. I got away with the lead, but the brute jumped into a wet nullah and lay down, and my horse went on some distance before I could stop him. The Boar being soon turned out, the chase recommenced, and after a short run, F. again secured first spear, disabling the Boar so much that he at once stopped, and was quickly killed. Another heavy Boar was roused, but soon crossed a deep nullah and was lost. We now beat for some time without seeing anything, but at length a Boar got up in the middle of the line. I was on the extreme right, and was racing up with P., when we suddenly came to a dry nullah: it was too wide to jump, and it was too late to pull up; my horse hit the opposite bank, fell, and rolled over. I was only a little shaken, and we were at once up and going again, but were only in time to be in at the death. F. had again secured first spear; making three in succession. We now went to the tents and breakfasted.

In the afternoon we again went out, and a very short distance from camp put up two Pig in long grass. One took to the open plain, and I followed her, and had all the galloping to myself for a long time: being only a Sow, however, she turned too quickly for my impetuous horse, and B., who had followed me, got first and second spears. I now got my horse straight, and spearing the Sow through the withers, dropped her dead: she fell under my horse's nose, and he jumped over her. When we rejoined the line, we found that two more Pig had been killed, C. getting both spears. Another fine Boar was soon on foot, and gave a capital run over rather broken ground. I secured first spear, and gave him another that disabled him as he charged. All our horses having now had enough, we returned to the tents, having had a splendid day's sport.

On several occasions we had very good sport on the 'Khádir.' On the 8th of April, 1866, six of us met at Hastnápúr and killed four heavy Boars. The second run was one of the prettiest I ever saw : an old Boar was found fast asleep in a clump of grass, and on being turned out, took to the open plain where the grass had been cut, and nothing remained but soft turf : the riding, therefore, was first rate, and we all rattled the Boar along at racing pace, each one striving for the lead, and the Pig swerving slightly from side to side as one or another pressed him rather closer than the rest : it was a good race, and for some time it appeared as if it might be any one's spear. At length he inclined towards me, and lengthening my spear to the utmost, I dashed at him : the spear point was not six inches from his quarters, and I had almost shouted 'first spear,' when the Boar pitched on his head and rolled over on his right side, just out of my reach : this of course let in the others, and P. took first spear.

We were marching down country in 1868, when near Sahárunpúr we heard news of Pig. Six of us went out, and proceeded to beat some sugar-cane fields, in which they were said to live. For some time we were unsuccessful, but we were at length informed that we should find the Pig lying in some green barley near a village. The crop was very high and rank, and when, after a time, there was a shout from the beaters that a Pig was on foot, we could not at first see him. P. was the first to sight the Boar at a considerable distance, as he reached some thinner corn, and he at once gave chase. I was not far behind, and had just reached his horse's quarters when we came to a wide piece of water. We took a pull at our horses, and I got through the deep mud and water with a struggle, but P.'s horse rolled over, and C., who came up directly afterwards, also came to grief. I now found myself alone, and pressed the Boar as hard as I could, but he had a tremendous start, and had got his second wind before I came up to him. My horse began to tire while the Pig still seemed pretty fresh : at length I succeeded in turning him several times, and the others came up. P. gave him the first spear, and S. the second : my horse coming again I gave the Boar two spears in quick succession, and he then became very savage and took to fighting. He made charge after charge, and though he received a spear each time, he seemed to care little for his wounds. He knocked C.'s mare off her legs ; and another horse, which was imprudently ridden *slowly* up to him, escaped being cut to pieces by a miracle. At last we despatched him, and had time to look over our horses : one only was slightly cut.

We next found an old Sow in the high corn ; she would not leave it, but kept running in circles, and, after I had given her a first spear, became desperately vicious. She charged everything that came in the way, including a coolie and a led horse, but fortunately did little harm. She, however, succeeded in slightly cutting my horse in the stifle before we killed her. The wound soon healed up, but afterwards the whole leg swelled to a great size and the horse was unable to leave the stable for three weeks.

My next encounter with a Boar was not quite so satisfactory. On the 17th of March, we were encamped about twenty miles from Moradabad on the Bareilly road. The country was a level plain covered with growing corn, which, although nearly ripe, was, owing to the poorness of the soil, not much more than eighteen inches high. Several of us were lounging about the mess tent, late in the afternoon, when we heard shouts of '*Jangli Súr*,' and on looking out saw a Boar galloping through some shallow water about three hundred yards from camp. Just then one of our men fired a charge of shot at him, which of course did him no harm, but only served to enrage him.

My horses were being cleaned, so that I shouted to a syce to saddle one, ran to my tent for a spear, and was in the saddle and in pursuit of the Boar in little more than a minute. He was about three quarters of a mile off, but I could plainly see him, and I sent my horse along as hard as he could go. The Pig was going leisurely, and I soon came up and made him quicken his pace. Just then he espied two wretched natives standing in the corn, and at once changed his course and charged them. They turned to run, but one was instantly knocked over. I was close behind and the Boar went on. I soon overtook him, and gave him three spears in quick succession, but, in my hurry, I had unfortunately brought a blunt spear, and I did not do him much harm. Each thrust was followed by a most determined and vicious charge which it took me all I knew to avoid. I had no spurs.

We now reached a field of higher corn, and the Boar, turning suddenly round, charged straight at my horse's chest. I had no time to get out of the way, and my horse was knocked off his legs, receiving a cut under the left knee. I was sent flying, but found myself on my feet in an instant, and had just time to lower my spear as the Boar rushed at me. The spear glanced and I was at once thrown down, and the Pig immediately attacked me on the ground, digging at me most savagely. I knew that my only chance was to prevent him from getting his tusks into my stomach ; I, therefore, kept my left arm well to the front, and let him rip at it, while I seized him by the foreleg with the right hand, and tried to throw him. He was too strong for me and kept on cutting me ; so finding that I could not get rid of him, I resolved to try the dodge of shamming. I therefore threw myself flat on my face and lay still, hoping the brute would leave me ; however, he went on digging at me as viciously as ever, inflicting two severe cuts on my head. This would not do ! so I jumped up, and grasping my spear with both hands, drove it with all my strength against his chest—but it would not penetrate, and I was again knocked down.

I now began to think that matters were becoming rather serious, when, to my delight, I heard horses galloping. I shouted for help, and as they approached the Boar left me. S., R., and S. then rode up, having by great good luck come the right way, for they did not even know that I was in front of them.

I was scarlet from head to foot, and my clothes cut to ribbons. S. looked after me while the others went for a dhoolie. I was carried into camp, and my wounds sewn up and dressed, a job which took nearly four hours ! I had received about fifty wounds ; two in the head, one in the foot, and the others pretty equally distributed between.

S. and F. went out next day in search of my enemy, but they were unable to track him.

They, however, beat a neighbouring jungle, in which they found a very savage Boar who may have been the same one, but they soon lost him.

I was luckily in very good health, so my wounds, many of which were very severe, quickly healed up, and I was on horseback again in a month. The tendons of my left arm, however, were injured, and I have never recovered the perfect use of that hand.

I shall always, in future, carry a large knife when out Pig-sticking, as, although an accident like mine is of rare occurrence, it is as well to be prepared for the worst and it is by no means pleasant to be cut to pieces, without the means of injuring one's antagonist.

CHAPTER XIV.

THE GAUR.

Bos Gaurus.

In the Terai.—*Gáori-gai—Mithan.* In Chotá Nágpúr.—*Gáor—Gail.*

This splendid animal is an inhabitant of most of the primeval forests of India, being found in suitable localities from the Terai to the southern coast. It is abundant in the Bhútán Dooárs, in the Assam valley, in the Central Provinces, in Chotá Nágpúr, Chaibássá and the neighbouring states ; in the Western Gháts, Travancore, and Canará.

It is commonly known among British sportsmen by the misnomer of Bison, a name which is as inapplicable as that of Buffalo to the American Bison. As I studiously avoid the use of misnomers, I have retained the name of Gaur as the proper English appellation, as it is recognised throughout all the districts of Northern India where I have hunted. In the Bhútán Dooárs and neighbouring jungles it is called indifferently ' *Gáori-gai* ' and ' *Mithan*,' the latter being the name of the closely allied domestic race of cattle usually known to Englishmen as the Gayal.

It is believed by many that a wild Mithan as well as the Gaur inhabits Assam, Chittagong, and the adjacent countries, but, although I have made many enquiries, I have been unable to obtain satisfactory evidence of the existence of more than one breed of wild cattle in those parts, and I much doubt the occurrence of the true Mithan in a feral state at the present day. The wild Gaur and the tame Mithan have many points of resemblance, but in addition to the heavier and clumsier formation of the Mithan, which might be due to long domestication, the skulls and horns of the two races differ very considerably.

The Gaur is the largest of all the known members of the bovine family, and in height it only comes second to the Elephant among the Large Game of India. I cannot help thinking, however, that its size has been considerably exaggerated, and although my limited experience of the animal necessitates my giving my opinion with some diffidence, I have great doubts as to the accuracy of measurements of twenty or twenty-one hands, which have been given by some authors.

Be this as it may, the bull Gaur is one of the most magnificent animals in creation, and its pursuit will always have great attractions for the real sportsman. An old bull stands at least eighteen hands at the shoulder, the withers being much elevated, and merging into a well defined dorsal ridge, somewhat like the keel of a boat, which extends to about the centre of the back, when it ends rather abruptly. The depth of girth is immense, and the

THE GAUR
BOS GAURUS
Young Herd Bull, Chotá Nágpúr, 22nd January, 1883

Published by Thacker, Spink & Co., Calcutta.

THE GAUR
BOS GAURUS
Old solitary Bull, Sátpúrá Hills, 21st May 1884

Published by Thacker, Spink & Co., Calcutta.

muscles of the shoulders and arms enormously developed. The neck is strong and massive, and supports a ponderous but high-bred looking head, which is set on at a rather peculiar angle. The hind quarters are full and rounded ; the limbs are comparatively slender and deerlike ; and the hoofs are small in proportion to the size of the animal. The tail is similar to that of the domestic cow, and is furnished with a tuft of longish hair.

The color is a deep chestnut, almost coal black in very old bulls, the hair being short and remarkably glossy. The belly and inside of the limbs have an ochreous tinge, and the hair is rather elongated on those parts. The frontal crest is arched and greatly developed, and both it and the forehead are cream colored. The legs below the knees and hocks are dirty white.

The horns are not remarkably large, a fine pair attaining a length of about thirty inches with a circumference of nineteen. They are yellowish at the base, of a greenish hue higher up, and jet black at the tips. They are highly polished, and in young bulls they turn inwards at the points, which are smooth and sharp. The horns of old bulls become rugged at the base, and lose their handsome sweep, the points becoming blunt, and being frequently broken off.

The cow is considerably smaller, and more slenderly built than the bull ; her horns are thin, and usually much curved.

The Gaur is never found except in extensive forests, and in more or less hilly country, although in the Terai a herd will occasionally stray to a considerable distance from the foot of the hills.

In the Bhútán Dooárs and Assam, the Gaur principally frequent the lowest spurs, at times ascending the higher ranges, or wandering down to level ground, according to the season and the abundance or scarcity of grass and other fodder. In places where the jungle has been burned, a crop of tender young grass springs up in a few weeks, and Gaur, as well as deer of all sorts, are very fond of visiting these cleared spaces by night, retiring to the densely wooded valleys during the day. Bamboo forest is a very favorite resort, the young shoots being greedily devoured.

In Chotá Nágpúr the Gaur inhabit low ranges of rocky hills, covered with tolerably open forest, consisting in great part of sál and bamboo, and intersected by numerous streams.

Gaur are generally to be found in herds, numbering from four or five to thirty, but old bulls are usually alone or in pairs. They appear to move about a good deal at night, and they may be found out feeding in open glades in the morning and evening, while they generally retire to some shady spot during the heat of the day.

They may be hunted like deer and other animals by simply searching for them in the most likely localities, but the usual method, and by far the most interesting, is by tracking. For this work it is absolutely necessary to enlist the services of some of the wild natives of the forests, who are frequently excellent trackers, although I have never witnessed any of the wonderful performances with which they are sometimes credited. I have heard that it is easy to approach close to Gaur on an Elephant, but I should be sorry to resort to that sort of shooting in a country where it was possible to stalk them on foot. Driving is also sometimes resorted to, but I do not consider it a very sportsmanlike proceeding, and it is attended with much uncertainty.

My opportunities of Gaur-shooting have been few, but I have seen just enough of the sport to acquire a keen liking for it, and I consider that it is perhaps only equalled in interest by the pursuit of the Ibex and the great Thibetan sheep.

I first made the acquaintance of the Gaur in May 1878, in the Sikkim Terai. I had been shooting on Elephants for a week with two friends ; we had bagged a Tiger apiece, a Rhinoceros, and several deer, and on my friends leaving me, I determined to see what could be done on foot along the base of the hills. I accordingly moved my camp to Sevook, on the right bank of the Teestá river, just where it leaves the hills. Here I found an intelligent Nepalese who told me that he could show me ' *Gáorí-gai*,' and by daylight on the morning after my arrival we had reached the top of a low plateau about a mile from camp. Here we found ourselves in a beautiful forest, and my guide assured me that we should probably find game. We had not gone far before we came upon fresh tracks of three Gaur, and we proceeded to follow them up, which was easy enough, as the soil was soft and moist from recent showers. Before long we heard branches breaking a short distance ahead, and on carefully stealing up in the direction of the sound, I found two Elephants quietly feeding. As they were forbidden game I contented myself with watching them for a few minutes as they unsuspiciously fed within a few yards of me, and then resumed the track of the Gaur. Three or four hundred yards farther on my Shikari drew my attention to two Gaur which were browsing on some low trees to our right, and I had no difficulty in stalking to within about seventy yards of the nearer of the two. He was feeding away from me, but halted at such an angle that I thought that I could send a bullet diagonally through him. I accordingly fired steadily at his flank, fully expecting him to drop on the spot. As the smoke cleared away nothing was to be seen, but my attention was distracted by a crash in the jungle to the rear. Running back to ascertain what it was, I was told that another Elephant had been disturbed by my shot, and had rushed past the Shikaris. I quickly returned to the spot where the Gaur had been standing, and soon found great clots of blood which showed us the direction that it had taken. Following up, along a steep hill-side, I again obtained a glimpse of the bulls, but they soon entered a nearly impervious thicket of tall grass and cardamums, which it was utterly useless to attempt to explore on foot.

In the afternoon I again went out on a pad Elephant, and rode through the forest in another direction. Coming upon tracks of Gaur, which a close examination showed to be perfectly fresh, I dismounted and took up the trail, directing the Mahout to remain well behind, and just keep us in sight. Easily read signs showed that the Gaur had been travelling leisurely, feeding as they went, and their course was a very erratic one. At length we reached a space nearly clear of trees, but covered with patches of high grass. I was entering one of these, in which the grass was just up to my eyes, and my Shikari was a pace or two to my left, when I suddenly caught sight of the muzzle and horns of a bull within ten yards of me !

I could see nothing more of him, but fancying that he must be facing me, I aimed just below his nose, expecting, of course, to hit him in the centre of the throat. There was a tremendous stampede, as all the Gaur rushed through the long grass, but I could see nothing. On going up to the spot where the bull had been, I discovered that he must have been standing with his broadside to me, so that my bullet must probably have only grazed his head or neck. There were only two or three drops of blood, but a broad trail through the high green grass plainly showed the course taken by the frightened herd. The cover was so tall and dense that I sent back for the Elephant and followed up on his back, until we had crossed the grass jungle and reëntered the sál forest. I then dismounted and resumed the chase on foot, and had gone but a little way, when I caught sight of the head and shoulders of a Gaur, standing in the shade of a tree. The sun was shining in my eyes, so that I could not see very distinctly, but concluding that it was the wounded bull, I whistled to my Shikari, who had not yet seen it, and fired at the Gaur's neck. I heard the sound of a fall, but as the smoke cleared away I could see nothing. I said to the Shikari, "It has fallen," but he replied, " No, it has gone away." I walked up to the spot where the Gaur had stood, and there lay a cow, shot through the neck. It then turned out that when I signalled to the Shikari, he had seen the bull, which was standing in full view of me, but which I had not made out owing to the cow having first attracted my eye. It being now too late to follow up the bull any farther, I returned to camp.

Next day I saw nothing, but on the 3rd June I crossed the Teestá and hunted through a large extent of country. It was not till we were on our way home that we discovered a fresh track. This led us through all sorts of cover, some of it being very dense and tangled. At length we descried the whisking tails of a bull and a cow, which were standing on the point of a nearly level and tolerably open spur, about a hundred and fifty yards off. The wind was all right, and the stalk appeared to be an easy one, but I had not advanced above fifty yards before another cow, which had been lying down unperceived in some thick cover, sprang up with a loud snort of alarm and dashed away. In an instant the bull wheeled round, tossed his massive head, and disappeared. I ran on, but saw no more of him.

The next day I again hunted on the left bank of the Teestá, but failed to find a single recent track, and on the following day I was compelled to abandon my trip owing to the whole of my servants and two out of three Mahouts being ill with Terai fever. The rains had commenced, and with them what is considered to be the most unhealthy season of the year, and out of the whole party of three officers and about nine servants who originally left Calcutta, one only escaped. Several were very ill, though only one servant died. I was not the exception, though I consider myself very nearly fever-proof, but I was fortunate enough to have a comparatively mild attack, which only lasted two days.

Four years elapsed before I again had an opportunity of hunting the Gaur, and this time I took advantage of an official visit to the station of Baxá in the Bhútán Dooárs, to explore the forests in the vicinity. Having obtained the loan of three Elephants, and having engaged two Nepalese Shikaris who knew the country, I left Baxá on the 14th March 1882 and encamped at a place called Gangáhatí, about two miles from the foot of the hills. The forest was thin and scattered, and wide tracts of jungle had been burned some time before, so that there was little cover; but it was evident, by numerous footmarks, that Gaur grazed on the tender young grass during the night.

Long before daylight the following morning I mounted an Elephant, and made my way to a spot which the Shikaris said was a favorite feeding place. Leaving the Elephant at dawn, we proceeded to search for fresh tracks, and had not gone very far before we came across those of a small herd. There was little difficulty in following them across the burnt plain, and we kept up the chase at a good pace, until we reached a dry river bed, on the farther bank of which the forest became rather denser. Crossing this, we found that the ground rose in a succession of terraces, so that it was impossible to see far ahead. The cracking of branches, however, attracted my attention, and on hurrying forward I found myself within seventy yards of about seven Gaur. I could not see a bull, but was looking about for him, when I detected my Shikari in the act of raising the spare rifle that he was carrying. I was obliged to rush at him and seize the rifle, and this movement frightened the Gaur, which commenced to move away. I had to fire hurriedly at what seemed to be the largest, and dropped it on the spot, but my second bullet was intercepted by a small tree stem, and the rest of the herd went off unscathed. The one shot proved to be a cow.

Moving camp the following day I found tracks of an old solitary bull, but after following them for a long distance, they led us up into the hills where the long dry grass rendered tracking impossible; and even had it not been so, the crackling dead leaves, which strewed the ground to the depth of several inches, would have effectually prevented us from approaching our game in silence.

Next day was also a blank one, so on the 18th it was determined to shift camp farther to the west. I started before daylight and hunted through the forest to our destination, having ordered my servants to follow me without delay. After a long march we reached the 'salt-lick' which was said to be a favorite resort of the Gaur, and as we saw a good many fresh tracks, we had hopes of good sport. We had sat for about two hours before we heard a man shout, and as we at once replied we expected every moment to see the Elephants appear. Another hour, however, elapsed, and there were no further signs of them, so we went back in search. To my disgust I found that although the servants had received minute instructions as to where they were to encamp, they had turned off the road a few hundred yards short of where we were awaiting them, and were then, doubtless, miles ahead. It was now late in the afternoon, so we at once replaced the howdah on the Elephant, and hurried in pursuit. Our progress soon became painfully slow: not only was there hardly a vestige of a track, but the boughs overhead had never been cut away so as to allow of the passage of a howdah, and consequently we had to make innumerable detours. As long as daylight lasted, we were able to follow the tracks of our Elephants, but as it became dark we had no guide whatever, and could only steer as nearly as possible due west.

After a most tedious journey through the forest we at length reached the banks of the Torsá river, and here we made sure that we should find our camp, but not a sign of it was to be seen. It was now pitch dark, and I shouted and fired frequent shots, but without eliciting any response. To add to our discomfort, a tremendous thunderstorm, accompanied by bitterly cold wind, had come on, and we were soon thoroughly soaked and shivering in every limb. Nearly blinded by the frequent and vivid lightning, which only served to make the darkness appear more impenetrable, we blundered along for an hour or two, following the course of the river, sustained by the hope that we should find some village. At last, our case being evidently hopeless, I gave orders to halt, and remain where we were for the night. Fortunately, although we had nothing to eat or drink, I had a small piece of candle and about half a dozen matches left, and having lighted these with infinite difficulty, and discovered an old decayed tree, we ultimately succeeded in kindling a splendid bonfire, by the side of which we spent a tolerably comfortable night.

Next morning we found the servants within half a mile, they also having lost their way. They had not been able to light a fire, for which I was not sorry, as it was a fitting punishment for their neglect of orders. Everything having been soaked, and the Elephants having had but little to eat the previous day, I was obliged to halt for the day; and with the limited time at my disposal it was then too late to retrace my steps, so I had to give up the Gaur, and set out for Julpaigorí.

In January 1883 I once more went after Gaur, this time in the southern part of the province of Chotá Nágpúr. A rather tedious journey of upwards of eighty miles from the military station of Dorandá, brought me to a place named Tinginná. My servants had again disobeyed orders, which necessitated my going more than ten miles out of my way to find them. My camp did not arrive until late at night on the 20th.

On the following morning I started for the jungles, my camp in the meantime being moved about ten miles to the south. During the day I found recent tracks of a small herd, but none perfectly fresh, and I did not see any game.

On the 22nd I went out in a different direction, and had a long walk over a succession of forest-clad ridges without seeing anything except a couple of Four-horned Antelope up to twelve o'clock. Having rested during the heat of the day, we worked homewards by a circuitous route. We were descending a gently sloping hill when the wild-looking aborigine who was guiding us suddenly halted and whispered 'Gáor.' Looking in the direction indicated I saw three Gaur in a small glade about two hundred yards below us. The bull was standing motionless gazing in our direction, while the two cows were quietly moving away. Ordering my men to remain perfectly still, I advanced carefully in the direction of the bull, and succeeded in stalking as far as the forest extended without being detected. I found, however, that an open space nearly a hundred yards wide intervened between me and the bull, and this it was impossible to cross. He still remained in the same position as when first seen, so I aimed at the centre of his chest and fired. Down came the bull on his knees, then recovered, and blundered away in a helpless manner that showed that he was grievously wounded. I ran after him, and had not gone two hundred yards before I heard a moaning bellow a short distance ahead of me, and directly afterwards I distinguished the outline of a Gaur standing broadside on among some high bushes, within thirty yards. Thinking that it was the wounded one, I fired behind its shoulder and rolled

it over, and on hastening up I found a bull and a remarkably large cow lying side by side.
I had struck the bull exactly where I aimed, and the bullet, as was afterwards discovered,
had shattered his heart to pieces. I was using my favorite 12-bore by Rigby, with hardened
spherical bullet, and seven drams of powder.

Next morning I sent men to remove the skins of the Gaur entire, as they were destined
to be mounted for the Calcutta Museum,* while I hunted on the opposite side of camp. We
saw nothing during the day, though pretty fresh tracks were numerous.

On the 24th we again visited the jungle in which I shot the bull and cow, and on
reaching a dense grove of bamboos we found perfectly fresh traces. We followed them up
cautiously, but the first intimation we gained of the presence of the herd was the resonant
snort of the bull as he detected us and moved away without offering a chance of a shot.
Hurrying in pursuit, I soon came up with the herd standing on a low hill among rather thick
sál forest, but though I managed to approach to within a hundred yards, I could not get a
clear shot at the bull, which kept in the middle of the cows. Having excellent trackers with
me I followed the herd for seven hours, but our progress was slow, owing to the stony nature
of the ground, and I never came up with them.

On the 25th, at the earnest solicitation of the hospitable native Zemindar, who attended
me with a number of his relations, I consented to try a beat. Several hundred of the
neighbouring villagers turned out armed with bows and arrows and axes, while a few of them
were provided with 'tom-toms' and most discordant horns of great power. The Zemindar
and his friends had guns of more or less primitive manufacture, and the sportsmen took up
their posts at the most likely passes, while the villagers formed line three or four miles away,
and beat up to the guns. The first beat was a blank as far as Gaur were concerned, and no
animal of any sort came past me ; but a boar and a Sambur hind were killed, the former
with an arrow, the latter with a matchlock. The second beat had also nearly come to a close
without any results, when a herd, which had been attempting to break on the left flank,
were driven across to where I was stationed, in the centre. As they crossed a rocky ravine in
front of me, it appeared as if they would come right up to where I was sitting on the ground
behind a small bush. Unfortunately, however, they bore away to their right, and passed on
the other side of some high bushes, which obstructed my view. The range was not a long
one, being only about eighty yards, but the herd came on in a compact mass, so that the
big bull was never clear of the cows, and I found it impossible to get a fair shot at him. A
fine bull, but inferior in size to the first one, brought up the rear of the herd, and I fired
at him as he passed through some thin bushes. A regular stampede ensued, but I could
see nothing but a cloud of dust, and the herd escaped untouched by the bullets of my native
friends. On following them up we found blood on the track and also on the stems of the
trees, but at such a height that it was evident that my bullet must have struck too high.

It was too late to follow up the same evening, but next morning I sent the two best
trackers on the trail of the wounded bull, while we tried another drive. The trackers reported

---

* The bull was admirably mounted, and the photograph which heads the present chapter is his portrait.

that the wounded bull had left the herd, but had gone away many miles without once stopping. Our beat was not a success, the only three adult Gaur seen, breaking back ; but we were fortunate enough to secure a female calf, which was surrounded by the beaters, and captured uninjured.

I presented it to the Calcutta ' Zoo,' where it lived for about four months, and then died rather suddenly.

As I had only two days more leave, and driving game is not at all in accordance with my tastes, I devoted the 27th and 28th to stalking, but there was no recent authentic information regarding the whereabouts of the Gaur, and I did not even see a track in the jungles that I visited on those days.

CHAPTER XV.

THE YÂK.

POEPHAGUS GRUNNIENS.

In Thibet.—*Donkh*. On the Indian Frontier.—*Ban Chdor.*

THE wild Yâk is generally found on the lofty plains and mountains in the interior of Thibet, where vast herds are said to exist. But few places, where it is found, are accessible to Englishmen, as the Thibetan Government jealously exclude all European travellers from their country. A few sportsmen have indeed succeeded in penetrating for several marches into forbidden ground (either by going in disguise or by cleverly eluding the vigilance of the Tartars who guard the frontier), and have shot Yâk in the mountains to the north of the Sutlej. Such expeditions are, however, still more difficult than they formerly were, as the Thibetans are more particular than ever, and are moreover too sharp to allow themselves to be again deceived by the stratagems which have already been successfully employed against them.

Formerly Yâk were always to be found in the valleys between the Nítí Pass and the Sutlej, and sportsmen were allowed to shoot there without interference, so long as they confined themselves to certain limits. The Yâk were so constantly hunted in this district, that of late years they appear to have grown shy of crossing the Sutlej, and there is but little chance of finding them in their old haunts.

Yâk have been shot on the northern slopes of the Kárá Koram mountains, but the best place to go to for them is undoubtedly the valley of Chung Chenmo. Here they are, certainly, only occasional visitors, but they are often to be found, and now that the new route to Yarkund has been discovered, it is only necessary to go a few marches farther north to be quite sure of finding them, if they don't happen to be on the southern side of the passes.

The male wild Yâk is a magnificent beast : he attains a height of fifteen hands or more, but stands on very short legs. He is nearly jet black, with the exception of a little white about the muzzle and a sprinkling of grey hairs on the head and neck. The hair is very long and shaggy, especially on the shoulders, thighs, and sides, where it hangs in heavy masses nearly reaching the ground ; so that one can hardly see daylight under an old bull in his winter coat.

YÀK

POËPHAGUS GRUNNIENS

Published by Thacker, Spink & Co., Calcutta.

The bushy tail of the Yâk is well known, being highly prized in India, where it is called 'Châorí.' It is used for switching away flies, and used to be considered one of the emblems of Royalty. The white tails which are brought for sale, are those of tame Yâk ; tails of the wild species are black and of much greater size.

The horns of the Yâk are not remarkably large in proportion to the size of the animal : they grow to about three feet in length, and fourteen inches in circumference. The head, however, is very grand ; the horns are finely curved, and the forehead broad and massive, the shaggy hair which nearly conceals the eyes adding much to the wildness of its appearance.

The neck is thick and muscular, and the withers rise very high, forming a sort of hump. The fore-quarter of the Yâk reminds one of the American Bison, but, unlike that animal, he does not fall away behind ; the back being nearly level, and the hind-quarters quite in proportion to the rest of the body. The legs are extraordinarily short and thick, and the hoofs large, the track of an old bull being nearly as large as that of a Camel.

The cow Yâk is considerably inferior in size to the bull, and her horns are small, but otherwise she much resembles him.

The Yâk inhabits the wildest and most desolate mountains ; it delights in extreme cold ; and is found, as a rule, at a greater elevation than any other animal. Although so large a beast, it thrives upon the coarsest pasturage, and its usual food consists of a rough wiry grass which grows in all the higher valleys of Thibet, up to an elevation of nearly 20,000 feet. On the banks of the streams in many places a more luxuriant grass is met with, and it is particularly plentiful in the valleys of Chung Chenmo and Kyobrung, forming the attraction which entices the Yâk from the still wilder and more barren country farther north. Yâk seem to wander about a great deal. In summer the cows are generally to be found in herds varying in numbers from ten to one hundred, while the old bulls are for the most part solitary or in small parties of three or four. They feed at night and early in the morning, and usually betake themselves to some steep and barren hill-side during the day, lying sometimes for hours in the same spot. Old bulls in particular seem to rejoice in choosing a command-ing situation for their resting place, and their tracks may be found on the tops of the steepest hills far above the highest traces of vegetation.

The Yâk is not, apparently, a very sharp-sighted beast, but its sense of smelling is extremely keen, and this is the chief danger to guard against in stalking it. In the high valleys of Thibet, where so many glens intersect one another, and where the temperature is continually changing, the wind is equally variable. It will sometimes shift to every point of the compass in the course of a few minutes, and the best planned stalk may be utterly spoiled. This is one of the chances which adds to the uncertainty of sport, and thereby, however provoking at the time, greatly enhances its charms.

Partially white wild Yâk have occasionally been seen, but these were probably the result of a cross between the wild cows and domestic bulls. The latter are frequently allowed to roam for months among the mountains where the wild Yâk are found, so it is not unlikely that the two species may sometimes inter-breed. The tame Yâk is smaller than the wild one, but there is little other difference : most tame ones are black, but many are more or less marked with white (the invariable result of domestication), and occasional brown, dun, and grey specimens are seen.

The flesh of the wild Yâk is excellent, the beef being fine in grain and of capital flavor, but that which I have tasted has always been very lean.   The tongue and marrowbones are delicacies not to be despised, especially in a country where one has so little variety of food.

It has been said that a wounded Yâk will not charge, but this is a mistake.   A friend of mine was charged by a wounded cow, which came at him in a most determined way ; and I have heard of several similar instances.   The only bull which I have shot showed every disposition to fight, but the poor brute had not much chance.

My first expeditions in search of Yâk were singularly unsuccessful, and it seemed as if the Fates had decreed that I should never get one : however, I persevered, and at last succeeded in bagging the fine bull whose portrait is here given.

I first visited Chung Chenmo in 1861, but I had very little time for shooting, and could only devote three days to hunting the Kyobrung valley ; and as two friends accompanied me, my chances of sport were of course not improved.   On the 27th of July, S. and I had fired at some Thibetan Antelope, and fancying that one was wounded, I went off alone in pursuit.   I had not gone far before I saw an old bull Yâk trotting up the ravine I was in, having evidently been disturbed by our shots.   He was far out of shot, but I followed up his tracks as fast as possible in hopes of overtaking him.   After tracking him along the valley for some way, I found he had turned up a narrow and very steep ravine, so narrow indeed, that he had only just room to pass between the lofty walls of rock on either side. I followed him up this gorge, and had a long and fatiguing climb to the top of a very high hill covered with loose shale.   It took me a long time to reach the summit, and when I at last arrived there, I saw the bull standing sentry on a rocky peak about half a mile off. I lay down and watched him for about two hours, during which time he scarcely moved, only occasionally turning round, and keeping a most vigilant watch.   At last he disappeared over the hill, and I hastened to the spot he had vacated.   From thence I again saw him standing perfectly motionless on the hill-side about three hundred yards farther on.   After watching for a short time and seeing that he did not appear inclined to move, I proceeded to stalk him.   Making a detour, I reached the top of the ridge under which he was standing, and on looking over I saw the tips of his horns, but a large rock concealed his body.   Drawing back, I went on a few yards, and on again looking over, fully expected to have had an easy shot within sixty or seventy yards ; instead of which to my horror, I saw the bull galloping straight down the hill, tail on end, about a quarter of a mile below me.   He had either got my wind, or, more probably, been alarmed by some of our men whom I heard shouting in the valley below.   I tracked him down to the river, and then, as it was nearly dark, returned to camp, fully intending to follow up the bull in the morning.

Next morning however, the ground was covered with snow, so tracking was out of the question, and though S. and I hunted every nullah to the head of the Kyobrung valley, we could find no traces of the Yâk.

Two days afterwards, as we were returning down the valley, we came upon the fresh traces of a bull (probably the same one), but though we followed the track at best pace for fifteen or sixteen miles, we never came up with him, and we unfortunately had not another day to spare.

In 1862 I again went to Chung Chenmo on purpose for Yâk, but, though I worked hard for a fortnight, I never had the luck to see one. My friend H., who was with me, was more fortunate ; he found Yâk at once in the first valley he went to, and killed a fine bull and a cow.

In 1864 I reached Chung Chenmo on the 28th of May, thinking that I should have a better chance early in the season—this I now believe to be a mistake. On my arrival I was laid up for four days with a severe attack of fever and ague, but on recovering I at once went up the Kyobrung valley. I had not gone above five miles when I discovered three Yâk on the opposite side of the river. I was not long in crossing, and had succeeded in stalking to within two hundred yards, when the wind, which had been perfectly favorable, suddenly veered round to the opposite point of the compass. The Yâk at once scented me and made off at full speed, and two or three wild shots which I fired after them were ineffectual. I hunted for a fortnight in hopes of finding either those three Yâk or others, but I never even saw a fresh track, and at last left the valley in disgust. About three weeks afterwards another Officer found a large herd on the same ground that I had unsuccessfully hunted !

In 1865 I crossed the Chor Hotí Pass and hunted in the valley of the Sutlej. This ground used to be a favorite resort of Yâk, but I was informed by the Nítí Shikaris that they had not been seen here for three or four years. An Officer who was just ahead of me however, found three bulls, wounded, and lost one. With my usual luck I never saw one, though I carefully hunted all the most likely places. I had intended to have crossed the Sutlej, but my rascally Shikari would give me no assistance, and even, I believe, informed the Tartars of my intentions.

In 1870 I once more visited Chung Chenmo, resolving to hunt there as long as my leave lasted, if I could not find Yâk at once. I went up the valley of Kyobrung on the 26th of June, but saw no recent traces of Yâk either on that day or the following one.

On the 28th, on reaching the mouth of a small lateral valley, I was delighted to see a herd of Yâk feeding on the grassy banks of the stream. It was impossible to stalk them where they were, as the wind was at present unfavorable, and in a short time they went up the stony hill-side above them and lay down on the shingle. I watched them all day, expecting them to come down to feed in the afternoon, but they did not move until it was very nearly dark, and then came down so slowly that I had to leave them and return to camp, which was fortunately only about two miles off. I had counted the Yâk and found that there were fifteen of them, but all cows.

Next morning I was up before daylight, and on reaching the valley where I had left the Yâk I saw the herd just leaving it. As they turned the corner to go up the next valley I followed them, and, taking advantage of the inequalities of the ground, got within sixty yards. As I was trying to make out which was the largest cow, one of them saw me, and started off. As she did so I fired and hit her hard, and then ran after the herd, reloading as I went. They did not go away very fast, being evidently confused by the firing, and I fired three or four shots, which had the effect of breaking up the herd into two portions. One lot of three now went straight up the hill above me, and I soon rolled over two of them quite dead. Two or three of the other lot had already shown signs of being badly wounded, but none of them had yet dropped. I now turned my attention to them, and saw that one very large cow had a broken foreleg and was limping slowly away. I followed her up, and soon overtook her in the bed of the river, and gave her a finishing bullet. The other wounded Yâk escaped with the rest of the herd. I had now shot three cow Yâk, so I determined not to fire at any more, but I was more anxious than ever to bag a bull.

Next day I went up to the very head of the Kyobrung valley, exploring all the small lateral valleys as I went, but I could not even see the track of a bull. I found one cow, which I would not attempt to shoot, but I bagged three fine Antelope.

On the 1st July I had several letters to write, so I did not go out in the morning, but sent men to bring in the Antelope, which I had left under a rock. About mid-day a man came in with the news that he had seen a bull. I at once started in pursuit, and after walking about six miles, reached the place where he had been seen. Here, sure enough, was a large fresh track, which I at once followed up: we had not gone far before we disturbed a flock of fine Burrell, which unfortunately galloped away in the direction that the bull had taken, and on tracking a mile or two farther we found that they had evidently disturbed him. He had been lying down on the steep hill-side, but on seeing the Burrell running away he had gone farther up the valley. Luckily he was not much frightened, and about a mile farther on we found him standing in a wide ravine far up the hill-side. He had chosen his position well, and it was quite impossible to approach him where he was, so I lay down to watch him. He soon lay down also, and remained in the same position till it was quite dark, when I left him and returned to camp, a rough walk of eight or nine miles.

I was quite determined that I would not lose a chance of shooting the bull by any laziness on my part, so I was up long before daylight next morning and set out for the place where I had left him. On reaching the spot, we found by the tracks that he had gone a little higher up the valley, and then descended to the river, which he had crossed.

We now discovered a herd of Yâk feeding two or three miles farther up the valley; so, thinking it probable that the bull might have joined them, we marked the place where we left his tracks, and went to have a look at the herd. We were not disappointed—the old bull was there, the remainder of the herd consisting of the twelve survivors of the lot which I had fired at two days before; and I was sorry to see that two of them were evidently badly wounded and very sick: (they were afterwards found, one dead, and the other so weak that it could not keep with the herd). The Yâk were feeding in a grassy nullah, which was so wide where they were, that it was impossible to get a shot; but I saw that if they moved up in the direction in which they were now feeding, I should probably get a good chance. I was very anxious about the wind, which was continually changing, but fortunately it did not blow towards the Yâk, and after waiting about two hours, I had the satisfaction of seeing them walk quickly up the nullah. All was now nearly spoiled by one of the wounded cows, which had lagged a couple of hundred yards behind the herd ; but fortunately a green patch of grass delayed the others, and she overtook them.

I now commenced the stalk : the wind was luckily steady for a short time, and I followed the Yâk under cover of the bank of the nullah. Having approached as near as I could without showing myself, I found that the range was still rather a long one, so I crawled quietly along in full view of the herd, and gained a good many yards without being seen. Two or three of the cows now raised their heads, and though they had not made me out, I thought it best to fire. The bull was feeding in a good position, and I pressed the trigger steadily. To my disgust the cartridge missed fire ! (the only one of Eley's 'gastight' that I had ever known to fail), but the distance was too great for the Yâk to notice it, and I put in a new cartridge and tried again. I did not see where the bullet struck, but it did not drop the bull as I had expected. One lock of my heavy double-barrel was out of order, so I changed the big rifle for a 'Henry' single-barrel, and hit the bull rather far back, but crippled him a good deal ; and again taking the double-barrel, I broke his foreleg with my third shot. He was now at my mercy, though he went off on three legs, and I missed one or two shots at a long range. This was useless, so I ran after him, and he soon turned and stood at bay, shaking his head and flourishing his tail in a threatening manner. Poor beast! he was too hard hit to charge far ; but as I had only one barrel to depend upon, I did not walk right up to him, but fired at him from the distance of about one hundred yards. Two bullets from my heavy rifle struck him on the point of the shoulder, but he never flinched, merely shaking his head angrily as each bullet struck him ; a few seconds after the last shot he trembled and rolled over dead. On going up to him I was quite astonished at his immense size. He had looked very big when alive, but it required a closer inspection to discover how enormously powerful he was.

As camp was seven or eight miles off, I cut off his tail as a trophy, and left the bull to be brought in on the following day ; first taking the precaution of fastening a rope in a circle round the carcase in order to keep off the Chankos, who will not touch any meat if they suspect the existence of a trap.

The flesh of the bull when cut up loaded several tame Yâk, the hide and head alone forming a considerable load. The hair was all coming out, so the skin was not worth keeping.

November would be the best month in which to shoot Yâk, as their skins would then be in good order, but unfortunately it is generally impossible for Officers quartered in India to get leave at that season.

In order to make sure of bagging Yâk in Chung Chenmo, it is advisable not to fire at other game until the country has been thoroughly hunted for the larger animals. Although the bull Yâk is such a splendid beast, I think it is hardly worth the while of any sportsman who may perhaps have only *one* opportunity of visiting Chung Chenmo, to lose the chances which he will probably get at other game, such as Antelope, Nyan and Burrell. Of this, however, everyone can judge best for himself.

CHAPTER XVI.

THE BUFFALO.

Bubalus Arni.

Generally throughout India.—Ban Bhaiñs.—Arná. In Bengal.—*Maiñs.*

SOME naturalists have endeavoured to make out that there are two distinct varieties, if not separate species, of Buffalo in India.

The alleged difference, however, I believe, consists more in the usual shape and size of the horns than in anything else, and is certainly not sufficient to warrant their receiving different scientific names.

The Assam Buffalo has been distinguished as *B. macroceros*, and that from the Central Provinces as *B. spiroceros ;* the horns of the former, being, as a rule, longer and straighter than those of the latter.

I believe that the Buffalo is not now found to the west of Philibít, but it extends eastwards all along the Terai as far as Assam, in which province it is extremely abundant. It is also to be met with in suitable localities on the banks of many of the great rivers and swamps in Bengal Proper, and immense herds inhabit the unreclaimed portions of the Sunderbuns.

The Buffalo of Bengal and Assam is the only one I have shot, and he requires but little description : everyone has seen a tame Buffalo, and the wild one only differs from the tame species in his superior size, greater plumpness and roundness, and the thickness and length of his formidable horns.

Although immensely massive and powerful, the Buffalo stands on short legs, and does not measure so much in height as his vast bulk would lead one to suppose. An ordinary full-grown bull measures fifteen hands at the shoulder, and I doubt if any measure over sixteen hands at the outside.

The color is a dark bluish grey, deepening to nearly jet black in old bulls, whose shiny hides are frequently nearly devoid of hair. The legs, below the knees and hocks, are of a dirty greyish white.

The horns of the bull are usually about eight feet in length, measured from tip to tip across the forehead and round the outside of the curve, and about sixteen inches in circumference at the base. Many horns far exceed these measurements, and I have heard, on the best authority,

BUFFALO BULL
BUBALUS ARNI

THE BUFFALO; Cow, 6th *April*, 1878

DEALER ARKI

Published by Thacker, Spink & Co., Calcutta.

of a pair of bull's horns measuring twelve feet seven inches from tip to tip, and thick in proportion.

Cows' horns, though much slenderer, are, as a rule, longer than those of the bull. I have heard of a pair measuring over thirteen feet.

Buffaloes usually frequent the densest covers, where shooting them on foot is utterly impracticable; and in such situations the only way of obtaining sport is with a line of Elephants, the guns being either distributed along the line, or sent on ahead, according to the extent and nature of the covert to be beaten. Not only would it be impossible to shoot on foot in many of these heavy grass jungles, but it is hardly possible to *move*. I know jungles not above a mile square, where I doubt if a man left alone without compass or food, would *ever* get out! It would be only by a lucky chance if he did, for no Fair Rosamond's bower was ever the centre of such labyrinths as are formed by the paths of the Rhinoceros and Buffalo, and to which no one holds the clue; and except along these paths, or rather tunnels, progression is impossible.

Occasionally, however, especially in the mornings and evenings, Buffaloes will venture out of their fastnesses to feed on the short grass on the open plains, or to drink in a river; and even during the heat of the day, they may sometimes be found wallowing in muddy pools at a considerable distance from cover. Under such circumstances they may be stalked and shot on foot, but as they are dangerous brutes, the sportsman must be well armed, and have all his wits about him. Their visits to cultivation are, as a rule, nocturnal, and the damage that they then do is frequently very great.

Although I infinitely prefer shooting on foot to any shooting off Elephants, there is still something very exciting in beating with a line of Elephants for Buffaloes. It is the chase on the very largest scale; and the necessity for being always on the alert, and ready for the momentary chance that may be offered, at the very time when least expected, keeps one's nerves strung to the highest pitch of tension. Frequently, although a herd of Buffaloes may be roused within a score of yards, the waving of the grass, and perhaps the glint of a polished horn tip, is the only ocular evidence of the presence of the animals; the probably nearly noiseless rush might be caused by other animals; and where the horns have not been seen, it is only by the strong sweet bovine scent—similar to, but much more powerful than, that of cows—that one can be absolutely certain as to what is in front of one.

At other times matters are reversed, and instead of a retreating herd, the first intimation one receives of their presence is a vicious charge, completely upsetting the equanimity of even steady Elephants, and creating general confusion along the line.

A Buffalo is not an easy animal to stop when he has made up his mind for mischief, a front shot especially requiring very powerful rifles. A Buffalo facing one is extremely difficult to kill on foot, as the head is usually carried with the nose level with the back of the head, rendering it almost impossible to lodge a bullet in the brain, while the other vital organs are so well protected by the muscles and bones of the brawny chest, that even with the heaviest rifles a shot must be very well directed to ensure penetration to the lungs or heart. As with all other animals, a shot behind the shoulder is the most likely to drop the beast on the spot, unless indeed one is near enough to shoot for the centre of the neck—a small mark, but the most deadly place in which any animal can be struck.

If only picked shots are taken, Buffaloes may be killed with a small-bore express, a solid bullet being substituted, if possible, for the hollow one; but it is cruelty to animals to fire small bullets in thick cover, where it is impossible to take an accurate aim. Under such circumstances, I agree with Mr. Sanderson and all experienced hunters of Large Game, that the heaviest weapons, which the sportsman can manage, should be used. Large rifles, however, require large charges, and nothing is gained by increasing the calibre of the rifle unless the charge of powder is in proportion to it. With properly constructed rifles, very heavy charges may be used without inconvenience, and I have habitually fired seven drams from a 12-bore, and nine drams from a 10-bore, without feeling the recoil in the least. A spherical bullet, hardened with mercury, driven by such charges, will frequently go clean through the largest animal.

I have heard of Buffaloes being shot from horseback in open country, and the sport has been described to me as most exciting: I have never had an opportunity of trying it. There is, of course, a certain amount of risk, and the hunter should be well mounted.

A friend of mine has also shot Buffaloes from small native 'dug out' boats in which he followed the animals in shallow water and among high reeds where he could have done nothing on foot. In this way he bagged some fine bulls and met with some stirring adventures; a large herd having on one occasion charged savagely to within fifteen yards of the boat, which they were only prevented from upsetting by heavy rifles and steady shooting.

In April 1878 I was shooting with two friends in the Bhûtán Dooárs, Rhinoceros and Buffaloes being what we were principally in quest of.

The second morning we were out, we obtained '*khubr*' of two 'Rhinos' from some woodcutters, and were endeavouring to track them through a belt of thick reeds, which, as it turned out, they had passed quickly through. I had gone on to the end of the covert, and as the line of Elephants approached within about a hundred yards, had just given up all hope of seeing anything, when suddenly a bull Buffalo, who had been hitherto lying perfectly quiet, rushed out within seventy yards of me. I got a good shot at his broad back, and believe that I hit with my second barrel also, but the bull blundered off, and a shot from one of the other guns also failed to stop him. Hurrying in pursuit along the well marked track, I soon heard him in the thick reeds, and forcing my Elephant along at his best pace, I fired shot after shot into the bull as he crashed through the heavy jungle, eventually compelling him to leave its shelter and take to the open plain. Here the old bull, finding flight useless, turned to bay, and shook his massive head, as he stood awaiting our approach, on three legs. One foreleg was broken, so he was unable to charge with any effect; another shot or two brought him to his knees; and several more, fired from a distance of a few yards, finally rolled him over.

It is a curious fact, which all experienced sportsmen have noticed, that wounded animals are the hardest to kill: shots that would have at once stopped a beast had they struck him at first, seem to have no immediate effect on him when he has been already severely hit.

Probably the shock to the nervous system caused by the first wounds prevents the subsequent injuries from being so keenly felt.

I measured the bull carefully, and found that the dimensions were as follows :—

Height	... 5 feet, or 15 hands.
Length from nose to root of tail ...	... 9 „ 7 inches.
Length of tail	... 3 „ 11 „
Girth	... 8 „ 3 „
Girth of forearm	... 1 foot 8 „
Length of horns from tip to tip along curve	... 8 feet 3 „

The following day we had only proceeded about a couple of miles from camp, when, on commencing to beat a grass jungle, I knocked over a Hog Deer. As we were padding it there was a great commotion among the Elephants at some little distance from us, and we were at first unable to discover the cause of the evident consternation, both among Elephants and Mahouts. On hurrying to the spot, however, with more expectation of finding a Tiger than anything else, we came upon a bull Buffalo, which had charged one of the Elephants without any provocation. Seeing us coming he made off, and I only got three long shots, two of which hit him, drawing blood pretty freely. Following him up we came to one of the thickest reed jungles I ever saw, in which tracking was quite out of the question, so we ordered the line of Elephants to beat through it, while we went to the far end. I will not now describe the beat, which led to the death of one Rhinoceros, and to at least one other being wounded, but will only narrate our experiences with the Buffaloes.

I was following up a wounded Rhinoceros through a tangled thicket of the highest reeds, where the grass was far above my head as I stood in the howdah, and I had frequently to cross my arms in front of my face as we forced our way through the thickest part. Suddenly there was a savage grunt just in front of me ; the Mahout in his terror shouted to me to look out ; and a huge bull Buffalo, carrying half a cartload of reeds on his horns, sprang at my Elephant with the agility of a goat. I could not see to shoot for a second or two, and my Elephant, although usually staunch, swung half round, and in another moment the bull was alongside, endeavouring to gore him. Holding on to the rail of the howdah with one hand, I fired my heavy 12-bore rifle, pistol fashion, into the Buffalo's back, the muzzle not being a foot from him. This somewhat astonished him, and caused him to turn tail and retreat into the reeds.

We had by this time approached the confines of the covert, which here ran out into a narrow tongue ; so getting the Elephants near me into compact formation, I proceeded to beat steadily onwards.

We were not above eighty yards from the end of the belt of reeds, when I heard the bull close in front of me, so, in order to obtain a clear shot, I went outside the covert. In another moment, however, there was a rush, and the bull, instead of facing the open, dashed back through the line of beaters, severely injuring one of the Elephants in his charge. On the opposite side of the tongue of jungle he encountered S. (one of my companions) and at once went straight at him. S. however was equal to the occasion, and having a clear shot, dropped the bull in mid career with a well directed bullet : he was a fine beast, with horns an inch or two longer than those of my bull of the previous day.

A few days afterwards we were breakfasting under the shade of some trees on a river bank, and were just about to remount our Elephants, when a large cow Buffalo came to drink on the opposite bank of the river about eight hundred yards off. After slaking her thirst, she walked into the river, and quietly lay down, apparently quite regardless of a number of natives who were resting on the sandy shore opposite her, and not more than three hundred yards distant.

Taking my double '450 Henry Express, I lost no time in crossing the river on a pad Elephant, and then dismounting, made the best of my way towards where the cow was lying. The walking was very rough, and the only way I could make much progress was by going along the water's edge at the foot of the steep bank of the river. At length I reached a place where the bank dropped perpendicularly to deep water, and here I had to ascend, and with great difficulty force my way through the reeds, which cracked loudly at every movement. A little farther on I was able to descend again, and advance under cover of the bank to within a hundred and twenty yards of where the cow was still enjoying her bath, in fancied security.

Beyond this point the river took a bend, so it was impossible to advance any nearer without again passing through reeds. This I accordingly did, and had gained about twenty yards, when, fearing that the unavoidable noise which I made would alarm the Buffalo, I resolved to fire. She was lying facing me with only her head above water, but seeing no chance of a better shot, I fired at her throat ; I believe that my bullet merely grazed her, and she stood up, but did not stir from the spot. My second barrel was quickly fired at her chest, and on receiving the shot she walked slowly out of the water, giving me a chance of a broadside shot, which had the effect of disabling her shoulder.

She was on the edge of a heavy jungle, so I lost no time in pouring bullets into her shoulder as quickly as I could load and fire, and after receiving seven or eight in all, she rolled over dead. She proved to be a very old cow, thin and covered with scars, but with a remarkably fine pair of horns, measuring ten feet two inches from tip to tip. Most of my bullets were grouped in a very small space behind the shoulder, and it was only by the rapidity with which I was able to load and fire, that I prevented her from gaining the shelter where she might perhaps have escaped, in spite of being crippled by my first shots.

NILGAO OR BLUE BULL

PORTAX PICTUS

Published by Thacker, Spink & Co., Calcutta.

CHAPTER XVII.

THE NILGAO.

PORTAX PICTUS.

Generally throughout India.—*Nil Gáo.*   In the Punjab.—*Roz.*

THE Nilgao does not hold a very high place among the Game animals of India, and is seldom shot by any but young sportsmen, unless meat is required for camp-followers. It is, however, one of the largest and most conspicuous of the ruminants to be found in the plains, and no records of Indian sport would be complete without some notice of it. In general appearance, the Nilgao more nearly resembles the *bovine* Antelopes of Africa than any of the Asiatic species, and the resemblance is heightened by the peculiar markings to which it owes its specific name. The Nilgao or Blue Bull (a literal translation of the vernacular name for the male) is widely distributed, being found in suitable localities in nearly every province of the Indian Peninsula. As far as I know, it is most common in parts of the Punjab and North-West Provinces, and in the Central Provinces.

The bull is a large and powerful beast, attaining a height of at least fourteen hands at the withers, which are high and narrow like those of a horse. The neck is long and compressed, and the head slender and deer-like ; the eyes being remarkably full and lustrous. The hind quarters fall away considerably, giving the animal rather an awkward appearance. The legs are slender and wiry, and the hoofs rather upright. The tail is tufted, something like that of the domestic cow, but it is not so long in proportion, reaching only to the hocks.

The color is a dark bluish grey, deepening to nearly black in very old individuals, while the legs are jet black, curiously marked with white patches about the fetlocks. The throat is white, and from the lower part of it depends a long tuft of blackish hair, while the hair on the withers is developed into a thin upright mane.

A friend of mine told me that the first Blue Bull he ever saw was standing facing him on a road in an out-of-the-way part of the country, and fairly puzzled him. He thought the apparition was more like the devil than anything else ! and it was not till the beast turned away that he saw that it was a four-footed animal, and not something less ' canny.' The short black horns which the bull possesses added much to the likeness to the conventional description of His Satanic Majesty !

The horns grow from the forehead, and incline slightly forwards ; they seldom exceed nine inches in length, so a Blue Bull's head is not much of a trophy.

The cow is of a light browh color, and is destitute of horns. The young males are like the females, but become gradually darker with age.

Nilgai inhabit extensive grass and tree jungles, but appear to prefer those that are not very thick, and interspersed with occasional bare open spaces. Their favorite cover seems to be that composed of the ' *dhák* ' or ' *palás* ' tree (*Butea frondosa*). They are also fond of resorting to sugar-cane fields, and they frequently commit considerable damage among cultivation.

They are generally to be found in herds, varying in number from four or five to twenty, and composed of both sexes ; but occasionally small parties of old Blue Bulls, and even solitary bulls, are to be met with. In places where they are not disturbed, especially in some of the Native States, Nilgai are absurdly tame, but in districts where they are much molested they become extremely shy and wary. It must not therefore be supposed that they can always be easily shot, but they afford such a poor trophy that, as already mentioned, they are not much sought after. When they can be found sufficiently far from thick cover, they may be speared, and they then show capital sport ; as they will probably lead a well-mounted horseman a chase of several miles. On hard ground, I doubt if a *cow* Nilgai could be speared by a solitary hunter : the bull, being much heavier, is more easily ridden down.

I have never succeeded in accomplishing this feat, never having had the good luck to find a Blue Bull sufficiently far from cover. A friend of mine, however, on one occasion speared an old bull single-handed off a little Arab horse. The bull gave a run of about five miles, and took nine spears before he died : he did not attempt to charge.

The Nilgao is occasionally domesticated, but like all pets of the deer and antelope tribe, becomes very dangerous. I have heard of their being broken to harness, but have never seen it. I once tried to tame a young bull by Mr. Rarey's plan, but after many long struggles, and getting the animal quiet for the time, I found that he became just as wild as soon as he recovered from his exhaustion.

The flesh of a cow Nilgai is occasionally excellent, and the tongue and marrow bones are supposed to be delicacies. They are, however, hardly worth shooting, except when one is in want of meat for Mahomedan servants : Hindoos, of course, will not touch the flesh.

In my early hunting days, I was, like most youngsters, extremely anxious to bag a Nilgai, and spent many days in some jungles where only a few existed, in unsuccessful attempts to secure a Blue Bull. Although traces of the animals were constantly met with, the Nilgai remained invisible, until at last one day, just as I had shot a Black Buck, I saw two Blue Bulls quietly feeding among some cattle in thin ' *bábúl* ' jungle. Under cover of the cattle, I found no difficulty in approaching within fair range ; but over-anxiety caused me to make a bad shot, and my bullet, instead of striking behind the shoulder, caught the poor bull somewhere about the centre of the body, and with a tremendous plunge and a kick he disappeared in the bushes, and I saw him no more.

There were a few in the ' Khádir ' near Meerut, and on one occasion, when out pig-sticking, three of us attempted to ride down a cow. This I believe to be nearly impossible as a general rule, the only chance being with a heavy old bull. On the 15th of April, 1866, D., N. and I had a good morning's pig-sticking near Jalálpúr, but had a stop put to our sport by N.'s horse falling (just as we were starting after an enormous boar), and stunning his rider. As he did not move, D. and I feared that he was seriously hurt, and pulled up to look after him, but luckily he recovered his senses in two or three hours, and in the afternoon was able to accompany us in search of the monster who had so unfortunately escaped from us. We beat for some time, but failed to find him. Having given up all hopes of him, we suddenly saw a cow Nilgai coming towards us, and as we had miles of open country before us, we resolved to attempt to spear her. I was mounted on a large '*waler*,' a fast horse, but cursed with a very bad temper, and too impetuous to be a good pig-sticker (he had jumped into a nullah sixteen feet deep with me that morning! but the bottom being soft and muddy he did not fall); he was now, however, in good humour, and went well. D. was on a nice little Arab, and N. on a slow but staying country-bred. As the cow passed within thirty yards, we at once gave chase. The stride of my horse told at first, and I led for more than a mile at best pace, keeping about the same distance behind the cow. I then began to feel that my horse was beginning to 'shut up,' and hallooed to D. to go faster (as if he was not already doing his best)! He could go no faster, but my horse went slower, and D. and at last N. succeeded in passing me, but without being able to gain an inch on the cow, who gradually increased her lead, and at last fairly ran us all to a standstill, after a run of at least six miles. D.'s horse fell heavily towards the end of the run, and lamed himself so badly, that we could with difficulty get him back to the tents. It was by far the fastest and most severe run I have ever seen. The tactics we pursued, of trying to burst the Nilgai by pressing her at first, were the only ones at all likely to be successful. Had we attempted to make a waiting race of it, we should have been left still farther behind. As it was, she had not the slightest difficulty in beating us on the hard ground.

In March, 1868, as we were marching down country, I hunted for Nilgao near Bárá, about halfway between Loodiáná and Umballa. I found a herd of cows, wounded one severely, and rode her down. I next saw twelve Blue Bulls on an open plain, and walked up to within shot of them. There was one immense bull, but when I wanted to fire, my horse would not let me, and the herd trotted off. Following them up, I got a long shot with an Enfield rifle, and hit the big bull. I then jumped on my horse with a spear, and gave chase. I was soon riding at their tails, and singled out the big fellow, who did not seem to be much the worse for his wound, and went away at a tremendous pace. I kept close behind him, and we soon came to cultivated fields enclosed by thorn hedges; after jumping three or four of these, the bull suddenly swerved to the right, and charged a high hedge with a rope in it. This brought him on his knees; and as he immediately turned to the left again, I went at a place between two trees, where the thorns were piled up very high, but there was no rope. My horse rose at it well, and I got through with the loss of my '*pugree*,' which remained hanging on the tree. The bull now gained on me a little, and on his jumping another impracticable place I was thrown out, and lost him among some high sugar-cane.

C. of my regiment was riding after a wounded bull on the same day, when he also got among hedges with ropes in them ; but fancying that they would break, he charged one, and of course came to grief, and lost his bull.

A few days afterwards I again went out in the Pitásí '*bhir*,' or grass preserve near Ungáná, and on this occasion I was well mounted on a powerful Arab, which I hoped would take me up to a bull should I chance to wound one. I had not been out very long when I discovered two old bulls and two small ones which I endeavoured to get near ; but they were shy and would not allow me to approach within a reasonable distance. At last they fairly took alarm and moved off at a fast pace, so I mounted my horse and followed them. The country was open, but just where we were, the ground was so full of holes and so dangerous, that, after being nearly down about twenty times in the space of about half a mile, I pulled up and contented myself with keeping the Nilgai in sight. After a time they came to a thick but narrow belt of jungle, and I took advantage of their passing through it to gain considerably upon them. Jumping off my horse, I saw them standing within a hundred and fifty yards, and at once brought my rifle to bear upon the largest bull. Unfortunately, just as I pressed the trigger, one of the small bulls moved into the way, and received the bullet intended for the large one. He at once dropped and lay struggling on the ground, apparently nearly paralysed ; but gradually recovering, he first dragged his hind quarters along the ground, and eventually regained the use of his legs and overtook his companions. I quickly remounted, and as a level open plain now lay before us, I urged my horse to his utmost speed. I had a fair start, and after going about a mile and a half, my horse was still fresh, while the big bulls began to show symptoms of distress. I had long ago passed the wounded one, being intent on securing a really good specimen ; and as the two old bulls now labored along, with tongues hanging out and foam dropping from their open mouths, I made sure that the victory was mine. I nursed my horse for a final effort, and again urging him on, had nearly reached the flanks of the bulls, when they gained the shelter of a thick '*dhák*' jungle, and farther pursuit was impossible.

In the autumn of the same year I was shooting in the neighbourhood of Cawnpore, and commenced operations by hunting for Nilgao in the grass jungles on the banks and islands of the Ganges, near Najafghar.

Here they were plentiful, but the grass was so high that little could be seen except from the back of an Elephant. I had one with me, and the first morning I went out I soon found a herd of Nilgao. My rifle missed fire at the first bull I fired at, but on my second attempt I dropped one apparently dead. Before we reached it, however, it had made off, and it was not until I had hunted for some time that we again found it, and a lucky shot finally rolled it over. A friend having joined me, we went out together the following day, when I mortally wounded another bull, and rode it down and speared it after a short chase. My friend also wounded one, but was unable to spear it without greatly distressing his horse, so he gave it up. On our last day, we were unsuccessful in finding any large bulls, but three small ones galloped into a muddy watercourse, where one of them stuck fast, and we caught him. As we had no object in keeping him, we extricated him from the mud and restored him to liberty.

From Najafghar I marched to a place called Dérápúr, where there were a number of ravines with scattered thorny jungle. Among these there was capital shooting ; Nilgao, Black Buck, and Chikara, all being plentiful.

One day, when returning homewards, I observed the head and white throat of an old bull peeping out of some bushes in a shady ravine where he had lain up for the day, and where he doubtless thought that he was perfectly concealed. He was only about a hundred yards off, and I hit him in the throat; but after struggling for some time, he contrived to scramble up the steep bank, and it took two or three shots to finish him. He proved to be a very old bull—a first rate specimen.

CHAPTER XVIII.

THE INDIAN GAZELLE.

GAZELLA BENNETTII.

Generally throughout India.—*Chikárá.*

In the Punjab.—*Herní.*

THE Indian Gazelle or Chikara is better known to sportsmen by its misnomer of
' Ravine Deer.'

In former days naturalists were few, and hunters in foreign lands had loose ideas of
nomenclature; for instance, the American Bison was called a Buffalo, a name which it has
retained to the present day; while no distinction was made between the hollow horned and
antlered ruminants, any horned animal of slender build being classed as a deer.

The prefix, in the present instance, is not inapplicable; for although frequently found on
open plains, the Indian Gazelle is undoubtedly partial to broken and slightly hilly ground,
much intersected by ravines.

The Gazelle is widely distributed throughout the drier parts of India, but is not, so far
as I am aware, to be met with in the moister regions, such as Lower Bengal. It is common
in the rocky and sandy districts of the North-West Provinces, and abounds in the Punjab,
particularly along the skirts of the Bikanír desert. It is found all along the north-west
frontier and in Sindh, and extends into Afghánistán at least as far as the Jalálábád valley.

Farther west its place is probably taken by *Gazella sub-gutturosa*, a very nearly allied
species, but I do not know the exact limits which separate the two.

The grace and elegance of the Gazelle, and the beauty of its soft dark eye, are proverbial; and the animal is almost too well known to require description. The color is a reddish
fawn on the upper parts, and white beneath, with lines of a darker hue on the face and legs.
The tail is about five inches long, it is jet black, and constantly in motion. The legs are
very slender.

The horns of the buck vary from ten to fourteen inches in length: they are ringed to
within three inches of the points, and are slightly curved: they are of close grain, black,
and sharp pointed.

The female is a little smaller than the male; her horns are thin, nearly straight and very
slightly ringed: they rarely exceed six inches in length.

XI

INDIAN GAZELLE

GAZELLA BENNETTII

Published by Thacker, Spink & Co., Calcutta.

The favorite haunts of the Gazelle are extensive wastes of sandy or rocky ground, sprinkled with low bushes, and interspersed here and there with patches of cultivation. Thick jungles they avoid ; and they are seldom to be met with in districts which are entirely under crop. During the day time, they resort to secluded spots where they are not subject to annoyance, and in the mornings and evenings they frequently repair to fields of young grain, sometimes in close proximity to villages.

In some places they are extremely wild, and can only be approached by the most careful stalking ; in other localities they are comparatively tame, and will allow the sportsman to walk openly to within easy range. At most times, however, they are restless little animals, continually on the move ; and they have a provoking way of trotting off with a switch of their black tails, the moment that they suspect danger.

On open plains, the best way of getting within shot of them is under cover of a steady shooting horse. As they afford but a small mark, and seldom remain still very long, quick as well as accurate shooting is required, and beginners in the art of rifle shooting will find them excellent practice.

The Officers of the Guides used to hawk the Gazelle in the neighbourhood of Hotí Mardán, the Falcons used for the purpose being nestling '*charghs*' (*Falco Sacer*). Adult caught birds cannot be trained for this sport, and the nestlings had to be obtained from the distant province of Balkh by the assistance of some of the Kabul Sirdars. In the present state of our relations with Afghánistán, the Falcons cannot be procured, and the sport has, for the present at any rate, died out. The hawks alone could not kill a Gazelle, but were assisted by greyhounds, which used to pull it down after the hawks had confused and stunned it by repeated blows. I regret that I never had an opportunity of witnessing the flight, which has been described to me as very interesting and exciting.

The flesh of the Gazelle, though rather dry, is by no means to be despised ; and a whole one, boiled down to jelly, forms splendid 'stock' for the foundation of a large 'all blaze' stew. I have pleasant recollections of such stews, of which hare, sandgrouse, chukor, quail, pigeon, wild duck and koolun, were among the ingredients !

Among the many days' sport which I have enjoyed at various times on the plains of the North-West Provinces, or amidst the low hills and intricate ravines of the Upper Punjab, not a few have been spent in the chase of the Antelope and Gazelle ; but I cannot recall to memory many incidents worth recording. Though pleasant enough at the time, the sport is not sufficiently varied to be interesting in narration.

I had a favorite 'Cape' shooting horse who was so steady that when leading him I could let him walk on while I prepared to shoot, and as he cleared me I could fire right under his tail without alarming him ; while on several occasions I killed from off his back.

I first met with Chikara when quartered at Delhi in 1863, and the two which first fell to my rifle were shot in a rather curious way.

On the 20th of June, when, as may be imagined, it was blazing hot, I rode out to Nangloí, a small village about seven miles from Delhi on the Rohtak road. Some low sandhills in the neighbourhood were said to be a favorite resort of Chikara, and it was not long before I discovered some. They were, indeed, tolerably plentiful, but so wild that for a long time I was unable to approach within shot. At last four does galloped past within about eighty yards, and I bowled one of them over: on going up to her I found that the bullet had merely severed the windpipe, cutting the throat as cleanly as if it had been done with a knife.

Shortly afterwards, as I was proceeding homewards, I saw a buck looking at me, and he remained motionless while I fired a steady shot at him at a hundred and fifty yards: he fell dead, and I found, to my surprise, that the bullet had cut his throat in exactly the same manner as the doe's.

The next time I went to Nanglo I was more successful, bagging four Chikara in the course of a day; and I never subsequently visited the place without killing at least one or two buck.

The best pair of horns that I secured fell to a neat but rather lucky shot. I had been hunting in vain for Chikara, which were, at the season, nearly all concealed in the standing crops. At length, as I was walking across a field where, owing to the sandiness of the soil, the crop was stunted and scanty, I observed a pair of horns showing just above the corn. The range was rather a long one, being upwards of a hundred and fifty yards, but as my only chance I aimed just below the horns and fired. On walking up to the spot I found a fine buck lying dead. His horns measured thirteen and a quarter inches.

There is not much variety in Gazelle shooting, and after shooting a few, a keen sportsman will tire of killing such beautiful little creatures, which neither afford valuable trophies nor greatly exercise the stalker's skill; but when there is no better game to be found, an occasional day after them will at least serve to keep the hunter from becoming rusty in the use of his rifle.

THIBETAN GAZELLE
GAZELLA PICTICAUDATA

Published by Thacker, Spink & Co., Calcutta.

CHAPTER XIX

THE THIBETAN GAZELLE.

GAZELLA PICTICAUDATA.

In Thibet.—*Goá.*

To the east of Ládák, along the frontiers of Chinese Thibet, and in the long tongue-shaped district of that country which lies between the upper waters of the Indus and the Sutlej, are vast expanses of undulating hills and valleys of great elevation, utterly destitute of forest, and with but scanty indications of vegetation of any sort. To the unaccustomed eye, indeed, the greater part of these wild uplands would appear to be a perfect desert, incapable of affording sustenance to the smallest animal ; but as a matter of fact there is hardly a slope however rocky, hardly an expanse of sand however thirsty-looking, on which an occasional tuft of coarse grass or bunch of some sweet-scented herb may not be found.

Where streams of water exist, either fed by perennial springs, or owing their transitory existence to the fast melting beds of the winter's snow which have accumulated in the more sheltered hollows on the higher ridges, their banks will be enamelled with the greenest of turf, studded with flowers of the most brilliant hues.

Where these streams are of considerable size, the grassy banks spread out until they almost attain the dignity of meadows ; and here may the famous black tents of the pastoral tribes be found pitched, while herds of yâk, sheep and goats graze peacefully around.

Even in the close vicinity of the domestic flocks the subjects of the present notice may be met with, but as a rule they avoid the neighbourhood of man, and must be looked for in more lonely places, where, if they find less food, they are at least more secure from molestation.

The Thibetan Gazelle or Goa (as I shall in future call it for the sake of brevity) is perhaps the loveliest and most graceful of a family proverbial for beauty and elegance.

It is about twenty-four inches high at the shoulder, and the color of the winter coat is a light creamy fawn, the hair being soft and of considerable length. On the rump is a snow-white patch or disc, the hair of which is longer than that on the rest of the body, and is partially erectile. The tail is about four inches long, jet black, and tufted at the end. In summer the Goa, like most other animals, becomes much darker upon shedding its coat.

The horns of the buck are somewhat similar to those of the common Indian Gazelle, but instead of being nearly straight, they are considerably curved backwards, with a tendency to again grow forwards at the tips. They are closely ringed, of very fine grain, and sharp pointed. The usual length is from twelve to thirteen inches, but I have shot them a little longer. The female has no horns.

The Goa inhabit the bleak country which I have already mentioned, the elevation of which varies from 13,000 to 18,000 feet; and are to be found scattered about here and there, in small parties, usually varying from two or three to about a dozen in number. In certain localities they are decidedly plentiful, while occasionally an isolated individual or a small herd may be met with, apparently many miles from any others. They are not generally very shy, though they will seldom allow the hunter to openly approach within shot. They seem to be very little frightened by noise, as I have known several instances of their going on grazing after being fired at: it is also said that, unlike most wild animals, they pay little or no attention to human beings passing to windward of them.

I first saw the Goa in 1861, on the plateau above the Tsomoriri Lake. I was following a Kyang which I had wounded, when, on coming to a ravine, I heard a sharp hiss, and saw two small antelope looking at me. I missed a longish shot at one and they went off, much to my annoyance, as I did not even know what they were, never having heard of the existence of such an animal.

In 1864, I saw a herd of seven on the top of the Nagpogoding Pass, but they were dreadfully wild, and I never could get within a quarter of a mile of them.

In 1866, I went to the Tsomoriri Lake and Hanlé, the Goa being one of my principal inducements to go there. I was accompanied by my friend B., and on the 2nd of June we pitched our camp at the corner of the lake and ascended the plateau above. We had not gone far before we discovered some animals feeding at a distance, and the telescope showed them to be Goa. We made a most careful stalk, and got within easy shot, but the small size of the animals deceived us in our estimate of distance, and we both missed. Soon afterwards we saw some more Goa, but I again missed a fair chance. We then separated, but I could see nothing for a long time ; at length I caught a glimpse of the heads of two or three Goa just as they were disappearing over a ridge ; I followed them, and shot a doe through the body as it was galloping away. A greyhound which I had with me gave chase, and ran into it after a long course.

The next day I determined to kill a buck, so I ascended the plateau very early in the morning : I soon discovered some Goa at a great distance, but after stalking to within seventy yards, I found that they were all does and young ones. I therefore would not fire at them, but lay watching the graceful little animals with much interest. Before long they caught sight of me, but being unable to make me out distinctly, they advanced towards me, occasionally rising on their hind legs to obtain a better view. I at length rose and showed myself, upon which they made off.

Farther on, I found some more does, and shortly afterwards three buck, but in a place where they could not be stalked, so I sent a man round to drive them. The drive failed, the Goa going off in the wrong direction, but the man who went after them informed me that he had seen five others, and pointed out the direction in which they had gone.

I crossed the plain, and saw them on the slopes at the other side, and after a détour found myself on the hill-side straight above them. I watched them for some time as they fed along the foot of the hill : at last they approached a deep but narrow ravine, which ran down the hill ; I entered this, which afforded me capital cover, and on reaching the plain and looking over the bank, I saw the Goa quietly feeding within about a hundred yards. Resting my rifle on the bank, I fired very steadily at the best buck, but to my surprise missed with both barrels, owing to over-estimating the distance. Dropping behind the bank, I reloaded, and on again looking over was astonished to see the Goa still feeding in the same place. I was more successful this time, wounding one with the first barrel and killing another with the second. Even now the Goa did not move far, and I had time to fire two more bullets, which, however, missed. Meanwhile I had sent a man to bring my dog, and on his arrival I slipped him at the Goa, but the wounded one seemed to recover completely, and it soon distanced the greyhound. The one I had killed had a very beautiful pair of horns.

The next Goa I shot were on the hills to the south of Hanlé, towards Chúmúrtí : here they were very plentiful, but the ground was not particularly well adapted for stalking. On one occasion after in vain trying to stalk some, three of them allowed me to walk up to within one hundred and fifty yards of them in the open. I dropped the first buck stone dead, and on the others standing to gaze about eighty yards farther on, I killed another.

I found that Goa generally stopped to look after a fallen companion; and on the 10th of July, I again bagged two buck, right and left, at two hundred and thirty yards.

In 1869, after a long tedious march from the Sutlej valley through Spiti, across the Párung-lá and Lának-lá, I, at last, reached the Gonpá, or Monastery, of Hanlé on the 1st of July, and pitched camp on the beautiful expanse of turf through which the Hanlé stream meanders.

The grassy plain is a mere oasis, and from its margin rise gently sloping barren hills, whose undulations stretch to the far distant horizon.

My previous visit had shown me that these hills were the resort of Nyan and Goa, and although I heard that they had already been shot over about a fortnight previously, I looked forward to good sport.

The day after my arrival I did not go very far from camp, and only saw a few female Nyan and Burrell, at which I would not fire. The following morning I determined to do a long day's work, so starting early, I crossed the wide grassy plain, and struck into the low hills in an easterly direction ; my object being to reach a well-remembered spot about nine miles off, where, on the occasion of my last visit, I had found a rill of water issuing from a steep hill-side. This spring was the only water to be found within a radius of three or four miles, and accordingly many Goa, Kyang, and other animals came here to drink.

I had walked about three miles, and was following one of the slightly worn tracks which traverse these barren hills in every direction, and whose existence may be accounted for by the fact that there is no traffic, no heavy rain, no falling leaf to obliterate a footmark ; nothing indeed except the slow action of time ; and where consequently the passing of two or three animals in the course of a week will, in a few months, wear a clearly defined path ; when the fresh impression of a tiny hoof caught my eye. There was no doubt as to what animal it was made by : it could only be a Goa, which probably used this path when going to drink at the river by which I was encamped. A short distance farther on I caught sight of the head of a buck Goa just showing over a rounded swell. He was evidently suspicious, and gazing in our direction. Signalling to my attendants to lie down and keep still, I crept carefully towards the Goa, and presently saw him facing me and still steadfastly gazing, at a distance of about a hundred and twenty yards.

I had a military short Snider rifle, the coarse sights of which were not well adapted for such a small mark as is afforded by the chest and neck of a Gazelle ; however I fired steadily. The bullet struck low, but the buck remained motionless. I slipped in a fresh cartridge and tried again : this time my shot went an inch or two to the left, but still the Goa never moved.

A third cartridge missed fire, but on trying once more I was at length successful, the bullet striking fair in the centre of the buck's breast, and dropping it dead on the spot.

All this, though it takes time to narrate, was the work of a few seconds, and the Goa had not time to recover from the surprise of the first shot, which it probably mistook for a clap of thunder.

After 'gralloching' the Goa we covered it up with stones, to preserve it from eagles, ravens, &c., until our return, and proceeded in the direction of the drinking place before referred to. On arriving there, however, I was disgusted at finding the spring dried up : there had been but little snow the previous winter, and so the fountain had been deprived of its usual source of supply. I saw one Goa, but he was very wild, and I could not get within a fair range. Going a little farther, I crossed a valley and ascended the opposite side to a wide level plateau strewn with huge blocks of stone, which lay about in all directions. Sitting down among a group of these stones, I proceeded to discuss my luncheon, but had not sat very long before I observed four buck Goa which came up from the valley on the opposite side of the plateau. After looking about them for a short time, two of them began to feed towards me, while the other two moved off in another direction. Placing two or three cartridges on the ground by my side, I remained perfectly motionless, while the Goa came nearer and nearer. At last they passed within about a hundred yards, when I fired at the second one, which had the finer horns of the two. I heard the bullet strike, and though the Goa did not actually fall, he staggered, and stood still in that peculiar helpless posture which the experienced eye at once recognizes as indicative of a mortal wound. Seeing that he was as good as bagged, I fired at the other buck, broke his leg, and again reloading finished him with my third shot. The first one had in the meantime fallen, and I was walking up to the slain when my attention was directed to another Goa which had come up to see what was going on, and was standing within shot. I fired at it but missed it, and it did not give me a second chance. I ought certainly to have made up the bag to four, however I was very well satisfied with having shot three buck, all with good horns.

After finishing our luncheon and enjoying a rest of an hour or two, we set off in the direction of camp, which had fortunately been ordered to be moved to our side of the grassy plain, thus shortening our return journey about a couple of miles.

My Tartars found a Goa each a sufficiently heavy load, and when we reached the one first killed, and one man had to carry two, I had to shoulder both my rifles. The extra weight did not, however, prevent me from going along at a good swinging pace; the sight of the white tent, which was visible from a great distance, suggesting visions of hot tea and a comfortable dinner, for which I was all the more inclined as I felt that I had earned them by a good hard day's work. The three Goa, as they lay where they had been thrown down by the door of the tent, formed a group that was very pleasing to a sportsman's eye; and I longed for the pencil of a Landseer to immortalize the event.

In 1870, I was again in Thibet, and towards the end of August I had once more to cross the plateau above the Tsomoriri lake on my return journey.

As it was probably the last day on which I was likely to see game, I sent my camp by the most direct route, while I made a long round over the hills. Towards the end of a shooting expedition one is in such splendid 'condition,' that the addition of six or eight miles to the day's work is thought nothing of, and as this was my last day I did not spare myself. I was in hopes of finding Nyan, which I had previously seen in the neighbourhood, but not a trace of them was met with.

Seeing a small herd of Gòa, I had to make a long détour to get above them, and on the way I saw a single buck. Proceeding to stalk him I found that he had been joined by another, and that both were very restless, and although I got a fair chance, I missed.

Three or four miles farther on I had to cross a lofty table-land, which was nearly level, but with a few slight hollows worn by the melting snows. Strolling along without much expectation of seeing anything, I suddenly discovered four Goa feeding on a grassy patch, and I at once saw that it would take all my generalship to get within shot.

There was nothing for it but to lie down and approach them by dragging my body along on my elbows, any attempt to creep up to them on hands and knees being out of the question on such open ground. Even by keeping myself as flat as possible there was not an inch to spare, for I could hardly keep my head low enough to avoid seeing them; and to see them was to *be seen*.

Those who have never tried the mode of progression which I mention, on stony ground, have little idea how delightful it is : crawling over wet moss or stumps of heather, is pleasant enough, but nothing to the sensation caused by the sharp edges and corners of the shingle of a Thibetan hill !

In the present instance I had to advance by inches for several hundred yards, remaining motionless whenever the Goa looked up, and gaining ground as they were feeding. At last, after the exercise of much patience, I found myself within a hundred and twenty yards, and obtained a fair broadside shot, which dropped the largest buck; and as the others looked round in astonishment for the cause of his fall, I had time to reload and bring down a second. The remainder of the herd did not again stop until they were at a respectful distance. These were the two last shots that I fired on a most successful trip.

o

CHAPTER XX

THE THIBETAN ANTELOPE.

PANTHOLOPS HODGSONII.

In Thibet.—*Tsoos—Choos.*

So far as we know, Thibetan Antelope are never found near the habitations of man, but frequent the plains and elevated valleys far above the limits of cultivation, where few human beings, save occasional wandering shepherds, ever disturb them.

The most accessible country to sportsmen where the Thibetan Antelope is to be found, is Chung Chenmo, a desolate valley to the north of the Pangong lakes. In this valley, and in those of the streams which flow down to it from the spurs of the Kárá Koram mountains, Antelope are usually plentiful; and they are also to be met with all over the lofty plateau which has to be crossed on the road to Yarkund. A few have been shot in the neighbourhood of the Mánsarovárá lake near the north-western frontier of Nipál, but there are great difficulties in the way of getting there, the Thibetans jealously excluding all foreigners.

The Thibetan Antelope is considerably larger than the Indian Antelope, and somewhat more heavily made; its remarkably thick coat of closely set brittle hairs also tending to increase its apparent bulk. The color is a light fawn, varying in shade on different parts of the body, and tending almost to white in old buck. The legs are dark colored, and the faces of very old males are nearly black.

The muzzle is very curious; instead of being fine and compressed, as is the case with most deer and antelope, it is considerably enlarged and puffy-looking; so much so, that properly stuffed heads are generally supposed by persons unacquainted with the animal, to be failures of the taxidermist.

The horns are perhaps the most graceful of those of any antelope: set close together at the base they diverge in an easy curve for about two-thirds of their length, and then converging more abruptly, approach each other, in some specimens, within three or four inches at the tips.

Out of twenty-five that I have shot, I have never seen a pair above twenty-four and a half inches, but considerably longer specimens are to be obtained, and I have recently heard of a pair twenty-eight and a half inches. The horns are jet black, of very fine grain, with a small central core, and being deeply notched on their anterior surface, they form perfect knife-handles and sword-hilts.

THIBETAN ANTELOPE
PANTHOLOPS HODGSONII

Published by Thacker, Spink & Co., Calcutta.

When seen in profile, the forward inclination of the horns has a curious effect, the two appearing like a single horn ; which has given rise to the belief that the Thibetan Antelope is the Tchirou or Unicorn Antelope mentioned by the Abbé Huc. Mr. Wilson, however, was inclined to believe in the existence of a real Unicorn, and when I have made enquiries from the Tartars in some of the more remote parts of Thibet which I have visited, I have almost always been informed that such an animal existed ; so I think it is still *possible* that the long supposed fabulous supporter of the Royal Arms may be discovered to be a reality.

The female of this Antelope has no horns.

The Thibetan Antelope has two greatly developed inguinal glands, the tubes of which run right up into the body. The Tartars say that the Antelope inflate these with air, and are thereby enabled to run with greater swiftness !

Although living in such remote and sequestered regions, the Thibetan Antelope is wary in its habits. In the mornings and evenings it frequents the grassy margins of glacial streams, which frequently flow between steep banks, which have been gradually scarped by the floods of centuries, and which are now remote from the ordinary water's edge.

These ravines have for the most part been cut through gently sloping valleys ; and on ascending their steep sides, slightly undulating plains will be found to stretch away, until they merge in the easy slopes of the rounded hills which bound the valley.

To these plains the Antelope betake themselves during the day, and there they excavate hollows deep enough to conceal their bodies, from which, themselves unperceived, they can detect any threatening danger at a great distance.

In addition to the concealment afforded by their 'shelter pits,' they have an additional safeguard against surprise in the constant *mirage* which prevails on these stony wastes during the bright hours of the day. This *mirage* not only distorts all visible objects in an extra-ordinary manner, but, like rippling water, refracts the rays of light to such a degree as to render objects altogether invisible at very short distances. It is, of course, worst near the surface of the ground, but in very hot days it attains a level of several feet ; and I well remember, on one occasion, observing the slender horns of an Antelope gliding past me within three hundred yards, apparently borne on the surface of a glassy stream, in which the wearer of the horns was submerged, and completely hidden from view !

When Antelope are feeding on the grassy flats by the streams is the time when they may be easily approached ; and then a knowledge of the ground, and of the habits of the animal, renders success in stalking them tolerably certain.

The first time I visited Chung Chenmo was in 1861. I was much pressed for time, and being accompanied by two friends, I did not shoot very much—in fact, I looked upon this year's expedition as merely a sort of reconnaissance—I only shot one small buck, and wounded but lost a fine one.

Neither on this trip, nor on any subsequent one, did I ever see a doe Antelope in the Chung Chenmo valley ; and I met with but few in the nullahs to the north.

In 1862, I again visited Chung Chenmo, accompanied by my friend H. We left S'rinugger on the 6th of June, and, after experiencing some difficulty in crossing two snow passes, on one of which we encountered a violent storm which caused the death of a pony and a sheep, arrived in the valley on the afternoon of the 28th.

I already knew the ground, so we ordered the camp to be pitched near a hot spring called Keum, and hurried on in hopes of finding Antelope. We were not disappointed—we had no sooner reached the place from which I expected to see them, than I discovered three Antelope feeding close to the river; we at once approached them, but the ground was very open, and we could not walk to within four hundred yards of them. Having got so near we lay down, and although the ground was very stony, we crawled and dragged ourselves along until we were within two hundred yards; but nearer it was impossible to go without being seen. We, therefore, lay still for a long time watching the Antelope, in hopes that they would feed towards us; but this they would not do, and at last began to move away from us. There were two good-sized buck and a small one, so I selected one of the former and fired; the bullet must have gone high, but the Antelope seeing nothing walked quietly on, giving H. a chance, but he also missed. My second barrel brought down a buck on the snow with a broken back, but H. again missed. The other buck now turned and walked slowly towards us, and as H. had a breech-loader, he had time to reload and shoot him at about a hundred yards, but had to follow and give him another bullet. The camp arrived shortly afterwards, and we had our buck carried to the tents; they were both fine ones, and we were much pleased at our first stalk proving so successful.

The next day we rested, and the following one we separated in search of Yâk. I went up a valley to the north-west, called Kyobrung, but never saw a Yâk. On the way down again I shot two more buck, one of them a very fine one with a remarkably handsome head. It was a nasty cold morning with drifting snow and a bitterly cold wind; I was up early, and started for some ground where I had seen Antelope the day before. For a long time I could not find any, but at length a solitary buck got up from behind some stones and went slowly up the hill; he was out of shot, so I ran towards him, and, having gained some distance, lay down behind a stone on which I rested my rifle, and took deliberate aim at his shoulder at about two hundred yards. I heard the bullet strike, but the buck went on untouched by my other two shots. Hastily reloading, I followed the track, but was disappointed at finding no blood; however, I soon came up with my friend lying down, but he saw me and made off. I saw the tips of his horns stop just over a ridge, so I ran for a shot, and as he rushed down a steep ravine, I bowled him over with a bullet through the spine. While preserving this buck's head, I employed a Tartar to assist me in holding it; on my opening the skull he took out a handful of the brains and swallowed them! I was not so well acquainted with Tartars then as I am now, and recollect that I was rather horrified at the time.

I rejoined H. on the 7th of July, and found that he had shot a fine bull and a cow Yâk. I hunted for the herd for some days and frequently allowed Antelope to go away unfired at for fear of disturbing the larger game, but I never had the good fortune to come across them.

I left Chung Chenmo on the 13th, as I was anxious to try for Markhoor, in Kashmir.

In 1864, I determined to reach Chung Chenmo as early as possible, and accordingly made a stay of only one day in S'rinugger, and at once pushed on for Ládák. I was detained at the foot of the Zojjí-lá, or Baltal Pass, for two days on account of rain and snow.

On the second of May, I persuaded my coolies to start, but a thaw came on soon after we set out, and we had a fearfully hard time of it in the deep soft snow. We had started at daylight, and continued marching until about eleven o'clock at night in hopes of reaching some stone huts in which we might find shelter. They were, however, completely buried in the snow, so we had to bivouac as we best could, pitching the tents by fastening the ropes to poles driven into the snow. Early next morning, we again got under weigh and arrived at Mataiyun, the first village on the Ládák side of the pass, in the evening: not having tasted food since the previous morning, I was dead beat; the coolies were much exhausted, and several of them were snow-blind and severely frost-bitten.

I reached Chung Chenmo on the 28th of May, but was laid up for four days with an attack of fever and ague; I found that the ravines were still full of snow, and the Antelope were on the higher and more open ground.

I had come up early on purpose to hunt Yâk, so as soon as I had shaken off the fever I went up the Kyobrung valley in search of them. I was unsuccessful, as elsewhere related, but on my return down the valley I shot a fine Antelope after an interesting stalk.

Not finding many Antelope near Keum, where the snow had not yet sufficiently melted off the grassy flats by the river-side, I crossed a low pass to Gipsung, and here, though there were no recent traces of Yâk, I found numbers of Antelope. I knocked over a young buck the first evening, mistaking it for a doe.

On the second evening I found a herd on some terraced ground, and placing myself in a favorable position, waited for them to feed up to me. A fine buck at length came within one hundred and fifty yards, and when he was broadside on, I fired steadily at him: he fell to the shot, but was up again directly and made after the others. Having reloaded I followed him and fired both barrels within easy distance, but I was so blown with running that only one of my bullets hit him, and it only grazed his foreleg. The first bullet had struck him high up in the hip and passed through the intestines, part of which were hanging out, but in spite of this he seemed to recover strength and went off at a great pace, luckily in the direction of camp. I followed as fast as I could, but was soon left far behind. I sent to camp for my two dogs (a retriever and a spaniel), and contented myself with watching the buck, who soon lay down in the middle of an open plain. On the arrival of the dogs I approached him, on which he got up and went off at a very fair pace. I hallooed on the dogs, who quickly entered into the spirit of the thing and gave chase. Antelope and dogs soon disappeared in a ravine, and on running up to the bank I had the satisfaction of seeing the buck on the ground, and the two dogs barking at him; strange deerhounds! but they did their work well. The kill took place not three quarters of a mile from camp.

During the next few days I hunted in vain for Yâk, but saw many Antelope, about which I gave myself little trouble.

On the last three days of my stay in Chung Chenmo I killed six buck; there was nothing remarkable about any of the stalks. On the last day I shot two fine buck; one of them by a drive, which is often a capital plan when they are feeding on the grassy flats by the river. The banks above are very steep, and it is only in certain places that the Antelope can ascend them : by placing oneself in the most likely path and sending a man round to drive them, a shot may often be obtained when it would be impossible by stalking.

On my last visit to Chung Chenmo, in 1870, I had my first stalk at Antelope completely spoiled by some Chankos, who seized the inopportune moment to carry out their designs on the herd which I had discovered. The Antelope, however, took the alarm and made off without giving the Wolves a chance, and the latter were equally careful not to give me an opportunity of punishing them for spoiling my sport.

The following day, I shifted my camp and marched several miles without seeing game. Having pitched my tent on a pleasant grassy flat, where the valley was nearly a mile wide, I was taking my ease and beginning to think of dinner, when one of my men came to tell me that two Antelope were feeding in a lateral ravine on the opposite side of the valley. From my tent door I could plainly see them—two yellowish specks on the bright green grass, a little way up a nullah with precipitous sides. My plans were quickly formed ; I went about half a mile down the valley, and then, when the Antelope were lost to view, forded the river, and gaining the plateau above the opposite bank, walked quietly up-wind in the direction of the nullah where they were feeding. It was now all plain sailing; and when, on approaching the nullah, I carefully crept to its edge, I had the satisfaction of seeing the Antelope still unsuspiciously grazing immediately below me, not more than forty yards off. There was little difference in size, so I selected the one in the best position, and dropped him on the spot. The other, startled by the shot, but ignorant whence the danger came, stood to gaze, and, slipping in another cartridge, I knocked him over also. Both had well-shaped perfect horns, about twenty-four inches in length.

The following day, I only found one lot of Antelope, and my rifle missing fire at the stalk shot, I only succeeded in wounding one by a long shot, as they went away.

Being in search of Yâk, I did not trouble myself about Antelope for the next two or three days, but when there was no longer any fear of disturbing the larger game, I again fired at all that came in my way.

One morning, I found a herd feeding near a watercourse, and had managed to stalk to within shot, when a solitary outlying buck, which I had not seen, came across some higher ground, and gave the alarm. He paid the penalty, however, for, as he stopped to gaze, my bullet laid him low.

I had a long walk that day, and as I returned homewards down the valley, I discovered another herd in such favorable ground that I was enabled to approach them within seventy yards, and knocked over the finest : as I remained perfectly still, the others stood hesitating where to fly to, and my second shot brought down another. I had to leave all three Antelope hidden under rocks, to be brought home in the morning.

I shot some more on succeeding days, but as there was nothing particular to record about the stalks, I need not describe them. But a singular piece of good fortune, which befell me on my return journey down the valley, is, perhaps, worth mentioning. Just before reaching the grassy camping ground above referred to, I espied an Antelope grazing on the very spot where I shot the first two buck ; and on stalking to within easy range, I found that there were four. I repeated my feat of the first day by killing the two finest fellows right and left, and I ought to have secured a third. As it was, I finished up my Antelope shooting by securing two as handsome heads as on the former occasion.

CHAPTER XXI.

THE INDIAN ANTELOPE.

ANTILOPE CERVICAPRA.

Generally throughout India.—*Heran.*

THE Indian Antelope, the male of which is universally known as the 'Black Buck,' is generally distributed throughout India, being found from the foot of the Himalayas to the extreme south of the mainland, and from Eastern Bengal to the river Jhelum.

There are, however, large tracts of country where it is not found, and it is essentially an inhabitant of the open cultivated plains, avoiding equally hills and dense jungles.

The localities in which I know it to be most abundant are the desert near Ferozpúr, in the Hissár District, and in the neighbourhood of Alíghar.

The male is one of the most graceful and beautiful animals in creation, combining symmetry of form and brilliancy of coloring, with marvellous speed and elasticity of movement. He stands about thirty-two inches at the shoulder, and when arrived at maturity, the upper parts are of a deep glossy black, with the exception of a light chesnut-colored patch at the back of the neck, and some markings of the same color about the face. The lower parts and inside of the limbs are snowy white, and the line between the black and white is most clearly defined. The hair is short and glossy, and the skin makes a very pretty mat.

The horns are remarkably handsome, being spiral and annulated nearly to their tips. They vary considerably in length, degree of spirality, in the number and prominence of rings, and in the angle at which they diverge. In Southern India they are said rarely to attain a greater length than twenty inches, but in the Punjab they have been found very much longer. I have *seen* two pairs of twenty-seven inches, and have *heard* of horns over twenty-eight. I was never fortunate enough to bag a buck with very remarkable horns, though I was once within an ace of getting a twenty-six-inch pair, as hereafter related. Young bucks are of a light fawn color, their coats gradually becoming darker with age, although I have seen full-grown buck with long horns, which had hardly a black hair.

The doe is of a light fawn above, and white beneath, with a light colored line along the side : she is not furnished with horns, except in very rare instances. When horns do appear they are slender and much curved, bearing no resemblance to those of the buck.

Antelope delight in extensive open plains, where there are alternate wide tracts of cultivation and waste land, repairing as a rule to the fields for food, and resting when they can on bare and sandy soil.

XIV

INDIAN ANTELOPE
ANTILOPA CERVICAPRA

Published by Thacker, Spink & Co., Calcutta.

During the rainy season, however, they are fond of concealing themselves among high standing crops, and only come out in the mornings and evenings.

Black Buck are very pugnacious, and sometimes fight so desperately that they will allow a person to walk close up to them without observing him. Many have their horns broken in their combats, and I have seen one, both of whose horns were broken off within three inches of the head.

Antelope are usually found in considerable herds, varying in numbers from ten or a dozen to a couple of hundred. A buck and one doe, or a buck and a couple of does, may however be frequently met with; and vast herds of many thousands have occasionally been seen.

When in large numbers they of course do much damage to crops, and it is with difficulty that the natives drive them away.

It is a beautiful sight when a herd of Antelope are first alarmed : as soon as they have made up their minds that safety is only to be found in flight, first one, then another, bounds into the air to a surprising height, just touching the earth, and again springing upwards, until the whole herd are in motion. So light are their movements that they seem as if they were suspended on wires. These bounds are only continued for a few strides, after which the Antelope generally settle down into a regular gallop.

The speed of the Antelope is wonderful, and it is seldom that greyhounds can pull down an unwounded one; but I know of one dog that has caught several, both bucks and does, on fair ground.

Antelope will go away when very hard hit, and a wounded one will often give a capital run, if ridden after with spear or knife; the latter is nearly as good as the former, for the buck runs so game, that he will not, as a rule, give a chance of spearing him until he is so completely exhausted, that he drops with fatigue, when one may dismount and cut his throat.

The sportsman can choose between riding down or coursing his wounded Antelope; but either a good horse or a brace of greyhounds should always be in readiness, or the best shot will have the mortification of seeing maimed animals escape to die a lingering death.

The Antelope is usually the first quarry which falls to the rifle of the young sportsman in India ; and although its pursuit is attended with far less excitement than in the case of rarer and wilder animals, there is quite enough interest attached to it to induce the oldest hunter to keep his hand in by an occasional day's Black Buck shooting ; while the tyro, if he is possessed by the true hunter's spirit, will probably, for the time, consider that there is no object in life so well worth striving for as the possession of a pair of horns, which seem to his unpractised eye at least a yard long !

Being for the most part found on open plains, it is but seldom that Antelope can be stalked,—i. e., approached under cover ; but the hunter must usually contrive to get within range by carefully watching their movements, and gradually edging nearer and nearer without exciting their suspicions. Except in remote and undisturbed places it is seldom that buck will allow any Englishman to walk straight up to within easy range, although they will take no notice of natives working in the fields close to them.

P

Usually the best plan is to observe the direction which they appear most likely to take, and then to advance obliquely so as to cut them off from their line of retreat. In doing this there should be no attempt at concealment, but the sportsman should walk quietly on, keeping his face steadily in the direction he is going, but gaining ground by stepping obliquely towards the Antelope. The rifle should be held on the side farthest from the herd, in such a manner as to attract attention as little as possible, and the movements of the animals should be carefully watched by a side glance, without turning the head, until the Antelope become unmistakably uneasy, or the distance is considered short enough. The hunter should then halt, if possible, behind a bush or tuft of grass, and take his shot as rapidly as he can. Success will depend a good deal upon the manner in which the approach is made, and there is scope for the display of a considerable amount of skill in manœuvring.

An able tactician will succeed in allaying the suspicions of a crafty old doe, who usually makes the safety of the herd her special business ; while the tyro unacquainted with the habits of the animals, will, by his very excess of caution, only succeed in alarming her to such a degree that the chance of a shot at *that* herd is gone for the day.

A steady shooting horse is a great luxury in Black Buck shooting ; not only saving one the labor of trudging over rough and dusty fields, but rendering it easier to get within shot of one's game. The horse may either be ridden up to within shot, or the hunter may have it led up, and walk behind it until within range, when the syce should walk on unconcernedly while his master sits or kneels down to fire. The latter is by far the best plan if your syce has been properly trained to incline to the right and left, diminish or increase his pace, and generally regulate his movements in obedience to your slightest sign and without the least hesitation. A new hand at the work will inevitably go exactly wrong, and frighten away the Antelope by his erratic movements and display of evident indecision.

When Antelope are so wild that they won't allow any one to come within shot, the only plan is to station yourself behind shelter which they are likely to pass, and have the herd driven towards you. This again requires some little knowledge of the country and the habits of the animals in order to be successful.

My first experience with Antelope was at Agra, on my way up-country in 1860. I went out one afternoon and wounded a fine buck very badly. Mounting my horse, I galloped as hard as I could, but at length lost the buck in high grass, to my great disappointment.

My next essay was at Thanésar, about twenty-five miles from Umballa, when I bagged two buck, one of whose portraits is here given. He afforded an example of the way in which Antelope will go away after receiving a mortal wound. He was lying in company with five or six does on a bare plain studded with patches of ' *dhák* ' jungle. They had apparently not observed me, and I stalked up behind a clump of bushes which was within easy shot of them. Something had alarmed them, however, for on looking through the bushes I saw them galloping away. Kneeling down, I fired both barrels at the buck, at a distance of about a hundred and fifty yards, but nothing showed that he was hit. The herd disappeared behind another clump of bushes, and presently the does reappeared, but no buck. I therefore ran on, and soon saw him on his knees, and before I reached him he was dead. The bullet had entered the flank and passed out at the opposite shoulder. His horns were about twenty-three inches in length.

On the march with my Regiment from Súbáthú to Delhi in 1863, when near the latter station, I one morning left the Grand Trunk road, and, accompanied only by a syce carrying my rifle, made a circuit across country in the direction of my next halting place. Before going very far I got a fair shot at a buck, which, however, galloped off on three legs. I had no dog with me, so remounting my horse, I at once gave chase. The ground was hard, but very rough, being principally ' *gram* ' fields, in which the clods are left unbroken, and although they crumble easily under the weight of the horse, they very much impede the progress of a lighter animal, especially a wounded one. So it proved in this case ; I had not galloped above half a mile before the buck began to tire, and a short distance farther on he fell completely exhausted.

In the course of the morning two more buck fell to my rifle and I was making for my tent, perfectly satisfied with the day's work, when I suddenly came in sight of a solitary buck with horns finer than any I had yet seen. I determined that I would spare no trouble to gain possession of such a trophy, but I soon found that the buck was very wide awake indeed, and knew the range of a rifle well (Express rifles had not then been invented). Although not apparently much frightened, he contrived to preserve a distance of at least two hundred and fifty yards, and all my stratagems to approach nearer were unavailing. At last he crossed a deep cut lane fringed by trees, and I thought that my chance had come, as by running down the lane I should probably be in time to get a fair shot if he continued in the direction in which he was then going. Just as I was about to put my scheme in practice, a puff of smoke issued from behind one of the trees, the crack of a rifle reached my ear, and the buck rolled over ! Running up I found that my friend R., from whom I had parted in the morning, had chanced to cross my route, had seen my ineffectual attempts to get near the buck, which I had driven in his direction, and had taken advantage of the unexpected chance.

Though of course disappointed at my own want of success, I was very glad that R. had bagged such a fine head. We measured the horns carefully ; they were just over twenty-six inches in length, and a very perfect pair. The head used afterwards always to hang in R.'s room, which I never entered without being asked whether I had ever shot a buck like *that !*

When quartered at Meerut, from 1863 to 1866, I made many expeditions after Black Buck. One of the best places that I discovered was in the neighbourhood of Súrujpúr, a village not many miles from the Gházíábád Railway station.

Having on one occasion driven over to Gházíábád, to which place I had sent on a horse, and my camp having preceded me a day or two, I made the remainder of the journey to Súrujpúr on horseback. There was no regular road, and I had to ask my way from time to time, frequently receiving the evasive and unsatisfactory answers which the tiller of the soil delights in giving, with a view probably to putting a stop to further questioning. Riding several miles through cultivated fields, fortunately without deviating very far from my proper course, I at last came to an open plain of beautiful turf, upwards of a mile in diameter, and in many places fringed by a belt of palm trees ; my tent was at the other side of this plain, and as I rode across the grass I soon saw that I had not come to the wrong place. Here and there, scattered about the plain, were herds of Antelope quietly lying down and chewing the cud in fancied security, little dreaming that the rider whom they hardly condescended to notice as he passed within a hundred and fifty yards of them, was bent upon their destruction. It seemed almost a pity to disturb or hurt such lovely animals, but the hunter's instinct gets the better of softer feelings, and that evening I was eager enough to possess myself of their trophies. I must also say that I did not find them quite so confiding when I had a rifle in my hand.

I had sent out a young greyhound which I was anxious to enter at Antelope, and next morning I strolled out with the rifle, the greyhound being led some distance behind me, and his leader having orders to slip him on a signal from me.

It was not very long before I found a small herd headed by a Black Buck with a good pair of horns, and I proceeded to lay my plans for getting within shot. There was no cover, so the only plan was to walk unconcernedly past them, and trust to their allowing me to approach sufficiently near. Not having been recently fired at, the Antelope did not appear to have any suspicions of my intentions until I was within a hundred and fifty yards, when, observing that they were beginning to look uneasy, I thought it best to fire. My bullet struck the buck, but too far back to drop him on the spot, and he at once bounded away, but in a different direction to that taken by the rest of the herd. Even if I had not heard the bullet strike, this would have been a sufficient indication that the buck was hard hit, and I at once signalled to let go the dog. He was soon in hot pursuit, and on the level greensward I had a splendid opportunity of witnessing a contest between two animals, each the swiftest of its family. Had the buck been unwounded he would soon have distanced his pursuer, but I hoped that his wound was just sufficient to put the two upon an equality : and this I at first thought was the case. After a few hundred yards, however, I saw that the poor buck had no chance ; the dog gained on him stride by stride, and just as he reached a small watercourse, the greyhound reached his quarters. They landed almost together at the other side, when the greyhound—puppy like—seized the buck by the tail ! This, of course, did not afford a very secure hold, but the buck was too exhausted to go much farther, and I soon came up and ended his sufferings with the knife.

I shot a couple more that day, and three more on the day following, but as far as I recollect, they all fell where they were struck, with the exception of one, after which I had a tedious track through fields of high ' *bájrá.*'

In August 1868, I varied the monotony of a hot season in the plains by a shooting trip in the vicinity of Cawnpore. Here I had very fair sport, killing Nilgao, Chikara, and Antelope.

On the last day that I intended to remain out, I found that I had expended all my rifle ammunition, so I had to rely upon a double barrelled No. 12 smoothbore (which was, by the way the best ball gun I ever saw). It was not very long before I found some Antelope among some scattered mimosa bushes, near which was a large mound, under shelter of which I was enabled to approach to within about a hundred and forty yards of the herd. This was a very long range for a smoothbore, but the shot before I had killed a buck galloping at full speed at a distance of a hundred and fifty yards, so I thought I would try my luck again. Accordingly, giving what I thought would be about the proper elevation, I fired steadily at the largest buck. The ball cracked loudly on him, and he disappeared with the rest among the bushes. I had to run back some little way for my horse, a small but well-bred and plucky beast, and quickly mounting him, I started on the tracks of the herd. The bushes only extended a short distance, and beyond was a perfectly open plain with only an occasional bush and tree dotted here and there. I rode on some distance, but could make nothing of the tracks on the hard ground, and could see nothing of the Antelope.

Retracing my steps to where the buck had been standing, I found a few drops of blood, and on following in the direction indicated by them I picked up a small piece of bone. Some distance farther on the buck jumped up out of a thorny bush in which he had been concealed, and went away at a great pace, and I could now see that one hind leg was broken just below the hock.

I was not fifty yards behind him, and my horse being by no means slow, I did not expect the chase to be a very long one, and although the buck at first went right away from me I rattled my horse along in the full expectation that I should soon regain the ground I had lost.

On we went at nearly full speed for at least two miles, when the severity of the pace began to tell upon my horse, but the buck seemed as fresh as ever, and the interval between us had not diminished. Until now we had been galloping on hard smooth ground, but on coming to some ploughed land I expected to see the buck laboring through the heavy soil, in which, through his superior stride, my horse would have the advantage. The Antelope, however, contrived to find some narrow paths which had not yet been broken up, and by following them he was enabled to go on at little diminished speed.

I now saw that it was useless attempting to ride him down by mere speed, and I therefore nursed my horse as much as possible and began to 'ride cunning.' In this way I was enabled to cut off several corners, and at length after crossing two or three ravines, and passing through some narrow strips of jungle in which the gallant buck seemed to scorn hiding himself, I again found myself not many yards behind him. Reaching a level piece of hard ground I roused my horse for a final effort, and at last the noble buck's course was run. Struggling gamely to the last stride he did not even then give in, but nature was utterly exhausted, the strained limbs at length gave way, and he fell to rise no more. Two minutes after he was dead his limbs were perfectly rigid. My horse was a good deal distressed, and it was altogether one of the most severe runs I ever rode. The total distance could not have been less than five miles.

The first time that I ever fired an Express rifle was at a Black Buck which I had considerable difficulty in circumventing.

I happened to pay the station of Sialkot a visit, and one day my friend D. proposed that we should go out and try for Black Buck, two or three of which were still to be found not far from cantonments, though, owing to their being constantly hunted, they were unusually wary.

Not having my own rifles with me, I borrowed a single-barrelled ·450 Henry Express from another friend. We had not ridden above three or four miles when we saw a buck and a couple of does lying on an open plain. When we were still a quarter of a mile off, he rose and trotted off, and as there was little or no cover, we found it quite impossible to approach him. As D. wished me to have the shot, I concerted a plan by which the buck was, if possible, to be driven up to me.

There were a few bushes scattered about at wide intervals on the plain, and we walked together with our horses led behind us until we had placed one of the bushes between us and the buck, who was now standing about half a mile from us. On reaching the bush I dropped behind it, while D. with the syces and led horses walked quietly on and made a wide circuit until they had placed the buck between themselves and me.

They then separated, and very skilfully proceeded to drive the Antelope towards me without unnecessarily alarming them. From my place of concealment I could watch every movement, and I soon saw that the Antelope were making straight for the place where I lay hidden. They came on very slowly, occasionally stopping to nibble at a bush or tuft of grass, but at last the buck approached to within one hundred and twenty yards, and offered a fair broadside shot. Not knowing the sighting of the rifle, I aimed a little too low, and my bullet, as I afterwards discovered, merely cut the lower part of the buck's brisket. He at once bounded off, and as he passed me at full speed with his horns thrown well back, I inserted another cartridge and let drive at him again. The bullet cracked loudly on one of his horns, which it knocked off, and the now dazed buck continued his headlong flight, and had placed three hundred yards between us before I could fire another shot. This third bullet struck just beyond him, and the buck, frightened and confused, at once changed his course and came past me within one hundred yards. My fourth bullet passed through his heart, and the buck was at last mine.

I was most favorably impressed with the Henry Express, the rapidity of its action being superior to anything that I had then seen ; and subsequent experience has confirmed me in my opinion that it is about the best weapon yet invented for Antelope and Deer shooting.

The chase of the Antelope by the Chíta or Hunting Leopard is a favorite sport with Native Princes and Nobles. As it involves no personal exertion, it can be enjoyed by those whose age, obeseness, or indolence prevent them from engaging in more active sports. Although it is well worth witnessing for once, it is not an amusement that an energetic sportsman will much care for.

To be of any use for training, the Chíta must be captured when full grown, and accustomed to kill game on its own account ; and there is a certain class of men in Central India who make their livelihood by Chíta catching. I believe that the course of training is on much the same principle as that of training Hawks, viz., first to thoroughly tame the animal and accustom it to the presence of man, and to strange sights and sounds, and then to enter it at captured Antelope under such circumstances that they will fall an easy prey.

The Chítá is invariably taken to the field on a light cart drawn by trotting bullocks, and it is kept hooded until within a short distance of the quarry.

The Chítá is built for speed, and for a short distance it is probably the swiftest quadruped in the world. It stands a little higher than an ordinary Panther, and the limbs are long and slender, the hindlegs especially being remarkably lengthened, and the hocks well let down. The head is small and round, and the jaws are somewhat short, while the teeth are not so developed as in most carnivora. The foot is more like that of the dog than of the cat, being small and upright ; while the claws are only semi-retractile. The body is slight and greyhound-like, the loins, though powerful, being much ' tucked up.'

The color is a reddish fawn, profusely dotted with round black spots. A singular dark streak extends from the eye down the side of the cheek. The eyes are rather round, of a brown color, and with a mild expression except when the animal is excited. The coat is generally smooth and glossy, except on the lower parts, where it is considerably elongated and of a much lighter tint ; and on the top of the neck and shoulders where there is a thin upright mane, from whence the animal derives its specific name (*Felis jubatus*). The tail is of great length, and slightly tufted at the end.

It was not until quite recently that I had an opportunity of seeing a trained Chítá at work. Being stationed at Ferozpúr during the hot weather of 1883 I obtained leave from the Rájá of Farídkot to shoot in his preserves, and he kindly sent out his Chítá to the shooting-box which he allowed us to occupy.

Early one morning at the beginning of June, M. (a brother officer) and I rode out with the Chítá cart, and had not proceeded very far across the fields, which were then almost destitute of vegetation, when some Black Buck were discovered in the distance. M. then took his seat beside the keeper in the cart, while I rode alongside, taking care to keep the cart between me and the Antelope. The herd had evidently been hunted before, and in spite of careful manœuvring would never allow us to approach within a hundred and fifty yards, which the keeper considered too great a distance for a successful slip. Several other Antelope were followed with a similar result, but at last a herd, that were grazing in a very rough field, permitted the bullocks to trot up to within a hundred yards. The Chítá was now unhooded, and on catching sight of the game he sprang lightly from the cart, but instead of at once giving chase, he walked quietly towards the Antelope, which, being now alarmed, were rapidly increasing their distance. I began to think that he had no intention of pursuing, and the Antelope were nearly two hundred yards off, when he gradually increased his speed, and after a few strides bounded after them with such amazing velocity that in a few seconds he was in the middle of the now flying herd. Passing several small ones, he singled out one of the finest buck, and in less time than it takes to describe it buck and Chítá rolled over in a cloud of dust. The chase had not extended much over three hundred yards.

Galloping to the spot, I found the buck lying on his back, while the Chítá crouched quietly by him, with his fangs buried in the throat. The keeper quickly came up, terminated the buck's existence with his knife, and catching the blood in a wooden ladle, presented it to the Chítá, who lapped it up with relish. A haunch was then cut off, and the Chítá seizing it bounded back into his cart, where he proceeded to devour it at his leisure. The buck was a fine one, with twenty-three-inch horns.

The Chítá having been fed, it was useless to slip him again that day, but two days afterwards we again took him out. Probably owing to the extreme heat he did not seem to be very eager, and allowed two buck to escape, although he appeared to have no difficulty in overtaking them. As on the first occasion, he allowed the Antelope to have a long start, but when he had once selected his victim he went up to it as if it were standing still.

———————

FOUR-HORNED ANTELOPE

TETRACEROS QUADRICORNIS

Published by Thacker, Spink & Co., Calcutta.

CHAPTER XXII

THE FOUR-HORNED ANTELOPE.

TETRACEROS QUADRICORNIS.

Throughout India—*Chársinghá.*   In Dérá Dún—*Choká—Dodá.*

In Chotá Nágpúr—*Cháorang.*

THE Four-horned Antelope is scattered pretty generally over India, being found in suitable places from the foot of the Himalayas to Central India. I have met with it in the Sewaliks, in the Terai, among the low jungles in the neighbourhood of Sítápúr in Oudh, and among the rocky hills of Chotá Nágpúr. Being of a shy and retiring nature I fancy that it often exists where its presence is little suspected.

The Four-horn is one of the smallest of the antelope tribe, being considerably smaller than the Indian Gazelle. The color is a reddish brown, becoming lighter on the under parts; the fetlocks are curiously marked with white, like those of the Nilgao. The hair is very coarse in texture, resembling that of a deer more than the usually glossy coat of an antelope. The hoofs are long, slender, and upright, and the animal always walks as if on tiptoe. The male only is furnished with horns, the upper pair of which are usually four or five inches long, while the lower pair never exceed an inch and a half, and are frequently mere knobs.

Four-horned Antelope are generally found alone, or frequently in pairs: they conceal themselves in long grass or among low bushes, and somewhat resemble hares in their habits. They are seldom to be seen out feeding, but usually jump up at the feet of the hunter and bound away at a great pace. I have observed that they generally make their appearance when least expected, and I do not recollect ever meeting with one among the Sewaliks when I have been actually hunting for them.

The only one I have ever shot was in the grassy jungles to the south of the Sewaliks in 1863. We had been out Tiger-shooting, and were on our way back to the tents, when a Four-horned Antelope galloped past my Elephant at full speed. I fired a snap shot, and unluckily hit the animal in the head with a 12-bore shell, blowing it to pieces and rendering it useless for preservation. The horns, as it happened, were very good ones, which made the destruction of the head the more unfortunate.

At Sítápúr I went out once or twice to try for Four-horns, but was not lucky enough to get a shot. The specimen here photographed was shot by a soldier in the Rifle Brigade, from whom I procured it.

In Chotá Nágpúr, in 1883, I saw several Four-horns, but as I was hunting Gaur I would not fire at them.

CHAPTER XXIII.

THE SEROW.

NEMORHŒDUS BUBALINUS.

In Garhwál and Kamáon—*Sardo.*   In the Sutlej Valley—*Imú.*

In Kashmir—*Rámú—Halj—Sálábhír.*   In Chambá—*God—Jhangál.*   In Nipál—*Táhr.*

THIS very curious animal, although nowhere actually plentiful, appears to have as wide a range as any ruminant in India. It is found all along the hills from Assam to the western frontier of Kashmir. It is perhaps most abundant in the neighbourhood of Nainí Tál and Mussourie, on the Shálí peaks near Simla, in the Sindh valley in Kashmir, and in some parts of Chambá.

The Serow is an ungainly looking animal, combining the characteristics of the cow, the donkey, the pig, and the goat ! It is a large and powerful beast, considerably larger than a Tahr, and longer in the leg. The body is covered with very coarse hair, which assumes the form of a bristly mane on the neck and shoulders, and gives the beast a ferocious appearance, which does not belie its disposition. The color is a dull black on the back, bright red on the sides, and white underneath, the legs also being dirty white. The ears are very large, the muzzle is coarse, and two singular circular orifices are situated two or three inches below the eyes.

The horns are stout at the base, are annulated nearly to the tips, and curve back close to the neck, growing to the length of from nine to fourteen inches : they are very sharp pointed, and the Serow is said to be able to make good use of them.

The sexes differ very little, less than in any ruminating animal with which I am acquainted : both are furnished with horns of nearly the same size, those of an old male being rather thicker than those of the female.

The Serow has an awkward gait·; but in spite of this it can go over the worst ground ; and it has, perhaps, no superior in going down steep hills.

It is a solitary animal, and is nowhere numerous ; two or three may be found on one hill, four or five on another, and so on. It delights in the steepest and most rocky hill-sides, and its favorite resting places are in caves, under the shelter of overhanging rocks, or at the foot of shady trees. It constantly repairs to the same spots, as testified to by the large heaps of its droppings which are to be found in the localities above alluded to.

XVI

SEROW

NEMORHŒDUS BUBALINUS

Published by Thacker, Spink & Co., Calcutta.

Although very shy and difficult to find, the Serow is a fierce and dangerous brute when wounded and brought to bay. I have even heard of an unwounded male charging when his mate had been shot. It is said that the Serow will sometimes beat off a pack of Wild Dogs, and I believe that Serow and Dogs have been found lying dead together. It is, therefore, advisable to be cautious when approaching a wounded one.

When disturbed, the Serow utters a most singular sound, something between a snort and a screaming whistle, and I have heard them screaming loudly when they had apparently not been alarmed.

The first year I visited Kashmir I might have had two or three chances at Serow, but in those days I thought more of getting a Bear! and took no trouble about the rarer animal. Since then I have only a few times met with Serow during all my wanderings, and never got a chance at one till 1872, when I went to Kashmir for the express purpose of bagging one.

I did not get away from Rawal Pindi till near the middle of June, and consequently I reached Kashmir at about the worst season for shooting. The grass and weeds had grown to a great height, the sun was very hot, and the Serow kept concealed in the thickest forests. I first hunted some likely-looking ground between Náoshérá and Bárámúlá, but though fresh tracks were to be found, I could not see a beast.

I then went on to the Sindh valley, and encamped in a wide nullah a short distance below the village of Wángat.

During the first day or two's hunting I saw nothing, though I constantly found fresh tracks. On the 1st of July I was out long before daylight, and went up the nullah behind our camp : having gone some distance to where the sources of the stream met, we were climbing up a steep ravine when we found quite fresh tracks of a Serow. I determined to follow them as long as I could, and accordingly took up the trail. It led us towards camp, along the steep hill-side ; through thick forests, long rank weeds and grass, and under over-hanging shelves of rock. We went along slowly and carefully, sitting down to reconnoitre wherever the ground was sufficiently clear to give any chance of seeing the object of our pursuit. We knew that he must have passed not long before us, so we patiently continued the chase for several hours. At last we heard a rush through a thicket a short distance ahead of us, but I only got a momentary glimpse of something black, and was unable to fire. On going forward about fifty yards, we found where the Serow had been lying under a thick yew tree, whose branches hung down to the ground and had completely concealed him. The tracks showed that, according to their usual custom when disturbed, the Serow had rushed down the hill. We followed quietly, and in a short time we again heard him bound away, this time uttering the peculiar screaming snort that showed that he had seen us, though I was unable to catch sight of him.

The next day I found another fresh track, but the Serow had been disturbed by my shooting a Musk Deer, and I did not think it worth while to track him far.

A badly fitting grass shoe had bruised a sinew in my foot; an abscess formed ; and I was unable to move for a fortnight. By the time I was able to go out again, the vegetation had much increased, and my chances of sport were proportionately diminished.

On the 16th, I made arrangements for sleeping out, and, accompanied by my Shikari and a couple of coolies, crossed the Wángat river and went up the banks of a stream opposite. The walking was very rough, over boulders and fallen trees, and through thick tangled bushes. At length we reached a place where the valley became narrower, being shut in by high steep rocks, and the forest was so dense that there was hardly any chance of seeing a beast. We, therefore, chose a spot to sleep on, and ascended a ridge where the forest was a little thinner than in other places. We had climbed some way when a heavy shower came on, so I sat down under a tree to watch while the Shikari went a little higher up. In a short time he returned with the news that he had found a Serow lying down, and I at once went in pursuit. The ground was precipitous and covered with pine leaves, and it was very difficult to walk without falling and making a noise. The Shikari led me up behind a large stone on the crest of a ridge, and on looking over I could indistinctly see the Serow standing under the overhanging branches of a pine tree within forty yards. I sent a bullet through its shoulder, but it did not fall, so I fired another shot to make sure. The Serow now rolled down the steep hill-side, and by the time we got down it was dead. It proved to be a very large female with a good pair of horns.

Skinning took some time, and it was dark before we reached our bivouac. My bed had been made under an overhanging rock, but there were unfortunately cracks in the stone, and as a heavy thunderstorm came on just after I had turned in, my bed was soon flooded. There was nothing to be done but to get up, make a heap of my blankets, and join the Shikaris and coolies under their rock, which afforded rather better shelter. With some difficulty we lighted a fire, and spent a tolerably comfortable night after all. I saw nothing on my way back to camp next morning.

On the 19th, I again went up the hill behind camp to hunt for a Serow, whose fresh tracks had been seen a few days before. After a long walk we heard a Serow scream at some distance, but it was a long time before we could find out where he had gone to. At last we found the tracks, and followed them till they brought us to a wide rocky nullah, the opposite bank of which was covered with pine trees. We sat down for a long time and carefully examined the opposite forest with the glass, but could see nothing. At last we sent a coolie down to reconnoitre a narrow nullah below us, and directly after he had rejoined us we saw the Serow moving off through the forest which we had been watching in vain. On going to the place where he had been lying at the foot of a tree, we found that he had been in full view of us all the time, and had we only made him out I must have got an easy shot. As he had only seen the coolie at a great distance, we hoped that he would not go far, but we followed the track for hours without coming up with him, and we had at last to give up the chase.

Next day I moved down to Chatargúl and hunted there for about a week without seeing anything. There were plenty of fresh tracks, but the Serow themselves remained invisible. Hunting at this season among the rank wet jungle is most unsatisfactory, and disagreeable work.

Early in the season, when the Serow, like other beasts, are compelled to wander in search of food, is the best time to look for them.

XVII

GOORAL

NEMORHŒDUS GORAL

Published by Thacker, Spink & Co., Calcutta.

CHAPTER XXIV

THE GOORAL.

NEMORHŒDUS GORAL.

Generally throughout the Himalayas—*Gúral—Ban bakrí.*

In Chambá—*Pij.*   In Kashmir—*Raiñ—Rom.*

THE Himalayan Chamois or Gooral has never become so well known, or been so much sought after, as its Alpine relative ; the reason probably being that it appears insignificant beside the larger and rarer objects of the chase which the Indian mountains contain. It is, however, well worth the attention of the sportsman who has no opportunities of penetrating far enough into the hills to reach the haunts of the Ibex, Burrell, or other members of the sheep and goat families : and its pursuit will thoroughly test his skill both as a mountaineer and a rifle shot. I think, indeed, that Gooral shooting has been undeservedly neglected, as I know of very few who have ever devoted much time to it ; and I confess that I have neglected it myself in favor of other and more varied sport.

The Gooral is found throughout the entire length of the Himalayas, from Kashmir to Bhútán, but is confined to the lower ranges and the valleys of the rivers, seldom or never ascending to a greater elevation than 8,000 feet. It seems, indeed, to prefer heat, being most abundant in narrow, precipitous gorges, and among the serrated ridges of the Sewaliks.

The favorite haunts of the Gooral with which I am acquainted are the valleys of the Ganges and Jumna and their tributaries, and the province of Chambá. In the latter State, Gooral are particularly numerous. I have several times seen, and have once shot, Gooral in the Sewalik hills.

The Gooral is about twenty-six inches in height at the shoulder, the back being rather rounded and the hind quarters higher than the fore. The color is a brownish grey, merging into a darker hue on the legs, and with a dark stripe along the spine. There is a conspicuous white spot on the throat, which frequently betrays the animal when it would otherwise be overlooked among withered grass and herbage. The horns are rather insignificant : they are jet black, annulated at the base, and taper to a fine point, curving gently backwards : they seldom attain a greater length than eight inches. The horns of the female are much thinner and shorter than those of the male. The texture of the coat is rather coarse, the hair being about two inches long, with a tendency to woolliness.

The Gooral is one of the commonest of the Himalayan ruminants, and it is certainly (with the exception, perhaps, of the Kakur or Barking Deer) the most regardless of the presence of man. It is often found within a few hundred yards of villages, and it appears to take little notice of the proximity of flocks and herds. It seems to be much attached to its own particular haunts, and will not desert a locality unless very frequently frightened and disturbed. It usually inhabits steep rocky hills, where there are occasional bushes and patches of forest, and it shows a marked preference for cliffs which overhang mountain torrents. Although, as has already been mentioned, it is not usually to be met with at very great elevations, it must not be inferred that it is generally found on easy ground : on the contrary, as every sportsman knows, the lower parts of the valleys are frequently the steepest and most difficult walking. It requires, indeed, a good cragsman to follow Gooral in their usual haunts ; and it often occurs that they betake themselves to utterly inaccessible precipices, or to places where, if shot, they can never be recovered.

Although Gooral are accustomed to seeing shepherds, woodcutters, grasscutters, and other hill-men, whose avocations lead them to the hill-side and the jungle, and therefore take but little notice of human beings at a distance, they are by no means easily approached by the stalker. I know of few animals that are more wide awake, and I consider it much easier to obtain a quiet shot at an Ibex than at an old buck Gooral. In the first place, a Gooral, from his small size and inconspicuous color, is by no means easy to see at a distance, unless on very open ground ; and in the second place, he is so quick in his movements, and so remarkably watchful, that great care must be exercised in approaching him. Even when a stalk has been successfully carried out, a Gooral affords such a small mark, that accurate shooting is required.

Gooral are not actually gregarious, but often feed in small parties, or may be seen scattered about at no great distance from each other. Old bucks are, as a rule, to be found alone. As the horns of both sexes are small, it is not always easy to distinguish bucks from does, unless there is time to examine them carefully through a telescope. This is rather a drawback to the real sportsman, who will always spare the females of all game as much as possible ; and as the number of does seems to be very much in excess of that of bucks, the hunter often only becomes aware of the mistake he has made in the sex of the Gooral fired at when too late to remedy it.

Gooral appear to dislike the sun, although they are indifferent to heat ; and in bright weather they only feed in the early mornings and evenings, retiring during the day to the shelter of overhanging rocks or shady trees. Under such circumstances, it is nearly useless to hunt for them, as they will not move until their hiding place is discovered, when they start off at a pace which seldom gives a chance of a successful shot.

Gooral are occasionally shot by being driven out of cover, the guns being posted in the most likely passes ; and under such circumstances, the shot gun is often employed instead of the rifle. Of course, they are more easily bagged in this way than by stalking them with the rifle ; but I do not consider it legitimate sport.

The best way to hunt them is (having discovered a good hill) to be on the ground by daylight, and work along the face of the hill, keeping as high up as possible. Every slope should be carefully examined, and on reaching the edge of each ravine, it should be thoroughly reconnoitred. Being good climbers, the Gooral may be found in all sorts of places—on narrow ledges on the face of steep precipices, on gentle slopes of young grass, and among scattered bushes or forest trees. As little noise as possible should be made; talking should never be allowed, for nothing frightens game so much. Frequently, after firing a shot or two on a hill-side, other animals may be found quietly feeding a little farther on, whereas if there has been any shouting or talking, the beasts will have been driven away. Shooting over a hill does not appear to have the effect of frightening Gooral away: when disturbed they seldom go far, and may be found again on their old ground in the course of a day or two. On detecting the presence of danger, the Gooral generally stands still and utters several sharp hisses before moving away.

In 1865, I went to the valley of Billing in Garhwál, a few marches beyond Mussourie. I had just returned from Thibet, and wanted to bag a Sambur stag or two, so I tried this ground. I was not successful in finding stags, but I had a few bye days at Gooral.

There was a steep hill-side, destitute of forest, but covered at that season (August) with long grass. Here and there were precipitous rocky places, and on walking quietly along a path which ran parallel to the stream below, but about half-way up the hill-side, Gooral might every now and then be observed feeding either above or below the road. As the grass was so long, doubtless many escaped observation, and I have no doubt that very good sport might be had here early in the year. I was suffering from bad toothache, which so upset me that for the first two or three days I could hit nothing; but having got rid of my tormentor (it was extracted or rather broken off by my *khidmatgár*), I made very good practice. I was unlucky in getting good specimens, and I only killed one buck with a good head. He was feeding in company with a doe some distance up the hill, and I had a steepish climb to get above him. Having at last got within easy shot, I sent a ten bore bullet through him, but as he managed to scramble along, I had to give him another shot.

In 1869, I was marching with my wife along the Pábar valley; and one morning on reaching the breakfast place—which as usual was about five miles from where we had slept— our coolies informed us that two Gooral had concealed themselves in the rocks overhanging the river on the opposite side. There were some boys herding cattle just above, so we shouted to them to throw down stones and drive the Gooral out. They did as they were told, and soon the Gooral made their appearance, taking some wonderful leaps from rock to rock. As the buck came within range I hit him hard, and he lay down on a narrow ledge behind a small bush. I now fired several more shots at him, but whether I hit him or not, they had not the effect of moving him, while we could see that he was still alive. We could not get the herd boys to go to where he was, so I sent some of my own men round by a bridge about a mile off. Just as they arrived opposite and were looking for a way up the rocks, the Gooral suddenly scrambled out from behind the bush, lost his balance, and fell into the river: he was at once swept away by the torrent, and we never saw him again.

In 1870, I halted at Kalél between Chambá and Tísá. The ground below camp looked promising for sport, so I devoted a day to hunting it: Gooral were very numerous. I killed a fair-sized buck the evening I arrived, and might have shot several next day, but would not fire at them for fear of disturbing Tahr. On the third morning as we were marching to Tísá, I saw a buck Gooral some way below the road : it was a longish shot, but I succeeded in killing him where he lay.

One day in April 1882, when marching in the province of Chambá, I was waiting for the breakfast coolies near a spring on the slopes above a foaming torrent, which roared along its rocky bed about two hundred feet below me. The hill-side on which I sat was steep, but covered with forest ; while on the opposite side of the stream nearly perpendicular cliffs overhung it, traversed by ledges overgrown with long grass and bushes, and here and there broken by ravines.

I had not sat long before my Shikari, (one of the most energetic of his class that I have ever met with), came to tell me that he had seen a Gooral in the opposite cliffs. Taking my Express rifle I accompanied him a short distance, and soon saw the Gooral feeding among some straggling bushes on one of the ledges just alluded to. The head and neck alone were visible, and the range was about a hundred and twenty yards ; but there was no possible way of approaching nearer. I therefore lay down, and fired as steadily as possible at the animal's throat. It rolled over to the shot, and fell down a few feet into a thick bush, in which, after a struggle or two, it hung suspended, apparently incapable of recovering its footing, though evidently still alive. I could have given it another shot with ease ; but, as the Shikari observed, it would have dropped into the river and been swept away : so I sat down to watch it, while he scrambled down to the water, crossed by some rocks which served as stepping stones, and commenced to climb up towards the Gooral. The little animal, in the meantime somewhat recovered, disengaged itself from the bush, and lay down on a small open space. I could now see with the telescope that my bullet had struck it on the side of the neck, inflicting a severe wound, which apparently paralysed it. I could still have easily shot it again ; but to do so appeared to be quite unnecessary.

I was now joined by a friend who had been at some little distance when I was first told of the Gooral, and presently his Shikari pointed out another Gooral lying in a sort of cave formed by an overhanging rock, just above where the wounded Gooral lay. F. fired at the second Gooral, which at once dashed off at a great pace ; and the wounded one, roused by the shot, also bounded away, and escaped into the jungle untouched by a shot which I sent after it.

After breakfast, we proceeded on our march, and as our path led up the opposite hill, I took the Shikari's advice and proceeded to hunt the rocky slopes above the road. After a steepish climb, I sat down to rest for a little, while the Shikari went to the point of a crag, at a little distance, to reconnoitre. He soon beckoned to me, and on my joining him told me that a Gooral was lying down just round the corner of the rock on which we were. I had a little difficulty in getting out to the end of the point, which projected in an awkward manner, and by the time I had screwed myself into a position to shoot, the Gooral's suspicions had been aroused. He only went a few yards, however, before my bullet crashed through his ribs, and he went rolling down the hill till brought up by a narrow path some five hundred feet below. As we had no coolie with us, the Shikari went to look for a man, while I remained perched on the rock. Soon a large vulture came sailing down the valley, and, after a few circles, settled by the dead Gooral, which it proceeded to tear. I rolled down two or three stones without effect ; so, as I did not wish the meat to be wasted, I had recourse to the rifle and dropped the foul bird dead on the spot. The Shikari, on his return, was rather astonished to see the result of my shot, and as this was the first day that he had been out with me, I was not sorry that I had an opportunity of showing him that I could hold pretty straight. I was fortunate enough to keep up my character for the rest of the trip, as I have seldom or never shot better.

It was about a month before I again went after Gooral, and one evening I was hunting along a steep hill-side, where slopes of short green grass alternated with sheer descents of rock. My Shikari was below me, and signalled that he had seen game. Going down to him I found that a Gooral was at the foot of a small precipice a little lower down. By the time that I had got within shot, the Gooral had become restless, and was walking away from me. It was rather an awkward shot, but I fired, and missed.

The Gooral galloped off in the direction in which we were hunting, and disappeared. Having reached the point from whence we expected to see game, we sat down to reconnoitre, and had not been there long before a Gooral looked over a ridge, but seeing us immediately drew back. Following quietly in the direction it had taken, we soon saw it standing on the hill-side about three hundred yards below us ; and as it evidently thought itself in a safe position, it gave me time to stalk to within a hundred and twenty yards, when I had no difficulty in knocking it over. Unfortunately, it proved to be a female, and it was almost undoubtedly the one which I had missed little more than half an hour before. Sending the Gooral home by a coolie, we reascended the hills and again sat down to watch.

My Shikari went a short distance to a point where he could command a view of another valley, and I sat for a long time without seeing anything. At last I heard some Moonal whistling not far off, and as no Gooral had made their appearance, I rose to see whether the Moonal were in a place where they could be stalked. I had hardly moved when I heard a sharp hiss below me, and on looking down had the mortification of seeing a fine buck Gooral bound away not twenty yards from me. It had crept up under the rocks in such a direction that I could not possibly see it coming ; though, had I been prepared for it, I could not have failed to bag it.

R

CHAPTER XXV.

THE TAHR.

CAPRA JEMLAICA.

In Garhwál and Kamáon—*Táhr* ; (The male) *Júlá.*   In Kashmir—*Jaglá.*   In Kishtwár—
Krás.   In Chambá and Pángí—*Kart.*   In Nipál—*Jharál.*

THIS wild goat is one of the most widely distributed of the Himalayan Large Game,
being found in suitable ground along the whole range from Kashmir to Bhútán.

It has been classed by some naturalists in a separate genus (*Hemitragus*), together with
the nearly allied Neilgherry wild goat, which has been misnamed an *Ibex* by Madras sportsmen.   The best authorities, however, do not consider it necessary to separate either species
from the true goats.

The Tahr is common in the Pír Panjál range to the south of Kashmir, and I have
known an instance of one being shot in the north-west corner of that valley, a few miles
from Islámábád.   It abounds throughout Kishtwár and Chambá, and in the upper valleys of
the Chenáb, Rávi, Beás, Sutlej, Jumna and Ganges and their numerous tributaries.

The Tahr is a fine looking beast, although his horns are small, and he cannot compare
with his majestic relatives, the Ibex and the Markhoor.   The male is about the same size as
the Ibex, but rather more heavily made.   The general color is a reddish brown deepening
into a much darker tint on the hind quarters ; but individuals vary a good deal, and I have
shot one which was of a yellowish white.   The face is covered with smooth short hair, and is
nearly black : the hair of the body is long and coarse, attaining its greatest length on the
neck, chest, and shoulders, where it forms a fine flowing mane reaching below the animal's
knees.

The horns are curious, being triangular, with the sharp edge to the front : they are very
thick at the base, much compressed laterally, and taper rapidly to a fine point, curving right
back on to the neck.   The largest horns attain a length of about fifteen inches, and are ten
or eleven inches in circumference at the base.

The female Tahr is very much smaller than the male, the hair is short, and the horns
diminutive.   The color is a lightish red, with a dark stripe down the back.

The Tahr is, like the Markhoor, a forest loving animal, and although it sometimes resorts
to the rocky summits of the hills, it generally prefers the steep slopes which are more or less

XVIII

THE TAHR

CAPRA JEMLAICA

Published by Thacker, Spink & Co., Calcutta.

clothed with trees. Female Tahr may be frequently found on open ground, but old males hide a great deal in the thickest jungle, lying during the heat of the day under the shade of trees or overhanging rocks. Nearly perpendicular hills with dangerous precipices, where the forest consists of oak and ringal cane, are the favorite haunts of the old Tahr, who climb with ease over ground where one would hardly imagine that any animal could find a footing. Tahr ground indeed is about the worst walking I know, almost rivalling Markhoor ground; the only advantage being that, bad as it is, there are generally some bushes or grass to hold on to.

The Tahr and Markhoor are indeed to be found together on the Pír Panjál, and it was on that range that I first saw them when I commenced my Himalayan hunting in 1861.

The ground in the neighbourhood where I was then shooting is about the most difficult I have ever seen, and extremely trying to those who are not gifted by nature with a " good head." This is undoubtedly a natural gift, and I do not believe that it can be acquired by any amount of practice, although a certain degree of confidence will be attained by habitually walking on narrow paths, and looking down deep precipices. For my own part, after many years' wanderings in the hills, I have never been able to shake off the sense of dizziness on looking down precipices, and although I generally manage to get along anywhere, except in the very worst ground, I cannot help being conscious of considerable nervousness in dangerous places, and frequently have to trust to a helping hand from my Shikaris. I have often felt very angry with myself at having to crawl along where a Shikari would walk with the utmost *nonchalance*, perhaps carrying two rifles; but I have usually comforted myself with the reflection that if *he* felt half as uncomfortable as I did, he would not venture on the hill-side at all!

Considering the unavoidable risks attending mountaineering, it is wonderful how few accidents take place in the Himalayas: during the last twenty-five years, I can only recollect about half a dozen Englishmen being killed by falls when out shooting. More fatal accidents have happened at our hill sanitaria, but the majority of them have occurred to people on horseback.

One morning I had a long and severe climb, and in the afternoon was descending towards my camp over very precipitous ground, among pine forest. The walking was extremely difficult, and I was picking my way carefully, and had just scrambled down from one ledge of rock to another, when I caught sight of a shaggy old Tahr moving away to my right. I quickly caught hold of my rifle and followed the narrow path along which he had gone, but he turned a corner, reached inaccessible ground, and I never saw him again. On subsequent days I again saw Tahr two or three times, but always among tremendous precipices where there was no possibility of approaching them.

Owing to the fact of its head being a comparatively poor trophy, the Tahr is not so eagerly sought after by sportsmen as its handsomer congeners, the Ibex and Markhoor, but it is quite as difficult an animal to stalk, and its pursuit involves equal labor and as much risk; while the hunter who keenly follows the sport will find that both his endurance and nerve will be thoroughly tested.

Owing to the ground it inhabits being so covered with jungle, the pursuit of the Tahr is attended with a good deal of labor and uncertainty. Forcing one's way for hours through tangled bushes is very fatiguing, and as it is impossible to do so without noise, chances are often lost which would be easy enough if the ground was more open. Frequently, although the tracks show that old Tahr must be near, in spite of the utmost care and caution, the first intimation one has of the presence of the game is a rush through the bushes, a clatter of falling stones, and perhaps a glimpse of the shaggy hind-quarters of the last of the herd as he vanishes over some precipice where it is perfectly impossible to follow him.

Early in the spring, when grass and leaves are scarce, and again in the rutting season, are the best times for Tahr shooting, as the old males then come out on the open slopes.

The Tahr is very tenacious of life, and even when mortally wounded, he will frequently make his escape into utterly impracticable ground. In autumn the Tahr becomes immensely fat and heavy, and his flesh is then in high favor with the natives, the rank flavor suiting their not very delicate palates. An Englishman would rather not be within one hundred yards to leeward of him! the perfume being equal to treble distilled " bouquet de bouc." Ibex is bad enough, but Tahr is " a caution." The flesh of the female is, however, excellent.

Somehow or other, it was several years before I made a special expedition after Tahr; the superior attractions of Ibex, Nyan and Burrell leading me to the higher and more distant ranges. At length I determined to add a pair of Tahr's horns to my collection, and accordingly in 1869 I marched from Mussourie to the valley of the Tonse, where I had heard of a place said to be famous for Tahr.

Times had changed, however, and I found that the ground, besides being continually disturbed by woodcutters, was frequently poached by professional Shikaris, those curses to sport in the Himalayas. Tahr still existed, but they were scarce, and confined themselves almost entirely to the thickest forests and most perpendicular precipices. For several days, although I worked hard, I only saw a few females, and did not even come across the track of a male.

At last, towards the close of a long day's work, I had the satisfaction of discovering a herd in an open glade, where I contrived to stalk to within fair range—about a hundred and twenty yards.

I was additionally anxious to make a good shot, as I was using a new rifle which I had never yet fired at game, but on carefully reconnoitring I was disappointed to find that there were no really large males in the flock. I selected the best, however, and aimed at his shoulder as he stood offering a fair clear shot. The rifle threw true, and the Tahr rolled dead to the bottom of the ravine.

On subsequent days, I two or three times roused male Tahr among the forest-clad precipices, but without their giving me a chance, and I left the valley without securing a first rate specimen.

Next year a friend recommended me to try Mangli in Chambá, and having obtained leave from the middle of April, I made straight for the place.

I reached the village on the 21st, and having engaged a Shikari, named Máhidr, I went out early in the afternoon. Crossing the river a little above the village, we ascended the opposite hill, and before long saw a flock of female Tahr among some steep cliffs. Leaving them alone, we went more to the right and still higher up, and my Shikari soon discovered eight or nine old males. They were coming down the hill to feed, and presently galloped down to an old sheep-fold, where there was plenty of young fresh grass. The stalk was an easy one, and after crossing several ravines and scrambling through a lot of jungle we arrived nearly within shot. As bad luck would have it, however, we had been seen by a second flock of females, which went up the rocks above us and gave the alarm to the old males. The latter had not seen us, but had collected together and now moved off along the hill-side. Máhidr's advice was to leave them alone till next day, and accordingly we began to descend the hill, but before we had gone far, we saw that the flock were again quietly feeding. We therefore reascended, and soon reached the ravine in which the Tahr were. Creeping carefully through the bushes, I saw them walking up the opposite slope, headed by a very light colored fellow. He was a large one, so I knocked him over with the double barrel, and fired the second barrel at another one, which also rolled over. Both Tahr now staggered down the hill, but the first one immediately stopped, and I finished him with a bullet from a Henry rifle. The second Tahr disappeared among the bushes, and reaching some inaccessible ground, was lost; a heavy thunderstorm, which came on immediately, washing out any tracks that we might have followed. The dead Tahr had a good pair of horns, and his coat, although short, was in very good order. On the way home I wounded a Black Bear, but though he fell twice he managed to escape.

Next day I went to look for Bruin, but heavy rain had washed away most of the blood, and we could not track him. Late in the afternoon we found a flock of Tahr, males and females. After an easy stalk I got within shot, but they were among thick bushes, and a small one gave the alarm before I could pick out a good one to fire at. I then fired a quick shot and missed, but hit one with my second barrel; however, it went off with the rest. Running after them as hard as I could, I was in time to see the flock going up the opposite side of a deep and wide ravine. I opened fire at them with a single barrelled Henry, and knocked over a young male stone dead. I hit two others, one a very fine fellow, and as he immediately lay down I felt sure of him. I crossed the ravine for the purpose of finishing him, but was just in time to see him cross a ridge of high rocks, to the top of which he contrived to climb in a miraculous manner on three legs. I scrambled up with great difficulty and followed the track by the blood for a long way, but had to give it up as it was very late. We reached the foot of the hill with difficulty, as the night was pitch dark. I was very glad to meet some men whom my wife had sent out with torches in search of me.

These torches are made of splinters of the Chíl pine *(Pinus longifolia);* they are full of resin and burn most brilliantly.

On the 24th we were out early, and after passing some small Tahr at which I would not fire, we saw three old males going up to some high rocks, and as we expected them to come down to feed in the evening we sat down to wait for them. Late in the afternoon they again appeared, and another solitary fellow also showed himself, but they remained high up till it was too late to go after them.

On the 25th I again went out early in a different direction, and high up the hill I disturbed some small Tahr. These gave the alarm to a flock of old males, which I first observed as they were making off up some steep rocks two hundred yards off. I fired with the Henry rifle and hit one, and as the flock stood to gaze I hit another, and then hit the first one again. Some of my cartridges (which had got damp) missed fire, and I now found to my disgust that I had no more, while the distance was too great for my heavy double barrel. The Tahr that had been twice struck, however, seemed unable to accompany the flock, and at once lay down. I therefore proceeded to stalk him, feeling sure that I should easily get him. I had to make a long round, and when I at last reached the place from which I expected to get a shot, the Tahr had gone. There was a great pool of blood, and there was plenty on the tracks, but after following them for a long distance over very precipitous ground and through thick bushes, the blood suddenly ceased and we were unable to track any farther. This was one instance of the uselessness of solid bullets and small charges from small-bore rifles: had I been using Express charges I should almost certainly have bagged both these Tahr ; as it was I went home empty handed, a succession of bitterly cold hailstorms making me seek the shelter of the tents earlier than usual.

I did not go out again till the following afternoon, when I went in search of the three old Tahr that we had seen on the 24th. After going very high up I found them close to where we had previously seen them. The stalk was a long and difficult one, but Máhidr's knowledge of the ground enabled us to get within about one hundred and twenty yards of our game. They were feeding unsuspiciously, and I was capitally concealed among some low bushes. I picked out the biggest one and hit him low in the shoulder with my double barrel. He did not fall, but at once turned down the ravine in which he had been feeding, and came past me at a great pace. The other two stood to gaze, but profiting by past experience I determined to make sure of the wounded one. I therefore followed him down the ravine as hard as I could go, constantly slipping and falling on the steep hill-side, but occasionally getting a shot at the Tahr. I was so shaky from the violent exertion that I did not shoot very well, and it was not until he had received four or five bullets from the Henry that the old Tahr finally rolled over. He proved to be a very fine specimen with good horns and a shaggy coat. His portrait is here given. I did not reach the tents till after dark.

I only went out once more after Tahr at Manglí, when I again lost a fine old male in an extraordinary manner. I had gone out with A.—a brother Officer—more with the intention of assisting him than of shooting on my own account. As usual when two people go together, we were unlucky, and did not get a chance at old Tahr till we were on our way home, when we saw a fine old fellow come out of the forest and commence to feed on a grassy slope. He was very wide awake and suspicious, but as he came down the hill I thought we were sure to get an easy shot. However, as we were stalking him, we had to cross a rather awkward place at which A. was delayed and made some noise. The Tahr either heard or saw us and set off at full speed. I ran for a shot, and fired at him as he stopped for a moment. I hit him hard and he stood still and began to scream. I fired another shot or two and hit him again, upon which he began to turn round and round in a most curious way : he then moved behind a rock and stood for some time, but finally went off into the jungle. I followed at best pace, but as he bled very little I was unable to track him.

To account for losing so many wounded beasts, I must explain that the ground was very rough and jungly ; none of the Shikaris had the remotest idea of tracking ; and heavy rain generally came on shortly after the animals were wounded. It rained nearly every day I was at Manglí.

Losing wounded animals is a misfortune which every true sportsman must regret, and although occasionally unavoidable, it is best guarded against by refraining from firing long and uncertain shots. The opportunity of firing off his rifle is a great temptation to a young sportsman ; but he may be more readily induced to withstand it if he will accept my assurance that the way to make a good bag is to get near his game, and seldom to fire a doubtful shot.

In 1882 I shot a few Tahr in the province of Chambá : it was rather late in the season when I commenced hunting for them, and as the ground had been already disturbed, I was not particularly successful. One morning I was perched on a lofty crag, which commanded an extensive view over most likely looking ground, when my Shikari called my attention to a female Tahr, which, accompanied by a tiny kid, was feeding far below us. I at once directed him to hurry to the spot, and endeavor to capture the young one, while I remained at my post to watch his proceedings. After a long scramble he reached the place, and he had slight difficulty in catching the little animal, which fortunately proved to be a male. I at once procured a milch goat, which the young Tahr quickly took to, and soon followed as if it was its own mother. I took the Tahr to the hill station of Bukloh, where I had a house for the season, and there it throve remarkably well, and eventually became as tame as a dog. Indeed it became rather a nuisance, as it would force its way into the house at meal times, jump on the table, to the imminent risk of glass and crockery, and steal the bread ! I sent it home to the Zoological Gardens, and I believe that it is still flourishing there. As it has two female companions of its own species it is to be hoped that they may breed.

CHAPTER XXVI.

THE SPIRAL-HORNED MARKHOOR,

CAPRA MEGACEROS.

In Kashmir and neighbouring states—*Már-khúr.*

OF all the trophies that an Indian sportsman can obtain, I think that none excels—or perhaps equals—the head of an old Markhoor.

He is undoubtedly one of the most majestic of all horned animals, and his appearance is quite in keeping with the wildness and magnificence of the rugged mountains which he inhabits.

There are at least four well marked varieties of the Markhoor, which are easily recognisable ; and even if all four have sprung from a common origin, I think that the two widely differing races of the spiral-horned and straight-horned are now entitled to recognition as distinct species.

Under the head of spiral-horned, *(Capra Megaceros)*, I would include the Kashmir Markhoor, found on the Pír Panjál and Káj-í-Nág ranges ; and the Markhoor inhabiting Astor, Gilgit, Chilás, and neighbouring provinces.

I consider the Kashmir Markhoor the finest of all, his horns being flat and massive, and rising in a fine open corkscrew form, with widely diverging tips, to a length of upwards of five feet measured along the spiral, and with from three to four twists. The horns of the Gilgit variety, on the other hand, although also broad and boldly sweeping, have a much more open spiral, there being seldom more than one complete turn in their length.

The straight-horned Markhoor (which has been distinguished as *Capra Jerdoni*) has also two representatives, *viz.*, the Markhoor found on the Sheikh Búdín and neighbouring hills, and that met with in Yúsufzaie, the Khaibar, and other parts of Northern Afghánistán.

The horns of both these varieties are rounded at the base and perfectly straight, but with a spiral groove running along their entire length, looking as if they had been originally smooth, but twisted when still in a soft and plastic condition. The Northern Afghánistán horns may be distinguished from those of Sheikh Búdín by their being heavier, longer, and with a more marked twist : the animal moreover more nearly approaches the spiral-horned race in size and general appearance.

XIX

SPIRAL-HORNED MARKHOOR

CAPRA MEGACEROS

Published by Thacker, Spink & Co., Calcutta.

The habits of the two races also differ considerably, but that may be owing to local and climatic influences; the spiral-horned species for the most part inhabiting lofty pine-clad mountains, whose summits are generally covered with snow; while the straight-horned have their home among barren and rocky hills of trifling elevation, where the heat during the summer months is frequently intense.

I have only shot the Kashmir and Sheikh Búdín Markhoor, and I will allot a separate chapter to each. I have only once marched through Astor, and had no time for shooting. I spent the summer of 1879 at Landí Kotal, which was then our advanced post in the Khaibar: I heard much about Markhoor in the neighbouring hills—where indeed they were occasionally seen by our reconnoitring parties—and I was making arrangements to hunt for them when Cavagnari's murder led to the resumption of hostilities.

I have, however, seen many specimens of all four varieties, so my opinion is formed from actual observation and not from hearsay.

The Persian name ' *Mâr-khúr* ' signifies *Snake-eater:* Shikaris all declare that Markhoor do eat snakes, which abound on the hills where this wild goat is found, and I see no reason to doubt the fact.

Having given my reasons for separating the Markhoor, and leaving the question as to whether I am correct or not to be settled by more scientific observers, I will proceed to describe the Kashmir variety.

As has been truly said, the Markhoor is the very *beau ideal* of a wild goat. Standing nearly forty-four inches at the shoulder, his flowing black beard, and long shaggy mane, falling from his neck and shoulders to his knees, give him a most imposing appearance; and as he stands to gaze on some jutting rock on the face of a rugged precipice overhung by dark pine trees, no sportsman nor lover of nature can fail to be struck with admiration at his noble bearing.

The general color of the body is a dirty bluish white, in the winter coat, but when this is shed, it is replaced by a shorter coat of a dark roan. The horns, as has been already mentioned, are long and massive, and at a distance an old male looks as if he bore two young withered pine trees on his head.

He is powerfully and compactly made, and in spite of his weight he has perhaps no equal in traversing difficult and dangerous ground. I know of no animal whose pursuit habitually entails so much difficult climbing, and to be successful one must occasionally venture into places where no less inducement would tempt one to run the risk.

Old male Markhoor are extremely difficult to find, especially where they have been frequently disturbed. Unlike the Ibex, which keeps to the rugged crags and steep ravines above the limit of the forest, the Markhoor delights in rocky forests, and although it occasionally comes out into the open glades, it seeks concealment as much as possible.

To hunt the Markhoor with success, the sportsman must exercise great patience, and more may usually be done by taking up a position which commands a good view of the favorite feeding grounds, than by walking for hours through the forests.

If Markhoor are in the neighbourhood (which can be ascertained by the tracks) they are pretty sure to show themselves sooner or later, and by sitting still there is much less chance of being observed first, than by scrambling blindly through tangled thickets, and displacing rolling stones. It is singular how wild animals sometimes appear when least expected: you may have been watching a hill-side for hours, carefully scanning every nook and corner with the most powerful glass, without seeing a vestige of a living creature; when suddenly—as if they had started out of the earth—a herd is feeding right in front of you. It may be that even after the game is viewed you find it utterly impossible to approach them; or, just as you have laid your plans, they are entirely upset by the approach of clouds which sweep along the hill-side and shut out everything from view.

How often have I been reminded of Tennyson's lines:—

> "The swimming vapour slopes athwart the glen,
> Puts forth an arm, and creeps from pine to pine,
> And loiters slowly drawn."

No description could be more graphic and expressive.

I have had my share of such disappointments, and have also had my successes.

The first year I was in India (in 1861), I commenced my hill shooting by visiting the Pír Panjál. Turning off the regular Kashmir road at Báramgallá, I spent several days in the vicinity of Chittá Pání, one of the best places for Markhoor, but though I saw several, I did not get a shot at an old male. Being quite inexperienced, I had not the requisite stock of patience to ensure success, and after a few days' hunting, I went on to Kashmir by a pass considerably to the left of the regular Pír Panjál one, without having bagged anything.

In August, 1862, on my return from Thibet, I again visited the Pír Panjál in search of Markhoor. Leaving the main road near Aliábád Serai, I came into another valley near Chittá Pání. On the first day, August the 20th, I had hardly reached the ground when I saw two female Markhoor. I wounded one of them badly, but lost her in a thick fog. For the next five days I worked hard, but only saw a few female Markhoor and Tahr among the highest rocks. Every morning the clouds came rolling up from the valleys below, enveloping us in thick mist and rendering it impossible to see farther than a few yards. In the evening they sank gradually down again.

I had not even seen the track of an old Markhoor, and was beginning almost to despair of success, when at last, on the 26th, we were blessed with a fine, clear day. Leaving my tent at daylight, and going to the top of the hill on which I was encamped, I proceeded along the face of a crescent-shaped range of high steep hills, much broken up by ravines. I had gone a very short distance when I saw five Markhoor feeding about four hundred yards below us. Two of them had fair sized horns, the others were smaller. We lay down to watch them, and while doing so, I discovered nine more farther along the hill: the glass showed them all to be fine old males, six in particular having splendid horns. They were near one horn of the crescent-shaped hill, while we were near the other, so it was impossible to approach them until they shifted their ground. In about half-an-hour they disappeared round the opposite end of the hill, and to my delight, they were speedily followed by the first lot. As soon as they were all out of sight, we went after them at best pace, and having reached the point round which they had gone (a distance of about a mile), we looked carefully over, and soon saw them not very far off. Some of them were moving slowly on, but others seemed inclined to stay where they were. There appeared to be two ways of getting near them, but the one which would give the best chance of a shot, if they remained where they were, would expose us to the danger of being seen, should the remainder of the herd move off in the direction which some had already taken : we therefore chose a rather more difficult approach. Retracing our steps a few yards, we then descended a rather awkward precipice, which I did not much like; however, we reached the bottom in safety. Keeping under cover of the hill, we at length arrived opposite a little hollow which ran down towards the Markhoor. Carefully descending this, I cautiously raised my head above the junipers and beheld two Markhoor, one lying under a rock, and the other feeding about a hundred and fifty yards off. The others were not visible, and there was no way of approaching any nearer, but the one feeding was a fine fellow, and he stood in a good position. After watching him for some time, and giving my nerves time to steady, I rested my rifle on a rock, and taking deliberate aim at his shoulder, fired. Nothing denoted that he was hit, he merely bounded forward, and the others, who had been lying concealed among the junipers, also sprang up. It was a grand sight, and one which I shall never forget, to see these noble animals standing on the rocks in various attitudes gazing about them, being as yet ignorant of where the danger came from. Conspicuous among them was one splendid old fellow with horns far larger than the rest, and at him I sent the contents of my second barrel. I could not see that he was hit either, and I am pretty sure that I missed with the single barrel which I discharged at a third one, and away went all the Markhoor in gallant style.

This would have seemed a pretty mess to a spectator, and I was almost speechless with disgust. In another minute I exclaimed "the large one is lame!" as he separated from the flock, and went slowly up the hill alone. As I was reloading and watching him, my Shikari called out "there is another one wounded," and, true enough, the first one I had fired at subsided into a walk, and, stopping every minute, went slowly down the hill. Having finished reloading, I gave my gun to Sádík, my Shikari, and told him to follow up the big one, while I went after the other one, which seemed hardest hit. Away I went as hard as I could run, slipping and frequently falling, for the steep hill-side was covered with grass and weeds. At first no blood was to be found, but after going some way, I discovered a few drops, and in a quarter of a mile came up with the Markhoor, who was slowly walking off about eighty yards below me. Dropping on one knee and holding my breath, I sent a shell through his neck, and he fell like a stone. He lay motionless for a few seconds, and then regaining his feet, rushed down the steep hill, splashing the grass and bushes with his blood. I followed, and slipped, fell, and scrambled (for it was too steep for me to keep my footing) for a couple of hundred yards, when I overtook him with his head in a bush, which he was too weak to force his way through. I seized him by his beautiful horns, and the knife finished him.

My Shikari, hearing me fire, relinquished his pursuit of the other Markhoor and rejoined me, saying he could find no blood. I was much annoyed, as I knew it was hit, but thinking that it might become stiff and lie down if left alone for a time, I allowed the Shikari to remain while we skinned the dead one.

This occupied some time, and when we had completed it and had something to eat, we took up the trail of the large Markhoor. We soon found a little blood, and when we came to ground where the footmarks could be distinctly made out, we came to the conclusion that he had a broken foreleg. We followed the track mile after mile, first down the steep hill, then for a very long way along a rocky watercourse, hoping all the time that as he did not attempt to ascend he must be badly wounded. Our hopes were at last destroyed by finding that the track turned up the face of a nearly perpendicular hill into thick forest : here the Markhoor appeared to have been joined by others, and we gave up the chase about dusk, several miles from camp. It was a steep ascent, through slippery forest, all the way home, and I was thoroughly tired out when I at last reached my tent long after dark. Having worn out all my grass-shoes, I had been walking nearly barefoot for a long distance, and had cut one of my feet on the stones.

I was too lame to follow up the chase on the following day, so I sent my second Shikari in pursuit, and managed to walk to Posháná. The Shikari came in in the evening, stating that he had seen the Markhoor, but had been unable to get near it.

In June 1871, I went to hunt in the Káj-í-Nág range ; a sportsman, who had been very successful there in former years, having kindly given me notes and a sketch of the ground.

I engaged my friend's old Shikari, but according to his account we found Markhoor much less plentiful than formerly, and for several days we had a succession of bad luck : I saw several Markhoor, but owing to no fault of my own, I never succeeded in getting a shot.

One disappointment was especially provoking : my Shikari and I had been sitting for upwards of an hour among some boulders in an open space in the forest, whence we had a clear view of the opposite hill-side : nothing was to be seen, and as we had not even found a track on our way up the ridge on which we had been sitting so long, we started to go higher up, to a place from whence we could see into another valley. Not expecting to see anything, I gave my rifle to my old Shikari, who usually followed close at my heels, and walked slowly up the ridge. We had gone about a couple of hundred yards when we came to a fallen tree, over which I stepped, while my Shikari took advantage of it to tie his grass shoe. I had not taken a dozen paces, when with a " *pst* " up jumped a fine Markhoor from the base of the tree where he had been lying, and stared me in the face within twenty yards! I put my hand back for my rifle, which, of course, was not forthcoming, and before it could be brought, the Markhoor had disappeared in the depths of the forest.

Several other blank days followed, until one morning, when I remained in camp to await the arrival of a coolie with letters, I sent my Shikari a short distance to reconnoitre a likely valley. It was not long before he sent back a man to say that he had seen game, and on joining him I found that two Markhoor were lying among some scattered birch trees on a spur at the other side of the valley. In order to stalk them it was absolutely necessary to cross some open ground, where we should be in full view ; but trusting to our being above our game, and to great caution, we contrived to pass the dangerous space without being detected.

Afterwards all was plain sailing, and in a short time I reached a ridge behind which the Markhoor were lying when last seen.

Looking carefully over, I saw a Markhoor standing about seventy yards off. It struck me that there was something unusual about his horns, but not liking to raise my head any higher to look for the other, I fired at the one in sight. He rushed down into the ravine in an evidently nearly helpless state, and then the second Markhoor gave me a fair running shot as he passed along the hill-side opposite to me. To complete the bad luck which had been haunting me, my rifle hung fire badly, and a miss was the result.

Meanwhile, the wounded Markhoor, whose shoulder was badly smashed, had scrambled down the ravine until he reached a larger one whose bed was filled with hardened snow. Down this he rolled and slid until the most active of my attendants overtook him, and managed to hold on till we arrived, although the task was almost beyond his strength. The buck was a fine old fellow, with gnarled horns, the right one of which measured forty-seven and a half inches. The left horn was seriously deformed, having apparently been broken off by an accident years before, after which it had acquired a peculiar lateral twist.

Urgent business recalled me from my hunting grounds a day or two afterwards, but the succeeding year but one saw me on the old spot in the month of September. The day I reached my old camp, after seeing the tents pitched in a secluded place, I went out in the afternoon on the chance of getting a shot in the immediate vicinity. I had not gone very far before we discovered Markhoor feeding some way below us in tolerably open forest. The hill-side was here intersected by numerous parallel ravines, running down to the rocky stream which drained the valley. These ravines were more or less clothed with bushes, while the ridges between them were more sparsely sprinkled with pines and other trees of considerable size. Descending towards the Markhoor I soon found myself most favorably placed behind capital shelter, immediately above where the Markhoor were still quietly browsing on the bushes. I could only see two, and it was extremely difficult to make out which had the best horns ; so, after waiting for some time, I fired at one which offered a clear shot. The smoke, which hung in the forest, prevented me from seeing the result, but my Shikari said that the Markhoor had fallen.

I quickly reloaded, but it was some time before I could see any of the others, and when at length four Markhoor went away below me to the right, where I had least expected them, I was in such an awkward position that I missed an easy shot. Directly afterwards another Markhoor, evidently lame, entered the bushes immediately below me, and as soon as he reappeared, I saw that he had a broken foreleg. Another shot or two finished him, and I thought at first that this was the one first fired at, but my Shikari declared that it was dead,—and so it proved. My first bullet had passed through the heart of the Markhoor I aimed at, and broken the foreleg of another which was hidden in the bushes just beyond.

Both heads were fair specimens, the first measuring forty one and a half, and the second forty inches.

CHAPTER XXVII.

THE STRAIGHT-HORNED MARKHOOR.

CAPRA JERDONI.

On North-West Frontier—*Már-khúr.*

IN the previous chapter I have given my reasons for considering that there are at least two distinct species of Markhoor, and I need not recapitulate them, but will merely give a brief description of the Sheikh Búdín, or, as it is sometimes called, the Trans-Indus variety of the straight-horned Markhoor.

This Markhoor is very much smaller than any of the spiral-horned races, and the beard and mane are much less developed. A reference to the photograph will explain the shape of the horns better than any written description, and will show how entirely they differ from those of the Kashmir Markhoor. I believe that the finest pair ever procured on the Sheikh Búdín hill measured thirty-two inches in length (direct measurement—not along the spiral). Those here photographed are about twenty-four inches long.

This wild goat inhabits the low but precipitous ranges on the right bank of the Indus to the south of Attock, and is perhaps most numerous in the immediate neighbourhood of the sanitarium already alluded to ; but I do not think that the exact limits of its distribution are at all accurately known, and I have good reasons for suspecting that it may be found in the hills between Attock and Kálábágh.

The hills which it inhabits being destitute of forest, and merely sprinkled with a few thorny bushes and stunted wild olive trees, the straight-horned Markhoor has fewer facilities for concealment than its Kashmir relative, and is therefore more easily found and stalked. It displays, however, the same fondness for precipitous ground, and frequently betakes itself to deep ravines with nearly perpendicular sides, separated by knife-like ridges of crumbling shale, where it is absolutely impossible to follow it.

A well-known old Indian sportsman assured me that he had, on more than one occasion, seen these Markhoor feeding in trees many feet from the ground, and from what I know of the habits of all the wild goats, I should have had no hesitation in believing the story even on much less reliable authority.

They are much less shy than the Markhoor of the Himalayas, and at Sheikh Búdín they wander all over the hill and are frequently seen from the roadside, and occasionally from the windows of the houses. It is even said that, during the winter months, when the station is deserted, they may be seen among the buildings !

XX

STRAIGHT-HORNED MARKHOOR

CAPRA JERDONI

Published by Thacker, Spink & Co., Calcutta.

In 1871, I had to visit the station of Dérá Ismail Khán on duty, and I took advantage of being so near Markhoor ground to obtain ten days' leave. The Deputy Commissioner kindly laid out horses for me, and I galloped over the dreary forty miles of sand that intervene between Dérá and the sanitarium.

On my way up the steep and rugged path which leads to the top of the hill, I saw some Markhoor by the roadside. I thought that this augured well for my chances of sport.

Having secured the services of a Shikari named Sháhzádá, I sent out my bed, some food, and two or three 'mussuks' of water on the evening of the 24th of September, and, accompanied by Sháhzádá, took a stroll over the hill in the direction of my sleeping place. We had not gone much more than half a mile when I discovered a male Markhoor feeding under some perpendicular cliffs: he was in a good place to stalk, and we were not long in getting within easy distance. On looking over the rocks I saw two small Markhoor within sixty yards, but I would not fire at them. Sháhzádá bothered me to fire, but I refused, saying that they were too small: he replied "it is a big one" and became so excited, and made such a noise, that the Markhoor took alarm and made off. It turned out that Sháhzádá *had* seen the big one, while I, being a little below him, could not possibly see it, as it was behind a thick bush. The Markhoor halted for a moment after running some distance, and gave me a long snap shot which I just missed. On the way to our bivouac we saw some more Markhoor in the distance, but it was too late to go after them.

At daylight next morning we commenced to ascend the hill on the opposite side of the valley in which we had slept, and we had not gone far before we saw some Markhoor above us. On reaching the crest of the ridge we found that there was a large flock, eight or ten of them being good-sized males. They were on the very top of the ridge, and it was impossible to stalk them where they were, so I lay down to watch them. They were about three hundred yards off, and Sháhzádá kept asking me to fire, which of course I would not do. After waiting for more than half an hour, the Markhoor suddenly took fright and made off, and I then found that Sháhzádá had again spoiled everything by sending a man for water, who had come straight up the hill and driven the Markhoor away. We marked the direction they went in, and after making a long round, we got to the head of the valley where they had stopped. Here we found eight or nine old fellows lying down in a capital place, but on our way to stalk them we unfortunately disturbed another flock, which went off and gave the alarm.

Two males were next discovered lying under a tree at the foot of a high precipice. We went round to the top, but I found that we were above three hundred yards off. We, however, managed to scramble down a nullah and reach a level place above the Markhoor. I could only see one; he was lying in the shade of the tree, and was fully one hundred and seventy yards off, but as he was nearly straight below me, I used the lowest sight and shot him dead. The other one then jumped up, but did not show himself till he was more than two hundred yards off, and I missed him. The one killed was a fair specimen of the species: his photograph is here given.

We were now a long way from home, the day had been very hot, our water was nearly exhausted, and my ' *Chaplis* ' (a sort of sandal) had been cut to pieces by the sharp rocks, so I had to borrow my Shikari's and get along as I best could. At last we halted to see if there was any water in a small spring ; we found it a mass of mud, having been trampled in by the Markhoor. As we reached it I happened to look up, and saw a flock of Markhoor within one hundred yards. I sent for my rifle, which had been left a short distance below, and had just time to put in two cartridges before the Markhoor began to move. I fired at the biggest one, and seeing him stagger, fired the other barrel at him. Unfortunately a small one got in the way and was knocked over, but the first one only went a few yards before he also fell.

We cleared out the spring, and managed to procure a few drops of water which we gladly drank—black as ink though it was. I thought I should never reach the top of the hill, and I was thoroughly tired out when I at last got home.

On the 26th I took a rest, and I was just going out shooting again on the 27th, when I received a telegram which necessitated my immediate return.

Having sent off all my baggage, I left Sheikh Búdín about 3 A.M. on the 28th, and went down to a ridge from which there was a good look-out. It was still dark when I got there, so I sat down and waited for daylight. Soon after dawn we saw Markhoor on the opposite hill, so we crossed over to look for them. They had gone, however, and though we explored some most likely-looking precipitous ravines, we could see nothing of them. Going along the ridge in the direction of Paniálá (the dâk bungalow at the foot of the hill) we met a flock coming over from the other side. They were only about one hundred yards off, but the sun was in my eyes, and I had to get Sháhzádá to shade them before I could fire. I picked out the biggest male, which galloped a short distance and then fell dead.

XXI

CHAPTER XXVIII

THE HIMALAYAN IBEX.

CAPRA SIBIRICA.

In Kashmir—*Kél.*   In Thibet—*Skín.*   In Pángí and Lahoul—*Tangrol.*

ALTHOUGH the name of Ibex is so familiar, there are few people, not naturalists, who really know what an Ibex is : the name is frequently applied to wild goats which have no resemblance to the real Ibex, of which there are several species inhabiting various parts of Europe, Asia and Africa ; and which, though differing considerably in some respects, form a very marked group.

The type of the group is the Alpine Ibex or Steinbok (*Capra Ibex*), now almost extinct in Switzerland, and only found in any numbers in the preserves of the King of Italy. Their pursuit was the favorite sport of that keen hunter Victor Emmanuel.

Other Ibex are, *Capra pyrenaica*, the Bouquetin of the Pyrenees ; *C. nubiana* from Africa ; *C. caucasica* from the Caucasus and parts of Persia ; *C. ægagrus* from Persia, Sindh and Bilúchistán ; and *C. Sibirica* from Siberia, Central Asia and the Himalayas.

All these Ibex have long gracefully curved horns, sweeping back over their quarters, and giving them a majestic appearance. The horns are generally more or less ringed or knotted.

Contrary to the general belief, the typical Ibex has not even a tuft on his chin, but both the species found in India have long flowing beards.

The Himalayan Ibex is found in Kashmir, Ládák, Pángí, Lahoul, Báltistán, Zánskár, Spítí, and Koonawur, but is not met with to the south or east of the river Sutlej, nor does it inhabit the extreme southern slopes of the Himalayas, but keeps more in the interior of the range. In Kashmir, for instance, Ibex are numerous on the mountains to the north of the valley, while none are to be found on the Pír Pánjál or Káj-í-Nág ranges. Similarly, in Chambá and Koonawur the sportsman must penetrate some distance into the hills before he has the chance of seeing an Ibex.

The old male Ibex is indeed a splendid animal, and living as he does amidst the most magnificent scenery in the world, there is a charm in his pursuit which can hardly be rivalled by that of any other animal.

He is very stoutly made, and attains a height of about ten hands. The general color of the coat is a dark chocolate, with large patches of dirty white, varying a good deal according to the age of the animal. There is a ridge of coarse dark hair along the back,

T

and the chin is adorned with a profuse black beard. The hair is rather coarse and brittle, and in winter there is a thick down or under-fleece called '*pashm*,' which, however, is also possessed by most of the animals inhabiting the higher Himalayas.

This '*pashm*,' and not the true hair, is the celebrated 'shawl-wool' of Thibet, of which the Kashmir shawls are made.

The horns are scimitar shaped, much knotted, and tapering; they are more massive than those of any other species: the largest pair of which I have authentic information were fifty-four inches long, and, if I recollect right, upwards of thirteen inches in circumference.

Female Ibex are about a third smaller than the males, with shorter hair of more uniform color, and their horns about a foot long.

The Ibex inhabits the upper portions of the hills where it is found, rarely descending to the limits of the forest, but preferring open and precipitous ground. Even during the winter Ibex do not, as a rule, descend very low, but resort to places where, from the steepness of the hill-side, the snow does not lie in any quantity.

Here they may be detained for weeks by a heavy fall, picking a scanty subsistence from the scattered tufts of withered herbage that here and there crop out of the crevices of the rock. At this season males and females herd together, but as the snow melts and the time for the birth of the young approaches, the old males forsake the females altogether, and, as the summer advances, retire to the most inaccessible mountains, frequently sleeping during the day above the limits of vegetation, and descending great distances to feed in the mornings and evenings. The best time to shoot Ibex is when the young grass is just beginning to sprout along the margin of the snow in May and June: after the hardships and frequent long fasts of winter they feed greedily on the fresh young shoots, and in secluded spots may even be found lying down on the grassy slopes during the day.

Most ridiculous stories have been told and repeated about the Ibex; such as their alleged habit of jumping down precipices and alighting on their horns, or hanging by them in dangerous places until they can make good their footing; while the popular belief appears to be that they pass their whole time far above the limits of eternal snow, perched upon needle-like pinnacles of ice, quite regardless of such considerations as rest or pasturage. Their powers of traversing precipitous and dangerous ground are quite sufficiently wonderful without needless exaggeration.

Although an excessively wary animal, the Ibex is usually found on such broken ground, that if due care be taken, it is not very difficult to obtain a shot. The grand rule, as in all other hill-stalking, is to keep well above the herd, whose vigilance is chiefly directed beneath them. In places where they have been much disturbed, one or two of the herd usually keep a sharp look-out while the rest are feeding, and on the slightest suspicion of danger the sentries utter a loud whistle, which is a signal for a general rush to the nearest rocks. Should the sportsman succeed in obtaining a shot before he is observed by the Ibex, he may often have time to fire several shots before they are out of range, as they appear to be completely stupefied and confused by the sudden noise, the cause of which they are unable to account for if they neither see nor smell their enemy.

The first time I ever hunted for Ibex was in June 1861, when on my way to Ládák I stopped at the small village of Kúlan, in the Sindh Valley. Having secured the services of a village Shikari, I crossed to the left bank of the stream, and ascended the mountain. For a long distance the path led through forest, the trees composing which changed in character as we got higher, until we at length emerged from the birch forest and found ourselves in an open grassy valley in which herds of sheep and goats were feeding. This valley was enclosed on both sides and at the upper end by high rocky peaks, which were still well covered with snow. A glacier blocked the head of the valley, and from this icy source a small stream took its rise. My Shikari assured me that Ibex were to be found here. It was pretty late in the afternoon when we reached the place, and having already had a long climb we selected a spot for a bivouac, and merely took a short stroll in the evening, seeing nothing but a Bárá Sing Stag.

Before daylight next morning I unwillingly enough left my comfortable blankets and began to mount the snowy ridge above us. We soon found tracks of Ibex, but only saw an old Bear and her cubs, who were, of course, allowed to remain in peace. Reaching the summit of the ridge, we carefully looked over, and soon discovered the horns of a fine male Ibex about four hundred yards off. As we were watching him we observed the remainder of the herd coming up a hollow straight towards us, so I lay quiet until they fed up to us. First, a female and her kid appeared, then two or three young males, but I waited for an old one. At last, however, a provoking young male jumped on to a rock and looked down on us, so I was obliged to fire, and knocked him over. The herd now stood to gaze, but the villager with my second rifle becoming excited, ran on with it. I had to follow him, seize my rifle, and fire a hurried shot, which I accordingly missed. The dead Ibex had meanwhile rolled down the hill a considerable distance into a ravine half full of snow, to which I had some difficulty in descending. I found that he had horns only about twenty inches in length, but as it was my first essay in Ibex shooting, I was tolerably pleased at having bagged a buck, my first shot. Having skinned him, we proceeded to explore another part of the hill, and saw some more Ibex, but in perfectly inaccessible places, and, as I had promised to meet a friend at Kúlan, I returned to that village.

In 1862, I made straight for Ibex ground. Passing through Islámábád I crossed the Margan Pass into the Wardwan Valley on the 7th of May. Fresh snow had just fallen, and the whole of my party suffered more or less from snow blindness. My own face was blistered all over, and my eyes were very painful for two or three days. Perhaps this interfered with my shooting ; at any rate, I succeeded in missing or only wounding several Bears at which I had shots on my way up the Fariábád river, which joins the Wardwan at Márú. At length, on the 17th, my luck seemed to change, and I bagged two splendid Snow Bears and two Ibex, but the latter were only small ones. During the next week I did not do much, only bagging a couple of immense Bears and a small buck Ibex, the latter by a 'fluke'; for I fired at a larger one who was standing alongside him. On the 23rd, I saw a herd of Ibex close to camp, but after a climb I only got a long shot as they were moving off, and missed.

Not long afterwards I saw a magnificent old male crossing some snow far above us ; I immediately started in pursuit, and in the course of the next hour came across seven Musk Deer, at all of which I might have had easy shots. At length we came to a narrow and very steep ravine filled with hard snow, and I was with difficulty climbing up this, when I suddenly saw the old Ibex on some rocks above me; he was accompanied by two or three females. Resting my elbows on a large stone, I had to get my Shikari to hold my feet while I fired at the Ibex, who was standing facing me; I felt sure of the shot, as the distance was not more than one hundred yards. On the smoke clearing away, however, the Ibex was still in the same position. I now tried the second barrel, but with no better result, and he made off. My Shikari then informed me that both my bullets had struck between the horns. I was much annoyed at missing such a fair chance, and inwardly resolved that I would not leave the valley until I had killed a similar beast.

I went on to the very top of the range of hills, until I arrived above the spot where I had killed a small Ibex a few days before. We lay down and watched the valleys beneath us nearly all day. Towards evening I made out three animals at an immense distance, and the telescope showed that they were fine old Ibex. I watched them go to some rocks where I hoped to find them in the morning.

Next day, long before daylight, I set out to look for the Ibex. When about a mile from the place where I had last seen them I discovered them feeding by the river. Descending into a broad green valley where we were out of sight, we made for the rocks above them. Several Bears were in our way, and I was rather alarmed lest in their retreat they should disturb the nobler game, but fortunately they all went off up the hill. Having reached the rocks we found that the Ibex had moved; so we climbed carefully along the crags above the river until we caught sight of six or seven fine fellows quietly feeding about six hundred yards below us. We lay down and watched them for about an hour, and a careful inspection through the glass showed them to be all grand old males with little to choose between them. All this while two Snow Bears lay on a rock within one hundred and fifty yards of us, coolly stretching themselves and looking at us. The Ibex having fed and played about for a long time, at length lay down, one by one, under the shadow of a large rock. After waiting a short time to see that they were comfortably settled, I began the stalk.

First going still farther up the hill, I made a circuit of half a mile, so as to get the rocks, under whose shelter the Ibex had lain down, between myself and them. Having again descended and reached their level, I cocked both barrels of my rifle, and crawled carefully and silently over the few yards of ground which still intervened between me and the rock, taking the utmost care not to rustle a leaf, and also keeping a sharp look-out lest any of the wary brutes should outflank me. Having reached the spot from which I hoped to get a shot, I paused a little to take breath, and then raising my head by inches, peered carefully over. There, within ten yards, lay a noble Ibex on his side, fast asleep, with his back turned towards me: the horns only of another were visible. Aiming between the shoulders of the unconscious animal I slowly pressed the trigger, and the fine old buck lay struggling on the ground. One other only went forward and stood at about fifty yards, when my second bullet crashed through his ribs; he made a spring or two, and again stood still; I took my other rifle and dropped him with a bullet through the neck. As he struggled towards the edge of the precipice, my Shikari, Sádík, seized him by the horns and called to me for assistance. I ran up and caught hold just in time to prevent the buck from going over, and held him fast while Sádík cut his throat. We now looked for the first one, who had managed to stagger to his feet, and then roll over the precipice. To my satisfaction we saw it lying on the snow by the river's edge far below us; had it rolled another yard it would have been swept away by the torrent. As it was, it must have fallen a sheer three hundred feet without touching anything, but fortunately the horns were uninjured. Sádík climbed down by a roundabout way and cut off the head. The horns (those photographed) measured forty-three and a half inches; the other pair measured forty-one inches. On my way back to camp I met an officer coming up to shoot, and as I was anxious to press on to Ládák, I resigned the shooting in the valley to him.

As I was bent upon securing as many different varieties of 'Large Game' as possible, I did not devote myself much to Ibex shooting for several years, and, although I shot a few in the interim, it was not till 1870 that I again spent much time in Ibex country.

In May of that year I crossed the Chéní Pass into Pángí, accompanied by my wife and A, a brother officer.

According to custom A and I had separated for about a fortnight, and our camps had, during that time, been many miles apart. On meeting at the appointed rendezvous we talked over all we had done, and formed plans for the future. I had had excellent sport, having bagged several fine Ibex, while A, who was quite a novice at the work, had not been successful, but was still most anxious to secure a fine pair of horns. From A's own account it was pretty clear that his ill-success might be attributed to his want of experience and ignorance of the native language, which prevented him from understanding his Shikari.

I therefore proposed that he should go out with me, the arrangement being that he was to have first shot. To this he agreed, and having heard of a very likely hill, we moved camp, crossed the river, and after ascending the opposite hill for about a mile, pitched our tents under the shelter of some pine trees on the banks of a mountain torrent.

Behind our tents rose a high steep hill, covered with short grass to its summit, but so smooth and open that it did not appear at all probable that it was a favorite haunt of the Ibex. At the back of this hill, however, we were assured, that there was a rocky valley, which was nearly a sure find, and we accordingly resolved to explore it next day.

Before daylight we were up and dressed, and after the welcome cup of tea, which one never enjoys so much as in camp, we commenced the ascent of the hill. Nothing is so monotonous or fatiguing as climbing a long hill, whose summit one can see from the base: the task appears nearly hopeless from the first; the progress one makes seems to be so terribly slow; there are no breaks in the dull sameness of the journey, no conspicuous marks by which one's brief halts for breathing time may be judiciously arranged; no hope of; possibly coming upon game. However, all things come to an end, and after steadily plodding along for nearly three hours, we reached the crest of the ridge, threw ourselves on the ground, crept to the edge of the precipitous valley beyond, and carefully reconnoitred it. The Shikaris had at least been right in describing the ground as being likely ; better it would be difficult to find. Far beneath us flowed a considerable stream, one of the affluents of the river which we had crossed the previous day, and from its farther bank rose a rugged mountain, whose face was furrowed by numerous rocky ravines, with frequent grassy slopes between them. Occasional groups of pine trees were dotted here and there, while juniper and other bushes were plentiful. Towards the top of the hill were numerous patches of snow, while away to our right the ridge on which we lay ran up to meet others, which terminated in a lofty peak, still clothed in its winter's robe of white. The slope between us and the stream was considerably steeper than the opposite one, but owing to its aspect, the vegetation was more advanced. We lay for probably more than half an hour anxiously scanning the slopes with our glasses, but neither we, nor the sharp-eyed Shikaris with us, could see a living thing. At last we rose, and went up towards the head of the valley, in hopes that we might find our game in some concealed ravine, or at least come across tracks which might show us in what direction they had gone. We saw nothing however, and having proceeded far enough to discover that there were no likely feeding grounds beyond, we retraced our steps, and began to explore lower down the valley.

We had not gone very far below where we had first looked down on the valley, when we saw a Snow Bear busily digging up roots on a grassy flat, some little way up the opposite hill-side. We sat down to watch him, and as we had seen no traces of Ibex, we were beginning to discuss the advisability of A's stalking him, when a white object, some distance above the Bear, caught my eye. Turning the telescope on it, I discovered a fine male Ibex, and a further scrutiny showed that there was a large herd lying among the rocks and bushes, and that several of them had large horns. The next question was, how to approach them. I thought I saw a way of doing so, by going to the head of the valley and coming round above the herd, but the natives with us declared it was impossible to do so, as we should be stopped by impracticable ground. This I afterwards discovered to be untrue, the fact being that the Shikaris did not like the prospect of a long extra walk.

There was evidently no other way by which the Ibex could be approached, so the only alternative was to sit still and wait patiently till they chose to move. I knew that they would shift their ground for their evening feed, and I trusted that they would select some place where we might be able to stalk them.

The hours of the long day passed slowly away, and the Ibex as usual remained on the spot which they had chosen for their midday siesta. Occasionally one would rise, stretch itself, perhaps nibble a few leaves, and lie down again ; and on one occasion two large males had a playful tilting match, rising on their hind legs and striking at each other like young kids.

Early in the afternoon two Snow Bears, who had probably not long woke up from their winter sleep, and were therefore anxious to make up for their lengthened fast, emerged from some bushes, and began feeding close to the Ibex, who paid but little attention to them.

At last, just as we were beginning to despair of their giving us a chance that day, there was a general movement among the herd. First, an old female rose, and after gazing earnestly down the hill for some time began to slowly descend. Another and another followed her example, until all that were visible were walking in our direction, and last of all six grand old males, conspicuous by their whiteness, came out from the shade of some trees where they had been lying all day, and joined the rest of the herd. This was the signal for a general advance ; the Ibex gradually quickened their pace and at last came down the hill at full gallop, evidently with the intention of crossing the stream a little lower down the valley.

Presently they were out of sight, and now came the opportunity for which we had waited so long. Seizing our rifles, we sprang to our feet and started at best pace down the hill. Having reached the watercourse I found that A, who had not had much practice in mountaineering, had been outpaced, and I had to wait for him. This was annoying, as moments were precious, although I was chiefly anxious on his account. However, he was not very far behind, and on his overtaking me, we followed the stream until we reached the place where, as we saw by the tracks, the Ibex had crossed it.

The wind was all right, and I knew that they could not be far off. Parallel ravines ran from the top of the ridge which we had just left to the bed of the stream : down one of them we had just come, and it was probable that the herd were in the one ahead of us. Climbing up some low rocks, we looked into it and saw the Ibex unsuspiciously feeding on the opposite side.

The large males were nearly a hundred and fifty yards off, but in good positions, so I pointed one out to A, and told him to take the shot, while I would look out for my opportunity. A's aim was true, and the Ibex fell dead. The startled herd rushed in various directions, and a fine fellow coming rather towards me, I hit him hard with a solid Henry bullet (I had no Express rifle in those days). He went slowly away and I fired two or three more shots, hitting him again, and at last stopping him.

We now went to inspect A's first Ibex, which had a very handsome and perfect pair of horns, nearly forty inches in length. We cut off the head, and then proceeded to recover my buck. I had a rather awkward climb to reach him, and finding him still alive, had to give him another shot. His horns, which measured forty-two inches, were much curved, and a very perfect pair.

It was now late, and it was evident that if we returned by the way we had come, it would be far on in the night before we arrived at our tents. Our attendants, however, said they knew of a short cut, and we accordingly started without loss of time. We had to go straight up the hill above where we then were, and we had not gone far before we came to a sheer wall of rock about twenty-five feet high, which seemed to be an effectual bar to our farther progress. At some little distance, however, we discovered the withered stem of an old tree, which grew close to the wall, and with the aid of one or two ropes, which we fortunately had with us, we contrived to climb to the top. This was the only serious obstacle we encountered, but we soon found that if this was the shortest way it was also the roughest and steepest, and the remainder of the ascent was one enormous flight of stairs with steps from three to six feet high! It was after dark when we at length surmounted the last step, and found ourselves on the open hill-side above our tents. There were no great impediments in the way now, but the hill being very steep and the grass slippery, we often had considerable difficulty in keeping our footing, and we were by no means sorry when we met some men who had come out with lights to show us the way to camp.

We had had a hard day's work, but that is little thought of when sport is good, and I look back upon that day as a most enjoyable one.

Circumstances prevented me from again visiting Ibex ground till 1882, when having obtained long leave, I made the best of my way to Pángí; and having crossed the *Pángí* Chéní Pass on the 26th of April, found that I was the first to arrive in the valley. The snow-fall had been unusually heavy, and although Ibex were not quite so numerous as they were twelve years before, I had excellent sport, and secured several good heads.

One of my last days' sport so well illustrates the difficulties and pleasures of my favorite pastime, that, at the risk of tiring the reader, I will describe it in detail.

At a point where the Chandrá-Bághá, or infant Chenáb, cuts its way between beetling cliffs, along the face of which rough stairs of stone and airy galleries of hastily trimmed pine trees form the road which rather tries the nerves of the unaccustomed traveller, a rushing torrent comes tumbling down a cleft between two deodar-clad hills, and contributes its quota to swell the volume of the great stream which ultimately exercises the utmost ingenuity and resources of our Engineers to span and restrain it. Along the margin of this torrent, in the direction of its icy sources, lay the path which I had to follow in order to reach my hunting ground. Path, in the proper acceptation of the word, there was none; but we had to pick our way over gravel and boulders, and occasional fallen trees washed down by the stream when in flood, until after a scramble of a little more than a mile, we reached a spot where the valley forked, and two streams of nearly equal size united their waters. Looking upwards, we could see that a huge rocky hill with craggy summit divided the two streams towards their sources, while from the main peak a long ridge ran down towards where we stood, terminating in a sharp tongue with precipitous banks which filled the acute angle at the junction of the two streams. Climbing the steep side of the sharp wedge which separated the waters, I found myself on a tolerably level spot, surrounded by young deodars; and here I determined to establish my bivouac.

Having reached the halting place pretty early in the day, there was ample time to make the few necessary camp arrangements, previous to going out to reconnoitre in the afternoon. These being completed, we set out to explore the upper parts of the valley; and in order to obtain the best possible view on both sides, we continued to ascend the ridge on which we already were established. After threading our way through a quantity of fallen timber which encumbered the ground over the space of several acres, and climbing for a consider-able distance through pine forest, we reached an open plateau where the bright green grass showed that it was the resort of shepherds with their flocks and herds, during the summer months. There we commanded a view of both valleys for a considerable distance, the beds of their respective streams at this point not being above half a mile apart. The right hand valley—that of the *proper* right branch of the stream—appeared to be the most likely for game ; and the local Shikari who accompanied me told me that he fully expected to find a good herd of Ibex in it.

Sitting down under shelter of a tree, we carefully reconnoitred both valleys, scanning every ravine and slope that was clear of snow, with both binoculars and telescope ; but for a long time without success. At length a solitary male Ibex appeared high up the hill on the opposite site of the left-hand valley, and after moving along its face for about half a mile, took up his position on a rocky ridge, where he lay down. His horns were not very large, being apparently only about thirty inches in length ; but as Ibex are rarely found alone, we thought it very likely that others might be concealed not far from him, and accordingly resolved to stalk him. It was easy enough to descend under cover of the forest to the bed of the stream, where we were perfectly concealed from the view of the Ibex ; and having crossed by a snow bridge, we commenced the long ascent. When about half our task was accomplished, a herd of Ibex, among which were several old males of conspicuous whiteness, suddenly appeared on a stony slope in the right-hand valley ; but having gone so far, we determined not to relinquish the pursuit of the solitary buck, and accordingly left the herd to be followed up another time. At length we reached the point for which we had been making, on a level with the spot where the Ibex had lain down ; and we now had no difficulty in making our way to a ridge from whence we could obtain a good view of the Ibex and develop our plan of attack. The ridge was gained, the wind was favorable, and the Ibex was lying, apparently quite unsuspicious, where we had last seen him. I had, however, hardly adjusted my telescope so as to make a careful inspection of the ground, when a mass of cloud came sweeping along the hill tops, and a bitterly cold gust was accompanied by falling snowflakes. This gust was in the opposite direction to that in which the wind had hitherto been gently blowing ; and we had hardly observed the change before it conveyed a warning to the delicate senses of the Ibex. In a moment he had risen, and, after a few minutes of hesitation, moved quickly up the hill and vanished from our sight. Pursuit under the circumstances was useless ; and, as it was now too late to follow the other herd, we descended and returned to our bivouac.

Before daylight the following morning we set out in search of the herd. Instead of going along the ridge as on the previous afternoon, we followed the bed of the right-hand stream, along which we went until we reached a point where nearly perpendicular banks of earth and gravel bounded the ravine on either side. Turning to our left, we had some difficulty in finding a way to the top of the cliff, but having at length surmounted the obstacle, we reached a level grassy plateau, on which were scattered clumps of fine deodars. From the farther margin of this plain extensive stony slopes stretched upwards to the foot of the frowning crags of the mountain above. A clear view could not be obtained from the plateau, so we took advantage of a small ravine which ran down the hill-side, and took up a commanding position from which the whole of the slopes were visible.

For a long time we could see nothing, but at last my Shikari discovered several old male Ibex which were grazing on a small hillock at the very foot of the crags, just where a water-course issued from a narrow gorge about three quarters of a mile farther up the valley.

U

This watercourse cut a deep channel for itself through the gravel of the slopes and soft soil of the plateau, and joined the main stream about a mile above where we left it. On the far side of the watercourse were some gentle grassy slopes from which the snow had partially melted, and beyond them again a semicircle of snow-clad hills and glaciers of considerable size enclosed the head of the valley.

In the basin thus formed the main stream took its rise. The scene was wild in the extreme, the whole of the valley being deeply covered with snow except the slopes before us ; and it was evident that the Ibex had no other grazing grounds, and must therefore necessarily descend during the course of the day. It was impossible to approach them where they were first seen, and there was nothing to be done but to exercise patience, and be in readiness to take advantage of any move on their part which would afford a chance of a successful stalk.

For a long time they appeared to be unwilling to leave their elevated position ; from time to time one or more would lie down while the remainder continued to crop the scanty herbage, and after a brief rest would rejoin their companions. At last there was a general move downwards, and the herd gradually worked their way along the nearer bank of the ravine through which the stream flowed, until they were little above our level. The old males first observed had, in the meantime, been joined by a number of smaller ones, and there were now about thirty Ibex of all sizes, and of both sexes, in sight. We were in hopes that they would have come down to the stony slopes, but it soon became apparent that they were making for the more tempting grassy slopes at the other side of the ravine. After the usual amount of hesitation, without which Ibex never seem to make up their minds to any combined movement, one after another crossed the snow, which nearly filled the ravine, at the point where they reached its margin, and commenced to feed greedily on the open spaces beyond. As they filed across we had a clear view of each against the white background, and could now make out that there were several good heads, and that one old patriarch carried a really fine pair of much curved horns. While the main body of the herd continued to feed in company, advancing slowly in an irregular line across a nearly level flat, two or three of the old males, including the largest one, held themselves aloof from the others, and after cropping a few mouthfuls lay down on the brink of the ravine.

Suddenly the main herd, for no ostensible reason, left off grazing and galloped back at full speed to the ravine, into which they disappeared ; and the swell of the ground prevented me from seeing whether they crossed it at once or remained in it. Beyond turning their heads to see what was going on, the old bucks took no notice of this movement of their juniors, and it was evident that they had no cause for alarm. One by one, however, at uncertain intervals, rose from his siesta, and followed the direction the herd had taken, the old patriarch being the last but one to move, and drop quietly down the low cliff on whose margin he had been lying. One only now remained in sight, a fair-sized buck with horns upwards of thirty inches long ; but his erratic movements gave us a lot of trouble. Instead of following his companions he continued to move down the hill, skirting the edge of the ravine, and apparently looking out for an easy crossing, while he occasionally turned aside to nibble some particularly inviting tuft. His progress was so slow that my patience was nearly exhausted when he at last reached the foot of the slopes and descended into a sort of shallow basin where he was concealed from view. No time was lost in commencing operations, but we had not gone far before a new difficulty presented itself. Not far above us were three or four juvenile Ibex which it was necessary to drive quietly away without alarming the herd. This was successfully done, and as they moved straight up the hill there was no possibility of their being seen by the lot that we were stalking.

So far all had gone well, but we were still in ignorance as to where the herd was lying. After resting a few moments we pursued our way, and soon reached a ridge from whence we hoped to have a good view. Cautiously raising my head, I caught sight of two or three Ibex lying on a gravelly slope not far above me, and a dip in the ground showed that there would be no difficulty in approaching them. Drawing back a little, I ascended the hill, and the ground proved to be so favorable, that I was enabled to walk without stooping until I had arrived within less than a hundred yards of the unsuspecting herd. A low juniper bush grew between me and them, and under cover of this I contrived to crawl quietly up, until, on carefully peering through the bush, I could see a young buck lying within twenty yards of me. He *seemed* to be gazing right into my eyes, but as he continued quietly chewing the cud and soon turned to watch the proceedings of some of his companions, it was evident that he had not observed me. Three or four females and young ones were grazing just beyond him, and on the top of a knoll, about a hundred yards higher up, several rounded arches showed the position of the old males, their horns alone being visible. For half an hour I continued to watch them, and I was beginning to get a little tired of my somewhat cramped position, when one of the old males rose, stretched himself, and then walked quietly away. The others soon followed his example ; the females and kids moved off in the same direction ; and finally the young buck thought it time to rejoin the herd, and he also disappeared over the knoll.

As soon as all had vanished, I slowly rose, and I could then see that the Ibex had crossed a low ridge, and I had only to follow them up promptly to be certain of obtaining an easy shot.

To my disgust, however, I discovered that a ravine which interposed between me and where the Ibex had been lying, and which I had previously been unable to see into, was impassable at the point where I stood, and it became necessary to go farther up the hill and seek for a practicable crossing. The hill-side was steep, and we had to climb nearly a quarter of a mile before we could cross the ravine, and then the crossing was by no means easy, as the banks were rotten, and nearly perpendicular. We accomplished it safely, however, and then descended as rapidly as possible to where we had left the Ibex. Being now well above them, we were pretty certain of success, but on looking over the ridge for which we had been making, we were just in time to see the last of the herd moving slowly along a ledge nearly straight below us. His horns seemed to be a fine pair, and I lost no time in sending a bullet through him, and I fired a second shot as he plunged forward after a momentary stagger. I could just see that this bullet struck also, as the Ibex disappeared round the corner of a steep cliff. But where are the rest of the herd ? Hastily reloading I ran forward to the edge of a deep ravine a short distance ahead, and from below me out dashed the big Ibex, whose horns I could not fail to recognise. He would not stand, but as he crossed some deep snow I sent the contents of both barrels after him in quick succession, and to my delight he went floundering down the snow in a helpless manner, that showed that he could not escape. He disappeared behind a rock, and as I could not descend into the ravine at the point from which I fired, I went back to look for the first Ibex. I soon found him standing just below where I had last seen him, and a third bullet stretched him lifeless on the spot. On going down to him I found that my first shot had been a mortal one, but that the second had only passed through the base of his horns. The horns, which had looked so large from above, proved disappointing on a closer inspection, as they only measured thirty-one inches. Meanwhile, the big Ibex, though grievously wounded, with both a fore-leg and a hind-leg broken, had contrived to scramble out of the snow, and was slowly and painfully endeavouring to ascend the opposite bank of the ravine. We soon overtook it, and the knife terminated its existence. It was with considerable satisfaction that I contemplated the splendid animal which it had taken us so long to circumvent. As it was early in the season, his coat was still in good condition, and the head, with the flowing beard and rugged arched horns, formed a trophy which any sportsman would be glad to hang on his walls. The horns, though nothing extraordinary, were a perfect and symmetrical pair, measuring forty-three inches in length. Skinning and cutting up the Ibex, for the benefit of the coolies in camp, occupied some time, but it was still early in the afternoon when we reached our camp, every one well satisfied with the day's work.

OORIAL

OVIS CYCLOCEROS

Published by Thacker, Spink & Co., Calcutta.

CHAPTER XXIX.

THE OORIAL.

OVIS CYCLOCEROS.

In the Panjáb—*Úriál—Úriár.*

THE majority of the known species of wild sheep inhabit lofty mountains, living at such an elevation that they are always in a cool atmosphere, and although none of them have the woolly fleece of the domestic sheep, their thickset coats of brittle and hollow hairs are admirably adapted to protect them from the icy blasts to which they are frequently exposed.

The Oorial is an exception to the general rule, being found among the rocky ravines of the Salt Range and other low stony hills in the upper part of the Panjab, and along the frontiers of Sindh, where the temperature frequently attains something very like furnace heat. I doubt, indeed, whether it would be possible to find, in the whole world, a fiercer heat than is to be experienced in those narrow gorges during the summer months ; when the rays of the midday sun have explored their lowest depths ; when not a breath of air is stirring ; when every leaf has been curled up and rendered dry as tinder by the radiation from the glowing rocks ; and hardly even an ant has energy to move. I have tried hunting under such circumstances, but should not care to repeat the experiment.

It was long supposed that the ' Shápoo ' of Ládák (*Ovis Vignei*) was the same as the Oorial ; but this has been proved to be incorrect : the ' Shápoo ' is a much larger animal, and differs considerably in other respects. It is not yet known for certain, whether the ' Oorren' of Astor and Báltistán is a distinct species or not ; it is at any rate very closely allied to the ' Shápoo.'

The male Oorial is a noble animal, and though really excessively timid, an old ram has a certain air of defiance as he throws up his head and gazes in the direction from whence he first suspects danger. Standing about thirty-six inches at the shoulder, he is well formed both for speed and for climbing, the body being compactly and strongly built, while the limbs are long and deer-like. The general color is a dark reddish brown above, while the lower parts and legs are of a lighter tint. Old rams have a peculiar saddle-shaped mark on the back. The throat and chest are adorned by a long flowing ruff of coarse black hair, which becomes hoary with age. The horns are somewhat like those of the domestic ram, but have only one twist, tending, when perfect, to form a circle. They generally attain a length of about twenty-six inches, with a circumference of ten inches, but they occasionally grow to thirty-two inches and even more. The eyepits of this sheep are very much developed, and secrete a gummy substance. The females are much smaller than the males and of a rather lighter color, without any vestige of a beard, and with very small horns.

Oorial are usually found in herds varying from six or seven to twenty or thirty in number : during the winter both sexes may be found together, but as the hot weather approaches the males live a good deal apart from the females.

The low ranges inhabited by the Oorial are for the most part stony and barren, some of them covered with low scrub or dotted here and there with thorny bushes ; occasionally, they are craggy and precipitous, while in the valleys between the ridges, where there is any supply of water, frequent patches of cultivation may be met with, to which the Oorial resort at certain times, especially when the young wheat is springing up.

The country being generally frequented by shepherds with their flocks of sheep and goats, the Oorial move about a good deal : after paying nocturnal visits to the crops in the neighbourhood of villages, they usually move slowly off at daylight towards some secluded ravine, where they probably take up their quarters for the day, lying under the shade of bushes or overhanging rocks, and so distributed, that most of the approaches are in full view of one or more of the herd.

Being accustomed to see goats and sheep with their attendants, they are not much alarmed by their proximity, and may even occasionally be found grazing in company with the domestic animals ; but they very soon recognise the presence of danger, and the sight of an Englishman in ordinary shooting costume, or the glitter from a rifle barrel, is quite sufficient to put the whole herd on the *qui vive*.

The ground is, however, so much broken, that, in spite of the disadvantages of its being nearly impossible to walk silently on the steep and crumbling slopes, there are many favorable opportunities of stalking, and I do not know of a better school for the young sportsman who is anxious to become a proficient in the art of rifle-shooting, as distinguished from mere target practice. For one good shot at game you will find a hundred who can make a good score at the target ; while the really brilliant performer in the field will nearly always hold his own on the rifle range.

In January 1868 I visited the Salt Range in search of Oorial. Commencing shooting from Sáhowá on the 10th, I walked many miles on that day, but only saw one young ram and a female.

On the following day I moved camp to Doméll, and walked across the hills. Having discovered a herd of Oorial at a great distance, I had a very long stalk, and at length got within about a hundred and thirty yards of them. They were lying on some precipitous ground where there had been a sort of landslip, and I could not make out the ram before one of the females had discovered me, and given the alarm. I had to fire hurriedly, and missed the ram with both barrels, but knocked him over at the third shot. He reared up and fell back down the precipice for a short distance, and I thought he was done for ; he soon, however, managed to regain his legs, and slowly made off, though apparently with great difficulty. I followed up the track for a long distance, but the blood, which had been at first pretty plentiful, gradually diminished, and at length all traces were lost on the stony ground. I went on in the direction which we thought most likely, and after a time I saw the head and shoulders of a ram showing over a bush about a hundred and sixty yards off. He was gazing at us, so I had to fire at once, thinking it was the wounded one. He at once made off at a great pace, and, as I thought, untouched, and I then saw that he was one of a fresh herd. I afterwards discovered that I had broken his foreleg.

Having lamed myself badly, I was unable to go out the next day, so I sent my Shikari with dogs to try and recover the wounded Oorial : they saw them both, but were unable to get near them ; the first one was eventually caught by a woodcutter.

Finding the Oorial very scarce about here, and my time being limited, after two or three days' unsuccessful hunting, I went across to another part of the range, and encamped at a village called Tháti, not far from Kotal Khúnd. The first morning I only saw three or four small ones, but in the afternoon I was more fortunate. Having ascended the range of low red hills behind the village, I carefully reconnoitred the various ridges below me, and soon made out two lots of Oorial. The herd which seemed to offer the best chance of a stalk were lying at the extremity of a sort of promontory with precipitous sides of bare red earth. Having made a long detour I went along this ridge, and on arriving at the end I saw the Oorial rush across the ravine and up the opposite slope. One ram was conspicuous among the others from his large horns and shaggy grizzled beard, and at him I fired. My second bullet from a 10-bore rifle struck him behind the shoulder blade and went out at his chest, but in spite of this he climbed the high cliff opposite, descended, crossed the next ravine, and had gone fully a quarter of a mile before I could come up with him! He proved to be a good specimen with horns twenty-six inches long. His portrait is the one here given.

On the following day I succeeded in getting within a hundred yards of another herd, but had only time to fire a snap-shot before they turned a corner ; the bullet, however, took effect, breaking the thigh of the largest ram ; he bled profusely, but it took me a long time to bag him, as I had to track him for fully two miles over rocky ground and ravines, before I could come up with him and give him the finishing bullet.

My stay in the Salt Range being limited, I did not shoot any more Oorial during this expedition, although I certainly had one or two fair chances.

Happening to be at the small military station of Talágong in March 1875, I determined to have a try for the Oorial which I had heard were numerous in the neighbourhood. I had not much time to spare, but I found that I had sufficient leisure to give me two clear days' shooting. I therefore sent a small tent and one or two servants to a village in the heart of the best country, and starting rather late one forenoon, rode slowly up the sandy bed of a river, above one of the branches of which my camp was to be pitched.

At this dry season only an occasional shallow pool remained to mark what frequently became, during the rainy months, a roaring torrent. On either side rose steep banks about a hundred or a hundred and fifty feet in height : in some places these were precipitous scarps ; in others they were so broken and irregular that there was no difficulty in ascending them ; while every here and there, the watercourse was joined by smaller ravines which brought the drainage of the surrounding country to swell the volume of the main stream.

On ascending either bank an extensive view was obtained of undulating ground intersected by an intricate network of ravines, stretching as far as the eye could reach in every
direction except to the south-east, where it was bounded by the more abrupt ridges of the
Salt Range.

From time to time, the tracks of Oorial were visible in the soft sand, where they had
either come to drink or merely crossed the valley; but I had gone several miles before I
observed a fresh footprint. At last I reached a place where the valley was rather wider
than usual, and here we found tracks so recent that it was evident that the herd could not
be far off. I was accompanied by a Sepoy, who did a little shooting on his own account,
and who had a very fair knowledge of the country; another man carried my rifle. Leaving
my horse, and ordering the syce to proceed to camp, I ascended the slopes to the right,
and soon gained a commanding position, from which I could see into several likely-looking
ravines. The sun was still high, and it was probable that the Oorial would be lying somewhere in the shade.

After carefully reconnoitring all the ground within sight, I went slowly on along a
narrow ridge, sending my gun-carrier and a shepherd whom I had just met, to explore two
ravines to the right and left. One of the men detached a few stones, which rattled down
a steep bank, and presently a fair-sized ram sprang out of some bushes among which he
had been concealed, ascended the opposite bank of the ravine, and after galloping a couple
of hundred yards, took up his position on a small level plateau. Seeing nothing—for we
had of course crouched behind shelter—he presently became reassured, and being apparently
convinced that his alarm was needless, lay down.

The stalk was an easy one, but I had to approach from the direction in which he was
looking, and on peering over the ridge which I had ascended, I found that I could only see
about half his body. I could not raise myself higher without the certainty of being seen,
so I took the best aim I could, and fired. The bullet went high and the Oorial sprang to
his feet and rushed across the plateau; before descending, however, he paused for a moment,
and half turned round to look for his still unseen enemy. That moment of indecision was
fatal: I had time to slip a fresh cartridge into my single-barrelled Express, and though
nothing was visible when the smoke cleared away, I knew that my aim had been true, and
on going up I found the ram struggling on the ground.

Having cut his throat, we were tying him up so as to form a convenient load, when we
heard a distant shepherd shouting, and soon made out that he wished to attract our attention to a herd of Oorial which had been disturbed by my shots. Following in the direction
which they had taken, I found that they had not been much alarmed, but had moved slowly
off, feeding as they went. It was not very easy to make out their tracks on the stony
ground, but here and there the slight indications which catch the eye of the experienced
hunter showed us where they had passed, and we soon came to a sort of basin in which it
seemed very probable that they might linger for a time. In spite of my caution, however,
the moment I looked over the intervening rising ground I was seen, and the herd, which
consisted entirely of rams, went off at full gallop. My first shot was successful, bringing down

a fine ram, and I had time to reload and fire two more shots before the herd reached the edge of the valley and plunged down the nearly perpendicular bank. One of the shots— I do not know which—took effect, for the largest ram lagged behind the herd, and was evidently lame. No blood, however, was to be found, and tracking proved to be impracticable, so we saw him no more.

We still had some distance to travel before we reached camp, and when within a mile of it, as we were again trudging along the sandy river bed, we saw an Oorial on the sky line of one of the highest neighbouring cliffs. It was nearly dark, but it never does to throw away a chance, so up we went, and after a stiffish climb reached the place where the Oorial had been. He had moved, but on proceeding a short distance along the hill-side, I found a young male and a female, which I of course allowed to go unmolested. It was dark before I reached my tent.

An intelligent villager (the Shikari of the place, of whom I had already heard) informed me, in reply to my enquiries, that Oorial were numerous in the neighbourhood, and that I should doubtless find plenty on the morrow. I also enquired about an old ram with one horn, of which the friend with whom I had lately been staying had told me, but I could gain no reliable information about him.

I was out very early on the following morning, and under the guidance of the villager above mentioned, went to some fields of young wheat, in the immediate vicinity of which were many deep and precipitous ravines. These were the strongholds to which the Oorial retired during the day, after their nocturnal visits to the crops. Although we were early on the ground, we did not find any Oorial feeding, nor were any fresh tracks to be seen, though footmarks, two or three days old, showed that they frequented the place. The fact was that they had been doing so much damage that the cultivators had taken to watching their fields by night and frightening the Oorial away. I hunted for a long time without seeing anything except a few Chikara, which were extremely wild and in such open ground that there was no chance of stalking them, although I certainly did not trouble myself much about them.

The sun became extremely hot towards midday, and I was glad to rest for some time under one of the few shady trees that were to be found at wide intervals on that rocky waste.

In the afternoon we recommenced our search, and after exploring a great extent of likely-looking ground without success, we at last found a herd lying on the stony slope of a deep ravine. Just below where they lay two ravines joined, and it was only necessary for me to gain the other branch without being perceived, in order to make pretty sure of an easy shot. With some little trouble I contrived to reach the ravine unseen by any of the watchful herd, and proceeded to descend the dried up watercourse as silently as possible. I had to keep a sharp look-out as I went along, for many of these ravines are so tortuous that on turning a sharp corner one may find oneself in full view of a spot, which one would imagine, from the lie of the ground, would be invisible. In this instance, however, no such bad luck attended me, and I reached the junction without being seen.

w

The banks of the watercourse down which I had come being perpendicular, and the place where the Oorial were lying being well above me and to my right, I could not possibly obtain a shot without being fully exposed to view. On turning the corner therefore, I was by no means surprised to see the Oorial spring to their feet at once. Before betaking themselves to flight, however, they stood a moment to gaze, and gave me time to select a fine ram which stood with his broadside to me, and seemed to be the largest of the herd. He fell to my shot, and the remainder disappeared among the rough ground before I had time to insert a fresh cartridge, rapid as that operation is with a modern breechloader. My surprise may be imagined, when, on going up to the fallen Oorial, I found that he was the big one-horned ram of which I had heard! One horn was broken off close to the base, the other, which was nothing very wonderful after all, measured thirty-one inches in length by ten and a quarter in circumference. I saw nothing more on the way back to camp, and next day I had to give up shooting.

BURRELL

OVIS NAHURA

Published by Thacker, Spink & Co., Calcutta.

CHAPTER XXX.

THE BURRELL.

OVIS NAHURA.

Generally throughout the Himalayas—*Baral—Barút.*　　In Thibet—*Nápú.*

THE Burrell inhabits the whole of the lofty Himalayan Range from Ládák to Bhútán, but is not found in Kashmir, nor in the mountains to the west of that country.

It is probably never found at a lower elevation than 10,000 feet, which prevents it from extending far to the south of the backbone of the great range, but we have no data to show how far its habitat may stretch to the north. To my own knowledge, it is to be met with in Ládák, Spití, Garhwál, Kamáon, near the Nítí and Chor Hotí Passes, and in all the valleys towards the upper waters of the Indus and the Sutlej; while I have seen live specimens brought down from Bhútán.

Jerdon was therefore mistaken in saying that it does not occur to the west of the Sutlej: 76° E. Longitude would, I should say, be very nearly the line of demarcation. The Burrell appears to be a sort of connecting link between the sheep and the goat tribe, both in appearance and habits; its horns especially differing widely in shape from those of the domestic ram, a type which all the other known sheep more or less closely follow; while it frequents precipitous and dangerous ground which goats delight in, and other sheep usually avoid. It has indeed been classed as *Pseudovis* by some naturalists, but I think that the generic name of *Caprovis*, (which has been applied to the Oorial [*Ovis Cycloceros*] and the Shápoo or Oorren [*Ovis Vignei*]), would be much more applicable.

The separation of genera, species, and varieties is, however, one of those knotty points which has led to great differences among naturalists; differences which become irreconcilable when the disputants follow different rules in their systems of classification.

The male Burrell is a fine-looking animal, and though the horns are not so graceful as those of some other species, they are quite unique in shape, and present a singular and striking appearance as he gazes at one from some lofty rock. The Burrell does not stand nearly so high as the Nyan, and is differently built, being stouter and standing on short legs; in fact, being adapted for climbing among dangerous precipices, at which probably no animal excels it.

The color is a light bluish grey above, and white beneath. The chest and throat, the legs, and a line along the side separating the grey from the white, are jet black. The hair is brittle and very closely set, and when killed in winter, the skin is one of the handsomest I know.

The horns are peculiarly shaped : they are set very close together, and at first diverge horizontally in two round arches ; then sweep backwards, upwards, and outwards, in a shape different to those of any animal with which I am acquainted. They attain an average length of about twenty-four inches, but occasionally reach thirty inches or more, with a circumference of upwards of twelve inches. Few very large pairs are perfect ; as with other wild sheep, old individuals usually have the tips broken off.

Female Burrell are not much more than half the size of the males : their color is similar, except that they want the black line along the sides ; and their horns are little, flat, stumpy excrescences.

Burrell are perhaps even more particular than Ibex in their avoidance of forest, for I have seen the latter among pine trees and bushes, but I have never met with the former exept on the barest and most exposed parts of the hill. They are, however, fond of good pasturage, when it is obtainable, and in Kamáon and Garhwál, they frequent the richest grassy slopes of the green but rocky hills of that region. In Thibet again, where vegetation is extremely scarce, Burrell have but little choice, and large herds may be met with on the most desolate and precipitous mountains ; but even there they prefer localities where the banks of occasional trickling streams afford here and there little oases of verdure. In a word, what they delight in is good grazing ground in the immediate vicinity of rocky fast-nesses, to which they can immediately betake themselves when disturbed. Except in most remote districts, they never stray very far from some stronghold, in which they take refuge on the slightest alarm.

Burrell are usually found in considerable herds, varying from eight or ten to one hundred or more in number. The males for the most part separate from the females during the summer months, but mixed herds may be seen at all seasons of the year. Few animals are more watch-ful while feeding, some of their number usually keeping a sharp look-out while the remainder are grazing, and a whistle from a sentinel at once causing the herd to seek safety by instant flight. It has been stated that Burrell usually *walk* away when disturbed, but my experience has been, that, except in very out of the way places, they lose no time in placing a safe dis-tance between themselves and their pursuer, and that they do not stop to gaze nearly so often as the wild goats do.

With regard to their tameness in very remote districts, Mr. Wilson relates an instance in the admirable "Summer Ramble in the Himalayas," and I have witnessed a similar case.

I was marching up the valley of the Indus, beyond the Chinese frontier, in 1866, with my friend B. We were endeavouring to reach the hills to the north of Gártope, where we hoped to find Yâk, and with that view had crossed the frontier in the dark, and, accompanied by a few Ládák Tartars, marched all night and concealed ourselves during the day. On the fourth morning we were proceeding up a ravine in which we intended to 'cache' for the day, when we observed four old male Burrell on the opposite side. They did not take the slightest notice of us, and being in a retired place where there was no danger of our shots being heard by the Tartars, B., who wanted a good head, walked across the boulders at the bottom of the ravine in full view of the Burrell, who allowed him to approach within eighty yards without betraying any symptoms of alarm! B. then quietly sat down and shot the largest one, upon which the others made off.

The same day our hiding place was discovered by the Tartars, who ordered us back ; and though we forced our way ' vi et armis ' for another march of thirty-five miles, we were after all compelled to abandon our project of reaching the Yák ground. The people turned out in hundreds ; several big wigs came down from Gártope ; and although we used every argument including threats and bribes, we could not obtain permission even for a few days' shooting, and had, most unwillingly, to retrace our steps.

There are few animals so difficult to detect as Burrell, when they are lying down on rocky ground : their color exactly harmonizes with the hue of the grey boulders and masses of shale which cover the hill-sides in their favorite haunts, and the keenest-eyed Shikari will frequently fail to discover a herd until some movement betrays their presence. I have indeed occasionally met Thibetans with telescopic powers of vision, who could see Burrell lying down at immense distances, when I could hardly make them out even with a powerful glass, after the spot where they lay was pointed out to me.

In out of the way places, Burrell will lie down on their feeding grounds ; and as they alternately feed and rest throughout the day, and never resort to cover, they may be found and stalked at all hours. This renders the sport peculiarly attractive; as in the pursuit of most other animals it is useless to work except early in the morning and again in the evening, and thus many hours of the long summer days have to be spent in enforced idleness.

To be successful in Burrell-shooting, the sportsman should be a first-rate walker, able to toil from morning till night with but little rest, and undeterred by the highest and steepest of hills from following up his game.

An old Burrell's head is a trophy worth working for ; and the meat is excellent, the flavor being a happy combination of Highland mutton and venison. Late in the year, Burrell become extremely fat, and a haunch is then hardly to be surpassed for tenderness, juiciness, and flavor.

I have few pleasanter recollections than those connected with Burrell-shooting, and I often long to revisit the scenes of many a good day's sport. How vividly I can recall to memory many a remote camping ground, where, by the margin of some clear trickling stream, my tent has been pitched on short green turf in the heart of wild rugged mountains. There, in the most bracing and exhilarating atmosphere in the world, I have been awoke at early dawn by the plaintive whistle of the Snow Cock from the barren cliffs, and on looking out from my tent door have seen the snow-clad summits of many a lofty peak catch the first rays of the sun ; each in succession being tinged with the rosy light, which gradually creeps downwards until the lower slopes and valleys at length become illuminated, and the frost-bound springs released from their icy fetters.

It is on such mornings that the Burrell may be seen on the grassy slopes, enjoying the comparative warmth, and so busily occupied in grazing, that they somewhat relax the vigilance which they display later in the day, when, having appeased their appetites, they lie down to rest and ruminate.

It is not, however, under such enjoyable circumstances that the chase can always be followed, and the hunter must make up his mind to encounter rough weather and undergo no small amount of toil.

In 1865, I was shooting in the country to the north of the Chor Hotí Pass, where I had very fair sport both among Nyan and Burrell.

On July 26th, while crossing from Keo into Leptel, I discovered two old male Burrell at the opposite side of the latter stream. After going a long way round, I got above them, and was nearly within shot when they moved off rather quickly : I waited until they had crossed a ridge, and then ran down as fast as I could, but on reaching the place, the Burrell were nowhere to be seen. I went on, much puzzled as to where they could have gone to, but at last came close upon them in a small hollow. As they galloped off I shot the larger one dead, but missed the other, my bullet striking just under him. The one I killed was a fine fellow with very large and perfect horns, measuring twenty-five and a half inches in length ; his head is capitally represented in the photograph.

My camp was pitched a mile or two lower down the valley, and I had not been very long in my tent when my Shikari came to say that he had seen some Burrell feeding on the flats above the river. I went after them, and found that the flock consisted of about thirty, many of them with fine horns. The main body of the flock was in a beautiful place for a stalk, but as bad luck would have it, there were several stragglers above them. I was obliged to fire a long shot at one of these, and hit him on the horn ; he was stupefied for a few seconds, and then went off all right.

The rest of the Burrell would not stop to look about them as they sometimes do, but made a simultaneous rush for the cliffs which were just below. I fired a snap-shot into a group as they reached the brink, but only broke the leg of one, which went away with the rest. I ran as fast as I could, in hopes of seeing the flock standing somewhere lower down, but they had disappeared. Another lot, headed by a very black old male, which had heard the shots, but were not much disturbed, were coming up the cliff a little farther back ; as they seemed inclined to come in my direction, I lay down to watch them. They were coming straight towards me when the cunning old black fellow, who was now last, suddenly turned back. I was so savage with him for this, that I fired all four barrels at him, although he was fully two hundred yards off : one of the shots broke his foreleg, and he went up to the flat above the cliff, crossed a corner of it, and went down the cliff again. These cliffs rose nearly perpendicularly from the Leptel river, and on looking over I could see the stream running hundreds of feet below me : narrow ledges traversed the face of this awful precipice in various directions, and here and there were jutting rocks affording barely standing room to the most surefooted of animals. Along one of these ledges the wounded Burrell had gone, as drops of blood testified, but he was not visible from the top, and I had to descend to a platform a little way down. I now caught sight of the Burrell, who had made his way to a point of rock from which even he was unable to move, except by retracing the difficult path by which he had reached it. If I shot him where he was, he would fall into the river below and be lost for ever, but my Shikari asked me to shoot him "to see the fun."

I was about to put the poor brute out of pain, when he turned round, and by a desperate scramble reached a small cave into which he went, only showing his head occasionally. I was about a hundred yards off, and fired four shots at his head when it appeared ; after the fourth shot it appeared no more. It was getting late, so nothing more was to be done that evening, but my Shikari said he thought that he and the other men would be able to get the Burrell next morning with the aid of ropes.

Early next morning a solitary Burrell appeared on the flat, but on reaching the place I found that it was only a female. The men had accompanied me with ropes, and now proceeded to attempt the recovery of last night's Burrell. Walking along a narrow ledge from which the loose stones rattled down to the river at every step, they reached a spot immediately above the cave. Sitting down on the ledge, and digging their heels into the shale, they let one of their number down the perpendicular rock to the mouth of the cave, a distance of about fifteen feet. He reached the cave.in safety, and announced that the Burrell was lying dead. I had expected the men to bring up the head only, but to my astonishment I saw the rope attached to the Burrell, and the heavy animal hauled up to the ledge, from whence he was transferred to a wider and safer place, skinned, and cut up. I found that all my bullets fired at him when in the cave had struck him, the last one having entered his eye. He had just shed his winter coat, and his summer coat was still very short, causing him to appear unusually dark coloured.

On my return from Thibet I hunted for a few days in the hills above Malárí, on the Indian side of the passes. Instead of the bright clear air of the northern or Thibetan slopes the climate was damp and foggy ; so much so, indeed, as to seriously interfere with sport. It was a long march to my first encamping ground, and it was late in the afternoon before my tent was pitched, where some birch trees and rhododendron bushes furnished an ample supply of fuel. In the evening, a flock of Burrell made their appearance on the top of a hill opposite my camp, and remained quietly feeding until dark.

Early next morning, the Burrell were again visible in the same place, and I lost no time in starting in pursuit. A long steep climb brought me to the summit of the ridge on which they were feeding, and I had little difficulty in stalking to within easy range. The morning was a bright one, the clouds not having yet rolled up from the valleys into which they slowly sink at night, and the rising sun, shining right in my face, rendered it extremely difficult to take aim. At length, however, I managed to cover the shoulder of the largest male, as he was feeding unsuspiciously on the verge of a rocky precipice, and dropped him on the spot. My second barrel was less successful, the bullet merely breaking the hindleg of another Burrell, which succeeded in effecting its escape into most difficult ground, where I could not follow it.

Being determined to be early on the ground the next day, and the hill which I intended to hunt being at a considerable distance, I made an early dinner, and gave orders that I was to be awoke an hour or two before day-light. I soon sunk into the slumber which comes so easily to the tired hunter, and no dreams disturbed my rest until my servant announced that it was near dawn and time to get up.   Hastily dressing, I made a very substantial breakfast, and, accompanied by my Shikari, shortly afterwards commenced the ascent of the hill.   The night was foggy ; not a star was to be seen, and my watch was *hors de combat* ; but I never doubted that daylight would presently appear, and patiently and slowly plodded upwards.   We must have walked for nearly two hours, and not a glimmer of light was yet visible, when the hiss of a Musk Deer was heard close to us.   I lay down and waited, momentarily expecting day to break, and at last, my patience being exhausted, I rolled myself in my blanket and went to sleep.   I had actually awoke and breakfasted about midnight, without discovering my mistake ! a fact which speaks volumes for the healthy appetite produced by hard work in a salubrious climate.

When my Shikari at length again aroused me, morning had really arrived, and we continued our journey ; but we were not repaid for our loss of rest, for I failed to get a shot at the only male Burrell which I saw throughout the day ; a herd of females and young ones having spoiled my stalk.   The clouds soon rolled up and obscured everything from view, and I returned to camp empty handed.

In 1869, I was hunting, principally for Nyan, on the high tableland to the west of Hánlé in Ládák.

The plateau is remarkable for two or three small lakes, which are probably among the most elevated sheets of water in the world, being at least 17,000 feet above the level of the sea.   The steep sides of this tableland are furrowed by ravines, some of them containing small springs of water, on the margin of which are little patches of verdure.

I had reconnoitred a number of these ravines without seeing game, when a blinding snow-storm came on, accompanied by a bitterly cold wind.   I was begining to think of returning to camp, when a man whom I had sent to a little distance to explore a small valley came back with the news that he had seen Burrell.   From my limited knowledge of the Thibetan language I was unable to understand exactly where they were, but going in the direction pointed out, I descended in search of them.

Presently, through the driving snow-flakes, I caught sight of the Burrell lying down under a ridge of rock about a hundred yards off.   I was in full view of them, and on my sitting down to fire, they all rose up.   Selecting the finest male, I fired at his shoulder as he stood with his broadside to me, but he turned round and dashed down the hill with the rest of the herd, who did not give me a chance for my second barrel.

I ran after them, but they crossed the rocky ridge, and, being favored by a dip in the ground, disappeared from view.   I knew that I had not missed, and, about fifty yards beyond the ridge, I found the Burrell I had fired at lying stone-dead, the bullet having struck him just behind the shoulder.   On cutting him up, I found that my bullet, a 12-bore one, had shattered his heart to atoms, and yet he had been able to gallop about a hundred yards before falling.

One can imagine an animal being struck in full career, and being carried on by his own impetus for a certain distance ; but here was an instance of a beast being hit when standing still, and having the vitality to turn in a different direction and accompany his companions over rough ground, although what is generally thought to be the seat of life was absolutely destroyed. It shows how careful one should be when hunting dangerous game, as the most accurately placed bullet will not always stop an animal on the spot, but may leave him with sufficient energy to strike down his foe before he dies.

The Burrell I had shot proved to be a very fine one, with handsomely arched massive horns ; but the skin was useless, the hair coming off in large patches.

x

CHAPTER XXXI.
THE GREAT THIBETAN SHEEP, OR NYAN.

OVIS HODGSONII.

In Thibet—*Nyañ.*

ON the wild bleak uplands of Thibet, where for hundreds of miles not a tree is to be met with ; where in every direction, as far as the eye can reach, there is nothing but a vast expanse of barren soil, rock and snow ; where there is no shelter from the glare of a cloudless noon, nor from the freezing winds that sweep the naked hills with relentless force towards the close of day ; here, in the midst of solitude and desolation, where animal life has apparently to struggle for existence under every disadvantage, is the home of this great wild sheep.

Several nearly allied species of large sheep inhabit the various mountain ranges of Northern and Central Asia, but their exact number has not yet been satisfactorily ascertained. According to the most reliable authorities there are at least four, *viz.*, the Siberian Sheep (*Ovis Ammon*); the Sheep inhabiting the Tián Shán range (*Ovis Karelini*) ; the Sheep of the Pámír Steppe (*Ovis Poli*) ; and the Thibetan Sheep (*Ovis Hodgsonii*),

The last named was long supposed to be identical with the Siberian Sheep or Argali, and to this day the scientific name of the Argali has been familiarly but erroneously adopted by sportsmen as the designation of the Thibetan Sheep.

Why a long Latin name should always be applied to this sheep, while the vernacular names of other Himalayan animals are in common use, I cannot imagine; and both brevity and scientific accuracy are best attained by dropping the scientific, and adopting the Thibetan, name, in descriptions of sporting adventures.

The favorite haunts of the Nyan with which I am acquainted are, near the Salt Lake, on the north-western side of the Pangong Lake, at Chúshul, and in the neighbourhood of Hánlé. It is also pretty numerous in the valley of the Sutlej beyond the Nítl Pass.

The *Ovis Hodgsonii* is the largest wild sheep which has yet been discovered, for although the horns of the *Ovis Poli* are longer (but not so thick) the animal is not so large. A full-grown male stands upwards of twelve hands at the shoulder. I have never seen one over twelve hands and one inch. The color of the upper part of the body is a dark earthy-brown, becoming lighter towards the lower parts. The rump is light-colored, and the tail is only about an inch in length. The throat and chest are adorned by a white ruff, the hairs of which are considerably lengthened ; those on the body being short, brittle, and very close-set.

XXIV

NYAN OR GREAT THIBETAN SHEEP

OVIS HODGSONII

Published by Thacker, Spink & Co., Calcutta.

The horns of this sheep are enormously massive in proportion to its size, and an old ram's head is *the* trophy most anxiously coveted by the Himalayan hunter, and very often longed for in vain. I believe horns have been found upwards of fifty inches in length and twenty-four in circumference; I have never had the good fortune to bag a specimen approaching these dimensions, though I once wounded and lost a splendid ram whose horns were much finer than any others that I have ever seen, and probably were not very far short of fifty inches. The average size of a full-grown ram's horns may be stated at about forty inches by seventeen.

The female is not much inferior to the male in size, but she has small horns, seldom exceeding twenty-four inches in length. She is darker-colored than the male, and may often be distinguished, when too far to see the horns, by the dark hue of her neck.

The legs of this sheep are long and deer-like, and I fancy that very few animals excel it in speed. The flesh, like that of all Thibetan ruminants, is excellent ; it is always tender, even on the day it is killed, and of very good flavor, possibly caused by the aromatic herbs which constitute so large a portion of the scanty vegetation of those arid regions.

Old rams are most difficult to find in the summer months, being apparently most fastidious in their selection of ground, where one would think there was but little choice. Females and young males may be met with day after day, while the old rams remain invisible until by some happy chance their feeding grounds are discovered. I know one or two small valleys where rams may *always* be found, while I have tramped over the surrounding hills for many a weary mile in every direction without even finding a trace of their presence.

I have hunted most kinds of large game in India and Thibet, and after a lengthened experience, I can unhesitatingly affirm, that there is no animal so difficult to stalk as a male Nyan. This is of course partly attributable to the open nature of the country it inhabits, but still more to the extraordinary watchfulness of the animal and the high development of all its senses of perception. To quote the words of ' Mountaineer' in the " Summer Ramble in the Himalayas" (about the best book on the subject that has ever been published) when the successful hunter at length " runs up to a fallen beast, lifts up his enormous head, and surveys the ponderous horns, he may rest assured that he has gained the highest step in the art of deer-stalking."

Some sportsmen, including such a good hunter as the late General Markham, have gone so far as to say that stalking these sheep is out of the question, and that driving them is the only plan by which success can be insured. This, however, is a mistake ; and although no one can expect to be almost invariably successful in his stalks (as a recent writer in *The Field* stated that he was), there is no doubt that, by the exercise of sound judgment and great patience, combined with the physical qualifications necessary for the endurance of considerable exposure to weather and much hard work, the Nyan may be fairly *stalked* and shot.

To be successful, the hunter should not spare himself, but should be out early and home late, and perfectly content, if necessary, to lie for hours on the hard stones, with a wind such as is only experienced in Thibet, penetrating the very marrow of his bones.

How often have I awoke with the knowledge that it was time for me to leave my warm bed and face the frosty air, the temperature of which could be guessed by a glance at the solid brown block which represented the half drunk cup of tea left by my bedside the night before. How distasteful has been the prospect of a couple of miles climb over loose shingle to the summit of a steep hill, which I must gain before it has been illuminated (not warmed) by the first rays of the rising sun, if I would not lose the most advantageous hour for seeing what game is in the neighbourhood.

How often have I again rolled myself in my blankets and wondered how I could be such a fool as to leave the comforts of a hill station where I might lie in bed till 10 o'clock if I chose—and for what? To walk hundreds of miles over hill and dale; to feed upon leathery '*chupatties*' and tough sheep (not worthy of the name of mutton); and to undergo a hundred discomforts for the chance of a shot at a big sheep!

"No,"—I have said to myself—"shooting is all vanity; why should life be wasted in such idle pursuits? Cultivate a taste for scenery; take to sketching, botany, geology— *anything* that can be carried on without the necessity for getting up in the middle of the night with shivering limbs and chattering teeth. Call *this* pleasure, indeed! A convict has no such miseries to undergo. No more shooting for me! What do I want with the Nyan? Leave the poor brutes alone!" But then comes the thought—" What a splendid ram that was which I saw yesterday! If he had only left the open plain and gone to those nullahs in the direction of which he was feeding when failing daylight obliged me to give up the chase, I should have probably got a shot. He is sure to be there to-day. If I could but get within a hundred yards of *him !*—such horns! must be fifty inches!"

Away with all ignoble thoughts of creature comforts and inglorious ease! The blankets are thrown off; the cup of tea is called for; the gun-carriers are summoned; and in another quarter of an hour we are plodding up the stony slopes, still cold certainly, but with the blood beginning to circulate more quickly; and with our hearts full of hope.

Although I had several times seen these sheep during my first two seasons in the hills, I never had a good chance at old rams until 1864. On the 23rd of June of that year I was encamped near Chúshul in Ládák, on the range of hills separating the Pangong Lakes from the Indus Valley.

The hills here were very steep and barren, being composed chiefly of loose shale, and they were, moreover, very high. I had not walked more than a quarter of a mile from my tent, and the sun was just rising, when I discovered three animals far up the hill above my camp. The Tartars pronounced them to be Kyang; I said 'Nyan,' and on having recourse to the telescope, I saw that they were fine old rams. As I was observing them, they lay down, and in such a position, that I saw that, if they would only remain where they were, I should be able to stalk them. A narrow ravine ran straight down the hill from near where the animals were lying; ascending this I had a hard climb till I had nearly reached their level, when, on turning to the right, I found that a dip in the ground concealed my movements until I arrived at the spot from which I expected to get a shot. Crawling up the last bit of slope, I carefully looked over and beheld the Nyan lying down within shot. In a moment they were on their legs and gazing towards me. Selecting the largest ram, I aimed most deliberately at his shoulder, and as I slowly pressed the trigger, I felt quite certain of the shot. To my disgust, however, the crack of the bullet on a stone reached my ears instead of the well-known and welcome 'thud,' and the Nyan instantly started off, much too fast for my second barrel. On standing up, I found that I had over-estimated the distance, the rams having been only one hundred and thirty yards off, instead of one hundred and eighty, which I had sighted for. This is a sort of mistake which one is very apt to make when lying down, and one which has lost me many a fine pair of horns.

I saw nothing more that day ; on the following day I saw seven old rams going off along a high ridge, but although I followed them at once I was unable to find them again, either on that day or the next.

Although I knew that there was plenty of shooting in this neighbourhood, I was compelled to leave it, as I was suffering so terribly from toothache, and could get no relief nearer than Léh, where I submitted myself to the tender mercies of a Thibetan barber ! I must confess that he handled his pincers with considerable skill, and soon extracted the offending tooth. I was not quite so fortunate on a subsequent occasion, when I allowed my *khidmatgdr* to try his "'prentice hand" on another aching tooth, which he only succeeded in breaking off, leaving me in great torture for nearly a fortnight. While making this digression I may offer a word of advice to sportsmen   " *See that your teeth are in good order before visiting Thibet ;* the cold winds there are sure to find out a decayed tooth, and no one who has not experienced it as I have, can have any idea of the misery caused by incessant toothache for weeks together without the possibility of relief."

In 1865, I crossed the Chor Hotí Pass, and found some female Nyan in the valley of Leptel. Going on through Keo and crossing the pass to Zunkum, I saw two rams, but was unable to get near them. Near the Sutlej are some low arid hills, which are known to the Nítí Shikaris by the name of the 'Lál Pahár' (Red Hills). I was informed that they were a favorite haunt of old rams, and I accordingly hunted among them for several days, but without seeing an animal. At last on the 6th of July, I sent my camp from Tálang at the west end of the range of hills to Shib at the other end, and proceeded to explore the only part of the ground which I had not yet visited. As I was crossing the plain at the foot of the hills, I made out five rams at the distance of about a mile ; they had evidently got my wind, and after looking very restless for some time, they went off. A little farther on I saw ten more which had also got our wind, and were following the first lot. I went round by the crest of the hills, and on getting well to leeward descended towards where I expected to see the Nyan ; I soon caught sight of the fifteen, who had formed one flock. They were all magnificent old rams, and I lay watching the noble animals until evening, hoping that they would leave the open plain where they were feeding, and move to some place where they might be approached ; but as they remained in the same place, I had to leave them and return to camp.

Next day I started early and walked to the place where I had left the Nyan, a distance of about five miles. I found them again on the same ground, but they were so scattered that it was impossible to lay any good plan for a stalk. At last seven of them fed on ahead of the others, so I determined to try and get a shot at them, and take my chance of being seen by the remainder. Having moved down the hill to the place from which I hoped to get a shot, I found that they were still two hundred and fifty yards off. Seeing little chance of being able to get back without being discovered by some of the wary brutes, I endeavoured to improve my position by crawling down the hill; in doing so I was seen, and had to fire at once. Selecting two in line I fired very steadily, but my heavy spherical ball rifle not being very accurate at such a long range, I missed, and they went off at a great pace. The eight remaining rams, who had heard the shots but seen nothing, after galloping about for a time, went round the end of the hill, but still kept in the open plain. Following them up, I observed six of them making for the hills, but two had stayed behind. Thinking they might be in a neighbouring large nullah, I went to it, but only found a flock of Burrell, out of which I shot two males. Having skinned them I was proceeding homewards, when I again saw the six rams in the wide valley ahead of us; it was too late to follow them, so I went up a deep nullah leading towards camp, so as not to disturb them. I had gone a mile or two up this, and it was becoming dusk, when I heard a noise on my right, and on looking up saw the six Nyan rattling along the high bank, two of them knocking their horns together. As they would not stand, I fired at one as he galloped past; I thought he staggered, so I fired the other barrel at him. My second gun-carrier, who was also carrying the Burrell's heads, had lagged behind, and now that my rifle was empty, the rams stood still and gazed at me within forty yards. By the time I had rammed down one bullet and put on a cap, they were just disappearing over the bank, and a snap-shot fired at the hind quarters of the last one missed. I was afraid that they had all gone off, but while I was reloading, my Shikari espied the horns and back of one evidently dying at the top of the bank, and on going up to my great delight I found a fine ram lying dead, shot through the shoulders. His horns, though not particularly large, were a fine pair, measuring thirty-six inches in length by sixteen in circumference. I did not reach camp until some time after dark, having had a long day's work, but being very well satisfied.

During the next four days I met with Nyan only once, when I stalked six old rams on the other side of the Shib River: I got within shot, but missed them as they galloped off.

On the 12th I sent my camp back to Tálang, and as my Shikari was ill, I hunted along the hills accompanied by only two Tartars. Among some ravines I found a flock of twelve Nyan, females and young males; they had just caught a glimpse of me, but were not much alarmed, so I ordered my gun-carriers to crawl quietly back out of sight. They moved back a few paces and then coolly stood up, and directly afterwards eight old rams, which I had not previously observed, went over the hill. The twelve others, after feeding for three or four hundred yards, lay down. To have stalked them properly would have involved making an immensely long round, which, as they were not large ones, I did not think they were worth, so I resolved to chance being seen while crossing one nullah, after which I should be safe enough. The wary brutes saw me, however, and went off at full speed. Going along the ridge of the hills towards Tálang I could see nothing, although I had expected to have found the eight rams again. Having come to the end of the ridge, I was descending a valley, when I suddenly saw a solitary old ram standing about half way up the hill-side. We instantly crouched, and he did not appear to have made us out clearly, but continued gazing without moving for several minutes. Thinking it just possible that he might remain long enough to give me time to stalk him, I left a man for him to look at, and crawling carefully out of sight, ascended the hill and got above him. As this occupied some time, I was much afraid that he would have gone, but on looking over the ridge I saw his horns. I walked down as far as I could without being seen, and then lay down and crawled along until I got within one hundred and forty yards. The ram had moved a little, but stood broadside on : I took a most careful aim, and though he rushed down the hill after the shot, I felt confident that I had not missed. When he had gone a few strides I saw blood on his side, he soon began to stagger, and finally rolled over after galloping about two hundred yards. I ran down to him and found that he was a fine fellow, not so old as the first one I shot, but with larger horns, measuring thirty-seven inches by seventeen. The head was a heavy load for my gun-carrier, so I had to shoulder my rifle and had a very long walk to camp.

I had one more chance at old rams before I left these hills, and lost it by bad generalship. I killed a small one on the last day.

In 1866 I hunted the big sheep in the neighbourhood of Hánlé. The first flock I saw was on the 9th of June, within two miles of the Lámáserai, or Monastery, on the opposite side of the stream : the herd consisted only of females and young ones, but I shot a large female for the sake of the meat. We had cut her up, and were proceeding homewards, when I saw her lamb galloping along the ridge of a hill. As I was watching it, a large dark-colored Eagle swooped down and fastened on its head. I hastened towards it, but long before I reached the place, the Eagle soared away far out of shot. I found the lamb lying dead with several holes in its throat : it was rather larger than a Gazelle. I should have much liked to have shot the Eagle, which was, I believe, the Golden Eagle, the ' Bearcoot,' about which Atkinson tells such wonderful tales.

Altogether I hunted for about three weeks in this part of the country, but with very indifferent success. I wasted a good deal of time in hunting the wrong ground before I met with a very intelligent Tartar, Thering Dorjé by name, who showed me the haunts of the old rams. Even then bad luck constantly attended me, as it sometimes will, something going wrong in every stalk, and I only killed a two-year old ram before the 16th of July. On that day I was encamped near the wide plateau which lies between the Lánák Pass and Nyima on the Indus ; the valley in which my tents were being a favorite resort of old rams. Very early on this morning I ascended the hill above camp and followed the course of the valley, keeping high up. Before long I discovered three Nyan lying on a steep slope, and had to make a very long detour in order to get beyond them. Having accomplished this, I found that the wind had changed, and the Nyan were moving restlessly about, but being favored by the ground, I managed to stalk to within fifty yards, and found that they were all only two-year olds. I shot one of them, and having covered him up with stones, proceeded towards camp, which had been moved a couple of miles. In the next wide ravine I found three more Nyan, but as they were all small ones, and in a place where it was impossible to stalk them, I resolved to try a drive, instead of waiting as I should have done if I had seen any big fellows. Accordingly I took up my position in the most likely place for them to pass, and sent a man round.

This plan answered admirably ; the instant the Tartar showed himself, the rams set off and rushed up the hill towards me, and, to my delight, I saw that there were eight or ten of them, some of them with fine horns. I lay still till they nearly galloped over me, and then, as they passed within twenty-five yards, I singled out the one which appeared to be the largest : he did not fall to the shot, so I reserved my second barrel until I saw whether he required it or not. I waited a little too long, and the others were just disappearing into a hollow as I missed a snap shot at the hind quarters of the last. The big one had meanwhile rolled over dead, having been shot just behind the shoulder. He was very old, and bore the scars of fights : his horns were a good deal broken, the one least injured measuring thirty-eight and a half inches by sixteen.

Next day I had to set out on my return.

It was not till 1869 that I again had an opportunity of revisiting the Nyan country, and as I had delayed on the way, shooting other game, I was rather late in reaching it.

Fortune did not much favor me during this trip, and my bad luck culminated in my losing the finest head I ever saw.

Not far from my favorite camp was a steep hill-side with wide ridges and hollows, running from the lofty and extensive plateau which crowned the summit of the hill to a wide plain, intersected by numerous ravines, which lay at its foot. In the hollows there were rills of water ; and grass and other plants, especially a species of furze, were unusually plentiful.

Early one morning I was hunting along this hill-side, carefully scrutinizing every little glen as I came to it, and occasionally sweeping the more distant slopes with my telescope. Having reached the end of my beat without seeing a trace of game, I had commenced to ascend with the intention of trying higher ground, when I suddenly observed four rams far below me. Two of them were fine ones, but one was a magnificent beast with enormous horns, which were conspicuous at a distance at which it is generally very difficult to judge at all accurately of the size of a ram's horns. Curving back, as they do, close to the neck, unless one is tolerably near the animal, or can see him against the sky line, I know of no horns whose size it is so difficult to estimate. In this case, as I have said, there was no doubt ; here was a trophy to win which would be an ample recompense for weeks of toil. Under the present circumstances there was nothing to be done but wait : the Nyan were feeding on open ground, and to move from where I was would be to run the risk of instant detection ; I therefore patiently watched them until they moved out of sight on lower ground, when I at once took advantage of the opportunity and gained the shelter of a high ridge, behind which I descended the hill and circled round to leeward of the rams.

On reaching the point I was making for, I found that the Nyan had lain down, and it was some time before a careful survey of the ground enabled me to lay my plans for approaching them. The ravine in which I was concealed was one of many with nearly parallel courses which joined the main watercourse of the valley (now nearly dry) a few hundred yards lower down, and I saw that by going round to the next ravine and again ascending under cover of its banks, I should probably be able to get within easy shot. This scheme I rapidly carried out, and on again peering over the bank of the nullah, up which I had to proceed in a crouching position, I found that I was within a long shot of the rams.

The wind was favorable, I certainly had not shown myself, nor had I made sufficient noise in my approach to render it possible for the wary animals to have heard me ; but on carefully peering over the bank, there were the two big rams apparently gazing straight at me, the two smaller ones peacefully grazing a short distance beyond them.

The two old rams were about a hundred and sixty yards off, a rather long range for the 12-bore rifle which I carried, and I waited a long time in the hope that they would move nearer to me. They remained immovable however, while the two smaller ones gradually increased their distance. At last I feared that the big rams might at any moment turn round and follow their smaller companions, in which case I should probably only get a stern shot as they walked away. There was little chance of my obtaining a more favorable shot than the old patriarch now afforded, and I accordingly resolved to risk it. I had had plenty of time to allow my hand to become perfectly steady, and slowly and carefully raising my rifle over the bank on which I rested, I aligned the sights on the ram's shoulder as he stood half facing me. Gradually I pressed the trigger, and never did I feel more confident of a shot. My confidence was justified by the sound which reached my ear, the crack of the bullet striking on bone and flesh—not the dull 'thud' so often talked of in the days of small charges and high trajectories, but the sharp stroke of a bullet travelling with the high velocity produced by the explosion of six drams of powder.

"What animal can stand the shock of such a projectile properly placed ? The glorious horns are mine !" Such were my thoughts, and although, on the smoke clearing away, I saw all four rams moving off, it was at a slow pace instead of the race-horse speed at which they almost invariably start when alarmed. Every moment I expected to see the wounded one stagger and fall, but they all crossed a low ridge at a fast walk, and disappeared from view. Hurrying forward, I saw all four going away together, and began to think that my ears must have deceived me, and that I had missed after all. But I knew that it was quite impossible for an animal to be struck by a bullet from that rifle without bleeding pretty profusely, and on examining the tracks, I soon found plenty of blood. Cheered by this discovery, I rapidly followed up the trail, expecting, as each ridge was crossed, to find the wounded beast lying down. After going about two miles however, I saw the large ram going up the steep face of a rocky hill towards which he had been making, and on having recourse to the telescope, I could see a large patch of blood on his side, my bullet having struck too high and too far back, probably owing to the strong wind which was blowing, but which I could not feel in my sheltered position in the nullah, and had not therefore made allowance for.

Y

The ram's breasting this steep hill was a bad sign ; but on the other hand, the fact of his having left the others was a good one. He went up slowly and painfully, constantly stopping for a few minutes, but before he reached the summit he had been rejoined by his companions, and all crossed the hill together.

It was now nearly dusk : I was about seven miles from camp, with a tremendous hill to cross : I was not prepared to bivouac : so I had to relinquish the chase and make the best of my way home. It was a bitterly cold night ; a howling wind seemed to pierce through and through me, while frequently my progress was interfered with by passing snowstorms. After a long weary trudge, the glimmer of the lights from my tent was indeed welcome, as it showed that I had only a few hundred yards to go ; and in a few minutes I was enjoying the luxury of a huge bowl of hot tea.

Those who have never undergone much hard work and exposure to weather, cannot really appreciate the blessings of tea. That it is the most suitable of all beverages for an inclement climate, is, I think, pretty well proved by the fact that the Thibetans (who, after the Esquimaux, are perhaps more exposed to the rigor of cold than any other nation) invariably drink tea on every opportunity. A Thibetan horseman, on a long journey, will probably make two or three halts during the day, and at each place, while his pony picks up a scanty meal, a bundle of dry roots, or a heap of the droppings of the Yâk will be collected, and the copper pot filled, perhaps with snow, for the preparation of the cheering cup. I do not think that the Thibetan's 5 o'clock tea would be much appreciated in a London drawing-room, for he makes it after a fashion peculiar to himself, with salt and rancid butter, with the addition of barley meal or even meat if procurable ! If well made with fresh butter it is not so bad as it sounds. The best I ever tasted was on an occasion when I had the honor of dining with the Rájá of Sikkim.

The wounded ram was too great a prize to relinquish without making every effort to obtain it ; so, early on the following morning, I ordered my camp to be moved to the valley where I had found the ram, and made the best of my way to where I had left the track the night before.

At first I found but little blood on the track, but after following it three or four miles, the blood became more plentiful, and my hopes accordingly rose. It soon became scarcer however, and at length entirely ceased, and after a fruitless chase of many miles, which led me back close to my camp, I at length gave up the pursuit as useless. Twice I found that the rams had lain down, but there was but little blood at either place, and it is clear that the wound must have been merely a superficial one.

The next day I again hunted for the rams, but without success, and as my leave was drawing to a close, I had to leave the ground without another chance of getting a big head.

The following year found me back in my old haunts about a month earlier in the season, and with my knowledge of the ground I anticipated great sport. Unfortunately, however, another sportsman had been before me, and although he had killed nothing, he had disturbed the game a good deal.

For the first three or four days I did not get a chance, although I saw several Nyan, which were always on the move ; but at last, early one morning, not far from camp, I saw five old rams on the hill-side far above me. They shortly afterwards lay down in a favorable position for a stalk, and by taking advantage of a neighbouring nullah, I was able to get above them without difficulty, and was delighted to find that they were still lying down on a gentle slope.

Just above them was a rocky ridge, on which were several large stones, under cover of one of which I was enabled to creep up to within easy range. Carefully peeping over the ridge I saw a fine ram lying broadside on within seventy yards, and not daring to risk showing myself any more I fired at his shoulder. He managed to rise, staggered a few paces, and then rolled over. One of the hammers of my double-barrelled rifle had been broken off some time before by an accident ; and now, as I hastily proceeded to reload the serviceable barrel, another large ram stood to gaze, giving me a splendid chance ; but before I could insert a fresh cartridge, he was off. Had I had both barrels to depend upon, I should undoubtedly have scored a right and left.

The ram killed had horns forty inches by seventeen.

CHAPTER XXXII.

THE BARKING DEER.

CERVULUS MUNTJAC.

Generally throughout the Himalayas *Kákur.* In Nipál and neighbouring States—*Ratwá.*

THE Barking Deer is only found in the lower hills, including the Sewalik range, and seldom ascends to a greater elevation than 5,000 or 6,000 feet. Although it may be met with nearly everywhere between Assam and the Indus, the Barking Deer is not exactly plentiful, except in certain localities. A well-known sportsman told me that he once stalked and shot *nine* in one morning, in a small valley in Kamáon. Usually, even where they are tolerably common, only two or three would be seen during a morning's walk.

The Barking Deer generally goes by its native name of Kakur ; it is also known to naturalists by the name of Muntjac, but I do not know in what country it receives that appellation—certainly not in any part of India with which I am acquainted.

The Kakur is one of the smallest deer, not being much more than eighteen inches in height. The body is long and flexible, and the legs very short, which enables the animal to make its way with ease through the low and tangled copses which it generally frequents.

The color of the skin is a bright red, and the hair is short, smooth, and glossy. The lower parts are white, including the under part of the tail, which is rather long, and is usually carried erect when the animal is running away. Frequently the whisk of the white tail is the first and last sign of the deer which catches the eye, as the little beast bounds into thick cover, on the edge of which it had previously been standing unobserved.

Two grooves or folds of the skin in the form of a V give a curious expression to the face, which is heightened by black tufts of hair over the eyebrows.

Above the folds in the face are two pedestals of bone covered with hair, on the summit of which the horns are situated : they are generally about five inches long, and bend inwards at the points in the form of hooks. In adult specimens there is also a small tine near the base of the horn.

The male is furnished with two strong and sharp tusks in the upper jaw ; these are formidable weapons, and small as the Kakur is, he can make uncommonly good use of them. I have heard, on the best authority, of powerful dogs being badly injured, and even killed, by a wounded buck.

When the Kakur runs, a curious rattling sound is sometimes heard, and various theories have been advanced to account for it. I have not succeeded in solving the problem to my

XXV

BARKING DEER

CERVULUS MUNTJAC

Published by Thacker, Spink & Co., Calcutta.

entire satisfaction, but I *believe* that the sound is produced either by the jaws being closed with a clash, or by the tongue being struck sharply against the roof of the mouth. The sound is not produced by the tusks, for I have heard it made by a female Kakur which I kept for some time. The little beast was very tame, and used to sleep in our bedroom, where it would frequently make a good deal of noise by champing its jaws and licking itself all over with its long extensile tongue.

The Kakur, like the Four-horned Antelope, has very upright hoofs, and it walks with singular stilty action. When galloping it keeps its head low, and bounds along in a peculiar springy manner.

Many visitors to the various hill-stations of the Himalayas, who may never have seen a Kakur, must probably be well acquainted with its voice, which is wonderfully powerful for such a small animal. It is rather difficult to convey a correct idea of it by words, but it may perhaps be best described as a hoarse, resonant bark. The cry may frequently be heard in the mornings and evenings, and it is also often uttered when the deer is alarmed, when it hears any loud or unusual sound, or suspects the existence of any danger. Occasionally a Kakur will continue to bark, at short intervals, for an hour at a time, and advantage may be taken of his thus betraying his whereabouts, to stalk him, and probably obtain an easy shot.

Kakur inhabit any wooded hills where there is plenty of cover ; they seldom stray into very open ground, but are generally to be found on the edge of thick bushes, or near shady ravines, in which they instantly conceal themselves when alarmed. In the mornings and evenings they move about in a stealthy manner, occasionally visiting fields of green corn in the vicinity of villages. They appear to be impatient of thirst, and when I have occasionally watched by pools of water in the Sewalik hills during the hot months, I have observed that the Kakur were nearly always the first deer that came to drink in the afternoon. On these occasions I seldom fired at them, unless I was in want of meat, as their horns were in the velvet. The venison is very good if it can be kept for a few days.

I have stalked and shot Kakur at various times, and have also had them driven out of cover : many may be found in this manner, but, unless one knows their usual runs, it is difficult to know where to post oneself. Like many other animals, the Kakur objects to being driven, and will break back through the beaters in order to make his point. As they probably only give a chance of a snap shot at short range, it is easier to kill them with a charge of shot than with a rifle bullet : the latter method is of course the more satisfactory and sportsmanlike.

CHAPTER XXXIII.

THE KASHMIR DEER.

CERVUS CASHMEERIANUS.

In Kashmir—*Hángal.* By Shikáris—*Bárá Singhá.*

THIS fine deer is very similar to, if not identical with, the Red Deer of Scotland ; the principal difference being in the superior size of the horns of the Kashmir stag.

It seems to be confined to the ranges surrounding the valley of Kashmir, and to the neighbouring districts of Gurais, Tilail, Kishtwár, and Badráwár. The Wardwan and Sindh valleys, and the lower hills near Islámábád, used to be favorite localities, but of late years I believe that the deer have been gradually working eastwards, and forsaking many of their old haunts.

The vastly increased herds of cattle, especially buffaloes, that are now annually driven from the plains of India to spend the summer months amidst the rich pasturage of the Himalayas, have had the effect of banishing the deer from many hills where they formerly abounded ; a result which, however satisfactory from a utilitarian point of view, is by no means welcomed by the sportsman.

Not only have the deer been driven away, but their numbers have been woefully thinned by the wholesale massacres perpetrated by the natives during the winter. It is said that Shikaris are sent out by the Kashmir authorities to shoot all the stags that they can find ; and after a heavy snow fall the villagers turn out with their dogs and hunt the unfortunate deer until they become exhausted and stick in the snow, when they are surrounded and either shot or knocked on the head with clubs and axes. I have been informed that during one winter five hundred stags were thus slaughtered.

Being, as I have said, so similar to the Scotch Deer, the Kashmir Deer requires but little description. In the winter coat I think that there is no difference in color between the two, but I am under the impression that the Scotch Deer is rather redder than the other during the summer.

The shape and character of the horns of the Hángal vary considerably, but as a general rule they are much more massive, and show a greater tendency to curve inwards at the tips than those of the Red Deer.

A full-grown stag usually has twelve tines on his antlers, hence the name *Bárá Sing* (twelve horns) by which he is generally known among the Shikaris and English sportsmen.

I have heard of fourteen and sixteen tines, but have never seen more than thirteen, and I think the finest pair of horns I ever saw had only eleven.

I have never shot a really fine stag, so I unfortunately possess no horns worth photographing.

It has so happened that I have only on one occasion been able to prolong my leave till the rutting season, and consequently I have had but scanty opportunities of shooting stags.

Bárá Sing usually shed their horns in March or very early in April, just before the time when officers can generally reach Kashmir.

Shortly afterwards the stags begin to work their way upwards as the snow melts, and eventually migrate to the highest ranges, and to distant and secluded forests. Here they remain while their horns are growing, and as soon as they are clear of the 'velvet' the stags begin to retrace their steps in order to rejoin the hinds, which have, for the most part, remained at lower elevations.

Before the rutting season actually commences the stags are extremely difficult to find, concealing themselves a great deal in the forest, eating very little, and not wandering far.

About the middle or end of September the stags begin to bellow or 'call,' and the fiercest rivalry prevails. The challenge of an old stag may be replied to from several directions, and the whereabouts of the belligerents being thus betrayed, they may be stalked and shot without much difficulty.

In order to be successful in Hángal-shooting, however, it is necessary to have good local information : the deer almost invariably return from their summer retreats by certain well-worn paths, and year after year they resort to the same shallow pools, in which they are fond of wallowing.

As I have already mentioned, my opportunities of Bárá Sing-shooting have been but few, and when I have hunted them my efforts have not been crowned with much success.

In August 1864, I tried the country on the Sindh valley side of the mountain of Harmúk. Leaving the village of Chatargúl on the 25th, after a long and steep march I encamped on the open flat above the forest. Next morning I did not feel inclined to go out, but in the afternoon, having sent my tent on a couple of miles, I went along the ridge of the hill, reconnoitring the steep ravines which lay below. Before long a Bárá Sing stag was discovered lying under a rock some distance down the hill, and I at once proceeded to stalk him. When within thirty yards of the place I saw his head and horns above the stone ; I could easily have shot him, but not wishing to spoil his head, I waited for a chance at his shoulder. The stag, however, did not move forward, and presently his horns disappeared ; I waited for a few minutes, and then, seeing nothing more of him, I crept carefully down to the rock under which he had been lying. To my astonishment he was nowhere to be seen. My Shikari having joined me, we both looked about and at last the Shikari discovered the deer's horns sticking out from under the stone a little to our right. I silently moved to the place and sat down on the rock above the horns, so close that I might have taken hold of them by leaning over ! The horns, although quite hard, were not yet clear of the velvet, which hung from them in strips. I sat for some time waiting for the stag to rise ; at last a fly got into my throat and I could not restrain a cough ; the horns moved quickly as the stag started—another cough—and he sprang up and gazed beneath him, but only instantly to fall dead with a bullet through his neck. Unfortunately the hill was very steep, and he rolled down a long way, breaking off one of his horns at the base ; we clambered down to him and found that he was a fine stag with ten points, but the horns were not very large. We found the broken one without much difficulty, and then had a pretty stiff climb back to camp.

I worked hard till the 31st, without seeing another stag ; on that day I found three lying down, and a Snow Bear feeding close to them. The stalk was an easy one, and I reached a juniper bush about one hundred yards from, and straight above, the deer. All had poor heads, so I chose the one that offered the best chance and shot him dead. A fourth stag, which I had not previously seen, now jumped up with the other two, and I should most certainly have got another, if my fools of Shikaris had not shown themselves instead of lying still, so that the deer galloped off without stopping to gaze.

I continued hunting until the 7th of September, frequently sleeping out on the hill-side, so as to be on the ground by daylight ; but I only saw one other stag, who came out of the forest one morning at dawn, and commenced feeding on a grassy slope in company with a number of hinds. I succeeded in approaching to within range, but I miscalculated the distance and missed with my first barrel, and my second barrel missed fire.

Until 1882, I never had another opportunity of hunting Bárá Sing, but in September of that year I went to the hills which divide the province of Chambá from that of Badráwár. Here, in former years, many splendid heads were obtained, and, as I had detailed accounts and sketches of the ground, I anticipated good sport.

To my great disgust, however, I found the hills overrun by innumerable herds of cattle, buffaloes, and sheep, with their attendant shepherds and dogs, which had utterly ruined one of the most perfect and beautiful deer forests imaginable.

The villagers who accompanied me assured me that the deer would return as soon as the cattle went down the hill, and I therefore remained for a month, during which time I patiently hunted all the favorite haunts of the deer without ever getting a single chance.

I once saw a small stag on the edge of the forest, and altogether I came across about half a dozen hinds, and heard another stag in the jungle, but I did not even find the tracks of any others. Not a single stag 'called,' and in fact the shooting on those hills is a thing of the past.

It must not be supposed, however, that these grand deer are as yet nearly extinct : I believe that they are still tolerably abundant in certain places, but they must be sought far away from the beaten tracks.

Although it is only during the rutting season, and again in March, that there is much hope of killing stags by legitimate stalking, the sportsman may chance to find them at other seasons ; but much time may be spent in searching for them without success, and even if one is found, either accidentally or by tracking it to its lair, probably a glimpse of the animal as he disappears in the forest, is all that is obtained.

I have often thought that grand sport might be obtained in some of the gently sloping valleys of Kashmir, by hunting the Bárá Sing with hounds, and either shooting the stags at the passes, or killing them with the knife when at bay in the water. To do this, however, one would require good and staunch hounds that might be depended upon to seize the stag and keep their hold. I have never had the opportunity of trying the experiment.

I do not, as a rule, approve of the use of dogs for hunting large game, but in the case of animals that will not leave the dense forests, I think that an exception may be made.

CHAPTER XXXIV.

THE SAMBUR.

CERVUS ARISTOTELIS.

Generally throughout India—*Sámbar—Sámar.* In Déra Dún—*Máhá—Maíd.*

In the Himalayas—*Jaráo.*

THE Sambur is one of the best-known game animals of India, and has been described by nearly every writer on Indian sport. It is found wherever there are forest-clad hills in almost every province from the Himalayas to Ceylon, but is not met with, as far as I am aware, to the west of the Sutlej, beyond which river, in the mountainous districts, it gives place to the Kashmir Deer.

The Sambur or Jaráo is common in parts of Garhwál and Kamáon, and in the Sewaliks, and from thence eastwards; it is extremely abundant along the whole length of the Terai and the spurs of the Himalayas, as far as Assam. In the Central Provinces, and in Chotá Nágpúr, Sambur are also plentiful in suitable localities.

The Sambur is one of the largest of the deer tribe, considerably exceeding both the Red Deer and Kashmir Deer in height and bulk. It is probably on account of its great size that it has received the misnomer of *Elk* in Madras and Ceylon.

The stag is a grand-looking beast, attaining a height of about fourteen hands, while he is very strongly made. The color is a dark brown, and when the coat has been recently shed, an old stag looks nearly black. The hair is extremely coarse, and at certain seasons the throat is surrounded by a shaggy mane, which is erected when the animal is excited.

The horns are massive, but have usually only three tines. The Sambur of the higher Himalayas however, has frequently more tines, which has given rise to the belief that it is a different species, but I believe that there is no doubt that the Jaráo and the Sambur are the same. I know of no deer whose horns vary so much in size as those of the Sambur, apparently irrespective of the age or size of the animal. Very large stags sometimes carry small stunted-looking horns.

The development of horn appears to depend more upon locality than upon anything else: I have seen some grand Jaráo heads, and I have come across Sambur stags with very fine horns in Chotá Nágpúr, but I have never seen a really good head from the Doon, the Terai, nor the Bhútán Dooárs.

There has been great discussion as to whether Sambur shed their horns annually or not: my own belief is that they do as a general rule, though there may be occasional exceptions. I know that I have hunted in the Sewaliks throughout May and June, and though I met with many stags I never found one worth shooting, all being either absolutely hornless, or with short velvet-covered stumps.

It is on this account that my experiences of Sambur-shooting have been very limited. As in the case of the Kashmir Deer, I have seldom been able to hunt Sambur at the seasons when they carried perfect horns, and I have never cared to shoot animals which afforded no trophies. My best, and, in fact, only chance, was when hunting Gaur in Chotá Nágpúr in January 1883: upon this occasion I might have bagged one or two fine stags, but I would not fire, for fear of disturbing the larger game.

I am therefore unable to give a portrait of a Sambur stag.

The hind much resembles that of the Red Deer, but it is darker in color, and probably rather heavier.

Sambur delight in stony hills, where there is plenty of cover, and where they can have easy access to water. They browse more than graze, and are nearly nocturnal in their habits. During the daytime they seek the most shady retreats, and old stags especially are most difficult to find, frequently betaking themselves to almost inaccessible places where the uninitiated would never dream of looking for them. The experienced hunter, indeed, has frequently to depend more upon fortune than his own knowledge of woodcraft.

Few animals will carry away more lead than the Sambur, and the two or three that I have shot for the sake of the meat, have given me some trouble before I brought them to bag.

One day in the Sewaliks I was returning from an unsuccessful search for a wounded Elephant, when I suddenly came upon a stag which was standing in a dry watercourse The larder was empty, so, although his horns were in the velvet, I fired at him with a 10-bore rifle. I struck him behind the shoulder, but a trifle too low, and he made off. A broad trail of blood showed that he was severely wounded, but I had to track him for a long distance across several ridges and valleys before I could overtake him, and give him a finishing shot.

Another, with perfect but small antlers, which I shot in the Sikkim Terai, led me a similar chase, although my bullet was apparently well placed.

In August 1865, I hunted for Jaráo in the hills near Billing in Garhwál: I frequently found fresh tracks, and several times at night I heard the singular trumpet-like call of the deer close to my tent; but though I worked perseveringly for more than a fortnight, I was never fortunate enough to obtain even a glimpse of a stag.

CHAPTER XXXV.

THE HOG-DEER.

CERVUS PORCINUS.

Generally throughout India—*Párá.*

THE Hog-Deer is one of the most insignificant of the beautiful family of the *Cervidæ*, and, owing to the nature of the country which it inhabits, its pursuit cannot be considered to come under the head of legitimate 'deer-stalking.' It is, however, one of the animals most frequently met with when shooting with a line of Elephants ; and, *magna componere parvis*, it may be said to take the place of the English rabbit in the Indian battue, where everything is on a magnified scale as compared with home scenes and game.

The Hog-Deer is found throughout the whole length of the Terai and in Assam, and I believe also in Burmah. It is also to be met with in the grass jungles on the banks of the Indus, Ganges, Jumna, and other large rivers, and is in many places extremely numerous.

The Hog-Deer somewhat resembles the Spotted Deer, but is not nearly such a handsome animal, being heavily made, and standing on short legs. Its English and specific names have been derived from the pig-like manner in which it rushes through the long grass when disturbed ; keeping its head low down, and galloping without that bounding action which characterizes most deer. The color of the skin is a dark reddish brown, occasionally more or less spotted with white ; the hair is rough and coarse in texture. The horns have three tines, but they are much smaller than those of the Chítal, and have a stunted appearance.

Like Chítal, Hog-Deer appear to shed their horns very irregularly, and deformed antlers are frequently met with.

The females are considerably smaller than the males and somewhat lighter in color : the young are invariably spotted.

Hog-Deer are not generally found in dense forests, but prefer those in which there are frequent open spaces, and still more delight in jungles composed of long grass interspersed with bushes of no great height. They are rarely found far from water, and when disturbed they frequently seek shelter in a neighbouring swamp. Though not gregarious, many may be seen at the same time in favorable localities, where they sometimes collect in large numbers, all, apparently, being quite independent of each other.

Many are usually put up when beating for Tigers, and they are a favorite prey of that animal.

Although they are, of course, unmolested when Tigers are expected, a bye-day is occasionally devoted to them when nobler game is not expected, and they afford capital practice to the young sportsman in the somewhat difficult art of shooting from a howdah : far more being missed than hit even by the oldest hands. The sound of a sudden rush,

XXVI

HOG DEER

CERVUS PORCINUS

Published by Thacker, Spink & Co., Calcutta.

the quick movement of high stalks of grass, and perhaps a glimpse of the white under part of a vanishing tail, are frequently the only indications to guide the sportsman's aim ; steady, deliberate rifle-shooting is out of the question, and the most rapid of snap-shooting must be resorted to. As in rabbit-shooting, you must fire where you *think* the animal is, or rather will be by the time your shot can reach him, though in these days of Express rifles, it is not necessary to hold so far forward as in the old times of small charges and high trajectories The commonest error made is usually firing *over* the deer, as the unpractised hand is extremely apt to shoot at the waving grass-tops, instead of directing his aim some three or four feet below them. When a hot corner has been found, the fusillade from a party of five or six guns occasionally becomes very heavy, as deer after deer rushes at headlong speed, sometimes from under the very trunks of the Elephants ; and the situation is not always a very safe one. The proportion of lead expended to each Hog-Deer bagged is often nearly as great as what has been calculated to be the amount required to kill each man in a general action.

Hog-Deer may be speared on favorable ground, and give splendid runs : they are very fast and usually give a much longer chase than a Boar. I have heard of instances of their deliberately charging a horse ; and with their sharp horns they can inflict a very severe wound. If they can be driven out of long grass on to the open plain, they can be coursed with greyhounds ; but they do not very often afford the chance.

As there is nothing in Hog-Deer-shooting which calls for the exercise of any special knowledge of woodcraft, its incidents do not admit of interesting description : one snap-shot is much like another ; and although one may feel well satisfied with one's-self, when a lucky bullet has bowled over a fat buck in full career, there is little in the attendant circumstances to impress itself on the memory, much less to be worthy of narration.

I shall not, therefore, give any detailed account of my own experiences in Hog-Deer-shooting, but I will relate a curious incident which once occurred to me, in which the conduct of the deer was quite unaccountable.

I was hunting Elephants on the left bank of the Ganges, a few miles above Hardwár, on the 24th of May, 1865. I had found a Tusker standing at the edge of a long belt of high reeds, bordered by a perfectly open plain covered with short grass. Taking advantage of an angle in the reeds, I was walking up to the Elephant ; when, within two hundred yards of him, I saw a fine buck Hog-Deer, with his horns in the velvet, lying out on the plain. He gazed at me, and as I was afraid that he would go away with a rush and alarm the Elephant, I tried to drive him away quietly by waving my hand, and then my handkerchief, at him. He would not move, however, but lay looking at me until I had advanced to within ten yards of him, when he started up and rushed into the reeds with a sharp cry.

I shot the buck whose portrait is here given, on the 10th May, 1867. I recollect that he took a tremendous deal of killing. Although first struck by a bullet from a 10-bore rifle, he went away through long grass, and my friend B. and I had to follow him up on our Elephants and give him several more shots before he could be secured. The horns are a remarkably good pair.

CHAPTER XXXVI.

THE SPOTTED DEER.

CERVUS AXIS.

Generally throughout India—*Chítal;* (The Male), *Jhánk.*

THIS beautiful deer is common all along the foot of the Himalayas from the Sutlej eastwards as far as the Nipál Terai, but it is not found in the Sikkim Terai, nor in the Bhútán Dooárs. Though as a rule it appears to prefer low hills or the vicinity of hills, vast numbers of Spotted Deer are met with in the low lying Sunderbuns and along the western coast of the Bay of Bengal, within a few hours' journey of Calcutta.

The Spotted Deer somewhat resembles the Fallow Deer, but its coloring is more brilliant, and it is a gamer-looking animal. Its color is a bright reddish chesnut, with a dark brown stripe along the back; the lower parts are white, and the whole body is beautifully spotted with white, the marks being arranged in horizontal lines. The tail is long, white beneath, and somewhat bushy.

When in good condition the skin is singularly glossy and very beautiful. The horns of the Chítal are large in proportion to the size of the animal; they vary very much in shape and thickness; they have only three tines, though occasional specimens may be found with four tines, but these are usually deformities.

A peculiarity about the Spotted Deer is, that it appears to have no regular season for shedding its horns, as is, I believe, the case with almost all other deer. I have shot stags with hard horns, others with horns in the velvet, and others again without any horns, in the same week; and this in different months. Others have remarked the same, and some have hence inferred that the Chítal does not shed its horns annually. This would be against all analogy, and I think that the real explanation of the fact is that the Chítal sheds its horns annually, not at any particular season, but according to its age. The breeding season is not restricted to any one month, and therefore deer would be born in various months, and would shed their horns accordingly.

The females are considerably smaller than the males, slightly lighter in color, and with smaller spots.

The Spotted Deer inhabits the forests at the foot of the hills, and is also found on the hills themselves to the elevation of a few hundred feet. It seems particularly to delight in low hills intersected by watercourses, such as the Sewaliks and the hills enclosing the various ' Dúns,' as the valleys which lie at the foot of the Himalayas are called. .

XXVII

CHITAL OR SPOTTED DEER

CERVUS AXIS

The Chítal is a shy and retiring animal, lying quiet in the densest thickets during the heat of the day, and if disturbed, generally attempting to elude observation by concealment, or by trying to sneak quietly away. I have often, when beating for Tigers, seen a cunning old stag with his head down silently creeping away through the jungle, sometimes passing almost under the Elephants. When on foot I have known a herd come quietly past within two or three yards of me in thick cover, and even at that short distance have had difficulty in getting a shot. It might be supposed that such a brightly colored animal would be very conspicuous in the forest, but this is far from being the case; unless it moves, few beasts are more difficult to see; the color of the skin harmonizes with the dead leaves and grass, while the white spots are indistinguishable from the little flecks of light caused by the sunshine passing through the leafy branches. Chítal generally assemble in herds of from ten to thirty, among which are probably two or three stags; but occasionally herds of hundreds are met with.

On being disturbed, and especially on detecting the presence of a beast of prey, the Chítal utters a sort of shrill bark, and many a time has this cry betrayed a Tiger to the sportsman. The stag's cry is a peculiar moaning sort of bellow, and is generally to be heard at night.

Immense numbers of Spotted Deer are frequently met with when beating for Tigers, and many are shot off Elephants in this way. In long grass it is of course only possible to shoot them from Elephants, but however satisfactory it may be to bowl over a stag in full career by a clever snap-shot from the howdah, it cannot, in my opinion, compare with the pleasure of stalking and shooting the same animal on foot, where the nature of the country renders it possible. I know places where splendid sport can be obtained in this way, among low hills covered chiefly with bamboo and sál, with, of course, a considerable undergrowth, but with many open spaces, and intersected by not infrequent streams.

Among such scenes I have passed many happy days, and I will attempt to describe a few of the incidents.

On the 3rd of May, 1863, I arrived at Futtehpúr bungalow, about sixteen miles from Roorkee. Going out into the jungle, I had not walked very far when I caught a glimpse of a stag Chítal galloping through the bushes. I ran for a shot, and fired as he was going straight away from me at a distance of about ninety yards. I heard the shell explode, and the buck staggered but went on. On going to the spot I found plenty of blood and *small pieces of flesh* lying about! We had to track him for fully half a mile and then he required another bullet. I found that the shell had completely shattered his hind-quarters. The same evening I stalked and shot another stag, but as it was late I had to leave him in the jungle.

Next morning I found that a Tiger had carried off the carcase: I tracked him to where he had left the remains, and sat by the place in the evening. The Tiger did not appear before it became quite dark, so I went home; but next morning I discovered that he had again visited the scanty remains.

Having met my friend M., who had a number of Elephants, he asked me to join him and beat for Tigers, and consequently I did not shoot many more deer for some days.

On the 23rd, M., having given up shooting and returned home, I was encamped by myself in the Andéra Kohl, one of the narrow valleys or glens which intersect the Sewalik hills. My tent was close to the stream, and a couple of Elephants were picketed within fifty yards. On awaking this morning I felt tired and disinclined to go out, so I called my Shikari and ordered him to go and shoot a peafowl. As I was speaking, a Kakur barked on the opposite bank, so I went out in my shirt and slippers to look for him, and immediately saw a stag Chítal standing in the water not more than seventy yards off. His tail was turned towards me, and I fired and missed him, but to my astonishment he never stirred! I fired again and broke his shoulder, but he still remained motionless, his fore-leg dangling loose! I sent my Shikari for my gun, which he brought me, and at the same time informed me that a Tiger had gone up the hill behind my tent. I finished the Chítal with a ball from my gun, and heard the Tiger growl in answer to my shot. On enquiry I found that the Tiger had been stalking the Chítal at the same time as myself. He was among some long grass, not twenty yards from me, nor fifty from the tents, when I fired the first shot, on hearing which he had jumped up with a growl and walked up the hill close to my servants. I immediately mounted an Elephant and went after him, but was unable to find him. The Chítal must have been aware that the Tiger was stalking him, and become paralysed from fear. I have been told of other instances where deer were so terrified by Tigers that they appeared to be unable even to make an effort to escape.

On the 25th, I came on a herd of Chítal in the rather open jungle at the foot of some low hills, to which they betook themselves. I carefully followed them, and at length succeeded in making a capital stalk at an old stag. He was quietly feeding in company with two or three hinds on a small open flat on the top of a hill. On reaching the summit and looking carefully over, I found myself within seventy yards, but the stag was feeding straight away from me. It was early morning, and as the rising sun shone on his glossy coat, I thought that I had never seen a more beautiful animal. At length he turned his head, and I instantly sent a bullet through his neck, dropping him stone-dead : he was in perfect condition, with a very bright skin, much splashed with white ; his horns were also very fine. In the evening I made a pretty shot at another stag at full gallop, sending him crashing down into a deep narrow ravine.

Another morning I ordered my camp, which was pitched by the edge of a small stream in one of the ' kohls,' to be moved to a place about five miles off. In order to reach this, my baggage animals had to descend the valley they were in to its mouth, and then skirt along the hills, which would take a considerable time.

I determined to take the short cut across the hills, in the hopes of meeting with game on the way ; and I accordingly took my rifle and a couple of attendants and strolled leisurely through the forest. A ridge or two were crossed without seeing any thing, but at length on reaching the brow of an undulating hill, I had the pleasure of seeing a splendid stag with about half a dozen hinds, on an opposite slope. They were quite unsuspicious as they cropped the short sweet grass which was just sprouting through the light coating of ashes left by the annual burning of the jungle ; a practice which, although highly detrimental, and indeed destructive to young trees, is innocuous to those of mature growth ; while by its fertilization of the soil it greatly encourages the development of grasses and other undergrowth.

It did not take me long to approach to within easy shot of the stag, and I was soon watching him and calculating the length of his shining white antlers from behind a small knoll, with the comfortable conviction that I could gain possession of the trophy whenever I chose. After observing his movements for a short time, I took advantage of his being in a good position, and dropped him on the spot. He was in excellent condition, and, even after being ' gralloched,' proved a sufficient load for the two men who had to carry him to camp.

Subsequently hearing that three Officers, with whom I was acquainted, were shooting in the jungles at the foot of the hills, I paid them a visit, and we arranged to join our forces and have a general beat with Elephants. By a general beat I mean that we were to fire at anything, for we had reason to believe that our two parties had already accounted for most of the Tigers that had been known to be in the vicinity.

We had hopes that we might, by good luck, add another Tiger to the bag, but we were not sanguine ; and were therefore not disappointed when the decomposing carcase of a small Tiger, which one of the party had wounded and lost on the previous day, was all that we saw of the feline tribe. Curiously enough too, although on previous days, when we were only after the nobler game, we saw any number of deer, to-day they were few and far between and it was seldom that the forest was disturbed by the echoes of a rifle-shot. In one particularly thick piece of cover, however, I espied an old stag Chítal with his head down, apparently shrinking into the smallest possible space, sneaking away through the bushes. Stopping my Elephant, I lost no time in bringing the sights of my rifle to bear on the rapidly disappearing form of the stag, and although the smoke hung in the heavy cover to such a degree that I could not at first see the result of the shot, on pressing forward we soon came upon the deer lying gasping on the grass. After duly admiring the beautiful animal we ' padded ' him and continued the beat, but though several other deer and some Pig were shot, I was the only one of the party fortunate enough to secure any trophy worth having, on that day.

The best Chítal's head I ever procured was the one here photographed. On the 12th of May, 1865, I was encamped in Dholkand in the Sewaliks. My friend F., who was with me, had gone out early in the morning to look for a Bear whose tracks he had seen the day before. I remained in camp, but after a time, my attention was drawn to some Chítal which were barking and making a great noise not far from the tents. I went out and soon found the herd, but they were in motion before I observed them. I followed them up, and got a shot at the stag at one hundred and seventy yards, as he went up the opposite side of a ravine. I broke his fore-leg and fired three other shots at him as he stood, hitting him with one. He then rushed down into the ravine, which became much narrower farther on ; I therefore sent a man round to head him, and then, following him up, hemmed him into a narrow place where I caught him by the horns. The antlers, as will be seen by the photograph, were very thick and symmetrical, and I have never seen a finer pair in any one's possession. I once, however, saw a stag in the Sewaliks whose horns seemed to be enormous—very much larger than any others I ever saw : unfortunately I could not get a shot at him.

A A

March, April, and May are the best months for shooting Chítal on foot in the Sewaliks. A good deal of the grass has then been burned, and the deer are easily found among the low hills, especially in the vicinity of water. This shooting in the Sewaliks is about the most delightful I know. A great variety of animals may be met with, and several shots may generally be obtained during the day.

XXVIII

MUSK DEER
MOSCHUS MOSCHIFEROUS

Published by Thacker, Spink & Co., Calcutta.

CHAPTER XXXVII.

THE MUSK-DEER.

MOSCHUS MOSCHIFERUS.

Generally throughout the Himalayas—*Kastúrá.*

In Garhwál and Kamáon—*Béná—Masak ndbá.*   In Kashmir—*Ráos—Roñs.*

THE diminutive subject of the present chapter is distributed in suitable localities, along the entire range of the Himalayas from Gilgit to Bhútán. It is also said to be extremely common in the interior of Thibet, from which country musk forms one of the most important articles of export.

It is, however, much less common, or rather less plentiful, than it used to be, for the value of the musk is well known, and no animal is more persecuted. In some of the more remote parts of Kashmir, such as Gurais and Tilail, and in the rugged district of Pángí, it is probably now as numerous as anywhere. The Ganges valley used to be a favorite locality, but I believe that few deer are now left there.

The Musk-Deer is very singular both in its form and habits: it is one of the smallest of the deer tribe, standing not more than twenty inches at the shoulder.

The hind-quarters are high and rounded, and the legs are long and slender, terminating in long, hard, delicately-shaped hoofs, the false heels especially being remarkably elongated. The tail is very short and nearly naked in males, and possesses a peculiar gland.

The prevailing color is a brownish grey, varying in shades on the back, where it is darkest, so as to give the animal a mottled or brindled appearance. The hair of the Musk-Deer is very curious, being coarse and brittle: it has been aptly compared to miniature porcupine quills: it always comes out very easily. That on the head and legs is shorter and finer than on the body. The head is small and narrow; both sexes are destitute of horns, but the male is furnished with a pair of tusks in the upper jaw: they grow downwards and slightly curved backwards, and attain a length of about three inches.

The singular product from which the animal derives its name, and which has been the cause of its being so much sought after, is a brown, gingerbread-like substance secreted by a gland situated on the abdomen of the male. For a more detailed description of the substance I must refer the reader to works on anatomy.

The quantity varies according to the season and the age of the animal.

Musk is valuable, a good 'pod' being worth at least Rs. 10 ; but as English sportsmen do not usually shoot for profit, Musk-Deer are not very much sought after by them.

Musk-Deer are solitary animals, very much resembling hares in their general habits : I have never heard of more than two being found together. Like hares, they are seldom to be seen moving about during the daytime, but make regular *forms* in the forest, and wander about in the mornings and evenings.

They may be found in all sorts of places at an elevation of over 8,000 feet ; but I have met with them oftenest in the birch forests.

Early in the year, when even the Ibex resorts to the lower parts of the hill, the Musk-Deer may be found far above the snow line, making its bed in the snow, and feeding on the buds and tender shoots of the bushes and trees which are just commencing to expand under the influences of spring.

No animal seems more indifferent to cold, from which it is well protected ; its thick coat of hollow hair forming as it were a sort of cushion, which acts as an insulator and enables the deer to lie even on snow without much loss of animal heat.

It is amazingly active and sure-footed, bounding along without hesitation over the steepest and most dangerous ground. Its usual food appears to be leaves and flowers, but the natives say that it will kill and eat snakes ! A friend of mine, an Officer in the Artillery, assured me that he had seen a snake which was taken out of the stomach of a Musk-Deer which he had just shot. I cannot remember, however, whether he actually saw it cut out or not, so it is possible that his Shikaris may have deceived him.

Musk-Deer differ considerably in their habits according to whether they are much or little hunted. Mr. Wilson describes how, when he first established himself in the Ganges valley and made hunting his profession, the Musk-Deer were easily procured. On seeing a hunter, they would stand watching him for a long time, occasionally uttering their hiss of alarm, but usually allowing him to approach within easy shot. I have myself witnessed similar conduct on the part of the deer in remote districts, and have even fired three shots at one without its moving ; but, as a rule, they are now excessively wary, and bound away as soon as they detect the approach of man.

There are two ways of hunting Musk-Deer : either by driving the jungles which they are known to frequent, or by quietly walking through the forest in the mornings and evenings. If the latter plan is adopted, the hunter should walk very slowly and carefully, and reconnoitre each ravine and glade he comes to ; for a Musk-Deer is most difficult to see among the grey stems of trees, unless he is in motion.

Natives snare many Musk-Deer by means of nooses placed in gaps in low, rude hedges, which are constructed in favorable localities, frequently running across the hills for a mile or two. These hedges form no real obstruction to the deer, which could bound over them with the greatest ease ; but the apparent aversion of animals to make an unnecessary effort, induces both the deer and pheasants of all sorts to seek for a gap. The result is that both deer and pheasants are soon almost exterminated where noosing is permitted.

When caught young the Musk-Deer may be easily domesticated, but many go blind and die. In 1865, I bought one from a shepherd-boy near Málárí, below the Nítí Pass. I got a milch-goat for it, but though the little thing soon took to its foster mother, she did not appear to reciprocate its affection, and always had to be held while it was sucking. This it did in a curious way, jumping up and crossing its fore-legs every instant, and uttering a singular plaintive cry. It would not remain long with the goat, but after satisfying its hunger it would go away and hide in some bush. I kept it for more than a fortnight, when it went blind and died, apparently suffering much pain.

A friend of mine was more fortunate. In 1867, he procured a young Musk-Deer in the hills near Murree: it soon became perfectly tame and seemed to thrive remarkably well on bread and milk, leaves, and flowers. It was very bold and fearless, and used to play with my friend's children, and with a little dog. The dog was equally fond of the deer, and it was amusing to see him attack any stranger who presumed to touch it. I saw the deer in November, after it had been brought down to the plains, and it was then in perfect health. I rather think that it was eventually sent to England. I have since seen another Musk-Deer that was nearly equally tame.

I have never gone out of my way to shoot Musk-Deer, and have let numbers go without a shot, but during numerous expeditions to the hills, I have shot a good many at different times; and when I am in want of meat and there is no fear of disturbing nobler game, I am always glad to have the opportunity of bagging one. The flesh is excellent, without the slightest flavor of musk, and it is a pleasant change from the leathery mutton which the higher hills afford in the early months of spring.

Those I have killed have been shot under varied circumstances: some have been come upon suddenly in the forest, affording an easy chance within a few yards: others have been first discovered at a great distance and regularly stalked: while others again have jumped up at my very feet and bounded away, only pausing for an instant to look back, and being knocked over by a lucky snap-shot.

After a long morning's walk in search of Markhoor, of which I had been unable to find any recent traces, I was one day sitting eating my breakfast on a grassy slope over-looking a wide ravine. I had not been there very long before I saw two Musk-Deer, one chasing the other, on the opposite slopes; and after playing about for some time, they dis-appeared among the bushes at the bottom of the ravine. Shortly afterwards, I saw one of them coming up the hill towards me. I sat perfectly quiet, and it approached to within a hundred and fifty yards, when, as it was about to enter the forest, I fired at it with my miniature Express. As it did not fall, I fired another shot, but could not see with what result. My Shikaris, who had gone to an old hut a short distance off to smoke, now came to see what I was firing at, and I sent one of them down to ascertain whether the deer was hit or not. On reaching the spot where I had last seen it, he drew back and beckoned to me. I at once ran down, and on looking over some low bushes, I saw the Musk-Deer within five yards licking the blood from its side, where the bullet had slightly grazed it. I knock-ed it over, and as it rolled down the hill, my Shikari seized it, and in doing so received a severe cut across the palm of the hand from one of its sharp tusks: the wound was, however, doubtless accidentally inflicted.

Not long ago I was returning to my camp down a wooded valley, when one of my coolies informed me that he had seen a Musk-Deer in the morning, and pointed out the patch of forest into which it had gone. I therefore proceeded cautiously, keeping a sharp look out, and on coming to a secluded spot, where scattered boulders and fallen trees strewed the ground, I caught sight of the object of my search, standing motionless half-hidden by the trunk of a tree, within thirty yards. At such short range a miss was impossible; but the deer bounded down the hill, to fall dead on the bank of the stream below.

The last Musk-Deer I shot afforded an instance of the extraordinary tenacity of life which animals will sometimes exhibit when mortally wounded, but not struck so as to injure the most vital organs, or break any of the limbs.

I was high up, close to the snow line, when I saw a Musk-Deer feeding in a small grassy ravine, which the rays of the rising sun had just lighted up. I had no difficulty in stalking to within about a hundred yards, and I fired a steady shot with a ·450 Express. The deer bounded into a small copse, on the edge of which it had been feeding; but I soon saw it struggling among the bushes, and presently it was still. I walked up to the spot, and seized the deer by the hind-leg, telling my Shikari to cut its throat. As he was about to catch hold of it, the deer made a struggle, escaped from my grasp, bounded down the hill for a short distance, and then stopped. I went down, got within ten yards, and threw three or four stones at it, striking it with the last, and sending it rolling down on to the snow which filled the ravine below.

We now went to pick it up, upon which the deer regained its legs and made off up the hill at a wonderful pace. I did not like to fire again, but followed it up the hill, expecting every minute that it would again lie down and give no further trouble. To our astonishment, however, it continued its course upwards as if nothing had happened, and went right out of sight, and I had to follow at least half a mile up a steep hill, and again shoot it across a ravine. On examining it I found that my first bullet had struck rather too low and too far back, but had cut out nearly the whole of the intestines.

Although so much persecuted, Musk-Deer are still tolerably plentiful in certain localities; but, except to the professional hunter, they do not offer much attraction.

CHAPTER XXXVIII.

MISCELLANEOUS.

ALTHOUGH I had hoped to have been able to give a description from my own personal experience, if not a portrait, of *every* 'Large Game' animal that inhabits the extensive area to which this book relates, I regret to say that there are still about half a dozen species which I have never succeeded in shooting. They are as follows :—

THE OUNCE OR SNOW-LEOPARD—*Felis Uncia.*

The Snow-Leopard is scattered all over the highest hills, but it is seldom that the English sportsman has the luck to meet with one ; I have never had that good fortune during all my wanderings.

The Snow-Leopard is one of the most beautiful of the feline race ; it is about the size of a medium-sized Panther, but the tail is far longer in proportion to the body, and it is also much more bushy than that of the Panther. The fur is long and beautifully soft ; it is of a light grey color, irregularly spotted with black.

I once obtained a good skin from a villager in Báltístán ; he had shot it during the winter.

THE CLOUDED-LEOPARD—*Felis Macrocelis.*

This very rare and handsome Leopard is said to be found throughout Sikkim, but it cannot be at all plentiful even there, as I have tried in vain to procure a skin in Darjiling ; and the only one that I have ever heard of being bagged, was killed by a Tea-planter of my acquaintance in his garden, with a charge of shot !

The color of the skin is a greenish-brown with large irregular blotches of a much darker hue.

The Clouded Leopard is said to prefer the densest forests, but I know nothing of its habits, never having met with one.

THE STRIPED HYÆNA—*Hyæna Striata.*

The Hyæna is not uncommon in many parts of Northern India, but being almost entirely nocturnal in his habits, he is not often seen, unless when beaten out of his retreat, when nobler game is being sought for.

The Hyæna is an ugly brute, having a large head, high withers, and drooping quarters. His shambling gait does not add to his appearance, and he has an unenviable notoriety as a robber and a coward.

His skin is of a brownish-grey color, with dark vertical stripes : the hair is long and coarse, and forms a sort of mane on the neck and shoulders.

I have never shot, and have only twice seen, a Hyæna ; on both occasions at night when I had no gun. The first was near Súbáthú, the second was in the station of Kasáoli. I was walking through the latter place one moonlight night, when I came upon a Hyæna on the road ; the brute merely moved a little to one side, and had the impertinence to growl at me as I passed.

Hyænas often carry off dogs and goats, but I believe that they will never attack a man. They are cowardly beasts, and, when speared off horseback, never attempt to show fight, though they often give a good run.

THE INDIAN BLACK BEAR—*Ursus Labiatus.*

The Indian Black Bear, or Sloth Bear as it is sometimes called, is found, though not in large numbers, throughout the Dún and Terai. It is more plentiful among the rocky hills of Bírbhúm, Singbhúm, and Chotá Nágpúr.

It is smaller than the Himalayan Black Bear, and is differently shaped, having a long head with largely developed lips, and slenderer limbs than the other species. The color of the coat is a rusty black, with a white V-shaped mark on the chest, and a greyish muzzle.

The hair is coarse and long, attaining its greatest length on the forequarters. The claws are most formidable weapons. Unlike most other Bears, which appear to delight in cold climates, this Bear seems to be regardless of heat, and inhabits some of the hottest localities in India.

Its favorite haunts are rocky hills, where it spends the heat of the day in a cave, or under some shady tree. It lives upon fruit, larvœ of insects, roots, &c., and it is excessively fond of the flower of the mhowa tree, to obtain which, it will travel great distances. I have never heard of this Bear eating flesh, either killed by itself, or carrion.

It is said to be extremely savage, and to attack people when quite unprovoked, but I do not believe that any animal, as a general rule, will go out of its way to attack man.

Common as this Bear is in certain districts, it has so happened that I have never been able to devote any time to its pursuit, and though I have two or three times hunted for it, it was under unfavorable circumstances. The only one that I ever saw was in the Bhútán Dooárs when I was beating for Rhinoceros, and as I only had an indistinct view of it in the long grass, I mistook it for a Pig till it was too late to get a shot at it.

THE JAVAN OR SUNDERBUN RHINOCEROS—*Rhinoceros Sondaicus.*

This comparatively little-known Rhinoceros is still tolerably abundant in the Sunderbuns or Gangetic Delta, where it inhabits the swampy islands near the sea face. It is also found, but rarely, in the Sikkim Terai, where, I believe its existence was not known for certain until I recognized it in 1878.

It is sometimes known as the Lesser Indian Rhinoceros, but when full-grown it is little, if at all, inferior in size to the other species.

It may be recognized by the different arrangement of the heavy folds of the skin, by the somewhat slenderer head, and above all, by the curious tesselated appearance of the hide, which is very different from the tuberculated armour of *Rhinoceros Unicornis.*

The female has no vestige of a horn.

In May 1878, I was hunting not far from the left bank of the Tístá river, with two friends, S. and L. One day we had pitched our camp at a place where we were told that Rhinoceros were to be found, and had spent the whole morning in a fruitless search for them. That there were 'Rhino' in the neighbourhood was evident from the fresh tracks, so we went out again in the afternoon.

After beating through a considerable extent of forest, we came to a wide grassy plain, and while crossing it, we roused a 'Rhino' out of a muddy watercourse. We did not catch sight of it, but the disturbed state of the water showed that it had just left, and we presently heard it moving through the high grass. We had not much difficulty in tracking, and in about a mile we overtook the 'Rhino,' which turned to gaze at us. S. fired and crippled it, and knocked it over with a second shot.

Our Elephants, which were all nervous untrained animals, refused to go near the fallen 'Rhino,' and as we endeavoured to force them in the proper direction, a calf, which we had not previously observed, rushed through the grass. L., who could not see how small it was, fired at once, and struck the poor little beast, which uttered a loud scream.

This was too much for the nerves of S.'s Elephant, which at once bolted at full speed in the direction of the sál forest, which he was only prevented from entering (to the imminent risk of his rider) by the Mahout's throwing a blanket over his eyes.

In the meantime L. and I were endeavouring to find the calf, but though we dismounted from our demoralized Elephants, and hunted for it on foot, we could find no trace of it in the heavy grass.

On going to examine our prize, I at once recognized it as *R. Sondaicus;* and on telling the natives who were with us that this was not the ordinary Rhinoceros, they informed me that they were aware that there were two kinds.

A Goorkha who was with me filled a soda water bottle with the milk of the dead Rhinoceros : I had the curiosity to taste it, and found it excellent.

S. had some very handsome shields and trays made from the hide ; which, when dried and polished, looks like tortoise-shell.

The Pigmy Hog—*Porculia Salvania.*

This tiny animal hardly comes under the heading of 'Large Game,' but being so nearly allied to the Wild Boar, I have mentioned it in its proper place.

It is an inhabitant of the Sikkim Terai and Bhútán Dooárs, but very little is known about its habits. As it lives in perfect forests of grass, there are not many facilities for observing it.

I can give no detailed description of the animal, never having inspected one. I believe that it is exactly like a miniature hog, only rounder in shape, and nearly tail-less. I have

B B

frequently seen its footmarks in the Sikkim Terai, and one occasion I followed a small animal, (whose course I could trace by the moving stems,) for some distance, but did not fire, because I could not see what it was. I was much annoyed when my Shikari afterwards informed me that it was one of the small breed of Pigs.

I believe that the Pigmy Hog does not stand more than twelve inches at the shoulder !

THE SWAMP-DEER—*Cervus Duvaucellii.*

This beautiful deer used to be much more widely distributed than it now is. In former days it abounded on the islands in the Indus, but it is now rarely to be found there. Not many years ago it was to be found in the Dérá Dún, and was fairly numerous in the Nipál and Oudh Terais. Now-a-days it is not to be found with certainty much to the west of the Bhútán Dooárs, but large herds exist in Assam.

The Swamp-Deer is considerably smaller than the Sambur, and much more gracefully made. The neck is long and elegant, and the whole appearance of the animal extremely *blood-like.*

The horns are peculiar, possessing basal, but no median tines ; while the terminal branches acquire a number of additional tines as the deer progresses in age. The usual number of branches of an adult head are about twelve ; but fourteen, or sixteen, are occasionally met with, when the horns acquire a somewhat palmated character.

The color is a bright red, becoming paler on the under parts.

The Swamp-Deer, as a rule, avoids dense forests, and lives principally in long grass on the banks of rivers, or in beds of reeds on the margin of swamps. During the heat of the day, however, it is fond of lying down in the shade of a tree, frequently a sál tree.

I have seen a few Swamp-Deer in the Bhútán Dooárs, but I have unfortunately never had a chance of shooting a fine stag.

The day after the death of the Rhinoceros described above, my friend S. shot a beautiful specimen, but its horns were not clear of the velvet : I recollect that the venison was the best that I ever tasted in India, being extremely fat. Most Indian deer, antelopes, wild sheep, &c., are very lean.

I have now mentioned every large animal that is to be found in the parts of Thibet and India which I have described ; and the reader can decide which he prefers to hunt, if his time is too limited for him to hope to be able to obtain specimens of each species.

It is not to be expected that anything like a complete collection even of the Himalayan game can be made in a single expedition, and it is a great mistake to attempt too much.

The sportsman should make up his mind as to what animals he wishes to hunt, and decide upon the route which he will take. This must of course be done with due regard to the seasons, as some of the best shooting grounds are inaccessible during great part of the year.

Plans having once been made should be carried out, and should not be changed, because, perhaps, sport is not met with at once.

Patience and perseverance are absolute essentials if success is to be attained. Some men seem to expect to find 'Large Game' as easily as they would find hares and pheasants at home, and become disgusted if they are not continually firing off their rifles.

Such men had better not attempt Himalayan shooting, for they will certainly be disappointed. There is still abundance of game in the Himalayas, but it is not to be obtained without hard work.

In many places the natives will deny the existence of game, and will tell any number of lies to induce the traveller to leave their village and go to some other one, where they assure him that he will obtain excellent sport. On his arrival at the place named, the same story will probably be repeated, and very likely the sportsman will be told that if he had remained at the *last* village he would have found game to his heart's content.

This anxiety to get rid of sportsmen is partly caused by the unwillingness of the people to furnish the supplies required by travellers; but I fear that it is partly to be attributed to the conduct of Englishmen, who have thrashed or abused villagers for not showing game, when they were doing their best.

It is, therefore, always advisable to be as independent as possible of the products of the country, and to limit one's requisitions to absolute necessaries.

If you have good reasons for supposing that game is to be found in any locality, do not believe any assertions to the contrary, but insist upon having a guide and look for yourself.

The presence or absence of tracks will show whether there is game or not, and it must be remembered that a hill may be full of game and yet that not a head may be seen for several days.

In almost every village at least one man may be found, who does a little hunting on his own account; and if you make friends with him and administer judicious '*bakshísh*' when he shows you sport, he will generally do his best for you.

Shepherds usually make the best Shikaris, and, even if they are not professional hunters, their knowledge of the country makes them valuable as guides.

The professional Shikaris who hover about hill stations, and the still more numerous *soi disant* Shikaris to be met with in Kashmir, are to be looked upon with the greatest suspicion. The latter especially are generally arrant impostors and rogues, who know little or nothing about '*shikár.*'

In conclusion I venture to give a few hints, which, though superfluous for experienced sportsmen—some of whom may also disagree with me on some points—may be useful to those who are beginners in the arts of rifle-shooting and stalking. If any of these hints are considered trivial, I can only say that it is by attention to small details that great successes are achieved.

I.

Never give a loaded rifle to a native if you can possibly help it. Now that breech-loaders are in universal use, it can seldom be necessary to do so, except when in pursuit of dangerous animals.

2.

Do not have 'safety bolts' on your rifles ; they are extremely dangerous, and have been the cause of fatal accidents. You can load and unload a breech-loader nearly as quickly as you can adjust the catches, which are, moreover, apt to get out of order.

3.

Never walk through jungle where Tigers or other dangerous beasts are known to exist without a loaded gun or rifle in your hand.

4.

Do not become careless because you do not find game at once ; the best chances nearly always occur when you least expect them.

5.

Make *sure* of easy shots. This is the grand secret of making a bag.

6.

Never fire long shots : you frighten away far more than you kill. Have patience and you will get near your game in time. Shots should seldom be fired at a longer range than a hundred and fifty yards.

7.

Always walk slowly, and often sit down and look about you.

8.

Avoid showing yourself against the sky line.

9.

Be as silent as possible, and insist on your attendants being the same.

10.

Always consider the direction of the wind, when hunting either in the hills or jungles.

11.

Always take out plenty of ammunition, and carry a large knife in your belt : you *may* never want it, but the time *might* come when your life would depend upon it.

DRAWING OF CAMP

Published by Thacker, Spink & Co., Calcutta.

CHAPTER XXXIX

HINTS ON TRAVELLING AND CAMP EQUIPMENT.

THERE is perhaps no country in which the sportsman who wanders beyond the reach of railways and metalled roads can travel in such comfort and at such small expense, as in the various provinces of India. Thanks to the comparatively low rates charged for the hire of country transport, and the cheapness of labor, he can penetrate to even the most remote districts without depriving himself of any of the ordinary conveniences of life. Adapting his equipment and description of transport to the districts which he proposes to visit, he may start from any part of India at the shortest notice, and roam for months as inclination prompts him, at considerably less cost than if he remained in his own house.

The means of transport upon which he must rely are, country carts, camels, bullocks, mules or ponies, yâks (in Thibet), and coolies or porters; and, in certain districts, elephants.

In most of the hill provinces he will have to depend upon coolies alone, at any rate as soon as he leaves the beaten paths.

TRAVELLING IN THE HILLS.

As the greater part of my book refers to the Himalayas, I will first give my ideas of the equipment most suitable for mountain travelling, which, with some modifications according to circumstances, will be found equally well adapted for other parts of India.

When travelling in the hills, it is desirable to restrict one's baggage as much as possible, consistently with reasonable convenience. It is a great mistake to stint one's-self unnecessarily, but at the same time comfort is diminished rather than increased by dragging about a quantity of superfluous luxuries.

The sportsman who works hard must be well clothed and well fed; but many changes of dress are not required, and very simple fare is relished in the bracing climate of the Himalayas.

I am no teetotaller, and I thoroughly enjoy the soothing influence of a cigar, but I strongly recommend any one who has much mountain climbing to do, to abstain as much as possible from liquor and tobacco, both of which are undoubtedly bad for 'the wind.'

In many parts of the hills inevitable delay is caused if a large number of coolies are required, as they frequently have to be collected from scattered and distant villages: and even when procurable, a long string of coolies is much less manageable on the march than a smaller number. Moreover, when the resources of a village are too heavily taxed, some of the coolies supplied are sure to be old or infirm, and they will probably either break down or throw away their loads on the march. Under such circumstances it will be found that the load abandoned or left behind is one of those most urgently required in camp—in nine cases out of ten, cooking utensils, bedding, or tent!

I do not think that any sportsman, whose baggage is well selected and properly arranged should require more than twelve coolies, the weight of each man's load being not more than 70 lbs. at the outside.

They would be thus accounted for—

Tent	...	...	...	1
Bedding	...	...	...	1
Servants' tent	...	...	...	1
Servants' bedding	...	...	...	1
Clothes, books, &c.	...	...	...	2
Cooking utensils	...	...	...	1
Stores and sundries	...	...	...	3
Guns	...	...	...	2
		Total	...	12

In very out of the way places, where food has to be carried for all hands for several days, additional coolies would, of course, be required.

Having stated what I consider to be about the amount of baggage which should be taken, I will now proceed to describe the camp equipment which I have found to best combine the requirements of portability and utility. I may as well mention, however, that the most careful arrangement of loads will be labor lost, unless the strictest supervision is exercised over native servants ; who, unless constantly looked after, will daily alter the disposition of the coolies' burdens, and accumulate rubbish of all sorts with most aggravating pertinacity.

When starting on a shooting trip, the first march should invariably be a short one, and after arrival in camp the baggage should be carefully inspected and overhauled, all useless and superfluous articles being ruthlessly destroyed. Similar inspections should be made from time to time at uncertain intervals, as thus alone will everything be kept in its proper place.

TENTS.

After a very long experience of camp life under all sorts of conditions, I have adopted the tent of which a photograph is given, and have found it answer every purpose in all climates. It is light, portable, weather-proof, and sufficiently roomy for a sportsman's wants.

The following are the dimensions :—

	ft.	ins.
Height	...	... 7 0
Length	...	... 7 6
Width at base		... 10 0

The tent poles are made of *male* bamboo, rather thicker than an ordinary spear shaft, and are jointed in the middle for facility of transport. The tent is made of American drill dyed '*khâkî*' color. As will be observed, no ropes are required except the guy ropes, the tent pegs being inserted in metal loops attached to the margin of the cloth, which should be double or treble.

The pegs are of iron, square in section, and about ten inches long ; twenty-one are required to pitch the tent properly ; they weigh 14 lbs.

The pegs are packed in a strong leather bag, which prevents them from chafing and wearing holes in the tent, which they soon do if rolled loosely up in it according to the favorite practice of servants.

The poles are contained in a strong canvas bag, and then rolled up with the pegs in the tent, which is again protected by an outer cover of strong canvas, the whole weighing under 80 lbs.

Though generally pitched as shown in the photograph, the upper fly may be dispensed with in cool dry weather ; or, by having a spare upright and an additional ridge pole, it may be pitched in prolongation of the inner fly, thus forming a sort of verandah, and more than doubling the space covered in.

For one's servants, the tent known as a 'bivouac pâl,' such as was used by some regiments in the late Afghan campaign, is very convenient : it is also most useful when one wishes to sleep a night or two on the hill, in places where it is impracticable or undesirable to take an ordinary tent. A bivouac tent may be of double cloth and the dimensions as follows :—

		ft.	ins.
Height	...	...	3	6
Length	...	...	7	6
Width at base	...	7	0

Such a tent will accommodate three natives with ease ; and I should recommend the sportsman to take two, one to serve as a kitchen in bad weather. The poles and pegs may be rather lighter than those of the larger tent. Canvas bags to contain everything should be provided for these tents also.

My tents were made by the Elgin Mills Company at Cawnpore, who have the patterns.

BEDS AND BEDDING.

Although I have slept on the ground for years, I think it is advisable to have a light camp-bedstead, to keep one off the damp ground, and to save one to a certain extent from the attacks of insects, as well as to raise one above the draught which must penetrate more or less under the walls of the best pitched tent.

Many sorts of camp-bed have been invented, but the majority of them are either too heavy and cumbrous, or too complicated and fragile.

After trying many different kinds I have at last adopted what I consider to be the best adapted to all circumstances, as it combines lightness, simplicity, portability and strength, with the additional advantage of economizing room in a tent.

It is a combination of travelling trunks and a stretcher, and is constructed as follows :—

The ends are composed of two strong square leather trunks or boxes known as 'yek-dáns,' to the corners of which are fixed iron sockets for the reception of four iron stanchions, which support the ends of the stretcher. The stanchions on one side are square, on the other round.

The stretcher consists of two bars of tough wood connected by strong canvas, which is firmly nailed to the bars along their entire length, with the exception of the ends which fit into the stanchions.

The length of the stretcher must of course depend upon the height of the person for whom it is intended : the width must be exactly equal to the distance between the stanchions.

The two 'yek-dáns' having been placed back to back at a proper interval, the ends of the stretcher bars (which are round in one bar, and square in the other) are dropped into their respective places ; the square bar of course remaining fixed in its square stanchions, while the round one readily revolves. The bed is now nearly complete, but however tightly stretched at first, it would be found that the canvas would become slack with use. To remedy this defect two strong iron eyes or 'dees' are fixed to the centre of the round bar, which is cut square for three or four inches in the middle. Through these eyes a tough but light wooden lever is passed, the lower end or point of the lever being furnished with a short strap and buckle firmly secured to it.

A strong leather strap is looped round the centre of the square bar, and, passing under the bed, is connected with the buckle at the end of the lever. According as this is tightened or loosened, so is the tension on the canvas increased or diminished.

Two small iron uprights fitting into sockets in the corners of the 'yek-dán' forming the head part of the bed, and connected by a belt of canvas, prevent pillows from falling off, and complete what I have found to be an extremely comfortable and very strong bed.

It is difficult to describe such a contrivance clearly, but I trust that by reference to the photograph, what I have written may become intelligible.

———————————

A combined valise and ground sheet of strong canvas lined with waterproof is a convenient arrangement ; as not only can bedding and many odds and ends be rolled up in it, but it forms a dry and serviceable bed when one is obliged to sleep on the ground.

The best sort of waterproof sheet which I know is that in which a wafer-like layer of cork is inserted between two layers of waterproofing : these sheets are generally lined with a tartan stuff, and those that I have seen measure six feet by three and a half.

Taking one of these sheets as the basis of my valise bed, I had the outer side covered with strong canvas, and a strip of the same material half the width of the waterproof sheet sewn to each margin and furnished with brass eyelets, so as to fold over and lace in the centre. A flap of canvas was also attached to the foot of the sheet, and a large bolster-shaped bag with circular ends to the head. This bag is the receptacle for a pillow, iron wash-hand basin with leather cover containing brushes, comb, soap, looking-glass, towels, &c., &c., while all blankets are neatly folded and laid on the waterproof sheet. The flaps are then turned in and laced, the whole rolled up commencing at the head, and secured by two strong leather straps which are kept in their places by loops sewn to the canvas.

The bedding thus secured is kept dry on the march, and can be got ready for the night in a few seconds. The stretcher should form part of the same load.

Four thick blankets should be sufficient for any climate, but in Thibet I recommend the use of an extra thick sleeping suit. Additional warmth may be secured by lacing the side flaps loosely over one, thereby effectually excluding all draughts.

Although the tired hunter will find that he will sleep soundly on the stoniest ground, there is no use in incurring unnecessary discomfort, and in the forest-clad hills a most luxurious mattress may be improvised from the young branches of the pine-tree. A bed composed of these twigs, piled to the thickness of about a foot, will be found to be deliciously soft and elastic, besides being delightfully fragrant.

Mosquito curtains are absolutely necessary in some places ; a very simple and portable arrangement is to suspend them from a cane hoop.

TRUNKS AND BASKETS.

The 'yek-dáns' (Persian for ice-box), already mentioned as forming part of the camp bed, should hold nearly all the clothes, books, and other small articles which a sportsman would require for a six months' trip ; but any one who wishes to travel more luxuriously than I consider necessary, can, of course, provide himself with one or more additional pairs. 'Yek-dáns' are made in all sizes, but the most convenient are twenty-three inches in length by eighteen in width and eighteen in height. The *length* of the 'yek-dán' becomes its *width* when utilized as part of the bed.

'Yek-dáns' may be procured in Peshawur, or from Messrs. Foy at Cawnpore, but care should be taken that they are properly made. They are sometimes lined with wood, and are sometimes constructed of leather alone : the latter are too limp to bear the weight of a stretcher, or indeed to stand much knocking about ; but I have found that the best plan is to have the leather ones strengthened by an interior frame of some tough hard wood, the sockets for the bed stanchions being firmly screwed to the frame-work.

Although these boxes are best adapted for all articles that are liable to damage from wet, they are unnecessarily heavy for the conveyance of stores, such as preserved soups, liquor, &c., which cannot be injured by rain. For this purpose nothing answers better than strong oval baskets made of cane, and covered with leather, such as are to be procured at Nainí Tál, but may be made by any basket-maker. These baskets are furnished with a hinged lid, hasp and staple, so as to admit of their being kept under lock and key. They are about twenty-four inches in length, by fourteen in width, and sixteen in height.

I have had these baskets fitted with a number of tin boxes to contain flour, rice, sugar, tea, &c. This plan answers admirably, ensures cleanliness, and prevents waste.

Again I must warn the stranger in India that he must look after everything himself, or he will find every device that he may have adopted perverted to strange uses. Native servants, especially the low class Mahomedans from amongst whom we obtain our cooks and table attendants, have no idea of order and are for the most part extremely filthy in their habits. Rather than make use of the best designed receptacles for the requirements of a kitchen, they will accumulate a heterogeneous collection of dirty rags and flimsy paper parcels, each of which will be found to contain some culinary ingredient destined for their master's table.

STORES.

The nature and amount of stores to be taken must of course depend upon individual tastes, upon the districts visited, and upon the duration of the expedition. Coarse flour and rice can be obtained in most villages in our own hill provinces and throughout Kashmir ; but in some districts wheaten flour is hardly ever eaten by the inhabitants, while in Ládák 'satú' or parched barley-meal is the staple article of subsistence. Under all circumstances the sportsman will do well to lay in a sufficient stock of fine flour and white rice to last him until he can make sure of visiting some good-sized bazar, or of having additional supplies sent out to him.

In remote districts it is frequently necessary to carry food for the whole of one's followers for many days : this is of course an additional reason for limiting the amount of personal baggage. One seer of flour per diem is the allowance for each man.

One should always be provided with a few tins of soup, and preserved meat, so as to be prepared for such emergencies as scarcity of fuel, bad weather, impossibility of obtaining fresh meat, being belated on a pass, &c., &c.

I have found Kopf's soups in small tin cylinders the most portable and convenient, and I think them excellent, especially the pea soup.

I cannot too strongly recommend Goundry's consolidated tea and coffee, which I consider most valuable inventions for adding to the comfort of the traveller.

Among other necessary and useful stores which no one should be without, I may enumerate carbonate of soda (a large supply for 'chupatties'), cocoa and milk, curry powder, sugar, Worcestershire and Harvey's sauce, a few tins of carrots, compressed vegetables, a few bottles of whisky or brandy, and one or two of ginger syrup.

COOKING UTENSILS.

I have now discarded all 'degchies' and saucepans in favor of Warren's cooking pots, which I consider unrivalled for convenience, portability, cleanliness, and economy of fuel.

With one of these, one of the corrugated combined gridiron and frying pans, and a spit, as good a dinner may be prepared as any traveller need wish for ; and with the addition of a kettle and a teapot no other utensils are required. Being made of block tin, the troublesome tinning, so necessary with copper vessels, is dispensed with ; the minimum of handling food is required ; and the only thing to be careful about is, that the cooking-pot should not be thrust into too large or fierce a fire.

A few enamelled iron plates should fit into the bottom of ' the Warren,' and a strong basket should be provided to contain the whole apparatus.

DRESS.

With regard to shooting clothes, color is most important : this cannot be too strongly insisted on. For the hills nothing can be more suitable than '*patú*,' a strong woollen cloth manufactured in Kashmir and other parts of the hills : it is soft, warm, durable, and usually of exactly the right color, a sort of brownish grey.

For the lower hills, the plains, and the dense jungles of the Terai, a lighter material is required, and American drill dyed ' *kháki*' color, or some of the light but strong cotton ' mixtures' manufactured in the Jabalpúr and other jails, will be found best adapted to the climate. For shooting on foot in thick forests the prevailing color of the dress should be a dull green.

The best dress is an easy fitting Norfolk jacket and loose breeches, which should fit closely from the knee to the ankle, where they may be with advantage laced instead of buttoned.

With these, gaiters and ordinary shooting boots or shoes, Kashmir bandages ('*patís*') and grass shoes, or ' Elcho' boots, may be worn.

Well fitting boots or shoes are most essential to the comfort of the sportsman, especially in the hills ; and even on the regular paths, want of attention to this most important point may entirely destroy the pleasure of a march.

The great requisites in boots and shoes are, that they shall be roomy enough to admit of two pairs of thick socks being worn, broad in the sole, low in the heel, and so constructed as not to press upon the toes, and thereby blister them when going down hill.

Strong English boots studded with nails, answer well enough on ordinary roads, on snow, or on turf, but they are not well adapted for walking on rocky and precipitous ground, and they are very apt to make the wearer footsore if long marches are made. It is moreover impossible to walk silently in them. Thick leather soles, without nails, are utterly useless on slippery ground of any description.

An admirable sole for mere road marching, or for wear on dry and rocky mountains like those of Thibet, or even in the stony ravines of the Salt Range, are composed of several layers of webbing or thick cotton rugs (' *durries*') sewn firmly together with fine twine. They give an excellent hold on rock, and they never cause foot-soreness, but they soon go to pieces in wet weather, and on steep grassy slopes they are very insecure.

Most hill provinces have their own peculiar *chaussure*, and the best is undoubtedly the Kashmir grass shoe or '*púlá*.' This gives a most secure footing on all sorts of ground, and when well fitted on it is very comfortable. It is made of rice straw, or occasionally of hemp or bark of trees, twisted into rope and ingeniously plaited into a sort of sandal.

In order to wear the grass-shoe properly, the great toe must be free to admit of a string passing between the toes, so socks made on purpose, with a separate division for the great toe, are usually worn.

The disadvantages of the grass-shoe are, that although admirably suited to the native, who usually treads perfectly flat, and has the free use of all his toes, it is not quite so well adapted to the Englishman, who generally throws his weight more on the fore part of his feet, and whose toes are of little use to him for grasping purposes. The consequence is that an Englishman is not only difficult to fit, but his grass-shoes are constantly twisting or coming off. The more flat-footed a man is the better will a grass-shoe fit him ; it is impossible to keep one in its place on a high arched foot. Another draw-back is that it is only in Kashmir and the provinces adjoining it that grass-shoes are procurable, so in the more eastern provinces some other shoe must be worn.

After trying nearly every imaginable sort of boot and shoe I have now adopted the Elcho boot, and find it admirably adapted for every purpose except wading. For ordinary work I have it made of brown leather ; but if I do not expect to encounter much wet, I wear boots made of Sambur leather, which are lighter, cooler, softer, and more comfortable than any others.

For stalking, both in the jungles and the hills, I have found nothing so good as the Indian-rubber soles* made for racket and lawn tennis shoes ; they are absolutely noiseless, and I find that they give a better hold on nearly all kinds of ground than any other material with which I am acquainted. They do not even slip on dead pine leaves—the most treacherous surface on which one can walk.

With regard to head-dress opinions vary. Most people feel the Indian sun more or less, and although I am firmly convinced that exposure to the sun is not half so deleterious as is generally supposed, it is advisable to have the head well protected.

'Sold topees' of enormous size, and helmets of various descriptions, are much in favor with some, but the ' Terai hat,' which is simply a broad-brimmed soft felt double wideawake, has lately become popular, and I think that with the addition of a 'pagri' it is far preferable to any stiff hat or helmet. Personally I prefer a 'lúngi' or turban, twisted Afghan fashion round a small conical cap, to any European head-dress, and I always wear it when I have to be much in a hot sun.

For stalking in the higher mountains there is nothing better than a close fitting tweed hat or cap such as is used by deer-stalkers in Scotland.

In Thibet I wear a knitted woollen 'Balaklava cap' with the addition of a mask, which covers head and face, leaving only two holes for the eyes. This I adopted after two summers in Thibet, during which I suffered terribly from the effects of the dry cold wind and sun on my face. My lips and nose used to be cracked and deeply fissured, and used to stream with blood when I ate, talked, or laughed. After adopting the mask I never suffered in the same way again.

---

* These soles should be made of thick, smooth, red, vulcanized rubber : the grey corrugated soles wear out very rapidly.

Thick warm gloves are by no means to be despised when the thermometer is below freezing point, and long gauntlets will be found most useful in some of the lower valleys, to protect the hands and wrists from the mosquitoes and '*pipsd*' flies, whose bites sometimes become really serious.

I need hardly say that flannel only should be worn next the skin, and that a good supply of thick woollen socks should be taken : the socks issued to soldiers wear better than any other sort I know.

Finally, a good thick 'ulster' with a hood will be found invaluable when you have to lie for hours on an exposed hill-side waiting for game to move, and if you always make one of your gun-bearers carry it or a good plaid, you may pass a night on the hill with comfort instead of being half-frozen to death.

SERVANTS.

Much of the comfort of a shooting expedition depends upon having good servants, and these are unfortunately most difficult to obtain. The best servants are frequently unwilling to give up the pleasures of their home, and the attractions of the bazar, for a rough life in the jungles ; even with the prospect of increased pay.

Fortunately the usual staff of Indian servants is not required in the hills, and two Mahomedan servants, who can cook and make themselves generally useful, should be enough to bring up from the plains. Strong active men, not liable to fever, should be chosen ; and I strongly recommend the sportsman to engage them some time before he starts on a trip, or he may find that he is saddled, when too late to remedy it, with some incompetent and lazy scoundrel, whose misdeeds will not only cause loss and inconvenience, but ruin the finest temper !

If you are fortunate enough to secure good servants treat them liberally. For a long trip I should recommend that each man should be provided with a waterproof sheet, a couple of blankets, at least one warm suit of clothes, and a pair of '*patis*.' For Thibet each man should have a '*poshtin*,' or sheepskin coat.

The clothes should be made up under your own superintendence, and should consist of a short jacket and lose '*paijámás*.' If left to their own devices, servants will infallibly buy long coats in which all the cloth is expended in the skirts, and skin-tight breeches which will split and wear out in the course of a few weeks.

Servants should not be permitted to take their own thin white garments with them, as they are utterly useless in the hills, and you will probably find that they are used for cleaning your plates and cooking pots !

For two men of the same class very few cooking pots should be required, and these should be made to fit into each other.

Men can always be obtained locally for such work as bringing water, cutting wood, &c.

If a really hardworking intelligent man, who can clean guns, skin birds and other animals, and make himself generally useful, can be obtained, he is well worth engaging as a permanent gun-carrier, and should receive an outfit the same as the other servants ; but regular Shikaris and gun-carriers should be procured in each district you visit.

No Shikari is of any use except in the country which he knows, and few have more than purely local knowledge.

MISCELLANEOUS REQUIREMENTS.

Having now given my ideas on camp equipment generally, I append a list of articles, most of which will be found indispensable in camp.

Portable waterproof tub. Waterproof bucket. ' *Chágal*' or leather water-bag. Strong lantern. Candles. Portable sundial. Green or neutral tint goggles. Hatchet. Two or three butcher's knives. Steel. Strong scissors. String. Needles and thread. Arsenical-soap. Powdered alum. Wax matches. Sticking plaister. Quinine. Chlorodyne. Cockle's pills. Lunar caustic. Holloway's ointment. Penknives. Some cotton wool. Plenty of dusters for servants. A spring weighing* machine to weigh up to 100 lbs. Common soap for washing clothes. Toilet soap. Stationery. A few favorite books. A measuring tape. Green gauze or goggles for servants when crossing snow passes.

A good rope should be provided for each load, as it frequently happens that coolies and owners of pack animals have no ropes, and much time may be lost in procuring them. The ropes should be collected and counted before coolies are paid off, or they will certainly be stolen.

PACK ANIMALS AND PACK SADDLES.

MULES, PONIES, YAKS, AND DONKEYS.

My recommendations, as regards camp equipment and the arrangement of loads, have been made for mountainous countries and narrow paths, where coolie-carriage only is available. No alteration will, however, be necessary, when mules, ponies or yâks can be obtained, but still more attention will have to be paid to the packing of loads and to their proper adjustment.

With properly packed loads marches can be much more rapidly performed with mules or ponies than with coolies, but if animals are badly loaded there will be much delay as well as breakage.

It would seldom be worth the while of any sportsman to purchase his own transport animals, unless for a very extended expedition where no difficult passes have to be crossed, but should any one determine to buy his own beasts I should advise him to get mules. They are more expensive than ponies, but they are hardier, thrive better on coarse fare, keep their condition better, and are much less likely to go lame.

With one's own pack animals good pack-saddles are required, and the Otago pattern is the one I prefer. If properly fitted it will never cause a sore back, and, as it is furnished with hooks, loads can be attached to it in a moment. If necessary it can be used as a riding-saddle.

---

* A light and handy weighing machine is made in the Government workshops at Roorkee.

As a rule, the traveller will have to depend upon the mules and ponies which he can hire at various stages along his road, and these animals will all be furnished with the common straw pad or '*paländ.*' This is a most inconvenient pack-saddle, and as the drivers are generally unprovided with ropes it is essential that the loads should all have their own cords (as I have already recommended), and that they should be carefully arranged in pairs, so as to balance one another. Here the spring weighing machine will be found indispensable. If pack animals are to be largely employed, each load should be furnished with two long leather straps, with 'dees' that can be hooked on to the Otago saddle or connected by cords over the back of the animal with the ordinary '*paländ.*'

The smallest baggage pony should carry two coolies' loads: a good one three—the third load being of course balanced on the animal's back, between the other two.

When travelling in Thibet, yâks will be the usual beasts of burden: they are furnished with small wooden pack-saddles, which answer very well. A good yâk will carry four ordinary coolie loads.

Although the yâk is well adapted to easy marching in a severe climate, it must be remembered that it will not stand a long succession of forced marches; and as it will not eat grain, it is useless in a country totally devoid of grass, such as that lying between the Chung Chenmo and Kárákásh rivers, on the road to Yarkund. If that country is visited, ponies or donkeys must be employed for transport, and barley carried for them.

TRAVELLING IN THE PLAINS.

CAMELS.

Throughout the greater part of the plains of India the camel is readily obtained, and is the most convenient form of transport. Camels always have their own pack-saddles, on which tents and similar loads can be easily packed ; but for all smaller articles I strongly recommend the use of '*Kajáwás*' (a sort of large pannier), which will save an infinity of time and trouble. A camel will easily carry 400 ℔s.

EKKAS.

For rapid marches, where there are tolerable roads, the small country pony-cart called an '*ekká*' is admirably adapted. The ratlike little '*tats*' which generally draw them have some of the best blood in India in their veins, and their powers of endurance are something marvellous. Some of the feats performed by these little ponies are almost incredible, and a journey of sixty or seventy miles, with a heavy load, within twenty-four hours, is no unusual performance.

BULLOCK CARTS.

'*Hackerries*' or bullock carts should never be employed if camels or '*ekkás*' are procurable. They are terribly slow, and only adapted for very heavy baggage on tolerable roads.

ELEPHANTS.

In the Terai, Assam, and parts of Lower Bengal, Elephants are the only available means of transport : they will carry at least 800 lbs.

GENERAL EQUIPMENT.

Although the whole of the equipment for the hills will be found useful in the plains, there is no occasion for the sportsman to restrict himself to the same amount of baggage.

A larger tent may with advantage be procured; either a 'Swiss cottage' tent, or a single-poled tent known as a 'hill tent,' about fourteen feet square, will be found quite roomy enough.

Strong tables and chairs will add to comfort; and there will be no longer any necessity for abstinence from beer and wine, or for dispensing with any ordinary comforts.

The usual staff of Indian servants will be found useful, and horses or ponies according to tastes and means will be indispensable.

EXPENSES.

The necessary expenses of a shooting expedition in the Himalayas are very small.

Not including rifles, guns, ammunition, stores, and other articles which would probably be already in the sportsman's possession, a complete camp outfit of tents, camp-bed, cooking utensils, trunks, baskets, &c., would cost about 250 rupees.

Monthly expenses might be calculated as follows:—

	Per mensem. Rs.
Twelve Coolies at four annas each per diem, or six Ponies or Mules at eight annas	90
Shikari	15
Gun-carrier	10
Two Servants at twelve rupees each	24
Flour, rice, &c.	10
Sheep or fowls when game is not procurable	10
Sundries, including carriage of supplies in remote districts...	41
TOTAL RUPEES ...	200

This is a most liberal estimate, and in many parts of the hills the expense would be considerably less, but it is best to leave a margin for possible contingencies.

When the sportsman has actually reached the district where he intends to shoot, and is likely to be out of the reach of villages for some time, I strongly advise him to hire or purchase two or three milch-goats, which will accompany his camp from place to place. A few sheep should also be taken in case of emergencies, though the flesh of nearly all the wild animals (with the exception of male Ibex, Tahr, and Markhoor) will be found infinitely superior to the mutton of sheep that have been half starved throughout the winter, and which do not generally regain their condition till late in the autumn.

Although the item of carriage will be considerably reduced in the plains, where camels can be hired for about nine rupees a month each, other expenses will probably be increased:

so that the expenditure may be estimated at about the same as in the hills ; without including the keep of horses, which may be fixed at about twenty-five rupees each.

No estimate of the cost of Tiger and other ' Large Game-shooting' in the Terai can well
be given. Extensive preparations are required, which are generally beyond the means of
private individuals to arrange.

Commissariat Elephants can occasionally be borrowed, but the best chance of obtaining sport is to get introductions to some of the higher Civil authorities in good shooting
districts. These officials frequently make up parties of their own, and they can obtain the
loan of Elephants, howdahs, &c., from Rájás and other rich natives.

A really staunch Shikari Elephant is extremely valuable ; from 3,000 to 5,000 rupees
being not infrequently paid for a perfectly trained and trustworthy animal.

CHAPTER XL.

RIFLES, GUNS, AND OTHER SPORTING REQUISITES.

—

RIFLES.

OPINIONS vary much as to what is the best Rifle for *general* purposes, but I think it must be admitted on all hands that the most suitable weapon for such heavy game as Rhinoceros and Buffaloes is not well adapted for small animals such as Antelope or the various species of wild goats and sheep.

For the former class of animals the hunter should employ the heaviest weapons that he is capable of handling, which may be said to be 10-bore for a man of average strength, and 8 or even 4-bore for those who are sufficiently powerful to use them.

It must be remembered that the weight of a rifle and the charge fired from it must be increased according to the calibre: nothing is gained by using a large bore unless heavy charges are used, and heavy charges necessitate heavy metal. Recoil is reduced to a minimum when the spherical bullet is used, and when this form of projectile is made of hard metal, I believe it to be the most effective yet invented.

The following may be taken as about the most suitable charges for large bore rifles on the Forsyth spherical ball principle:

Bore.	Weight of rifle.	Charge of powder.	
12	11 lbs.	5 to 7	drams.
10	13 lbs.	6 to 9	„
8	15 lbs.	8 to 10	„
6	17 lbs.	10 to 12	„
4	20 lbs.	12 to 16	„

No shoulder will stand much more than the last named charge; which, however, I have frequently fired.

For Deer, Antelope, Ibex, and animals of similar size, the Express rifle has justly become a favorite, and no weapon is better adapted for the purpose; as it possesses the advantages of comparative lightness, accuracy, low trajectory, and great killing power on thin-skinned animals.

The commonest bores of the Express rifles in use are ·500, ·450, and ·360. With proportionate charges of powder their power may be said to be in about the same ratio as the weight of their bullets.

The charge of powder for a ·360 bore should be about 2 drams, for a ·450 bore 4½ drams, for a ·500 bore 5½ drams.

The principle on which the Express hollow bullet has been constructed is, by weakening the projectile and increasing the charge of powder, to insure the bullet's breaking up when it strikes an animal, and thus cause extensive laceration and shock to the system. This end is attained with thin-skinned animals of medium size, but if these light projectiles are employed against such ponderous beasts as Rhinoceros or Buffaloes, it will be found that the result will generally be a merely superficial wound.

Again the lightness of the bullet renders it peculiarly liable to the influence of wind, and materially lessens the value of the rifle at the longer sporting ranges.

It has been found moreover that Express bullets are not to be trusted in jungle shooting, as they are apt to be broken up or diverted from their course by contact with twigs or even with thick grass.

Both the drawbacks just alluded to have been overcome to a certain extent by substituting solid bullets for hollow ones, but it must be remembered that this entails additional recoil, and increases the curve of the trajectory. The solid bullet, moreover, if used for the smaller deer and antelope, would not meet with sufficient resistance to cause it to break up or 'set up a head,' so that one of the principles of the Express system would be sacrificed.

It is evident therefore that it is highly desirable that different weapons should be used for different purposes; and I should recommend any one who is likely to have extensive opportunities of shooting, and who has ample means, to procure a pair of double barrelled large bore rifles, and a pair of double barrelled Expresses; the weight and calibre of each being that best suited to his strength.

If means are limited, one rifle of each description will still form an excellent battery; indeed I only recommend a pair of each in case of any accident happening to one of the rifles, or for heavy game-shooting on foot.

The cost, however, even of two double barrelled rifles is considerable, and to those who can only afford *one* rifle, I say without hesitation that a 12-bore rifle on the Forsyth system, to carry a spherical bullet with a large charge of powder, is the best of all weapons for *general* purposes. It will be found sufficiently powerful for the largest animals if the shots are at all well placed, and accurate enough up to a hundred and fifty yards for all practical purposes; while its trajectory is nearly, if not quite, as flat as that of the Express rifle at short ranges.

Such a rifle, not exceeding 11 lbs. in weight, will carry seven drams of powder without inconvenient recoil, and will be found perfectly manageable by any man of average strength.

I have used a rifle of the above description for several years, and have rarely lost an animal hit with it; while my shooting has been better than I ever remember to have made with any other rifle. With it I have killed Rhinoceros, Buffalo, Gaur, Panther, Bear, Sambur, Ibex, Tahr, &c.

As an extra rifle, in case of anything happening to the 12-bore, a single barrelled ·450 Express will be found most useful: a very efficient and cheap one may be obtained by using express charges with the regulation Martini-Henry rifle; the only alteration necessary being a raised bead foresight to fit on to the ordinary foresight, so as to reduce the elevation given by the lowest sighting.

For an extended trip a pea-rifle will be found a most desirable accessory, as it will enable the sportsman to shoot hares, pheasants, &c., for the larder, in places where firing a gun would be certain to disturb game.

GUNS.

I need say nothing about guns, as whatever suits one in England, will be found equally serviceable in India; though I would not take a valuable gun to the Himalayas, where it is exposed to rough usage, and a cheap gun would answer just as well.

I may, however, mention that I am opposed to the use of bullets in guns, a practice usually adopted by those who will not take the trouble to learn to shoot with the rifle.

GUNMAKERS.

Most experienced sportsmen have their favorite gunmaker, and I believe that there is little to choose between eight or ten of the best known, whose names are a guarantee for the excellence of the weapons which leave their hands. Most of them, however, have their *specialité*, one being famous for match rifles, another for Express, a third for large bores, a fourth for pigeon guns, and so on.

It is always best to go to a good maker and to buy a *first quality* rifle. Cheap double rifles by obscure makers are to be avoided. If possible, a rifle should be made to order, and tried by the purchaser before it is finished. However perfect in other respects, there are very few rifles that shoot *exactly* alike with both barrels. In my experience I have not found one in fifty that would.

GUN-CASES, IMPLEMENTS, &c.

Elaborate cases and the numerous implements usually supplied with a first class gun or rifle add much to its cost, and are in my opinion quite unnecessary.

Wooden gun cases are rather incumbrances in India, and I think that solid leather gun covers, lined with waterproof, the shape of the rifle or gun, and furnished with slings, answer every purpose. They can always be carried on the march or on the hill-side, and afford quite sufficient protection. They should be loose enough to admit of an inner cover of flannel or serge being placed on the rifle.

A cleaning rod with 'jag' and wire brush, a bullet-mould, a turn screw, a lock cramp, a pair of spare strikers, and a spare foresight, are all the implements required with a rifle. I should never dream of reloading *Rifle* cartridges, as the number fired in the course of a year is seldom sufficient to make the economy worth considering, while the chance of miss-fires is undoubtedly increased by using cartridges more than once.

On a sporting trip plenty of Rangoon or other mineral oil should, of course, be taken, also a good supply of rags for cleaning guns.

CARTRIDGES.

For rifles of all descriptions I now use solid drawn metal cartridges, which possess many advantages over the best paper cartridges. The latter frequently swell in damp weather, rendering loading difficult or impossible, and if wet they become useless. Metal cartridges, if properly loaded, are nearly waterproof, and they increase the shooting powers of the rifle.

Bottle-shaped cartridges are now nearly universally used with Express rifles, and the proper method of loading them is generally understood.

Large bore spherical bullet cartridges are, however, frequently improperly loaded, and, as this injuriously affects the shooting, it may be well to describe how they should be loaded.

In the first place, the cartridge cases (which are made in several lengths) should be exactly the length of the chamber of the rifle.

This point having been seen to, and the charge of powder determined upon, the powder charges should be carefully weighed or measured, well shaken down in the cartridge, and secured by a thin black jute wad. Over the thin wad a greased felt wad or wads should be inserted, of such a thickness that nearly half the bullet shall project beyond the cartridge case, and thus at once take the grooves of the barrel when started by the explosion of the powder.

On the top of the greased wad pour a small quantity of melted beeswax, and before it has cooled, place the bullet in the mouth of the case, and press it firmly down. The bullet will be imbedded in and secured by the wax, and no choking or turning down of the case will be required.

Cartridges thus loaded will keep in almost any weather for a very long time. I should mention that bullets are best made of hardened metal, $\frac{1}{13}$ of tin (by weight) being added to the lead.

If gun-cartridges are not reloaded, the brown sort will be found quite good enough

For a six months' trip in the Himalayas I would advise that three hundred rifle and two hundred shot cartridges should be taken. Nos. 4 and 6 shot are the most useful sizes.

The allowance of rifle cartridges is a liberal one, and it is unlikely that so many would be fired, but it is best to err on the safe side.

Cartridges should be made up in packages of ten, sewn up in cloth or waterproof, the gauge, &c., of the cartridge being written on each packet.

KNIVES AND BELTS.

Some writers have disparaged the use of hunting knives, apparently considering that to wear one marks a man either as a foreigner or as a cockney sportsman.

Having experienced the want of one at a time when it would have been invaluable, I have been careful to carry one ever since; and I strongly recommend every one who shoots in India to be provided with one, and never to go after dangerous game without it.   The knife is indeed but a poor weapon to depend upon; but when everything else has failed and you find yourself at close quarters with a Panther, Bear or Boar, you may find that one well directed thrust may decíde the fight in your favor.

A hunting knife, to be practically useful as a weapon of offence, should be double edged, the blade being about eight inches in length and one and a half in width, tapering rather suddenly to a fine point.   It should always be kept as sharp as a razor, and should not be used for hacking or rough work.   It should be kept in a wooden sheath, in which it is secured by a spring, which is released by the hand in the act of grasping the hilt.

A knife is most conveniently worn, not in a frog, but diagonally on the left side, the scabbard being firmly attached to a broad leather belt.   In this position the knife is always ready to the hand; it is not in the way even when going through thick jungle; and in the event of a fall with one's horse there is no danger of injury from it.

Cartridges are most conveniently carried in leather pouches forming part of the belt, with separate stalls for them; eight or ten are enough to carry, four or five on each side of the belt buckle; a strong leather flap should hang over and protect each pouch.   At the back another small pouch to contain odds and ends, may be attached, and the belt should be made to unfasten behind, so as to allow of a binocular case being slipped on to it when required.

TELESCOPES AND BINOCULARS.

Binocular field glasses are very useful when looking for game, but when it has been found, a good telescope is required to enable one to judge of the size of horns and other details.   I, therefore, advise every sportsman to provide himself with both.

CHAPTER XLI.

PRESERVATION OF SKINS, HEADS, AND HORNS.

MANY fine trophies are utterly ruined for want of knowledge how to preserve them, or by their being left to natives who *profess* to know all about them.

There is no difficulty whatever in *preserving* them properly, but the *curing* should be left to professionals. There are very few places in India where you can get skins properly cured, and native '*mochis*' almost invariably spoil them by using salt, lime, and other deleterious '*massálás*.'

Few Indian skins are worth preserving : Tiger, Panther, Leopard, Bear, Spotted Deer, and Black Buck are the only skins that, in my opinion, are worth the trouble and expense. The skins of Yák, Burrell, Thibetan Antelope, and a few other dwellers at great elevations, are very handsome if procured in winter, but at the seasons when sportsmen can usually visit their haunts the skins are quite worthless.

The following simple directions will enable any sportsman to bring back his trophies in proper condition for curing or mounting.

SKINS.

The manner in which a skin is removed depends upon whether it is required to be dressed flat and used as a mat, or whether it is to be ultimately stuffed and mounted. Few sportsmen care to have entire specimens of large animals set up, but as they are occasionally desiderata for museums, I will describe both methods of skinning.

First, let us suppose that a flat Tiger-skin is required.

Lay the Tiger on its back, and have it securely held while you make a long incision from the point of the lower jaw to the tip of the tail, being careful to cut quite straight along the very centre of the belly. The cut should be merely deep enough to divide the true skin.

Next, from the centre of the chest, cut a line to the elbow, and from thence down the forearm to the ball of the foot, taking care that the two forelimbs are held in the same position during the operation, and that the direction of the cuts is exactly the same in both fore-legs.

The hind-legs should be similarly treated, two slits being cut from a point in the central incision, a few inches from the root of the tail, to the point of the hock, and thence down to the ball of the hind foot.

The skin should then be detached from the flesh, one or two men working on each side until they have cleared it right down to the spine, and as far as the paws. In doing this, care should be taken not to leave pieces of flesh, fat, or cartilage adhering to the skin, as their removal hereafter will merely entail double labor. The feet may now be cut off and left hanging to the skin for the present, while the tail is carefully skinned.

The next process is to remove the skin from the skull, when precautions must be taken against cutting the cartilage of the ears too short off, enlarging the eyelids, or injuring the roots of the whiskers when separating the lips from the jaws.

The carcase may now be dragged away, the skull being first cut off if it is required, and one man should be told off to skin each foot. The pads of the sole and of each toe should be cut away with a sharp knife, and all the bones of the feet carefully dissected out, until nothing is left attached to the skin but the last articulations with their respective claws.

The skin of the head should next be cleaned, care being taken to remove all flesh from the base of the ears, and to pare down the lips as closely as can be done without loosening the whiskers, which add so much to the appearance of a skin.

While the skinning was going on, a clean level place should have been selected in a shady situation ; and a number of thin pegs made of hard wood or of stout iron wire should be in readiness.

The skin should now be spread out hair downwards, and having been stretched a *few inches* longer than the measurement taken of the dead Tiger, a peg should be driven through the nose, and another through the tail, near the tip.

The four limbs should next be stretched out at right angles to the central line and firmly pegged down, the position of each peg being carefully measured, so as to insure the skin being perfectly even.

In like manner the whole skin must be carefully stretched and secured by numerous pegs along its margin, remembering always that each peg on one side must have a corresponding peg on the other.

The skin having been thoroughly stretched—and the more quickly this is done the better—it should be carefully examined, with a view to removing any flesh or fat that may still adhere to it, and then well rubbed with a flat stone. Powdered alum should then be thickly sprinkled on the skin and thoroughly rubbed in, while the lips, eyes, ears, paws and tail may be advantageously anointed with arsenical soap.

Should the weather be very hot it is well to sponge the skin both inside and out, as soon as it is removed from the carcase, with a solution of carbolic acid, which will arrest putrefaction.

The skin should remain stretched until it is perfectly dry, being well rubbed from time to time, and arsenical soap or diluted carbolic acid being freely applied to any part where there may be any suspicion of taint. When quite dry, the pegs should be carefully removed, and the skin hung up in the shade until camp is moved, when it should be rolled up with the hair inwards.

A still better method of drying the skin is to stretch it on a large wooden frame on the same system as that used by ladies for stretching their canvas for worsted work. The edges of the skin should be laced to the frame by small iron hooks attached to stout cord.*

Second—Let it next be supposed that a Bárá Sing stag has been shot, and that it is proposed to preserve it entire.

Lay the stag on his back and divide the skin of the belly from the centre of the breastbone to the root of the tail ; and it will aid matters if you also make two incisions a few inches long down the inside of the thighs, but these are not absolutely neces-sary.

Proceed with the skinning in exactly the same manner as in the case of the Tiger, until the skin is separated from the flesh as far as can be done without further cutting. Then amputate one of the hind-legs at the hip joint, skin it as far as possible below the hock, turning the skin inside out like a stocking. Strip the whole of the flesh from the bones, scraping them perfectly clean, and then proceed to skin the tail and to treat the other hind-leg in the same manner as the first one.

Next turn the stag over on his belly, pull the skin forward over the shoulders, and separate both fore-quarters from the body.

Continue to skin the neck until the base of the skull is exposed, and then sever it at the last vertebra.

The fore-legs may now be skinned as far as possible below the knees, and all flesh removed from the bones, which must remain intact, with the exception of the scapulæ or shoulder blades, which are not absolutely required.

The skull has now to be removed from the skin ; in order to do which a longitudinal incision must be made in the nape of the neck as far as the base of the horns, between which another cut must be made. The skin has now to be detached from the back of the skull, the ears severed at the roots, and the skin carefully cut away from the inside round the base of the horns.

The skull is now pulled through the opening in the back of the neck, and the skinning proceeds until the lips and cartilage of the nose are detached and the skin remains like an empty glove.

It must be cleaned with as much or even more care, than if it was merely intended for a mat ; and the feet and lower parts of the legs still remain to be disposed of.

Inserting the point of a knife between the heels, make an incision up the back of the leg nearly as high as the knee in the fore, and as the hock in the hind-leg. Dissect

---

* Since the above went to press, Mr. Sanderson, the well-known author of " Thirteen Years among the Wild Beasts of India," has published a detailed description of a frame such as I have advocated. The only drawback to his invention appears to be its great weight. This is, of course, of little importance when plenty of Elephants are available for transport ; but those who have not the facilities at Mr. Sanderson's command can probably improvise a rough wooden frame which will answer the purpose.

the skin away from the bone all round, and remove all cartilage and sinew both from the foot and shank.

The skin is now best left to dry inside out, being plentifully dusted with alum, and the extremities liberally dosed with arsenical soap and carbolic acid. It should be hung up or propped up with sticks, not laid on the ground.

The skull should be thoroughly cleansed of all flesh, and, if there is time, soaked in cold water; but it should on no account be boiled.

The lower jaw should be preserved, and should be ticketed with a distinctive mark corresponding to similar marks attached to the skin and skull.

STUFFED HEADS.

Stuffed heads are difficult to keep in good preservation, especially in India, as they are liable to destruction by many sorts of insects.

They are, moreover, unsatisfactory, unless really artistically mounted, and such mounting is expensive.

For my own part I am quite satisfied to have one good specimen of each species mounted, and prefer merely to keep the skulls and horns of the others.

Stuffed heads are best protected from the ravages of insects by being occasionally sponged or brushed over with a solution of corrosive sublimate in alcohol. Nothing will preserve them, however, if they are not properly prepared in the first instance, and the treatment which I recommend should be strictly carried out.

I may begin by stating that the throat of an animal, whose head or entire skin it is proposed to mount, should never be cut, as a blemish is thereby caused which the cleverest taxidermist will be unable entirely to conceal.

Choosing an old Markhoor as a good subject to experiment upon, the procedure should be as follows:

Sever the neck from the body where it enters the shoulders, so as to retain the whole of the long mane which adds so much to the appearance of the animal.

Skin the neck until it can be severed from the skull; cut an opening in the back of the neck, cut away the skin from the base of the horns, and proceed with the skinning of the head in exactly the same way as was done in the case of the Bárá Sing.

The skin of the head must in the same manner be thoroughly cleaned, dressed with alum and arsenical soap, allowed to dry inside out, and marked with a corresponding number to that hereafter to be attached to the skull.

Arsenical soap and other preservatives should be liberally used. As long as a skin does not decay nor become infested by insects, it does not signify how dry and shrivelled it may become.

In the case of the Bárá Sing, the skull had merely to be fairly cleaned, and no farther preparation was necessary. The Markhoor, however, being a hollow or sheath-horned animal, further precautions are required. Between the bony cores or standards, and the horns which they support, are a mass of blood vessels and tissues, which would rapidly decay and form a *nidus* for insects, whose larvæ would soon pierce and destroy the horns, eventually reducing them to mere dust.

To prevent this the horns must be removed ·from their cores, and the sooner this is effected the better. If the skulls are placed in water, or even exposed to damp heat, when quite fresh, the horns will generally come off in two or three days ; but if the cartilages have been allowed to dry and harden, they will sometimes require soaking for a considerable time.

When they become detached, they should be thoroughly cleaned and then repeatedly washed out with diluted carbolic acid.

The skulls should be allowed to soak until all flesh and cartilage rots off, although if the head is to be stuffed, it is not essential that the bones should bleach until they attain a snowy whiteness. As soon as the skulls are dry, the tops of the standards should be sawn off, leaving only about half their length to support the horns. Both core and horn should be thoroughly poisoned with arsenic and corrosive sublimate, and heads thus treated will last for many years.

SKULLS AND HORNS.

I have already described how skulls and horns should be preserved when heads are to be stuffed. When the bare skulls only are required, exactly the same process must be gone through, but more care should be taken to bleach the skulls and to insure their being absolutely perfect.

If heads are set to macerate when perfectly fresh, they will make more satisfactory skulls than if they had been previously half cleaned and dried, and then placed to soak.

They will moreover become clean more rapidly, and they will not be so liable to fall to pieces as skulls, which have had to be soaked for several weeks.

When skulls are macerated, the water should be frequently changed, and all teeth that drop out during the process should be carefully collected.

Teeth of Tigers, Bears, &c., may be fixed with beeswax, and if coated with that substance they will not split, as they are otherwise apt to do in hot dry weather.

To make Arsenical Soap.

Arsenic in fine powder	...	2 ℔s.
White Soap ·	...	2 ℔s.
Spirits of Turpentine	...	quant. suff.

The white soap should be cut into fine shreds ; a small quantity should then be placed in a mortar and the arsenic gradually added, the whole being most carefully incorporated with a pestle. Spirits of turpentine should be added from time to time to prevent the arsenic dust from getting into the mouth or nostrils of the person who is mixing the ingredients.

POSTSCRIPT.

Owing to the negatives of the Illustrations of my original 1st Volume having unfortunately been lost or destroyed, much delay has occurred in bringing out the present work; and many months have elapsed since my MSS. were first placed in the hands of the publishers. The present Illustrations, which have been reproduced from the originals by a new and beautiful process, are, in my opinion, so good, that I personally do not regret the delay.

During the past year I have enjoyed unusually good sport, and I am tempted to add an account of my recent adventures to what I fear is already a rather too lengthy record of my own doings.

In March last, accompanied by a brother Officer, I went to the borders of the Bikanír desert, about ninety miles south of Ferozpúr, to see if we could manage to shoot some of the long horned Black Buck, for which that district is famous. We found Antelope extremely numerous, and although they had lately been a good deal disturbed by another sportsman, they were by no means wild.

We might have shot a great number had we fired at all that came in our way, but we restricted ourselves to shooting only those that bore good heads. In the course of six days I bagged fourteen fine buck, while my companion killed nine or ten, his best pair of horns measuring twenty-six inches in length. I was still more fortunate, and procured one of the finest heads that I have ever seen.

I had observed a very black old buck lying by himself on a plain, and had attempted to approach within shot without success, but by good luck a herd of does came up from another direction, and as they passed near me the buck joined them. In their society he lost some of his caution, and I eventually obtained a fair broadside shot as he was walking after the does at a distance of about a hundred and fifty yards.

The bullet laid him low, and on walking up I at once saw that I had secured a prize. The measuring tape was soon laid along his horns, and I had the satisfaction of finding that they measured exactly twenty-six and three-quarter inches.

On a subsequent day I came across an immense herd, whose numbers I computed to be not less than fifteen hundred.

They extended in a broken string from one horizon to the other, and the proportion of Black Buck was unusually large. Conspicuous among them was a magnificent buck, the length of whose horns far exceeded any that I have ever seen, and I believe that I am quite within the mark when I estimate them at not less than twenty-nine inches.

F F

For hours I followed the herd with the greatest patience, and refrained from firing easy shots at many fine buck, in hopes of getting within range of the one on which I had set my heart.

It was not to be, however; the big buck was too careful of his personal safety, and always contrived to keep on the side of the herd farthest from me, while he never halted even for a moment. At length, in despair, I fired two shots at him, as he was walking or trotting at upwards of two hundred yards—both shots were unsuccessful. Had the buck been a small one, not worth shooting, I should probably have knocked him over!

I was also exceptionally fortunate in the pursuit of Gaur during a short shooting trip in Central India, and my account of it will, at any rate, give a more complete idea of the circumstances attending the fascinating sport of Gaur shooting than is afforded by the slight experiences recorded in Chapter XIV.

I must, however, warn the young sportsman that such good fortune as befell me, falls to the lot of few, and that, under ordinary circumstances, the bag which I was lucky enough to make in a few days, would be considered a good one for a month's labor.

I purposely avoid mentioning the exact locality where I enjoyed such excellent sport— not that I would not willingly assist a brother sportsman, but because publishing particulars about good shooting ground spoils the sport of many, by sending numbers of sportsmen to the same place. A recent author, with the best intentions, has done much to destroy the shooting in the Himalayas, by giving details of all the best localities. The result has been that all the best valleys are invaded by crowds of keen sportsmen, who interfere with each other and probably return disappointed.

I shall therefore only state that my shooting trip led me to the Sátpúrá hills, and will limit myself to a general description of the country, and of the incidents of sport, omitting all names of places.

It was on the 12th of May 1884 that, after a march of nearly a hundred and fifty miles from the nearest cantonment, I found myself at a village situated at the foot of a range of hills which had been recommended to me as holding plenty of Gaur. The village officials were very obliging, and the headman sent for four or five inhabitants of neighbouring jungle hamlets, who were well acquainted with the haunts of the game. On the following morning I took advantage of a moon that was near the full, and started for the hills at 3 A.M., leaving tents and all heavier impedimenta at the village, and taking only absolute necessaries with me. It was just daylight when I reached the top of a plateau of considerable extent, where a large spreading tree and a good well afforded every requisite for a comfortable bivouac. We were now on the summit of the main range, which stretched away as far as the eye could reach from east to west, while its width varied from fifteen to thirty miles. The average elevation was somewhere about 2,500 feet, while here and there loftier peaks rose from 500. to 1,000 feet higher. Towards the north the land trended away—not in regular slopes but in broken ridges of diminishing height—towards the distant plains; while on the southern side, steep scarped cliffs overlooked the low hot valleys, which ultimately merged in the level country a few miles beyond. Our plateau was one of a succession of similar table-lands which crowned the main ridge, from the sides of which numerous ravines of varying depth and width, and of more or less devious course, ran towards the main valleys.

The forest consisted mainly of teak, the trees being, for the most part, of no great size, and at this season destitute of leaves. The jungles had not long been burned, and the cover was therefore very scanty, the bare black hills and naked stems presenting rather a desolate appearance, only relieved by occasional bright spots where peepul, banyan, and other non-deciduous trees somewhat enlivened the landscape. In some of the deeper ravines patches of long withered grass still remained, while the wide valleys which lay at the feet of the abrupt precipices on the southern side were adorned with groves of feathery bamboo. Water and pasturage both being scarce, and the thin jungles affording but little concealment, the season was most favorable for hunting.

Having made a few necessary arrangements, I set out, with four or five trackers and gun-carriers, to explore the hills and ravines to the south of the spot chosen for our bivouac. It was not long before we found tracks, and we had not walked above an hour, when we saw a herd of Gaur feeding leisurely through the forest about five hundred yards ahead of us. They were ascending a gentle slope, and it would have been easy to follow the crest of the ridge and stalk them from above, had not the wind been unfavorable. As it was, I had to descend into the valley below the Gaur, and approach them up hill. It did not take long to carry out the stalk, but, on reaching the place where the herd had been last seen, they had moved away. Advancing cautiously, on crossing a low swell in the ground I came face to face with two cows, which, having gazed at me for a few seconds, uttered a snort of alarm, and trotted off. I could easily have killed one, but as there might be a bull with the herd I let them go, and ran on in the direction which they had taken. A couple of hundred yards farther on I reached some bamboo jungle, and almost met three cows which were quietly walking along, apparently unconscious of danger.

I sat down to watch for a bull, but as none appeared, and I wanted a specimen of a cow, I fired at the shoulder of one which was standing within sixty yards. She rushed forward, but I knew that my aim was certain at such a short range, and after going about a hundred yards she rolled over dead. Leaving the fallen cow to be skinned hereafter, I continued my hunting, and had not gone above a mile before some Gaur were seen ascending a steep ridge at the opposite side of a small valley. I at once attempted to stalk them, but they had evidently been alarmed by my shot, and they hurried away before I could get near them. The tracks showed that there was a bull in the herd; so, after giving them time to recover from their fright, we followed in pursuit.

The tracking was easy, but we had not gone far before we saw the herd, consisting of three cows headed by a jet-black bull, hurrying along the open crest of a hill about half a mile ahead. They soon stopped to gaze about them, and then went on at a leisurely pace. They were apparently making for a lofty spur, where several large peepul trees afforded ample shade and would be likely to tempt them to stop. I therefore determined to make an attempt to head them instead of following them up, and accordingly we made a considerable detour, and ascended the spur on which they were last seen, from the opposite side.

On reaching the summit I had the satisfaction of finding that my surmise was correct, and that the Gaur were standing under one of the large peepul trees. I had no difficulty in stalking to within a hundred and twenty yards, but I then found that a deep ravine intervened between me and the Gaur: this it would be impossible to cross without being seen. I crept to the edge of the ravine, and, under cover of a small bush, carefully reconnoitred the herd. The cows were standing in the open, but the bull was at the other side of the tree, and I could only see his head and neck, and, occasionally, his tail. I lay watching them for a long time, but although the cows occasionally moved about, and one eventually lay down, the bull remained almost motionless. With the naked eye it was difficult to make out his exact position, owing to the flickering shade cast by the peepul leaves; but, with my binoculars, I could see that his head and a considerable portion of his neck were clear of the stem of the tree. I was lying out in the sun, slowly roasting, and I had in my hands a rifle in which I had the utmost confidence, so, although the range was rather a long one, I resolved to fire for the neck. I must have taken a false aim owing to the deceptive light, and my bullet probably struck the tree; at any rate it did not touch the bull.

I had been lying in an awkward position when I fired, and the recoil of the heavily charged rifle drove one of the hammers into my forehead, covering my face with blood, and momentarily interfering with my sight. Hastily sitting up, and dashing away the blood, I saw the bull standing clear of the tree and offering a capital chance, and I at once fired my left barrel at his near shoulder. With the activity of a deer he bounded across the ravine, and passed me within twenty-five yards before I could insert a fresh cartridge. I had, however, the satisfaction of seeing a crimson patch behind his shoulder, and immediately following him up I saw him moving off through the thin forest at a very slow pace. Hurrying in pursuit, I kept slightly above his track, as he went along the steep hill-side, but I had not gone above a hundred yards before he became aware that he was being followed and turned to seek his foes.

Back he came, at a fast gallop, evidently looking out for some one on whom to wreak his vengeance. I was ahead of my men and stood my ground, while they, being unarmed, very wisely scrambled up trees. I allowed the bull to come on to within forty yards, when I fired my right barrel at the point of his shoulder, reserving the other in case he came to close quarters. The shot did not check him, but he slightly swerved, and passed me within twenty yards. He had no sooner passed, than I gave him the left barrel, on receiving the contents of which he floundered forward about fifty yards, and fell to rise no more, the last bullet having smashed his shoulder to pieces. On going to examine my prize I found that my three bullets had all struck within a foot of each other: any one of them would have been ultimately fatal. An old man who had accompanied me as gun-carrier was sitting on the ground within a few yards of the fallen bull, which he declared would have caught him had I not broken its shoulder. The old fellow was not active enough to climb a tree like the others, and seeing that he was unfitted for such work I did not again take him out.

The bull was a fine one, with an almost hairless skin: he probably would not have remained much longer with a herd.

His horns were somewhat splintered at the tips, and measured sixty-six and a half inches from tip to tip, along the curve and across the forehead ; their circumference at the base being seventeen inches.

We were barely two miles from camp, to which I now returned, and the remainder of the day was occupied in skinning the dead Gaur—a labor of considerable difficulty with unskilled men.

On the following morning we hunted at first in the opposite direction from camp, but during a long walk we did not even see a recent track, so we made a wide circuit and revisited yesterday's ground. We had sat down to smoke, when a movement in the jungle attracted the attention of one of my men, and, on going to ascertain the cause, I found fresh tracks of Gaur. Following them up, I saw a small bull against the sky line, but he at once disappeared, and on reaching the top of the hill we saw an old bull and a young one in full retreat, having evidently got our wind. They went right away over a distant hill, and as it was late in the forenoon, I returned to camp. Early in the afternoon I sent men to see if they could find the bulls that we disturbed in the morning, while I remained to superintend the preservation of the heads. · Shortly afterwards a man came in with news of a herd that he had seen in a valley several miles off. I at once started, and, after a hot walk of five miles down a steep hill I found—a herd of tame cattle ! I was naturally considerably annoyed, as a walk of ten miles up and down hill on a May afternoon is not what one would undertake without some inducement ; and I was not much better pleased at hearing from my men that they had ascertained that all the Gaur had left the jungle and had gone to a favorite haunt several miles away.

I had been told of a very good place about eight miles to the west of my camp, and I accordingly, marched to it on the morning of the third day. On my arrival, however, I found that the hills had been cleared and brought under cultivation within the last three or four years, and that no Gaur were ever now seen there. A villager whom I questioned assured me that he had recently seen the fresh tracks of a herd in a valley about five miles to the south, so on the fourth day I made for the spot, only to find that the valley was full of woodcutters, and that all the game had left. There was nothing for it but to return to the village where I had left my tents, and make a fresh start.

I had lost three days by my westward move, but by daylight on the 18th I was again on the hill tops, this time to the south-east of the village. We had just reached the plateau, and walked perhaps four hundred yards, when a herd was discovered. I had no difficulty in stalking them, and got right in among them, but I found that they were all cows, so I left them unmolested.

Continuing our walk along a long level ridge for upwards of a mile, we at length saw another herd among some trees on a hill about a mile and a half away. We could not make out whether there was a bull among them or not, but we at once set out for the spot. We had gone about half way when a bull appeared among some thick bushes almost on our path He was about five hundred yards off, and the ground was favorable for stalking, so I lost no time in approaching him. He was now concealed among the bushes, but after a careful advance, I found him standing under a tree, on the branches of which he was browzing. I was within forty-five yards before I could get a clear view of him, and then I found that he was standing facing me. I aimed at his throat, and he dropped without a struggle. Another bull, which I had not previously seen, now rushed forward a few paces and stood to gaze, giving me a fair shot at his shoulder. He did not fall, but, on running after him I soon saw him slowly and painfully crossing a ravine immediately below me, and a couple more shots rolled him over dead.

I sent off a man at once to bring the skinners and some breakfast, and went on in search of the herd which we had previously seen. We arrived just in time to see the last of them moving off, but half a mile farther on I again found them quietly feeding. I had to go some way round in order to stalk them, and the wind was very shifty: and by the time I had reached the place from which I expected to get a shot I found them all collected together on the top of a narrow ridge along which I had come: they had evidently winded me, and were very uneasy. Just beyond them the ridge ran up into a rocky knife-like edge, with a deep precipice on each side; along each side of the ridge ran a narrow path which, I supposed, communicated with another path beyond the rocks. The Gaur, all huddled together, presently hurried along the left hand path: they were within a hundred yards; but, as I could not see a bull, I would not fire. As soon as they disappeared I ran after them, and found that they had managed to scramble along a narrow shelving bank with barely footing for an Ibex, above which, on the right hand side, the rocks rose perpendicularly, while below was a sheer precipice at least a hundred feet deep. So bad was the path that I only followed it for a few paces, and then returned and followed the path that led along the other side of the ridge. About fifty yards farther on, this path ended abruptly at the edge of a deep precipice, and I stood for a minute or two wondering where the Gaur could possibly have gone to. Presently I heard them clattering at the other side of the rocks, and on running back I nearly met them; the whole herd passing me within ten yards at the junction of the paths. They did not seem to know what to do, and stood in a confused mass within a hundred yards. There was no bull, so I would not fire, but amused myself by whistling to them, and watching their consternation and indecision. It was like herding tame cattle. On examining the path along which the Gaur had gone and returned, I found that it was a *cul de sac:* had I followed them along it, either I or the whole herd *must* have gone over the cliff: *I* should probably have been the sufferer!

Leaving the scared herd, I went back to where the dead bulls lay, and having set the skinners to work, I set out for my bivouac, which had been established by the only water that was to be found on the hill. The men who came with the skinners had brought me news of a solitary bull having been seen near the bivouac, and when within a mile of it, we saw a bull standing under a large tree on the top of a hill some way to our left. It was now nearly one o'clock and blazing hot, and it was unlikely that the bull would move for some time, so I went on to the water to let my men quench their thirst. A muddy greenish puddle, much trampled by animals, was all that we had to depend upon, and I had to keep a strict watch over it to prevent my followers from still farther defiling it.

At two o'clock we started to look for the bull. It was a long hot climb to the top of the hill, and I was slowly walking up the last few yards of the ascent, when one of the men behind me whistled, and, on looking up, there was a bull standing on a rock just above me, not seventy yards off. He gave me plenty of time for a steady shot, on receiving which he rushed down the hill in front of me, followed by a much larger, jet-black bull. I ran after them and saw the smaller bull walking slowly along, evidently very sick, while the big fellow seemed to be waiting for his companion. I fired my second barrel at the big one, and then, reloading, fired right and left at the pair. A dip in the ground now concealed them for a few moments, but on again reloading and running forward I found the old bull lying dead, and the other hardly able to limp along.

As wounded beasts always carry off most lead, this bull took two or three more shots before he died, and received more bullets than any bull that I killed, although he was certainly the smallest.

His companion was about the same size as the first bull that I shot ; the other two bulls were both rather younger.

I saw nothing the following morning, but, in the afternoon I again went out. We had walked a considerable distance without finding even a fresh track, and were following the crest of a long level ridge, nearly devoid of cover, when I heard a rustling in a patch of tall dry grass a few paces to our left. I thought that it was probably caused by a deer, but a few moments afterwards I saw a solitary bull trotting off, out of shot. We watched him as he crossed a wide valley, and disappeared over the opposite hill, when we started in pursuit. Arrived at the place where the bull was last seen, we took up his tracks and followed them down into another valley in which there was a dense bamboo covert. There was no time for systematic tracking, so, having ascertained the direction that the bull had taken, we made a wide cast ahead, in hopes that we might somewhere intercept him. We were not disappointed : after walking for about an hour we saw him crossing a ravine not more than four hundred yards from us. He was moving slowly, and had apparently got over his alarm, for on reaching the top of the opposite bank he began to saunter about and crop the branches of the trees. Waiting till he was out of sight, I hurried across, and on looking over the edge of the ravine I saw the bull standing within seventy yards. He loomed rather indistinctly in the shade of the bamboos, and the stem of a small tree covered the vital spot behind the shoulder, so I had to take him rather farther forward than I liked, and fired at his neck. He turned round and crashed through the bamboos into the ravine beyond, down which I quickly tracked him and soon found plenty of blood. A little farther on frothy pools showed that he was desperately wounded, and although he had strength to cross another ravine and ascend the opposite bank, I found him standing not four hundred yards from where he was first fired at. He could not have gone much farther, having been shot through the throat, but I had to fire three more shots before I finally secured him. Although a solitary bull he was not a very old one, and his horns, though massive, were still perfect at the tips : they measured a little more than those of my first bull.

As I was anxious to preserve the heads and skins properly, and knew that they would be spoiled if left to the natives, I remained in camp the following morning to superintend the skinners, and sent out men to reconnoitre. One of them soon returned with news, and I at once accompanied him to where the others had remained to watch, little more than a mile from camp. The Gaur had been seen on the summit of a low ridge, and along this I walked, expecting to see them in the valley below. Suddenly, I came upon them lying down in a small hollow : they were within twenty-five yards, but quite unconscious of my presence. Presently they rose slowly and stood gazing at me for nearly two minutes : there was absolutely no cover, so they had a perfect view of me, but they seemed to know that I would not molest them. There were one very young bull and two cows, so I refused to fire, although my men were anxious that I should do so. At last the Gaur walked quietly away, and descended into a wooded valley. In the evening I had a long walk, but only saw some small Gaur, probably the same that I had seen in the morning.

The next day the men with me declared that all the Gaur must now have left the neighbourhood, but before making any farther plans I despatched three or four men to the jungle where I commenced my shooting, with orders to ascertain whether any Gaur had returned to it. I also ordered other men to reconnoitre in the vicinity of camp, while I again looked after the skins.

As I was at breakfast a man returned, stating that he had found the track of a solitary bull close to camp, and had followed it until it had joined others, shortly after which he had actually seen the animals, which two other men were remaining to watch. I was not long in getting ready, and half an hour's walk brought me to the place where the men were keeping watch on the top of a hill. They informed me that there were several Gaur, which had separated into two lots, and were now lying or standing in the shade, several hundred yards apart. Each lot was said to be headed by an old bull, and the finer of the two was now lying on a flat immediately below us. They pointed him out to me, and I at once saw that the stalk ought to be an easy one.

The bull was lying at the foot of one of the few trees which grew on the nearly bare flat, which was bounded by the steep hill-side above, and by deep ravines on each side, the ravines uniting a short distance below where the bull lay.

Going well to leeward along the hill-top, I took advantage of a ravine which ran down the hill-side to descend under cover until I was well below the level of the flat. I then worked up the bed of one of the ravines until I believed that I must be very near the bull. Cautiously ascending the bank, I looked over, and soon observed a black mass lying at the foot of a tree about two hundred yards off. I thought that this must be the bull, but it remained absolutely motionless, and after examining it for some time with my binoculars, I came to the conclusion that it was only a rock. I therefore slowly advanced, but had fortunately only moved a pace or two, when a whisk of his tail betrayed the bull. Very carefully I crept back into the ravine and went along its bed, until I knew that I must be just opposite the bull. Stepping as lightly as possible, I re-ascended the bank, and on reaching the top, found myself within thirty-five yards of the bull, who at once rose to his feet. The trunk of the tree under which he had been lying was between him and me, and I could only see his head and hind quarters; I therefore waited for him to move and expose his shoulder.

For at least a minute he remained perfectly motionless, gazing at me, and then turned slowly round and walked two or three paces. I raised my rifle, and as the movement caught his eye he wheeled rapidly round and faced me, lowering his head in a threatening manner. I was on lower ground, so I could still see his chest, and I fired for the centre of it, sending the bull staggering back. He only went about ten yards, and then halted and again faced me, apparently meditating a charge. If such was his intention I forestalled him, for stepping forward, I gave him another shot which stretched him lifeless. My attention was now directed to two other bulls, which trotted across the flat, and began to ascend the hill. I opened fire on these and dropped one dead, but failed to secure the other, which I either missed or only slightly wounded. I hope the former.

I now had time to examine the big bull, which proved to be a grand specimen. His horns were very massive and rugged, and his head was scarred and abraded by fighting; a curious horny excrescence on his forehead giving him a peculiarly savage appearance.

His horns measured sixty-nine inches from tip to tip, but were a good deal broken at the tips: the sweep was thirty-six inches. His hide was nearly devoid of hair on the back and sides, and was of a curious purplish hue, like Indian rubber.

The heat was so intense that the hair was blistered off both the Gaur before the skinners could arrive, although they were on the spot in less than two hours after the bulls had fallen.

I was now thoroughly satisfied with my bag, and as the rainy season was rapidly approaching, when travelling becomes extremely difficult, and in fact impossible for carts, I gave up shooting and returned home.

It may not be out of place to mention that I killed all these Gaur with a 12-bore rifle, with seven drams of powder, and a hardened spherical bullet. Such a rifle has been condemned by many people,—including some high authorities on sporting matters—as an inefficient weapon against large game. After very considerable experience I am convinced that, if the shooting is careful, there is seldom any *necessity* for the employment of 8 bores and 4 bores against anything smaller than Elephants.

A. A. A. K.

FERÓZPUR,
December, 1884.

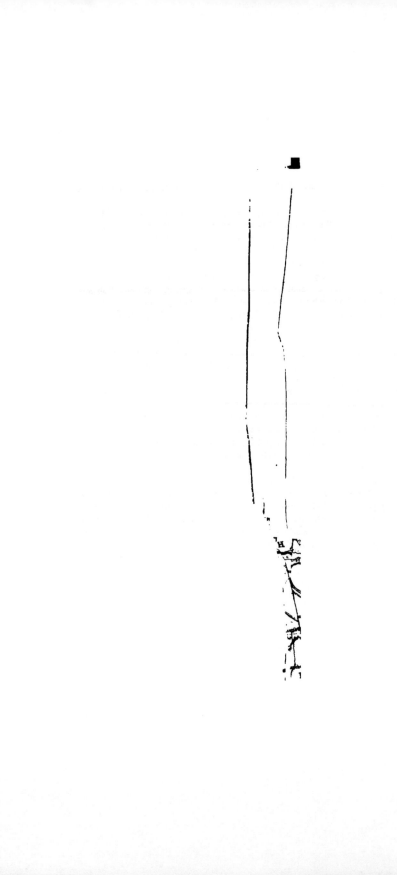

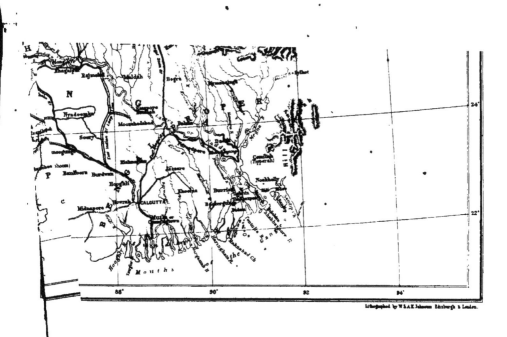

CATALOGUE OF ILLUSTRATED WORKS

PUBLISHED BY

THACKER, SPINK AND CO.,

CALCUTTA.

Just Published; in Demy 4to; Rs. 25; elegantly bound.

LARGE GAME SHOOTING
IN
THIBET, THE HIMALAYAS, AND NORTHERN INDIA.

Containing Descriptions of the Country and of the various Animals to be found; together with Extracts from a Journal of several years' standing. With Thirty Illustrations, and Map of the District.

"An attractive volume, full of sporting adventures in the valleys and forest hills extending along the foot of the Himalayas. Its pages are also interesting for the graphic description they give of the beasts of the field, the cunning instinct which they show in guarding their safety, the places

which they choose for their lair, and the way in which they show their anger when at bay. Colonel Kinloch writes on all these subjects in a genuine and straightforward style, aiming at giving a complete description of the habits and movements of the game."—*British Mail.*

BY COLONEL ALEXANDER A. KINLOCH.

Formerly published in Two Series, which were quickly out of Print. The present Work embraces those Volumes with Additional Excursions, a Map and Thirty Illustrations from Photographs in the Finest Style of Art.

STERNDALE'S
MAMMALIA OF INDIA.
One Hundred and Seventy Illustrations.   *Rs.* 12-8.

REVIEWS.

"STERNDALE'S MAMMALIA OF INDIA.

"The compiler of this exceedingly valuable treatise on the Mammals of India tells us in the preface that it was designed to meet the existing want of a popular manual, and having looked carefully through the book, we are bound to state our opinion that it is in all respects the most serviceable handbook we have any knowledge of, and that it is especially one adapted for the sportsman or naturalist in a country where large collection of books are difficult to carry."—*Army and Navy Gazette.*

"Has contrived to hit a happy mean between the stiff scientific treatise and the bosh of what may be called anecdotal zoology."—*The Daily News.*

"It is the very model of what a popular natural history should be."—*Knowledge.*

In Imperial 16mo. Uniform with "Riding," "Hindu Mythology," and "Indian Ferns." Rs. 12-8.

A NATURAL HISTORY
OF THE
MAMMALIA OF INDIA.

By R. A. STERNDALE, F.R.G.S, F.Z.S., &c.
AUTHOR OF "SEONEE," "THE DENIZENS OF THE JUNGLE," "THE AFGHAN KNIFE," ETC.

WITH 170 ILLUSTRATIONS BY THE AUTHOR AND OTHERS.

A WORK designed to meet an existing want—*viz.*, a popular manual of Indian Mammalia. The only work of the kind hitherto has been one which treats exclusively of the Peninsula of India, and therefore the more interesting types found in Assam, Burmah, and Ceylon, as well as the northern countries bordering the British Empire, have been left out. In the present work the geographical limits have been extended to all territories likely to be reached by the sportsman from India, and thus its field of usefulness has been greatly enlarged. It is copiously illustrated, not only by the author himself, but by careful selections made by him from the works of well-known artists.

REVIEWS.

"The notices of each animal are, as a rule, short, though on some of the larger mammals—the lion, tiger, pard, boar, &c.—ample and interesting details are given, including occasional anecdotes of adventure. The book will, no doubt, be specially useful to the sportsman, and, indeed, has been extended so as to include all territories likely to be reached by the sportsman from India. . . . . Those who desire to obtain some general information, popularly conveyed, on the subject with which the book deals, will, we believe, find it useful."—*The Times.*

"An amusing work with good illustrations."—*Nature.*

"Full of accurate observation, brightly told."—*Saturday Review.*

"The results of a close and sympathetic observation."—*Athenæum.*

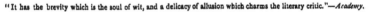

"It has the brevity which is the soul of wit, and a delicacy of allusion which charms the literary critic."—*Academy.*

THE TRIBES ON MY FRONTIER.

By EHA. Seventy Illustrations by F. C. MACRAE.

AN ANXIOUS MOMENT.

REVIEW.

"TRIBES ON MY FRONTIER."

"One of the most entertaining books it has been our hap to come upon for many a day. . . . The book is cleverly illustrated by Mr. F. C. Macrae. We have only to thank our Anglo-Indian naturalist for the delightful book which he has sent home to his countrymen in Britain. May he live to give us another such."—*Chambers' Journal.*

THE CHAPTERS ARE—

Second Edition. In Imperial 16mo, uniform with "Lays of Ind," "Riding,"
"Hindu Mythology," &c. Rs. 5-8.

THE TRIBES ON MY FRONTIER:

An Indian Naturalist's Foreign Policy.

By EHA.

WITH SEVENTY ILLUSTRATIONS BY F. C. MACRAE.

THIS remarkably clever work most graphically and humorously describes the animal surroundings of a Mofussil bungalow. The twenty chapters embrace a year's experiences, and provide endless sources of amusement and suggestion. The numerous able illustrations add very greatly to the interest of the volume, which will find a place on every table.

REVIEWS.

" It is a very clever record of a year's observations round the bungalow in ' Dustypore.' . . . . It is by no means a mere travesty. . . . The writer is always amusing, and never dull."—*Field.*

" The volume owes something to illustrations by F. C. Macrae, which, if not very unfinished works of art, are often as unconventional and humorous as the text. It is a book to be read, and has the advantage of needing no preliminary knowledge of natural history for its enjoyment."—*Westminster Review.*

" A most charming series of sprightly and entertaining essays on what may be termed the fauna of the Indian bungalow. . . . . We have no doubt that this amusing book will find its way into every Anglo-Indian's library."—*Allen's Indian Mail.*

" This is a delightful book, irresistibly funny in description and illustration, but full of genuine science too. . . . . There is not a dull or uninstructive page in the whole book."—*Knowledge.*

" It is a pleasantly-written book about the insects and other torments of India which make Anglo-Indian life unpleasant, and which can be read with pleasure even by those beyond the reach of the tormenting things ' Eha ' describes.'—*Graphic.*

" The volume is full of accurate and unfamiliar observation, and the illustrations prove to be by no means without their value."—*Saturday Review.*

" It has the brevity which is the soul of wit, and a delicacy of allusion which charms the literary critic."—*Academy.*

Imperial 16mo. Rs. 12. 8. Uniform with " Lays of Ind," " Hindu Mythology," " Riding," " Natural History of the Mammalia of India," &c.

A POPULAR HANDBOOK
OF
INDIAN FERNS.

By COLONEL R. H. BEDDOME,

AUTHOR OF THE "FERNS OF BRITISH INDIA," "THE FERNS OF SOUTHERN INDIA."

THREE HUNDRED ILLUSTRATIONS BY THE AUTHOR.

REVIEWS.

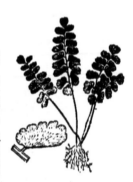

" It is the first special book of portable size and moderate price which has been devoted to Indian Ferns, and is in every way deserving of the extensive circulation it is sure to obtain."—*Nature.*

" I have just seen a new work on Indian Ferns which will prove vastly interesting, not only to the Indian people, but to the botanists of this country."—*Indian Daily News.*

" ' The Ferns of India.' This is a good book, being of a useful and trustworthy character. The species are familiarly described, and most of them illustrated by small figures."—*Gardeners' Chronicle.*

" Those interested in botany will do well to procure a new work on the ' Ferns of British India.' The work will prove a first-class text book."—*Free Press.*

" The great amount of care observed in its compilation makes it a most valuable work of reference, especially to non-scientific readers, for in preparing it as many of the technicalities as could be safely dispensed with have been left aside. This excellent book, which is intended to meet a want that has long and acutely been felt by all lovers of ferns, will be all the more welcome coming, as it does, from an author whose thorough knowledge of the subject is already well known through his former works."—*Garden.*

Fcap. 8vo. Elegantly Bound. Rs. 4.

INDIAN LYRICS.

By W. TREGO-WEBB, M.A.,

PROFESSOR OF ENGLISH LITERATURE, PRESIDENCY COLLEGE.

REVIEWS.

" A volume of varied and graceful verse which, while appealing to the sympathies and experiences of all Anglo-Indians, will not be without its value as illustrating for English people at home the various phases of an Indian sojourn."—*Englishman.*

" He presents the various sorts and conditions of humanity that comprise the round of life in Bengal in a series of vivid vignettes. . . . He writes with scholarly directness and finish."—*Saturday Review.*

" A pleasant book to read."—*Suffolk Chronicle.*

" The style is pretty pleasant, and the verses run smooth and melodious."—*Indian Mail.*

" One of the main objects of the author is to throw some fresh light on Indian things for English readers, and we are happy in being able to introduce him in this way to our readers. This is a pleasant book to read. The verse is mostly strong and vigorous; a quiet humour sparkles on the page: few pieces are long, and the subjects are varied. The reader may trip from piece to piece, ever finding something which will interest him."—*Suffolk Chronicle.*

Seventh Edition. Profusely Illustrated.

LAYS OF IND.

By ALIPH CHEEM.

COMIC, SATIRICAL, AND DESCRIPTIVE POEMS,

ILLUSTRATIVE OF

ANGLO-INDIAN LIFE.

Handsomely bound. Cloth, gilt edges. Rs. 7.

REVIEWS.

" This is a remarkably bright little book. ' Aliph Cheem, supposed to be the *nom de plume* of an officer in the 18th Hussars, is, after his fashion, an Indian Bon Gaultier. In a few of the poems the jokes, turning on local names and customs, are somewhat esoteric ; but, taken throughout, the verses are characterised by high animal spirits, great cleverness, and most excellent fooling." — *The World.*

" Aliph Cheem presents us in this volume with some highly amusing ballads and songs, which have already in a former edition warmed the hearts and cheered the lonely hours of many an Anglo-Indian, the pictures being chiefly those of Indian life. There is no mistaking the humour, and at times, indeed, the fun is both 'fast and furious.' Many portions remind us of the 'Bab Ballads.' One can readily imagine the merriment created round the camp fire by the recitation of ' The Two Thumpers,' which is irresistibly droll. . . . The edition before us is enlarged, and contains illustrations by the author, in addition to which it is beautifully printed and handsomely got up, all which recommendations are sure to make the name of Aliph Cheem more popular in India than ever."—*Liverpool Mercury.*

" Satire of the most amusing and inoffensive kind, humour the most genuine, and pathos the most touching pervade these ' Lays of Ind.' . . . From Indian friends we have heard of the popularity these ' Lays' have obtained in the land where they were written, and we predict for them a popularity equally great at home."—*Monthly Homœopathic Review.*

" Former editions of this entertaining book having been received with great favour by the public and by the press, a new edition has been issued in elegant type and binding. The author, although assuming a *non de plume*, is recognised as a distinguished cavalry officer, possessed of a vivid imagination and a sense of humour amounting sometimes to rollicking and contagious fun. Many of his ' Lays' suggest recollections of some of the best pieces in the ' Ingoldsby Legends,' or in the ' Biglow Papers' of Russell Lowell, while revealing a character of their own. Anglo-Indian terms and usages are skilfully employed, and even what appears to some the uneventful life of a secluded station is made to yield incidents for humourous description."—*Capital and Labour, May 17th, 1876.*

" The ' Lays' are not only Anglo-Indian in origin, but out-and-out Anglo-Indian in subject and colour. To one who knows something of life at an Indian ' station' they will be especially amusing. Their exuberant fun at the same time may well attract the attention of the ill-defined individual known as ' the general reader.'"—*Scotsman.*

" To many Anglo-Indians the lively verses of 'Aliph Cheem must be very well known, while to those who have not yet become acquainted with them we can only say read them on the first opportunity. To those not familiar with Indian life they may be specially commended for the picture which they give of many of its lighter incidents and conditions, and of several of its ordinary personages. . . . We have read the volume with real pleasure, and we have only to add that it is nicely printed and elegantly finished, and that it has several charming wood-cuts, of which some are by the author, whom Indian gossip, by the way, has identified with Captain Yeldham, of the 18th Hussars."—*Bath Chronicle.*

Third Edition, revised, enlarged, and newly illustrated. Crown 8vo. Rs. 7.

VETERINARY NOTES FOR HORSE-OWNERS.

AN EVERY-DAY HORSE BOOK.

By CAPT. M. HORACE HAYES.

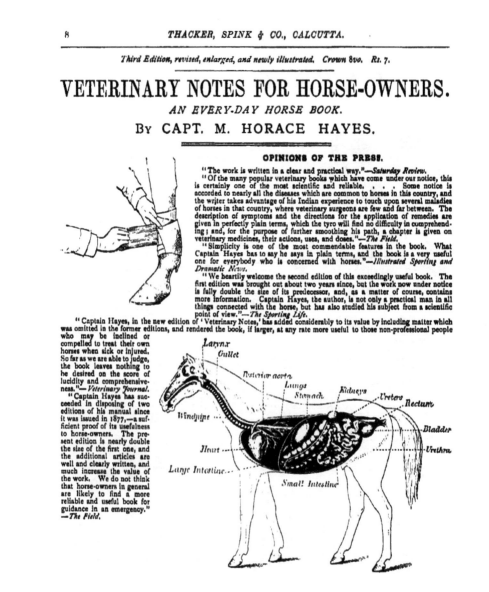

OPINIONS OF THE PRESS.

"The work is written in a clear and practical way."—*Saturday Review.*

"Of the many popular veterinary books which have come under our notice, this is certainly one of the most scientific and reliable. . . . Some notice is accorded to nearly all the diseases which are common to horses in this country, and the writer takes advantage of his Indian experience to touch upon several maladies of horses in that country, where veterinary surgeons are few and far between. The description of symptoms and the directions for the application of remedies are given in perfectly plain terms, which the tyro will find no difficulty in comprehending; and, for the purpose of further smoothing his path, a chapter is given on veterinary medicines, their actions, uses, and doses."—*The Field.*

"Simplicity is one of the most commendable features in the book. What Captain Hayes has to say he says in plain terms, and the book is a very useful one for everybody who is concerned with horses."—*Illustrated Sporting and Dramatic News.*

"We heartily welcome the second edition of this exceedingly useful book. The first edition was brought out about two years since, but the work now under notice is fully double the size of its predecessor, and, as a matter of course, contains more information. Captain Hayes, the author, is not only a practical man in all things connected with the horse, but has also studied his subject from a scientific point of view."—*The Sporting Life.*

"Captain Hayes, in the new edition of 'Veterinary Notes,' has added considerably to its value by including matter which was omitted in the former editions, and rendered the book, if larger, at any rate more useful to those non-professional people who may be inclined or compelled to treat their own horses when sick or injured. So far as we are able to judge, the book leaves nothing to be desired on the score of lucidity and comprehensiveness."—*Veterinary Journal.*

"Captain Hayes has succeeded in disposing of two editions of his manual since it was issued in 1877,—a sufficient proof of its usefulness to horse-owners. The present edition is nearly double the size of the first one, and the additional articles are well and clearly written, and much increase the value of the work. We do not think that horse-owners in general are likely to find a more reliable and useful book for guidance in an emergency."—*The Field.*

Uniform with "Lays of Ind," "Hindu Mythology," "Indian Ferns," "Mammalia of India," &c.

Second Edition. Revised and Enlarged. Imperial 16mo. Rs. 7.

RIDING:

ON THE FLAT AND ACROSS COUNTRY

A Guide to Practical Horsemanship by Capt. M. H. HAYES.

ILLUSTRATED BY STURGESS.

" The book is one that no man who has ever sat in a saddle can fail to read with interest."—*Illustrated Sporting and Dramatic News.*

"The general directions are in most cases in accordance with our own opinions; and Mr. Hayes has supplemented his own experience of race-riding by resorting to Tom Cannon, Fordham, and other well-known jockeys for illustration. 'The Guide' is, on the whole, thoroughly reliable; and both the illustrations and the printing do credit to the publishers."—*Field.*

" A master of his subject."—*Standard.*

" An excellent book on riding."—*Truth.*

"It has, however, been reserved for Captain Hayes to write what in our opinion will be generally accepted as the most comprehensive, enlightened, and 'all round' work on riding, bringing to bear as he does not only his own great experience, but the advice and practice of many of the best recognised horsemen of the period.—*The Sporting Life.*

"An eminently practical teacher, whose theories are the outcome of experience, learned not in the study, but on the road, in the hunting field, and on the racecourse."—*Baily's Magazine.*

In Imperial 16mo. Illustrated. Rs. 5. 12.

INDIAN RACING REMINISCENCES:

BEING

ENTERTAINING NARRATIVES AND ANECDOTES OF MEN, HORSES, AND SPORT.

ILLUSTRATED WITH TWENTY-TWO PORTRAITS AND A NUMBER OF SMALLER ENGRAVINGS.

BY M. HORACE HAYES (*Late Captain, " The Buffs "*).

Author of " Riding : On the Flat and Across Country," "Veterinary Notes for Horse Owners," etc.

"Captain Hayes shows himself a thorough master of his subject, and has so skilfully interwoven technicalities, history, and anecdote, that the last page comes all too soon."—*Field.*

"No racing reminiscences have ever been recorded so graphically, with such a loving lingering over the days that were, and with such a wide personal acquaintance with the horses, the men, and the times, as Captain Hayes has done in his new book."—*The Indian Planter's Gazette.*

Crown 8vo. Rs. 4 4.

THE STUDENTS' MANUAL OF TACTICS.

BY CAPT. M. HORACE HAYES.

SPECIALLY WRITTEN FOR THE USE OF CANDIDATES PREPARING FOR MILITARY COMPETITIVE EXAMINATIONS, AND FOR PROMOTION.

CONTENTS.

Definitions.	V.—Formations : Time and Space.	XI.—The Attack.
I.—Composition of an Army.	VI.—Outposts.	XII.—The Defence.
II.—Infantry.	VII.—Screening and Reconnoitring.	XIII.—Villages.
III.—Artillery.	VIII:—Advanced Guards.	XIV.—Woods.
IV.—Cavalry.	IX.—Rear Guards.	XV.—Machine Guns.
	X.—Marches.	

"There is no better Manual on Tactics than the one which Captain Hayes has written."—*Naval and Military Gazette.*

"The Students' Manual of Tactics is an excellent book. Principles are reasoned out, and details explained in such a way that the student cannot fail to get a good grasp of the subject. Having served in both the artillery and infantry, and being a practical writer, as well as 'a coach,' the author of this manual had exceptional qualifications for the task he has accomplished."—*Broad Arrow.*

"Is a well-considered treatise on tactics, giving not merely rules, but also principles and reasons. We would particularly draw attention to the chapter on the defensive, which subject is treated with more fulness than is usually found in English books. A valuable chapter on machine guns winds up the work."—*The Times.*

Fourth Edition. Crown 8vo. Rs. 5.

TRAINING AND HORSE MANAGEMENT IN INDIA.

By Captain M. HORACE HAYES,

Author of "Veterinary Notes for Horse Owners," "Riding," etc.

"No better guide could be placed in the hands of either amateur horseman or veterinary surgeon."—*The Veterinary Journal.*

"A useful guide in regard to horses anywhere. . . . . Concise, practical, and portable."—*Saturday Review.*

"We have always been able to commend Captain Hayes's books as being essentially practical, and written in understandable language. As trainer, owner, and rider of horses on the flat and over country, the author has had a wide experience, and when to this is added competent veterinary knowledge, it is clear that Captain Hayes is entitled to attention when he speaks."—*The Field.*

NEW WORKS BY CAPTAIN HAYES; IN THE PRESS.

In Demy 8vo.

SOUNDNESS IN HORSES.

WITH ONE HUNDRED AND SEVENTY ILLUSTRATIONS.

A Complete Guide to all those features which require attention when purchasing Horses, distinguishing mere defects from the symptoms of unsoundness, with explicit instructions how to conduct an examination of the various parts.

CHAPTERS.

I.—Soundness.
II.—Defects which are Absolute Unsoundness.
III—Defects which are not necessarily Unsoundness.
IV.—Method of Examination.
V.—How to Handle a Horse.

VI.—Examination of the Mouth.
VII.—Examination of the Eyes.
VIII.—Examination of the Head, Neck, and Trunk.
IX.—Examination of the Limbs.
X.—Lameness.

Oblong 4to.

THE POINTS OF THE HORSE.

A Familiar Treatise on Equine Conformation.

Illustrated by J. H. OSWALD BROWN.

Describing the Points in which the perfection of each class of Horses consists; illustrated by very numerous reproductions of Photographs of Living Typical Animals: forming an invaluable Guide to Owners of Horses.

CHAPTERS.

I.—Names of the Different Parts of the Horse.
II.—Structures of the Body.
III.—Sketch of the Anatomy of the Horse.
IV.—Heart and Lungs.
V.—Mechanism of Breathing.
VI.—Levers.
VII.—Distribution of Weight.
VIII.—Paces of the Horse.
IX.—Mechanism of Locomotion.

X.—Proportions of the Horse.
XI.—Head and Neck.
XII.—Fore Limb.
XIII.—Trunk.
XIV.—Hind Limb.
XV.—Weight Carrying and Staying Power.
XVI.—Skin and Hair.
XVII.—Characteristics of the Various Classes of Horses.

New Edition in Oblong Folio.

DENIZENS OF THE JUNGLES:

A SERIES OF SKETCHES OF WILD ANIMALS, ILLUSTRATING THEIR FORM AND NATURAL ATTITUDE.

WITH LETTERPRESS DESCRIPTIONS OF EACH PLATE.

By R. A. STERNDALE, F.R.G.S., F.Z.S.

Author of "Natural History of the Mammalia of India," "Seonee," &c.

"ON THE WATCH."   *(Reduced from Original.)*

CONTENTS.

IN THE PRESS. Imperial 16mo., with Numerous Illustrations.

IN SADDLE AND STABLE:
𝔗𝔥𝔢 𝔠𝔬𝔪𝔪𝔬𝔫 𝔖𝔢𝔫𝔰𝔢 𝔬𝔣 ℜ𝔦𝔡𝔦𝔫𝔤,

By Mrs. POWER O'DONOGHUE.

Authoress of " Ladies on Horseback," " A Beggar on Horseback," &c.

CHAPTERS.

I.—OUGHT CHILDREN TO RIDE?
II.—"FOR MOTHERS AND CHILDREN"
III.—FIRST HINTS TO A LEARNER.
IV.—SELECTING A MOUNT.
V.—THE LADY'S DRESS ON HORSEBACK.
VI.—DITTO.
VII.—BITTING.
VIII.—SADDLING.
IX.—HOW TO SIT, TO WALK, TO CANTER, AND TO TROT.
X.—REINS, VOICE, AND WHIP.
XI.—RIDING ON THE ROAD.
XII.—PACES, VICES, AND FAULTS.
XIII.—A LESSON IN LEAPING.
XIV.—MANAGING REFUSERS.
XV.—FALLING.
XVI.—HUNTING OUTFIT CONSIDERED.
XVII.—ECONOMY IN RIDING DRESS.
XVIII.—HACKS AND HUNTERS.
XIX.—IN THE HUNTING FIELD.
XX.—SHOEING.
XXI.—FEEDING.
XXII.—STABLING.
XXIII.—DOCTORING.

In Post 8vo. Cloth limp. Rs. 5.

THE STEEPLECHASE HORSE:
How to Select, Train, and Ride Him,

WITH NOTES ON ACCIDENTS AND DISEASES, AND THEIR TREATMENT.

By Capt. J. HUMFREY.

CHAPTERS.

I.—GENERAL REMARKS.
II.—HOW TO SELECT STEEPLECHASE HORSES.
III.—AGE.
IV.—HOW TO PUT IN CONDITION.
V.—HOW TO BREAK IN.
VI.—SCHOOLING.
VII.—TRAINING.
VIII.—STABLES AND STABLE MANAGEMENT.
IX.—HOW TO RIDE.
X.—ACCIDENTS AND DISEASES.
XI.—MEDICINES — RECIPES TO IMPROVE CONDITION—SHOEING.

THE INDIAN COOKERY BOOK.
A PRACTICAL HANDBOOK TO THE KITCHEN IN INDIA:
ADAPTED TO THE THREE PRESIDENCIES. Price Rs. 3.

Containing Original and Approved Recipes in every department of Indian Cookery; Recipes for Summer Beverages and Home-made Liqueurs; Medicinal and other Recipes; together with a variety of things worth knowing.

By A THIRTY-FIVE YEARS' RESIDENT.

Third Edition, Demy 8vo, Rs. 10.

A MANUAL OF GARDENING
FOR
BENGAL AND UPPER INDIA.

By THOMAS A. C. FERMINGER, M.A.

PART I.

OPERATIONS OF GARDENING.

Chap. I.—Climate—Soils—Manures.

Chap. II.—Laying-out a Garden—Lawns—Hedges—Hoeing and Digging—Drainage—Conservatories—Betel Houses—Decorations—Implements—Shades—Labels—Vermin—Weeds.

Chap. III.—Seeds—Seed Sowing—Pot Culture—Planting—Cuttings—Layers—Gootee—Grafting and Inarching—Budding—Pruning and Root Pruning—Conveyance.

Chap. IV.—Calendar of Operations.

PART II.

GARDEN PLANTS.

1. Culinary Vegetables.	3. Edible Nuts.
2. Dessert Fruits.	4. Ornamental Annuals.
5. Ornamental Trees, Shrubs, and Herbaceous Perennials.	

Crown 8vo, Rs. 5.

MANUAL OF AGRICULTURE FOR INDIA.

By LIEUT. F. POGSON.

1. *Origin and Character of Soils.*—2. *Ploughing and Preparing for Seed.*—3. *Manures and Composts.*—4. *Wheat Cultivation.*—5. *Barley.*—6. *Oats.*—7. *Rye.*—8. *Rice.*—9. *Maize.*—10. *Sugar-producing Sorghums.*—11. *Common Sorghums.*—12. *Sugarcane.*—13. *Oil Seed.*—14. *Field Pea Crops.*—15. *Dall or Pulse.*—16. *Root Crops.*—17. *Cold Spice.*—18. *Fodder.*—19. *Water-Nut.*—20. *Ground-Nut.*—21. *Rush-Nut or Chufas.*—22. *Cotton.*—23. *Tobacco.*—24. *Mensuration.*—*Appendix.*

REVIEWS.

"The work seems to us both in thoroughness of execution and in clearness or arrangement entirely to fulfil all the hopes that have been formed of it. We cannot doubt that the Government will heartily take up this most valuable book, and circulate it both in the original and vernacular translations throughout the length and breadth of the land; nor should a moment be lost, for it represents one of the most important and most promising lines on which we can meet that terrible 'Malthusian difficulty.'"—*Allen's Indian Mail.*

"A work of extreme practical value."—*Home News.*

"Mr. Pogson's advice may be profitably followed by both native and European agriculturists, for it is eminently practical and devoid of empiricism. His little volume embodies the teaching of a large and varied experience, and deserves to be warmly supported."—*Madras Mail.*

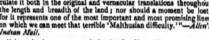

Complete in one Volume, Rs. 5.; Interleaved, Rs. 5-8.

WITH 240 ILLUSTRATIONS.

A TEXT BOOK OF INDIAN BOTANY:
Morphological, Physiological, and Systematic.

By W. H. GREGG, HUGHLI COLLEGE.

Uniform with "Lays of Ind," "Riding," &c. Rs. 7.

HINDU MYTHOLOGY:
VEDIC AND PURANIC.

BY

Rev. W. J. WILKINS,

OF THE LONDON MISSIONARY SOCIETY, CALCUTTA.

Illustrated by very numerous Engravings from Drawings by Native Artists.

"His aim has been to give a faithful account of the Hindoo deities such as an intelligent native would himself give, and he has endeavoured, in order to achieve his purpose, to keep his mind free from prejudice or theological bias. To help to completeness he has included a number of drawings of the principal deities, executed by native artists. The author has attempted a work of no little ambition and has succeeded in his attempt, the volume being one of great interest and usefulness; and not the less so because he has strictly refrained from diluting his facts with comments of his own. It has numerous illustrations."—*Home News.*

"Mr. Wilkins has done his work well, with an honest desire to state facts apart from all theological prepossession, and his volume is likely to be a useful book of reference." —*Guardian.*

"In Mr. Wilkins' book we have an illustrated manual, the study of which will lay a solid foundation for more advanced knowledge, while it will furnish those who may have the desire without having the time or opportunity to go further into the subject, with a really extensive stock of accurate information."—*Indian Daily News.*

Crown 8vo. Rs. 5.

A TEA PLANTER'S LIFE IN ASSAM.
By GEORGE M. BARKER.

WITH SEVENTY-FIVE ILLUSTRATIONS BY THE AUTHOR.

Few efforts have been made to bring the people of this strange country and their quaint customs before English readers in book form; for although some works exist on the technical working of a Tea plantation, no one has in recent times attempted to describe the country and people that form the surroundings of every Assam planter.

This book aims at conveying to all interested in India and the Tea industry an entertaining and useful accound of the topographical features of Assam; the strange surroundings — human and animal — of the European Resident; the trying Climate; the Daily Life of the Planter; and general details of the formation and working of Tea Gardens. The Illustrations, by the Author, add greatly to the interest of the work.

NAGA WOMAN.

ASSAMESE.

"In case anyone dreams of visiting that delightful spot, we can heartily command to him Mr. Barker as a guide."—*Literary World.*

"Mr. Barker has supplied us with a very good and readable description, accompanied by numerous illustrations drawn by himself. What may be called the business parts of the book are of most value."—*Contemporary Review.*

"Cheery, well-written little book."—*Graphic.*

"A very interesting and amusing book, artistically illustrated from sketches drawn by the Author."—*Mark Lane Express.*

MISCELLANEOUS WORKS.

Tales from Indian History; Being the Annals of India retold in Narratives. By J. TALBOYS WHEELER. One Vol., small 8vo. Rs. 3-6. Forms a Complete History of India from the earliest period to the present day, drawn up as a series of "Narratives" for general reading.

"Will absorb the attention of all who delight in thrilling records of adventure and daring. It is no mere compilation, but an earnest and brightly-written book."—*Daily Chronicle.*

"The history of our great dependency made extremely attractive reading."—*Broad Arrow.*

"No one can read a volume such as this without being deeply interested."—*Scotsman.*

Thacker's Indian Directory, embracing the whole of India and Burmah. Published annually, royal 8vo., half bound. Rs. 16.

For twenty-one years this work was known as the "BENGAL DIRECTORY," and was confined in its information to the Bengal Presidency. With the 22nd issue, in 1884, its range was extended to every town and station in India. The importance of a work thus embacing in an extremely compact form the vast territories of the British Indian Empire, cannot be exaggerated; and it is hoped that the costly efforts of the Publishers to present a great increase of information without any increase in the price of the volume, will secure it an enlarged circulation commensurate with the labour and expense bestowed upon it.

Goodeve's Hints for the Management and Medical Treatment of Children in India. Re-written by EDWARD A. BIRCH, M.D., Surgeon-Major, Bengal Establishment. Seventh Edition. Crown 8vo. Rs. 7.

"I have no hesitation in saying that the present edition is for many reasons superior to its predecessors. It is written very carefully, and with much knowledge and experience on the author's part, whilst it possesses the great advantage of bringing up the subject to the present level of Medical Science."—*Dr. Goodeve.*

Merces' Indian and English Exchange Tables from 1s. 6d. to 2s. per Rupee. New Edition. In this Edition the rate rises by 32nds of a penny, to meet the requirements of Financiers. The progression is by units; thus, in most instances, saving a line of calculation. Facility of reference and accuracy render it the most perfect work in existence. Demy 8vo. Rs. 12.

"We heartily recommend these tables, both for their reliability and for the great saving in time that will be gained by their employment."—*Financier.*

Hydraulic Works: Rivers, Canals, Storage, Irrigation, Sewage Farms, Water Analysis, &c. Under the patronage of the British Indian Government. Embracing Works in England, India, the Continent, China, Egypt, and America. By LOWIS D'A. JACKSON, author of "Canal and Culvert Tables," "Survey Practice," "Hydraulic-Manual," &c. Royal 8vo.

Calcutta to Liverpool by China, Japan and America, in 1877. By Lieut.-General Sir HENRY NORMAN. Second Edition. Fcap. 8vo, cloth. Rs. 2-8. The only book published on this interesting route between India and England.

Reconnoitring.—The Reconnoitrer's Guide and Field Book, adapted for India. By Major M. J. KING-HARMAN. Second Edition, Revised and Enlarged. Small 8vo, in leather with tuck. Rs. 3-8. Intended as an aid to the memory of those who might be called upon at any time to make a military survey or reconnaisance.

"To the officers serving in India this guide will be invaluable."—*Broad Arrow.*

Bose.—The Hindoos as they are: a description of the Manners, Customs, and Inner Life of Hindoo Society. Bengal. By SHIB CHUNDER BOSE. Second Edition. Revised. Crown 8vo. Rs. 5. Shib Chunder Bose is an enlightened Bengali of matured conviction and character, and his extended and varied experience eminently qualify him for lifting the veil from the inner domestic life of his countrymen.

Busteed.—Echoes from Old Calcutta: being chiefly Reminiscences of the days of Warren Hastings, Francis, and Impey. By H. E. BUSTEED. Crown 8vo. Rs. 4.

"Dr. Busteed has made an eminently readable, entertaining, and by no means uninstructive volume; there is not a dull page in the whole book."—*Saturday Review.*

"The book will be read by all interested in India."—*Army and Navy Magazine.*

Mookerjee.—A Memoir of the late Justice Onoocool Chunder Mookerjee. By M. MOOKERJEE. Third Edition. 12mo. Re. 1. The Biography of a Native Judge, by a native, forming a most interesting and amusing illustration of Hindoo life and character.

"The reader is earnestly advised to procure the life of this [gentleman, written by his nephew, and read it. —*The Tribes on my Frontier.*

Milton Keynes UK
Ingram Content Group UK Ltd.
UKHW021914091023
430259UK00004B/112